Best Practices in Customer Service

BEST PRACTICES IN CUSTOMER SERVICE

Edited by

Ron Zemke and John A. Woods

HRD Press
Amherst

AMACOM
American Management Association

New York • Atlanta • Boston • Chicago • Kansas City • San Francisco • Washington, D.C.
Brussels • Mexico City • Tokyo • Toronto

This book is available at a special
discount when ordered in bulk quantities.
For information, contact Special Sales Department,
AMACOM, an imprint of AMA Publications,
a division of American Management Association,
1601 Broadway, New York, NY 10019.

This publication is designed to provide accurate and authoritative information in regard to the subject matter covered. It is sold with the understanding that the publisher is not engaged in rendering legal, accounting, or other professional service. If legal advice or other expert assistance is required, the services of a competent professional person should be sought.

Library of Congress Cataloging-in-Publication Data

Best practices in customer service / edited by Ron Zemke and John A.
   Woods.
         p.   cm.
   Includes bibliographical references.
   ISBN 0-8144-7028-9
   1. Customer services.   I. Zemke, Ron.   II. Woods, John A.
HF5415.5.B484   1999
858.8'12—dc21   98-31888
                                                 CIP

Printing number

10   9   8   7   6   5   4   3   2   1

CONTENTS

Part Eight. Customer Service and the Rest of the Organization

INTRODUCTION

This book is a tool. It's designed to help you learn about the best practices in customer service. But even more important, it's designed to help you implement these practices in your organization.

Many of you are managers of customer service departments, supervising people who interact with customers to help them solve problems. Some of you are general managers who are concerned with growing your division or company and you want to know more about building long-term relationships with your customers. A number of you are customer service representatives who want to better understand your role and what you can do to perform your job better. Whoever you are, you will find lots of material here to help you improve how you, your staff, and your organization perform in the crucial area of customer service.

What we've done is commission consultants and practitioners to prepare articles that do three things:

○ Help you understand the connection between excellent customer service and organizational performance,
○ Help you deliver a higher level of customer service for lower costs, and
○ Provide you with a wide selection of practical customer service tools and techniques.

They've contributed 35 articles, which we've organized into eight parts.

Part One. Great Customer Service, Customer Retention, and Growth

First of all, it's important to know *why* it's vital to be concerned with customer service. Explaining that is the purpose of Part One, which is all about retaining the customer base that will fuel growth and profitability.

We begin with an article by co-editor John Woods that looks at the systems view of organizations and how that view supports the development of exceptional service. We follow this with an article by Jerry Fritz on taking the journey to get to what he calls "Wow!" service. This involves three stages in leading your employees and gaining commitment to ever-higher levels of service. The next article, "Quantifying the Impact of Great Customer Service on Profitability" by John Goodman of TARP (Technical Assistance Research Programs), gives you a way to understand the substantial positive financial impact of caring about your customers and solving their problems. Eb Scheuing then further explains the strategic imperative today of better customer service, in "Delighting Your Customers: Creating World-Class Service." We conclude Part One with an article in which Terry Vavra and Doug Pruden break down the stages of service after the sale and indicate which types of service are appropriate at each stage.

Part Two. Practical Models for Managing Customer Service

The articles in this part of the book provide you with practical frameworks for planning, organizing, and delivering excellent service.

We start with "How to Create a Plan to Deliver Great Customer Service," in which Susan Smith outlines five basic steps. In the next article, "Building a Picture of Perfect Service," Michael Vandergriff uses a cause-and-effect diagram as a tool for understanding the set of causes that yield the effect of "perfect service," with vivid examples to show how such service comes about and where things might break down. Kristin Anderson, co-author on the "Knock Your Socks Off" series books on customer service, then explains the importance of having standards for the quality of your customer service and how such standards, especially for transactions with the customer, keep customers coming back.

But sometimes we might get confused in setting standards, believing that we need to deliver ideal service, when all customers really expect is a moderate level of service. An article by Georgette Zifko-Baliga explains the difference between perceived quality and customer satisfaction. Then, Chip Bell shares an important insight into making customers your partners in delivering service. He explains how you do this—and how you don't. Finally, in the article "Training for Success Through Service: How Delta Air Lines Does It," Nora Weaver and Tom Atkinson share an example of making customer service a competitive advantage, as they explain how Delta Air Lines trains and coaches its representatives to provide better customer service through its Success Through Service program.

Part Three. Practical Methods for Leading Customer Service

While Part Two provides you with some useful management frameworks, Part Three is more tactical, with specific techniques for leading customer service.

The first article, by Anne Bruce and James Pepitone, provides you with 10 techniques for being an effective coach, with special emphasis on the needs of CS reps. In the following article, JoAnna Brandi presents her CARE³ formula for managing customer service—"Create **A** **R**elationship **E**nthusiastically, **E**nergetically, with **E**veryone"—and then includes ideas for implementing this approach among representatives. In the last article in Part Three, "How to Let Customer Value Drive Customer Problem Solving," Eric Reidenbach, Gordon W. McClung, and Reginald W. Goeke examine the importance of knowing what customers value when you go about providing service and how to create a "value map" to ensure that service and value expected coincide.

Part Four. Customer Service on the Front Line

Here we've provided five articles that provide specific techniques customer service managers and reps can use to do their jobs better.

We start with Rebecca Morgan, who gives you "Six Tools for Improving How You Deliver Service to Customers." Then, Janelle M. Barlow (author of *A Complaint Is a Gift*) and Dianna Maul provide a baker's dozen techniques for maintaining superior levels of service even during periods of high demand. In the third article, Kathleen Brown provides a detailed overview of techniques to ensure that a rep's voice and demeanor over the phone create a positive relationship with the customer and facilitate quick solutions to problems. Donna Hall then explains several generic methods that phone reps can use to effectively solve problems for customers. Finally, Marlene Yanovsky, another TARP consultant, explains how to set up automated telephone response systems that help customers, rather than turn them off.

Part Five. Improving Customer Service: Strategies and Techniques

Our goal in this part of the book is to give you an eclectic selection of ideas you can use to improve the quality of service your department delivers.

We start with "The Ten Practices of Exceptional Service," in which Mark Sanborn shares his views on what constitutes great service, with specific examples. Michael Cafferky then explains how to serve your customers better, to inspire them to brag about your company and the service you deliver.

We then change gears slightly, with a card sort customer service training exercise developed by Sharon Wulf, author of HRD Press's "Card Sort Activities" series. In the next article, Lisa Ford presents a series of ways to change organizational culture to value customer loyalty and explains how to do what it takes to earn this loyalty one transaction at a time. In the fifth article in Part Five, Pat Alea and Rebecca Chekouras of Age Wave Communications describe how the aging population presents new challenges and opportunities in delivering customer service, and they suggest ways for effectively dealing with the challenges to make the most of the opportunities. We conclude Part Five with an article in which Bob Shaver explains step by step how to develop surveys that will help you gather customer information that you can use to learn what your customers expect and what changes you can make to better accommodate them.

Part Six. Customer Problems and Problem Customers

Do you want some techniques for effectively handling upset customers and recovering when you blow it with your customers? That's the purpose of the two articles in this part. The first is a review of service recovery methods by co-editor Ron Zemke. He explains how, if you do it right, you can actually build a stronger relationship with customers through problems. Then, John Hartley presents a four-step procedure (characterized by the acronym HEAT) for helping reps deal effectively with upset customers, lowering the level of emotion, and raising the possibility of a win-win solution.

Part Seven. Customer Service and the Internet

The Internet is becoming ubiquitous, providing great opportunities as a customer service tool. In this section we provide three articles that will help you become familiar with this customer service tool.

We begin with Jim Sterne, author of *Customer Service on the Internet*, who provides an overview of how to take advantage of the World Wide Web to better serve your customers. John Chisholm then explains how to use the interactive capabilities of the Web to survey customers and measure customer service and loyalty. Finally, Keith Loris of ServiceSoft explains how to take advantage of Web capabilities to deliver self-service support to your customers.

Part Eight. Customer Service and the Rest of the Organization

The customer service department does not operate independently of the rest of the organization. What CS does affects the rest of the organization, and what goes on in the rest of the organization affects the level and nature of assistance the customer service can provide. In Part Eight we explore these relationships from a variety of perspectives.

We start with an article in which Jody Hoffer Gittell explains how Southwest Airlines provides better service through employee cooperation, detailing how several different groups of employees collaborate in the departure process. Then Mark Rosenberger presents the metaphor of the "trapeze buddy," as he explores five steps you can take to facilitate internal cooperation to efficiently deliver higher levels of service. In our third article, Gary Connor describes how to develop and maintain the vital relationship between sales and customer service to enhance both sales and service.

Then Scott Davis makes an interesting point: since customer service reps deal constantly with customers and their problems, they have a unique window into customer needs and opportunities to develop innovative new products and services. In his article, "Customer Service: A Key to Innovation Success," he describes how CS reps can be part of a cross-functional team to develop innovative new products. We close with an article titled "Great Internal Service Creates Great External Service," in which Lee Meadow explains the importance of creating an internal company culture where service to others inside is a primary value and how that naturally translates into superior service to external customers.

Appendices

We have included three references for you at the end of the book:

- ○ A series of 20 graphs documenting some of the most useful findings from the 1996 ICSA Benchmarking Study. You can use these to benchmark your company's performance and approach to customer service.
- ○ A directory of magazines, journals, and newsletters that deal with customer service. This directory includes publication and subscription information and a brief description of their content.

○ A directory and more of customer service on the Internet. This includes an annotated listing of Web sites, discussion lists, and other information about customer service available online.

How to Use *Best Practices in Customer Service*

The best way to use this book is to selectively read material that will help you answer questions about how to proceed in some area. To help you find what you might be looking for, here are some suggestions based on questions you might ask:

Why should I and my employees (and my boss) care about delivering great service?

To answer that question, we suggest the following:

○ Start with John Woods's article on the systems view and how that logically suggests the importance of caring about customers (article 1). The welfare of the company and the welfare of the customers are inextricably connected.
○ Read John Goodman's "Quantifying the Impact of Great Customer Service on Profitability" (article 3). He explains how to quantify the payoff and shows the dramatic difference customer service can make on your bottom line.

What do I need to know about my customers to deliver great service to them?

You need to have some sense of their expectations and what you might do to meet and exceed them. Here are some articles to read to learn more:

○ Terry Vavra and Doug Pruden's "Customer Retention and the Stages of Service After the Sale" (article 5), where the authors spell out what customers expect at different points after you've sold them something.
○ Georgette Zifko-Baliga's piece on what customers really want (article 9) will help you realistically understand what level of service you should be delivering to satisfy them.
○ If you're interested in the rapidly growing segment of consumers 50 and older, read Pat Alea and Rebecca Chekoura's article, "The Care and Handling of the Mature Market" (article 24), to better understand how to serve these customers.

How can I learn more about customer needs and expectations?

Check the following articles for how to effectively learn more about your customers:

○ Eb Scheuing provides an overview of several methods for collecting customer information in "Delighting Your Customers: Creating World-Class Service" (article 4).
○ In "Customer Surveys That Deliver Actionable Information" (article 25), Bob

Shaver explains each step in the process of putting together surveys to get the information you need to make changes.

○ For ideas on how to get customer information using the Internet, read John Chisholm's "Using the Internet to Measure Customer Satisfaction and Loyalty" (article 29).

What's involved in developing a plan for designing and delivering great customer service?

In other words, how do I figure out just how to get the whole process organized inside the company? Here are three answers to that question:

○ Check out Susan Smith's "How to Create a Plan to Deliver Great Customer Service" (article 6), in which she takes you step-by-step through the planning process.

○ Michael Vandergriff's "Building a Picture of Perfect Service" (article 7) helps you understand the different aspects of delivering customer service.

○ Finally, Kristin Anderson explains the importance of establishing service standards (article 8) in developing your service plan.

How do I help my representatives improve their ability to deal with customers?

If you're looking for ways your representatives can help customers more quickly and with higher levels of satisfaction, check out the following:

○ Anne Bruce and James S. Pepitone's article, "Authentic Coaching: Getting the Best From Customer Service Providers" (article 12), gives specific ideas for helping employees one-on-one.

○ Kathleen Brown's "Creating the Sounds of Quality: Delivering Great Service on the Telephone" (article 17) provides lots of practical advice on how to come across on the phone in a more friendly and positive manner.

○ Donna Hall's "Problem-Solving Tips for Phone Representatives" (article 18) provides a series of specific techniques to help reps interact more effectively with customers.

○ Eric Reidenbach and colleagues' article, "How to Let Customer Value Drive Customer Problem Solving" (article 14), helps reps get to the heart of a problem from the customer's viewpoint, rather than the company's.

How do other companies deliver superior service?

An intensely service-oriented industry is the airlines. Two articles explain how two of the best carriers do it:

○ Jody Hoffer Gittell explains how Southwest Airlines coordinates services across functional boundaries in its departure process (article 31).

○ Nora Weaver and Tom Atkinson explain how Delta Air Lines uses service as a key competitive advantage to hold on to customers and how it uses training to help employees deliver that service (article 11).

What are some key practices that characterize excellent service in any organization?

Here are some articles that give you lots of specific answers to this question:

- In "The Ten Practices of Exceptional Service" (article 20), Mark Sanborn reviews his choice of key customer service practices and gives several examples.
- Chip Bell explains the innovative practice of making customers partners in the delivery of service, in "Customers Care When They Share: How to Nurture Loyalty Through Inclusion" (article 10).
- Marlene Yanovsky's "Customer-Sensitive Automated Response Systems" (article 19) gives you sound advice on how to make automated phone service easy for customers to use. Share this with your tech people.
- JoAnna Brandi's "Unleashing the Power of Customer CARE in Your Organization" (article 13) describes how reps can establish a service-oriented attitude resulting in better service to customers.

What about customer loyalty and the role of customer service in engendering it?

You'll read frequently in this book about the importance of customer loyalty in building a successful company. Articles that directly address this issue include:

- Michael Cafferky's "Beyond Loyalty: Inspiring Customers to Brag" (article 21) provides specific ideas for identifying potentially loyal customers and then engendering that loyalty through specific actions.
- Lisa Ford in "Strategies That Foster Customer Loyalty" (article 23) provides techniques for moving beyond mediocre service to exceptional service that keeps customers loyal.
- Terry Vavra and Doug Pruden's article "Customer Retention and the Stages of Service After the Sale" (article 5) helps you understand that, at different times, customers have different needs and expectations.
- Ron Zemke's "Service Recovery: Turning Oops! Into Opportunity" (article 26) shows how taking the time to deal with specific problems reinforces the connection and loyalty customers feel to your company.

How can I use the Internet to deliver customer service?

We're glad you asked, because we have three articles and an appendix on this:

- Jim Sterne provides a great overview of the strengths and potential of the Web in "The World Wide Web Was Made for Customer Service" (article 28).
- John Chisholm teaches you how to use the Web to survey customers in "Using the Internet to Measure Customer Satisfaction and Loyalty" (article 29).
- An innovative way to use the Web so customers find service answers is profiled in Keith Loris's piece, "Internet Self-Service Support: Beyond Search Engines to 'Smart Answers on the 'Net'™" (article 30).

- Appendix C, "Customer Service Resources on the Internet" includes lots of information on finding CS sites and lots more.

What do attitude and culture have to do with implementing superior customer service?

The simple answer is nearly everything. You can't sustain great service when there isn't a service-oriented culture in place where employees cooperate and support one another. The following articles provide more insight into this:

- Lee Meadow's "Great Internal Service Creates Great External Service" (article 35) vividly shows what a service-oriented culture is like and the results you can expect.
- Mark Rosenberger's "Swing With Your Trapeze Buddy: Working Together Internally to Serve External Customers" (article 32) explains how to develop the internal relationships that help cement your external relationships with customers.
- Jody Hoffer Gittell's "Coordinating Services Across Functional Boundaries: The Departure Process at Southwest Airlines" (article 31) describes the type of service-oriented culture that every organization might emulate.

There are many more questions we could list here, but the ones above give you a good sense of what you'll find in this book. Every article is aimed at answering practical questions like these. We're committed to practicing what we preach by creating a book that gives you strategies and tactics you can use today and tomorrow to enhance your service capabilities. We hope it works well for you.

Of course, we'd be glad to have feedback. You can contact us at the addresses given just below in the paragraphs that tell who we are. We also invite you to visit the HRD Press Web site (http://www.hrdpress.com) and John Woods's Web site featuring *Best Practices in Customer Service* (http://www.execpc.com/cwlpubent/bpcs.htm).

Acknowledgments

First, we want to thank the contributors who took the time to prepare the articles you'll find in this book. They are all professionals in the field of customer service. At the end of each article, you will find a little information about the author(s). At the end of the book, you'll find a listing of all the contributors, along with their addresses, phone numbers, e-mail addresses, and, if available, Web site URLs. We also want to thank Chris Hunter of HRD Press for suggesting this book and working with us in its development. At CWL Publishing Enterprises, Robert Magnan prepared Appendices B and C, the directories of publications and customer service on the Internet. He also copyedited the articles and did lots more to facilitate the delivery of this book. He did a terrific job. Finally, we want to say thanks to you for purchasing and using this book. We hope it serves you, our customer, well.

About the Editors

Ron Zemke is president of Performance Research Associates, a Minneapolis-based consulting and training company specializing in service quality audits and service management programs. He is a senior editor of *Training* magazine and a columnist for the American Management Association's President's Newsletter. Ron is the author or co-author of several best-selling books on customer service, including *Service America!*, *The Service Edge: 101 Companies that Profit from Customer Care*, and the "Knock Your Socks Off" series of books from AMACOM Books. Ron received the 1994 MOBIUS Award for his contributions to the customer service profession. You can contact Ron at PRA, 821 Marquette Avenue, Suite 1820, Minneapolis, MN 55402, phone: 612/338-8523, fax: 612/338-8536, e-mail: zemke@aol.com.

John Woods is president of CWL Publishing Enterprises based in Madison, Wisconsin. His company develops business books in a variety of fields, with special emphasis on quality management. He is co-author or co-editor of *The Quality Yearbook, The ASTD Training and Performance Yearbook, QualiTrends: 7 Quality Secrets That Will Change Your Life, 10-Minute Guide to Teams and Teamwork*, the *McGraw-Hill Encyclopedia of Quality Terms and Concepts, Sales Games and Activities for Trainers*, and a college textbook, *Supervision*. You can contact John at 3010 Irvington Way, Madison, WI 53713, phone: 608/273-3710, fax: 608/274-4554, e-mail: jwoods@execpc.com, Web site: http://www.execpc.com/cwlpubent/.

PART ONE

Great Customer Service, Customer Retention, and Growth

1

CUSTOMER SERVICE, VALUE, AND THE SYSTEMS VIEW

John A. Woods

Many times we read about the importance of serving customers well, but poor service is still all too common. Why is this? This article by the co-editor of this book suggests that managers often do not relate excellent customer service to excellent business results. It also shows the fallacy of not understanding this and provides a model for demonstrating the inextricable connection between organizational success and customer satisfaction. Finally, it provides a context for all of the articles that follow.

What is customer service? That's a basic question—and yet it's frequently misunderstood. Customer service is not just about how you handle a transaction. It's about a relationship with people who are an essential part of everything you do.

Customer Service and the Marketing Concept

Sometime in the 1950s, organizations began to discover that customers were not a necessary inconvenience but vital to the business and that their needs provided direction for what the organization should be about. One of the earliest articulations of this understanding came in the 1952 General Electric annual report, where management stated that marketing should drive company behavior. They defined marketing as the activity that helped the company understand and serve the customer. The following paragraph was part of that report:

> *The marketing person [should come] at the beginning rather than at the end of the production cycle and marketing should be integrated into each phase of the business. Thus, marketing, through its studies and research, will establish . . . what the customer wants in a particular product, what price he or she is willing to pay, and where and when it will be wanted. Marketing will have authority in product planning, production scheduling, and inventory control, as well as sales, distribution, and servicing of the product.*[1]

1. Annual Report of the General Electric Company, 1952, p. 21.

In other words, figuring out how to serve customers and making sure this drives all organizational activities were fundamental to success. This idea is regularly taught, if not completely understood, in business schools today.

If you were to read any textbook on marketing, one of the first things you'd read about is the importance of pleasing the customer, of making the customer the focus of the business. This is known as "the marketing concept." Here's how some textbooks actually state this:

> *The* marketing concept *holds that the key to achieving organizational goals consists in determining the needs and wants of target markets and delivering the desired satisfactions more effectively and efficiently than competitors. (Philip Kotler,* Marketing Management, *6th Edition, Prentice-Hall, 1988)*

> *According to the marketing concept, an organization should try to satisfy the needs of customers or clients through a coordinated set of activities that, at the same time, allows the organization to achieve its goals. Customer satisfaction is the aim of the marketing concept. (William Price and O.C. Ferrell,* Marketing, *3rd Edition, Macmillan, 1983)*

> *The marketing concept calls on management and employees (1) to be consumer-oriented in all matters, from product development to honoring warranties and service contracts, (2) to stress long-term profitability rather than short-term profits or sales volume, and (3) to integrate and coordinate all marketing functions and other corporate functions. (William Zikmund and Michael D'Amico,* Marketing, *3rd Edition, Wiley, 1989)*

The way I express the marketing concept is like this: *The purpose of the organization is to create a mutually beneficial relationship between itself and those that it serves.* Each of these textbook quotes emphasizes and, indeed, equates the importance of satisfying the customer with achieving organizational goals.

What are these organizational goals? Conventionally they involve growth and profitability. But it's very important to appreciate that growth and profitability should not really be organizational goals. Of course management has to be concerned with profit, but a focus on profit will not tell you what you need to do to generate profit. What will, however, is figuring out how to serve customers.

The fact is that being more concerned with profit than customer needs is at the heart of poor management and the cause of many problems for organizations. The rise of consumerism and laws that protect consumers demonstrates, Peter Drucker has observed, "that not much marketing [effectively serving customers] has been practiced." Drucker also reminds us that profit is not a goal but "a measurement of how well the business discharges its functions in serving market and customer."[2] That's an important point because it shows that profit and customer service are intimately related. The company's profit is a measure of the value and quality of the service it delivers to customers.

2. Peter Drucker, *Management: Tasks, Responsibilities, Practices* (New York: Harper & Row, 1993), pp. 64, 98–99.

What Customers Value—Benefits

The marketing concept is a very useful idea for understanding why paying attention to customers and their needs is so important. But what are these needs of customers? They have all kinds of needs. These mainly center around work, family, recreation, entertainment, shelter, food, education, communication, and transportation or some combination of these. But however we categorize their needs, the important thing to remember is that people *never* buy *products* or *services*. They *always* buy the *benefits* they expect to derive from those products or services.

What organizations offer and what has value to customers is really a *bundle of benefits*. Benefits have to do not with the item itself, but what that item allows the customer to do to fulfill some need or solve some problem. Benefits are what customers pay for and what they value. Focusing on the delivery and improvement of benefits is what gives one company a competitive advantage over another.

These benefits can be divided into four categories, all of which directly or indirectly involve customer service before, during, and after the sale:

- **Form** (the item is easy to use, attractive, durable, and so on),
- **Place** (the place where the item or service is located is convenient),
- **Time** (the item or service is available when the customer wants it), and
- **Possession** (the item or service is easy to buy and take ownership of).

Let's review each of these in a little more detail to see the role of customer service in helping the company put into practice the marketing concept, or, said another way, to secure, build, and sustain customer relationships. In doing this review, I am not suggesting that only customer service personnel are responsible for delivering these benefits. Every department in the organization plays its role, some more direct than others. And the success of any one group depends on others properly executing their roles. With that stated, let's look specifically at the role of the customer service department.

Customer Service and the Form Benefit

Initially, product development is responsible for creating the form benefit. However, once the customer has made a purchase and has questions or problems with how the product works, then customer service has an important role to play. Customers are unlikely to feel satisfied if the product does not work as expected or they can't figure out how to make it work. In the computer hardware and software business, for example, customer service reps are often called on to help customers figure out how to get the new product up and running.

If customers did not believe that such help was available, that a part of the benefits they purchased was help in getting started, then they might not have made the purchase. Later on, when they might need additional help, it's customer service they call on. For some products, in fact, this benefit has so much value that customers are willing to pay extra for it. But whether they pay extra or not, one benefit customers expect when they buy a product is that the vendor or manufacturer will be there to help make sure they can use it and that it will work properly.

Customer Service and the Place Benefit

If customers need service, they want the service provider to be located in a convenient location. This might mean that the service location is near where they live or it might mean that it is available right from their phone at an 800 number. The point is that a benefit most customers expect and that has value to them is that service is accessible at a convenient location.

Customer Service and the Time Benefit

This benefit isn't hard to understand. Service being available *when* customers are looking for it is often one of the most valuable benefits a company can offer. This means that service providers are available whenever a problem arises, and it means that the customer service rep can provide a speedy response that actually solves the problem. Time is money, and offering service that is very timely helps cement a long-term relationship between seller and buyer.

In terms of both place and time, FedEx is a wonderful example of a company that takes these benefits into account. Even though it usually costs more to send a package via FedEx, the company makes it so easy to do business with in terms of package pickup and delivery, as well as instant tracking of the package, that it's worth the extra cost. FedEx sets the standard in the package delivery business because of its ability to provide great time and place benefits.

Customer Service and the Possession Benefit

Issues that deal with warranties, credit terms, and return of faulty products are another set of benefits that customers value and that are especially the purview of the customer service department. Customers want to be able to easily pay for and take ownership of whatever they purchase and feel secure that it will work as promised. Having customer service reps who are empowered to respond to and deal with warranty claims promptly and with an attitude of making sure things work right raises the level of customer comfort in any transaction. It eliminates the "buyer beware" feeling that all customers want to avoid when possible, and further reinforces a positive relationship between organization and customers.

Value and Customer Service

So a major influence in what customers purchase and what brings them back is the belief that they will receive the bundle of benefits just described—form, place, time, and possession. Of course, all these aspects of service have costs for the organization. However, since their value to customers should outweigh their costs, their delivery helps to ensure profitability and growth. If this isn't the case, then it means you have not properly understood what customers want and value or you do not have good control of the processes by which you deliver your products and services.

The Systems View of Organizations

The main point up to now in this article has been to demonstrate the connection between the effective implementation of the marketing concept in organizations and the role of customer service in doing this. I'm sure most people would assert that they understand this point, at least in principle.

But there are many organizations that are still not very good at putting this principle into practice. Managers in these organizations often view customer service as a separate department that's supposed to take care of customer problems and questions, and they don't think much more about how it's actually the responsibility of the entire organization, each department contributing in its own way. They may not see the connection between customer service and satisfaction and everything else that goes on in the organization.

There is, however, a view of organizations that is useful in helping managers see more directly that customer service and satisfaction is central to organizational success. The marketing concept is not just an abstraction from this view, but at the heart of the organization's existence. What I am referring to is the *systems view of organizations*. I want to describe this approach to understanding organizations and show how it helps us better understand *why* customer service is vital to the survival of any organization.

Let's start with a definition. A system is *a group of components whose functions are interdependent, and which, through a series of processes, transforms inputs into outputs*. This is also an excellent definition of an organization.

In other words, a realistic way to understand what an organization is and what it does comes from this idea of a *system*. All organizations take in various raw materials, parts, tools, equipment, and other inputs and, through a series of process steps, transform and add value to these inputs to create outputs of various sorts.

Why do organizations do this? Because some group of people (customers) is willing to pay for these outputs. If that weren't the case, all this effort would be wasted. If the organization is a manufacturer, the output will be products that will be delivered either to other manufacturers for further processing or to final consumers. If the organization is a service company, it will bring together its resources to provide the output of its service to some group of customers. (Although I refer to outputs here as products and services, what I mean is that these companies deliver some bundle of benefits centered around a particular product or service.)

If we were to graphically depict an organizational system, a simple way to do it would be as shown in Figure 1-1. The significant point to note in reviewing this figure is that the correct way to understand the organization is to include, as parts of the system, both suppliers (who provide inputs) and customers (who purchase the outputs). To not understand and not take into account the vital role of both parts in the operation of the system will result in problems.

In other words, any borders that you put up that separate the company and its assets and employees from either its suppliers or its customers are artificial, arbitrary, and detrimental. An accurate view of the organization is one that includes customers and suppliers as *parts*. This means that looking out for the interests of the

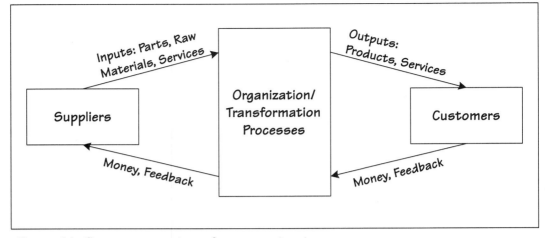

Figure 1-1. The systems view of an organization.

organization by definition means looking out for the interests of all the organization's parts, including customers and suppliers.

The Systems View and Sound Decisions

This point is a significant switch from the more traditional approach of seeing the organization as somehow separate from the customers with whom it does business. The reason this is important is because of how it affects decision making. Sound decisions from this perspective require taking into account the interests of the entire system—suppliers, "company," and customers—in making business decisions.

We can contrast the systems view as the foundation for decisions with the more traditional approach of viewing the company as a separate entity. That often leads to decisions that may compromise the delivery of benefits to customers. Or it may even suggest taking advantage of customers to the immediate "profit" of the organization. Experience, however, shows that such decisions are actually detrimental to the company. When managers do not take into account the interests of that part of the organization made up by customers, they do not look out for the organization itself.

Imagine a company where all decisions are driven by a desire to look out for all the parts of the organization. Customers are not an afterthought. Managers will continuously look for ways to improve the system, which means improving the company-customer relationship. The employees will view their jobs in terms of better understanding customer needs and how the organization can efficiently deliver benefits that will fulfill these needs. And, in fact, if you were to examine America's most admired companies, from Southwest Airlines to 3M to Hewlett-Packard, you would see that in fact this is an important part of their cultures and how they operate.

That's the main point of this article: companies that understand and apply the systems view consistently and conscientiously will succeed in serving their customers, making a profit, and growing. They will provide benefits that their customers value and the relationship that they establish will ensure their financial success.

But What Can I Do?

If you're a customer service manager or representative, you cannot necessarily directly affect your company's culture or way of operating. You can, however, understand just how important it is to continuously improve your ability to help customers fulfill their needs by doing business with you and your organization. And you can translate this into an attitude and a set of actions that result in more effectively building a mutually beneficial relationship between company and customers.

If you're a general manager, you can use the systems view to drive the decisions you make. In considering any question, you should ask *how does this help us add value for our customers?* Then you can look at the bottom line, not just as what's left over after you pay all the costs, but as a *measure* of how well you've done at figuring out what customers value and then delivering it.

This is the most realistic approach to understanding what an organization is, what it does, and why it prospers or fails. Whatever you read about customer service in this book or learn at any seminars you attend, you can use the *systems view* to better understand the principles and practices you're learning about. The *value* of these practices will come from how they help you to do two things: (1) improve the efficiency of your processes for delivering service and (2) improve on the benefits you deliver to customers. That is the ultimate definition of "best practices."

2

Traveling the Highway to "Wow!" Service

Jerry Fritz

Do you want your customers to be excited about what you have to offer? Do you want to create positive impressions consistently above the normal customer expectations? This article maps out three checkpoints along the road to "Wow!" service: establish a compelling reason for making customer service a primary goal, create a common service language and focus within your organization, and identify some of the potential barriers.

Introduction

"Wow!" service leaves customers with such a favorable impression of the organization that they grab the first person they see, look them in the eyes, and shout, "You ought to do business with that company!" If you want your organization to be "that company," then it is time to travel the highway to success. Are you ready?

As on any trip you take, you want to be sure of two things: where you're headed and that you're prepared for the trip.

To help you with number one, you and your organization are making a commitment to follow the highway to quality customer service. This road is not always smooth and clear of obstacles, but if you drive carefully, you can successfully navigate down this road. One of the things you'll learn on this trip is how to drive your commitment to customer service up, down, and laterally throughout the organization. Many of you have already traveled the road to customer service commitment. However, if you have not yet begun on this journey or have only recently gotten under way, then carefully read on.

To help you prepare for the trip, I've included directions for proceeding along the highway. And I've noted the following checkpoints that you'll encounter along the way:

- Checkpoint 1. You'll establish a compelling reason *why* customer service must be a primary goal for your organization.

○ Checkpoint 2. You'll create a common service language and focus within your organization.
○ Checkpoint 3. You'll identify some of the barriers that may exist and could potentially interfere with your customer service commitment.

Prepare now to take the wheel and follow the highway to superior customer service. Then when you return to your office, you'll want to share your experiences with everyone and invite them to take this "excursion" with you.

Checkpoint 1

The objectives for Checkpoint 1 are (1) *to create compelling reasons why your organization needs a customer service culture* and (2) *learn the financial value to your company of satisfied customers.*

Checkpoint 1 takes you on a quick side trip to Vermillion Bay, Ontario, Canada. You stop for breakfast at a restaurant and you see a sporting goods store next door. The sign on the roof says, "Bobby's Sport Shop." You read this sign on the door:

> *Hi, my name is Allan. My home phone number is 123-4567. My hours are long, but if you come by and I'm closed, just call and I will come up because you, my customer, are number 1, and it's been that way for the 32 years that I've been here and, besides, I love my job! —Al*

Having read this sign, what kind of customer service would you expect from Bobby's Sport Shop? Outstanding, world-class customer service! As a matter of fact, it's been said that Al actually can be seen driving up in his truck at 3 o'clock in the morning in his pajamas—taking care of a customer! Al believes that you take care of a customer when the customer wants to be taken care of.

Do you and your organization know how to take good care of your customers like this? And if you do, how do you move on to an even higher level? How do you take your customer service from good to world-class? Where do you start the whole process of customer strategy? The answer starts with understanding why you should do this.

Establishing the *Why*

Having procedures in place to serve customers will just not be good enough in the late '90s and beyond. You must be looking for ways to move performance to ever higher levels, to transform things from simply knowing you should do it to having everyone in the organization with his or her own compelling reason *why*.

Have you ever tried to lose weight? Perhaps your doctor hinted that you needed to drop a few pounds, but you found that the suggestion didn't really motivate you enough—there just wasn't a compelling reason for going on a diet. But then the 20-year class reunion invitation arrives, and the motivation clicks in. Now you have a compelling reason *why* you need to lose those pounds.

You can apply that same principle in your organization. Many times the behavior and attitude displayed by employees stem from lack of awareness. Once a compelling reason for superior customer service is established, the employees see both personal and professional benefits of doing better. If the *why* is not strong enough, you're going to face resistance. But when the *why* is there, you can figure out a way to get it done.

Of course, the *why* is that it is the customers who pay the bills. When the company delivers high value to customers, they're willing to do business with you today and tomorrow. And that means people keep their jobs and progress in their careers. Great words, huh? But once employees see that you mean it and that they will be recognized and rewarded for delivering great service, then the *why* will be in place for them.

Create Value

The goal of business every day is to create more value for the customer in the hopes of getting and holding on to their business. Doing this is simply stated: create more value, get more money. The important thing is this—the value must be in place before you can expect business.

Value = The Utility to Customers of Your Products + Your Services

Who's responsible for creating value for your organization? Everyone is! What if you don't serve customers directly? Are you still responsible for creating value? You bet! Perhaps you've heard someone inside the organization complain, "Those darn people in logistics!" The unspoken part of the message is that some employees in the organization don't relate what they do to adding value for customers. The fact is that the job of every employee, directly or indirectly, is about serving customers. Every employee is an extension of the company. And in every transaction, the customer is thinking, "Is there value here? Is it consistent with my expectations? Is it improving?" The challenge you face is putting together and driving forward a commitment to adding value for customers in every individual in your organization.

And when everyone in the organization understands that their job is to serve customers and the company delivers on that, it:

- Creates goodwill and enhances the positive reputation of the company
- Reduces instances of "poor quality"
- Increases opportunities to up- and cross-sell
- Raises the rate of customer retention
- Lowers employee turnover
- Increases margins and profit
- Provides for a more positive work environment
- Produces an objective and clearly visible performance measure
- Establishes a competitive advantage
- Can be an important point of differentiation from the competition

The Value of a Customer

If you were to write a check for the worth of one of your customers, what dollar amount would you put? Impossible task, you say? No! Customers have value. Everyone knows that happy customers have value. But how much value?

There is power in establishing the specific dollar value of a happy, repeat customer who brags about you to friends and associates. Take the following restaurant example as an illustration of how a dollar value can be placed on one customer. Then note how the dollar value of that one customer can impact a business further by indirect or word-of-mouth advertising. If you're looking for one idea to create a compelling reason *why*, determine the exact dollar figure of one of your customers.

Example: Restaurant
Direct Value

A.	Average customer revenue per transaction	$25
B.	Number of transactions per year	12
C.	Revenue per year (A × B)	$300
D.	Customer lifetime in years (average)	5
E.	Customer lifetime value (C × D)	$1,500

Indirect Value (Word of Mouth)

F.	Happy customer tells five people on average (E × 5)	$7,500
G.	Revenue generated from referrals (assuming only 25% purchase from you) (F × .25)	$1,875

Total Value of *One* "Wow!" Customer (E + G)   **$3,375**

And this calculation of the value of a customer is conservative.

STOP

○ Have you established a compelling reason *why* you and your organization need to be committed to customer service?

○ Were you able to establish a dollar value for your customers?

If so, you're ready to move on to Checkpoint 2.

Checkpoint 2

The objective for Checkpoint 2 is *to create a common service language and focus within your organization.*

How do you take what you're doing in terms of customer service and drive it to the next level? One way to move forward is for everyone in the company to understand the definition of "Wow!" service. "Wow!" service is the process of creating positive impressions consistently above the normal customer expectations. Does your company offer "Wow!" service? Are you offering service beyond customer expectations?

Creating Impressions

Does your company create an impression on its customers? Absolutely! People in the company create impressions every single day. Those impressions fall into three basic categories. Some customers are saying, "Wow, that was pretty amazing!" Others are saying, "It was nothing to write home about." Then there are customers who might say, "Ugh!" What do you want to hear from your customers? "Wow!" is a good answer to that question.

Stop and look at where customers form impressions about your business. Look at the service that your customers are receiving and challenge yourself and your team to make changes to get to the level of "Wow!" service.

Who Are Your Trapeze Buddies?

The people you can count on to complete a task or function or provide you with information so that you can get your job done are called "trapeze buddies" (a term developed by Mark Rosenberger of WOW Seminars, who describes it in greater detail in his article in this book, "Swing with Your Trapeze Buddy"). Do you have trapeze buddies? Of course! If you're in the lending business, for example, your trapeze buddies are those people who help you with your job, such as the appraiser or the loan originator.

Trapeze buddies work together to get a job done. They work together to make a positive impression on customers. In everyday life, you and others in your organization are like trapeze artists in a circus: you climb way up, you jump, you spin . . . hoping that someone will catch you. But in business, there's usually no safety net. You need your trapeze buddies to help you successfully perform your act—providing "Wow!" customer service.

Who are your trapeze buddies? Think of others within your organization on whom you depend so you can successfully do your job. And how about those who depend on you so they can do their jobs? Both of you are part of your company's trapeze act. Encourage your trapeze buddies to discuss with you the ways in which you can work together more efficiently, so you can create positive impressions for your customers.

STOP

○ Have you defined "Wow!" service for your organization? Are you prepared to offer it to your customers?

○ Have you identified your trapeze buddies?

If so, you're ready to move on to Checkpoint 3.

Checkpoint 3

The objective for Checkpoint 3 is *to identify the barriers that may impede plans to improve customer service in your organization.*

As on any road, you may encounter barriers along the way. Each organization has its barriers. Now it's time to identify them, before you "return home."

Potential Barriers

1. **Performers**. You probably already know what you're going to face with some people in the company. Think about how you can be proactive in addressing these people, not reactive.

2. **Processes**. What do the customers like? Generally, they like companies and people that are easy to deal with. So make it simple for customers to do business with you. Remove unnecessary steps, cut red tape, and reduce paper flow as best you can. In other words, look at your processes and eliminate steps that complicate how you deal with your customers before, during, and in delivering after-the-sale service.

3. **Policies.** Reread your policy manuals. Are they written so you can empower people to have some flexibility to do what's right for the customer without being hamstrung by bureaucratic rules? Do the policies interfere with the company's ability to provide superior customer service? If so, change them. Or, better yet, eliminate as many of them as possible.

Using the exercise below, capture your thoughts on how you can reinforce customer-focused quality by removing work barriers in your work unit.

1. What do you see as the major barriers to delivering customer-focused quality in your unit?
   - What are the barriers to delivering hassle-free transactions for your work unit?
   - What are the barriers to making customers feel good about doing business with your work unit?
2. What do you suspect are the causes of these barriers?
   - Performers?
   - Processes?
   - Policies?
3. How will you involve your employees in identifying barriers and developing plans to remove them?

STOP

- Have you identified potential barriers to delivering customer-focused quality in your unit?
- Have you thought of ways in which you will involve your employees in removing these barriers?

If so, you're ready to "return home" to your company, with ideas you received from the three checkpoints you encountered along the highway to success.

Your Trip Has Been Successful

The plan, now, is for you to take these ideas and begin formulating ways in which you can implement them for your unique situation. Your initial "trip" is over. Now the real work begins. Getting everyone committed to "Wow!" service will not happen overnight. It will take time, patience, and dedication.

The key to success is to plan in advance what has to happen, and then follow through and follow up on those plans. Use those ideas that you picked up along the highway's checkpoints. And invite others to commit to "Wow!" customer service. Be sure to load everyone in your organization into your vehicle as you travel down the highway to success. Follow the road less traveled—and you, your employees, and your customers will find that the journey is the destination, and you will continue to get better and better at what you do.

About the Author

Jerry Fritz is the Director of Sales and Customer Service Programs for the Management Institute in the School of Business at the University of Wisconsin, Madison. In 1996 he was named marketing educator of the year by Sales and Marketing Executives International. He's also a member of the National Association of Sales Professionals Education Institute Advisory Group "to help provide national standards defining sales professionals and a certification exam."

3

QUANTIFYING THE IMPACT OF GREAT CUSTOMER SERVICE ON PROFITABILITY

John Goodman

Is the customer service department a cost or a profit center? In this article, John Goodman dramatically demonstrates that it is, indeed, a profit center, one which can generate revenues many times greater than the cost of providing service. In addition, Goodman provides a methodology for measuring the profitability of a customer service department.

Quantifying the Bottom-Line Impact of Improved Quality and Service

In many companies, management believes that customer service is a necessary nuisance. Service and product quality often fail to win sufficient investment because of a lack of understanding of how to link such investments to revenue and profits. The market damage model developed by TARP (Technical Assistance Research Programs) has helped scores of companies understand how investing in great service and quality translates into higher sales and profitability. This article will explain this model and show how service problems affect customer loyalty and produce negative word of mouth, and how you can estimate the effect on your revenue for such problems.

The Effects of Market Damage

What is the impact of problems on customer loyalty and negative word of mouth? Figure 3-1 provides the answer to that question in six very different industries. It compares customers who have had a problem and those who have not had a problem in terms of their loyalty and willingness to buy again.

Figure 3-1 shows that, on average, customer loyalty will drop by about 20% if the customer has encountered a problem. What does that mean for your bottom line? Out of every five customers who experience a problem, one will leave or purchase another brand the next time he or she goes into the marketplace. If your average customer is worth $1,000, then you can estimate that for every five customers with problems, you are losing one customer and $1,000 in revenue.

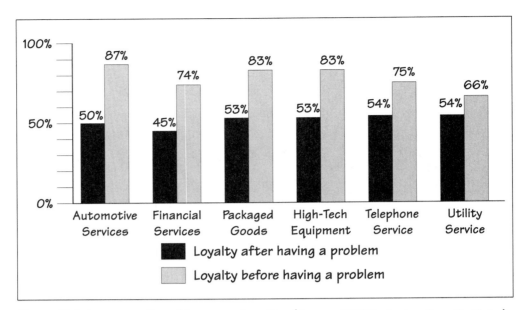

Figure 3-1. Impact of problems on loyalty. (Source: TARP Industry-Specific Data.)

TARP calls this reduction in loyalty due to a problem "market damage." Market damage is the loyalty and revenue lost because of customer-perceived service and quality problems. Quantifying the level of market damage can help motivate top management to fix the problems and allocate the resources to provide world-class service. This motivation is what TARP calls "the economic imperative." (We'll go more into this idea later in this article.)

Once you have the linkage of problems to loyalty, you can then reverse the analysis. The reverse is that if you prevent five problems, you will retain one customer worth $1,000. You can now justify quality initiatives that reduce problems. This analysis and justification of problem prevention is a critical job of service managers. And by undertaking such an analysis these managers can act as internal consultants to the rest of the organization on how to enhance bottom-line performance.

Customer Service and Retaining Customer Loyalty

When a problem occurs, you can retain the loyalty of customers only if they tell you about the problem. Customer service systems have an impact only if customers make use of them. Unfortunately, many customers never contact the company when they need assistance or have a problem. TARP's research across all industries shows that many customers with problems never complain, thereby depriving companies of a chance to retain the loyalty of these customers. Said another way, if customers don't get in touch with the customer service department, the company will likely lose these customers, a situation the company needs to attend to. On average across all industries, TARP has found that 50% of all consumers and 25% of all business customers with problems never complain to anyone. They often just take their business someplace else.

A company can, however, win back all of a customer's loyalty if it can get the

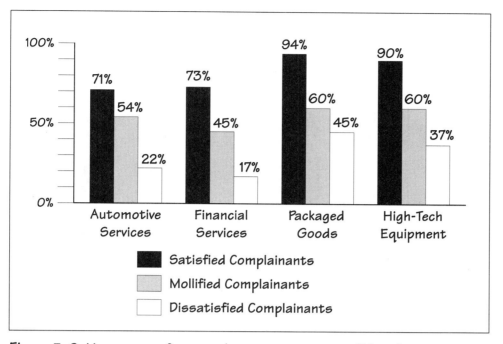

Figure 3-2. How many of your unhappy customers will buy from you again? (Source: TARP Industry-Specific Data.)

customer to call with a problem and then provide a solution that satisfies this customer. Figure 3-2, from four of the six industries shown in Figure 1, illustrates that complaining customers who are then satisfied have loyalties approaching those of customers who had no problem. It also shows that if they are at least mollified, you have a good chance of retaining their loyalty, but if they are left dissatisfied, their loyalty is reduced to a level below what it was before the company tried to deal with the problem. In other words, if you're going to offer customer service to help retain customer loyalty, you better solve the problem. Otherwise, you have a customer who has been dissatisfied, not once, but twice.

In many industries, a complaining customer whose problem is solved becomes more loyal than a customer with no problem. This, we believe, is because, until the customer has a problem, "service" and "quality" are merely advertising slogans. Once the customer encounters a problem and the company acts to resolve it, the customer thinks, "Wow! They really *do* have great service." Every Nordstrom and FedEx story is a recovery story. Figure 3-3, from the computer industry, illustrates the above principle. Notice that a satisfied complainant for both personal computer systems and medium computer systems has a higher sense of loyalty than those customers with no problem.

Finally, service also impacts a company's ability to influence word of mouth. Figure 3-4 gives word of mouth data for small and large transactions. Twice as many people hear about a bad experience as about a good experience. Also, people tend to pay more attention to bad word of mouth. TARP's general assumption is that negative word of mouth has twice the negative impact as positive word of mouth has positive impact. Our usual factors are that 1 out of 50 customers hearing negative

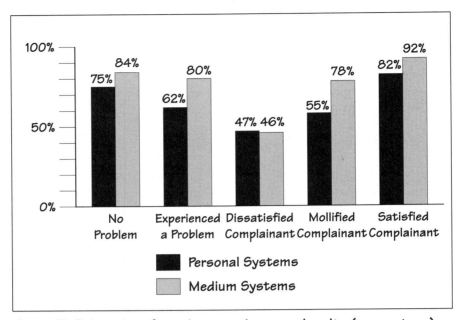

Figure 3-3. Impact of service experience on loyalty (computers).
(Source: TARP Industry-Specific Data.)

	Satisfied	Dissatisfied
SMALL TRANSACTIONS	5	10
LARGE TRANSACTIONS	8	16

Figure 3-4. Word of mouth behavior (median persons
told of experience).

word of mouth will not buy, while 1 out of 100 hearing positive word of mouth will buy.

You should use the data in these figures cautiously. TARP has seen wide variation by industry. For example, in the personal computer industry, TARP has observed the effects of word of mouth to be as follows: A customer with a good service experience tells one person, a customer with a neutral experience tells two people, and a dissatisfied customer tells six people.

Across all industries, TARP has found that if customers complain and are satisfied, their loyalty approaches that of customers with no problems. On the other hand, if they are not satisfied, loyalty decreases by 50%. Therefore, a good service system that can effectively solve customer problems will increase customer retention by up to 50%, meaning that for every two customers processed, the equivalent of another will be retained.

At a macro level, we can perform a simple cost-benefit analysis to calculate the payoff of world-class customer service. If the service transaction costs $40 and increases loyalty by 50% and the customer is worth $400, the result is a 500% return on investment.

We can easily understand and accept the above analysis on a macro level, but there sometimes is a strong current of "we're different" or "our customers don't behave that way." How do you rigorously calculate the market impact of improved quality and service in *your company*?

Market Damage Model

The following section will show you how to use the market damage model to calculate two key sets of numbers: how much it is costing you not to give perfect quality and service and how much improved service will return on various investments.

Overview of the Market Damage Model

To perform an analysis, you need five pieces of data:

- The long-term profit value of a customer,
- The number of customers who experience problems,
- The impact of problems on loyalty,
- The impact of the service system on loyalty, and
- The percentage of customers who bother to complain about problems.

(A sixth desirable data element is the impact of service on word of mouth.)

With this data, you can quantify the return on investment of problem prevention, enhanced service accessibility, and improved satisfaction with service. Let's look at the following example (Figure 3-5), in which a customer will buy a widget once a year, for a profit of $25.

We calculate the sales lost from customers who had problems (SL_{Prob}). We then estimate the sales lost from customers who had no problems and who would have gone to competitors for reasons not related to quality (SL_{NoProb}). Remember that there are other factors that lose customers, such as price, product features, and convenience. For example, FedEx, a world-class delivery service, is losing sales even though its service is very good. This is because of fax machines and the ability to e-mail attached files; you do not need a delivery service in certain cases when the document is only 10 pages long, and a faxed copy is sufficient. These sales are subtracted from the total loss because we would have lost them even if perfect service

SL_{Prob}	SL_{NoProb}	=	SL_{Yr}	X	P_S	=	PL_{Yr}
82,716 Sales	19,125 Sales	=	63,590 Sales	X	$25 Profit per Sale	=	$1,589,750 Lost Profit Annually

Figure 3-5. Baseline analysis results.

had been given. (Exactly where all these numbers came from will be explained later.) The result (SL_{Yr}) shows us that problems are costing us 63,590 sales. At $25 profit per sale, that loss can be valued at $1.59 million annually. This loss is due to 54% of the customers experiencing a problem and only 45% complaining. When they do complain, only 31% are satisfied. (Again, these figures will be explained shortly.)

Once we have this baseline calculation, we then estimate the impact of changing the three major parameters available to us: (1) reduce problems that customer encounter, (2) get customers to tell us when they encounter a problem, or (3) make every effort to satisfy them when they do complain. This analysis is called the *sensitivity* analysis, because it quantifies the sensitivity of the revenue stream to problems encountered (level of quality) and accessibility and effectiveness of the service system in satisfying customers (level of service). We can then use different service strategies to change one or more of these three parameters (Figure 3-6).

If a company implements a program to reduce problems by 5% (Program A), it will reduce lost sales by 5,888 and add $147,200 to our profit. If it implements a second program (Program B), such as having an 800 phone number that allows customers to reach empowered reps who have clear effective response rules, the company will have an opportunity to solve more problems. This is because such a system will increase *both* the complaint rate and the satisfaction rate. By having more unhappy customers call and more of them having their problems solved, the company can retain many more sales and cut the loss in profits by (in this example) almost $700,000.

In Program B, we also observe another common impact of the service system on basic quality. If complaints are actively solicited, the front-line staff tend to raise their level of service to avoid complaints. By soliciting complaints and increasing the rate of customers who complain, you create an environment where the number of complaints actually goes down—because the levels of quality and customer service go up.

Formula Terms	Baseline	Program A	Program B
Percent Experiencing Problems	54%	49%	45%
Percent Complainining	45%	45%	60%
Complainant Satisfaction	31%	31%	60%
Annual Sales Lost	63,590	57,702	35,897
Annual Sales Saved		5,888	27,693
Additional Annual Profit		$147,200	$692,313

Figure 3-6. Sensitivity analysis results. (Note: The decreases in annual sales lost for Programs A and B are calculated using the methodology described in the Appendix to this article. Only summary results are given here.)

Think about the environment of a car dealership. Consider a 23-year-old service writer talking to a difficult customer. He says, "I'm sorry, we can't finish your car today," and the customer looks upset. At that point, the service writer, if the dealership has a strong commitment to customer service, will know immediately to call the service manager and have a technician stay late to finish the job. But the foundation of this commitment to customer service is *not just* a desire to mollify the feelings of a difficult customer. *It is also to increase customer retention and the profitability of the dealership.* In other words, it is a win-win approach where the company is building a mutually beneficial relationship that results in long-term customer retention.

Once you have quantified the profit impact of an investment in quality and service, you can then estimate the return on investment, in Figure 3-7. If Program A costs $50,000 and Program B costs $150,000, your return on investment would be much higher for Program B ($692,000) than for A ($147,000), even though it costs three times as much.

The ROIs portrayed in Figure 3-7 are not at all atypical. In one computer company, TARP found the ROI of an aggressive, high-visibility customer support hotline, where reps could resolve about 60% of customer problems, was over 800%! A pharmaceutical company CFO estimated that, for every dollar saved through quality improvement, over 10 dollars of revenue were retained.

The above examples illustrate the most important audience for the economic model, CFOs or, as we term them at TARP, the resident financial cynics. If they understand and believe the model, invariably they will see the tremendous payoff derived from investment in service and they will become the strongest advocates for investment in higher levels of customer service.

Appendix: Market Damage Model in Detail

The objective of the market damage model is to **quantify the *overall* bottom-line impact** of:

- The impact of the customer problem experience and
- The financial impact of an effective customer response system.

$$\frac{\text{Annual Profit Saved}}{\text{Annual Cost of Program}} = \text{ROI}$$

	Program A	Program B
Annual Cost of Program	$50,000	$150,000
Additional Annual Profit	$147,200	$692,313
Return on Investment	294%	462%

Figure 3-7. Calculation of annual return on investment.

Overview of the Methodology

The methodology in developing the model consists of three steps:

- Collecting data from both the company and the customer,
- Processing the data via a simple set of linear equations,
- Interpreting the data for decision-making.

The first type of data required is company-provided data on the value of the customer. The basic data needed is how much the average customer is worth. At TARP we used to think that this data was universally available. We have learned that only about one-third of companies have this data at hand. If neither the marketing nor the finance office has it, you must assemble the data from the following four data elements:

- Number of annual sales to average customer
- Period of loyalty of average customer
- Number of customers who buy in a year
- Average profit per sale

Combining the four data elements provides the value of the customer over the total period of loyalty. The data does not have to have three-place accuracy. In fact, it is better if it is a rounded-off number that management can remember. At one copier company, for example, TARP found that the average customer had two copiers and bought enough supplies to be worth $25,000 as a customer per year. The actual number was $26,736, but it was more useful to round off to an easily remembered number. That way, in the future, when you told management that the problem was endangering 1,000 customers, they could quickly do the math in their heads and say, "1,000 times $25,000 . . . Gee, that's a $25 million problem!"

The second set of data required is derived from a survey. There are five categories here:

- Percent of customers who experience one or more problems during a one-year period
- Percent of customers who experience one or more problems and complain
- Satisfaction level of complainants in terms of those who are completely satisfied, those who are mollified (the response was acceptable, but they are not completely satisfied), and those who are dissatisfied (usually completely dissatisfied and no action taken)
- Brand loyalty by level of satisfaction in terms of the customers who will buy again and/or recommend if they are satisfied, mollified, or dissatisfied
- Word of mouth by level of satisfaction in terms of the number of people told by satisfied, mollified, and dissatisfied complainants as well as by non-complainants

Note: If the customer buys several times per year, the annual problem rate is calculated using the following mathematical equation:

$$P = 1 - Q^N$$

where P = Problem Rate, Q = Probability of Not Having Problem, and
N = Number of Purchases/Year

For example:

- For one purchase, $P = 1 - 0.7^1 = 0.3$, or a 30% chance of a problem
- For two purchases, $P = 1 - 0.7^2 = 1 - 0.49 = 0.51$, or a 51% chance of a problem

The calculation then consists of two numbers: the sales lost from customers who encounter problems minus those sales which would have been lost even if they had not encountered a problem. The first number, sales lost from customers encountering problems, is made up of two groups of customers—those who will not come back and those who will be lost due to the negative word of mouth produced by the unhappy customers. Figure 3-8 illustrates this idea.

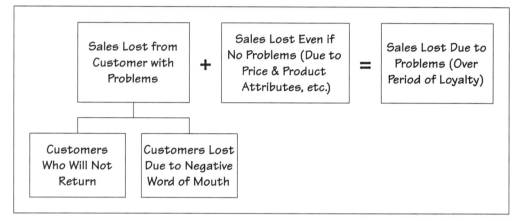

Figure 3-8. Calculation of market damage.

Detailed Example of This Calculation: The ABC Company

The following figures are data from the ABC Company on the value of customers and data from a survey on problem experience, complaining behavior, and the impact on loyalty and word of mouth.

- Number of purchases over five-year period of loyalty · · · · · · · · 10
- Number of customers · · · · · · · · 500,000
- Profit per purchase · · · · · · · · $20
- Percent of customers experiencing problems annually · · · · · · · · 70%
- Percent of customers complaining · · · · · · · · 50%
- Percent of complainants satisfied · · · · · · · · 40%
- Percent of complainants mollified · · · · · · · · 35%
- Percent of complainants dissatisfied · · · · · · · · 25%
- Repurchase intention:
  Customers Without Problems · · · · · · · · 88%

Noncomplainants   55%
Satisfied Complainants   95%
Mollified Complainants   75%
Dissatisfied Complainants   30%
○ Word of mouth (number of people told by each):
Noncomplainants   2
Satisfied Complainants   1
Mollified Complainants   3
Dissatisfied Complainants   6

The assumption about the impact of negative word of mouth is that *1 customer is lost for every 50 potential customers who hear negative word of mouth.* This factor was negotiated with over 400 marketing executives over the last 10 years as being a very conservative assumption of the impact of word of mouth. There have been few empirical studies of word of mouth impact in a commercial setting. In one, an auto company suggests that 12 customers will be lost for every 50 due to negative word of mouth, while an over-the-counter drug company suggested that 8 per 50 was realistic. For the sake of this discussion, we use the very conservative estimate of 1 per 50.

We first calculate the sales lost over a five-year period from customers who encounter a problem and do not buy again (Figure 3-9).

An important lesson here is to observe which aspect of the service delivery system loses the most customers. Note that the highest number of customers in

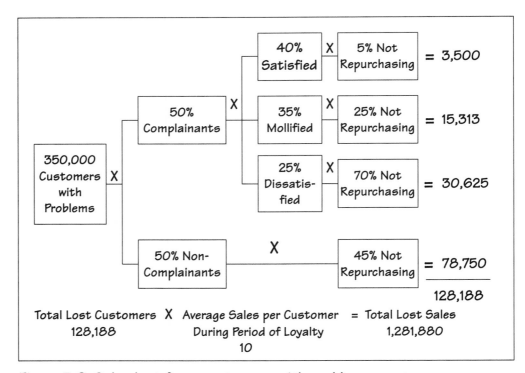

Figure 3-9. Sales lost from customers with problems: customer nonrepurchase.

Figure 3-9 (78,750) is lost from those who never contact the company. This makes a strong case for aggressively soliciting complaints and making customer service easy to access.

The next step is to calculate the impact of the negative word of mouth produced by those customers who have encountered problems (Figure 3-10).

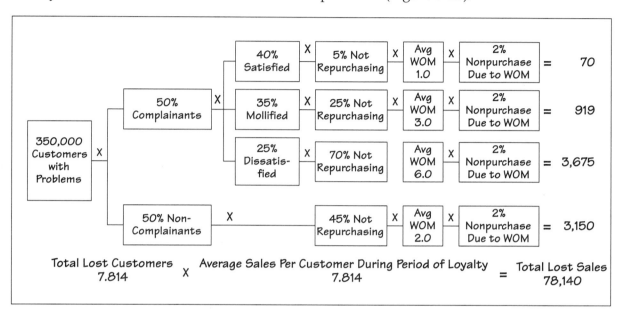

Figure 3-10. Sales lost from customers with problems: nonpurchase due to word of mouth.

The third step, shown in Figure 3-11, is to calculate the amount of sales that would have been lost even if there had been no problems. We do this by taking the number of customers encountering problems and multiplying by the rate of attrition of customers who have no problem. This is the customer loss that would take place if the service and quality were perfect but with pricing, product features, and convenience remaining the same. While all of these factors can be addressed, they are the domain of product development and marketing, not customer service and quality.

Figure 3-11. Sales lost even if no problem.

The three calculations are combined in Figure 3-12 to show the sales stream lost over a five-year period.

One objection some have here is that a five-year sales stream is very speculative because of the changing market. Therefore, to obtain a very conservative estimate of the lost profit per year, we divide the lost sales by five and convert to profits lost

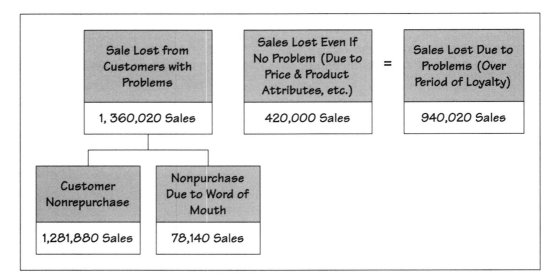

Figure 3-12. Calculation of lost sales over a five-year period.

over just the next year (Figure 3-13). The outcome of the data will be similar to the table (Figure 3-14), which is similar to the data in Figure 3-6.

The three programs in Figure 3-14 are evaluated by simply changing the parameter in the calculation and rerunning the numbers. For instance, for program A, which could be better customer education or improved delivery reliability, the 70% problem rate declines to 65%, which results in 325,000 customers with problems, rather than 350,000. The rest of the calculations are then the same. For Program C, which could be more empowerment and training or representatives, satisfaction goes from 40% to 55%, and the equations are recalculated.

Collecting the Data to Build the Model

There are several questions that you need to ask to build the model. There is also a secondary set of questions that will assist in diagnosis of the problems inherent in any service system. Both sets of questions are outlined below.

Core questions you need to ask customers to build the model:

- Did you have any problems?
- Which was most serious?
- Did you complain?

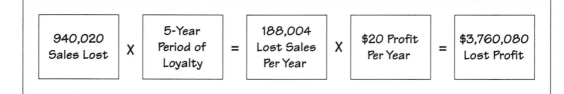

Figure 3-13. Profit lost per year.

Formula Terms	Baseline	Program A	Program B	Program C
Percent Experiencing Problems	70%	65%	60%	70%
Percent Complaining	50%	50%	65%	50%
Complainant Satisfaction	40%	40%	60%	55%
Annual Sales Lost	188,004	174,574	99,795	149,520
Annual Sales Saved		13,430	88,209	38,484
Additional Annual Profit Earned		$268,600	$1,764,180	$769,680
Program Cost		$85,000	$400,000	$77,500
Return on Investment		316%	441%	993%

Figure 3-14. Sensitivity analysis results: ABC Company.

○ Are you satisfied?
○ Have you remained loyal?

Diagnostic questions include, among others you might ask:

○ What type of problems have you had?
○ To whom did you complain?
○ How well was the problem handled?
○ How many times did you contact us?
○ Did you feel we were very responsive and concerned?
○ Did our response elicit delight?

Use your answers to collect the data necessary to use the economic model to understand the impact of customer service on your company's profitability.

About the Author

John Goodman is the president of TARP (Technical Assistance Research Programs), a leading research and consulting organization specializing in customer service toll-free telephone systems and loyalty measurement systems. He has managed more than 600 customer service studies, including TARP's White House–sponsored evaluation of complaint-handling practices in government and business. He has developed methodologies for integrating customer problem data with other types of market feedback to estimate the market implications of quality and service decisions. Goodman and TARP's clients include many companies in the Fortune 100 as well as numerous international firms.

4

DELIGHTING YOUR CUSTOMERS: CREATING WORLD-CLASS SERVICE

Eberhard E. Scheuing

This article highlights the crucial role of world-class service in building an organization's competitive advantage. As the author notes, "For organizations to survive and prosper, creating competitive advantage through customer loyalty is the strategic imperative." He shows how the effort to deliver world-class service begins with finding out what your customers want and expect from your company, and he recommends some means for doing so.

Customers are the lifeblood of any organization. Without them, it loses its meaning and purpose. Customers provide incentive, vitality, and growth. Serving them well requires a customer-focused culture and customer-friendly systems. And it requires unrelenting effort toward continuous improvement. But the rewards are well worth the effort: unflinching customer loyalty, sustainable growth, and impressive performance.

Listening to Customers

To deliver world-class service and delight its customers, an organization needs to engage in an ongoing dialog with them. Figure 4-1 illustrates the one-way communication that organizations have traditionally practiced. Customer delight is all but impossible to achieve in this manner because the organization will never know what the customers' requirements are and whether it has met them. This kind of short-sighted approach leaves an organization highly vulnerable to more sophisticated, customer-focused competitors. In contrast, closed-loop communications allows information to flow both ways—to and from the customer. Customers are proactively asked about their service expectations and requirements. They are encouraged to offer ideas, comments, and suggestions. But they are also periodically requested to provide feedback by rating the performance of the organization as a whole as well as that of individual employees. This process helps identify and reward employee excellence and pinpoint opportunities for improvement. Customers appreciate being asked and listened to, and tend to reward closed-loop communications with loyalty.

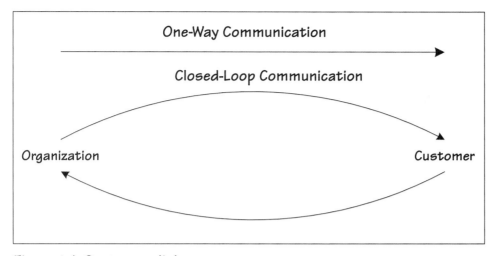

Figure 4-1. Customer dialog.

There are various tools available to resourceful service leaders eager to tune in to customers. Here are five of them:

- ◯ *Focus Groups*—roundtable discussions with small customer groups.
- ◯ *Surveys*—questionnaire studies of large numbers of customers.
- ◯ *Critical Incident Reports*—experiences told in customers' own words.
- ◯ *Advisory Panels*—representative groups of customers offering advice.
- ◯ *One-on-One Conversations*—personal contacts with individual customers.

Focus Groups

Focus groups are informal roundtable discussions with small groups of customers that are facilitated by a skilled moderator. The purpose of focus group sessions is to encourage free-flowing discussion of issues relevant to an organization's customers and thus to the organization itself. Refreshments are usually served to create a relaxed atmosphere, and it is useful to record the results at least on audiotape for subsequent replay and review. It is the moderator's role and responsibility to keep the discussion on the topic and cover all important issues. Toward this end, it is helpful to draw up a moderator's guide or checklist of issues to be addressed during the discussion.

Major benefits of focus group sessions are their spontaneity and the synergy that arises when participants build on each other's comments. Also, the moderator has the unique opportunity to probe for details when an unexpected line of thinking emerges. The dynamics of group interaction make the serendipitous discovery of previously unknown concerns or opportunities a key benefit of focus group discussions.

Due to their versatility and speed, focus groups can be used for a variety of purposes in an organization's dialog with its customers. They can be utilized to provide input into or feedback on the organization's actions and to guide the design and/or interpretation of customer surveys. Focus group sessions are powerful research tools that must be used with care to avoid their potential pitfalls, which include domination of the discussion by an outspoken participant.

Surveys

Surveys are large-scale customer studies conducted with the help of questionnaires. Questionnaires are formal lists of questions that are usually followed by multiple-choice answers from which respondents are asked to select one or more that fit their particular situations. These forms can be administered in person, over the phone, by fax, or through the mail to a sizable number of customers. In contrast to focus groups, which are qualitative research tools and thus can provide insights but no numbers, surveys are means of quantitative research that can generate numerical measurements, such as frequency distributions.

Questionnaire design is both an art and a science. Concerns relate, for instance, to the wording, sequencing, and number of questions to be asked. All too often, questionnaires are written from the perspective and in the language of the researcher, not those of the customer. This may well lead to misunderstandings in the interpretation of questions or even meaningless results. Ideally, questionnaires should be designed with the help of customers and pretested with a small group of respondents before being rolled out on a large scale. Focus groups can be very helpful in this effort.

Critical Incident Reports

Critical incident reports are statements made by customers about recent experiences with an organization. In the customers' own words, such reports represent top-of-mind awareness of incidents that matter to them. Customers are asked to recount recent interactions with employees of the organization and report how satisfied or dissatisfied they were with the service process and/or its outcome. Although such reports are somewhat difficult to quantify, they provide a treasure trove of information about moments of truth.

While questionnaires present preconceived notions that may be of little concern to customers, critical incident reports reflect occurrences that continue to either bother or delight customers. Their memories of these incidents will not only impact their own future behavior but will also be shared with others via word-of-mouth conversations and thus have a ripple effect on what other customers do.

With critical incident reports, customers have the opportunity to express their perceptions and feelings from their own perspective, not in reaction to the company perspective represented in survey questionnaires. If a company neglects the use of critical incident reports, management is deprived of valuable insights into the current quality of service, where the company is doing the right things, and in which areas it needs to improve. Too many organizations display an attitude that "no news is good news." This is a head-in-the-sand approach that says, "We are not receiving any complaints, therefore we must be doing well." Nothing could be further from the truth for mediocre organizations that continue to exist mainly for lack of effective competition. Most likely, the lack of complaints is not due to a lack of deficiencies but to a lack of an effective mechanism for reporting them.

Advisory Panels

Advisory panels are groups of customers who advise an organization on a regular basis. Telephone companies, for instance, use such panels as sounding boards for new initiatives and services and to help them assess the nature and severity of complaints. The panels essentially act as spokespersons for the organization's customer base and assist in guiding its actions in a direction beneficial to both parties. Typically serving in a voluntary capacity, panel members tend to be vocal advocates of their constituencies, providing a vital and dynamic link to the marketplace.

One-on-One Conversations

Last but definitely not least, *one-on-one conversations* involve invaluable personal contacts between individual employees and customers. A few organizations have developed this tool to the level of an art. Intuit, a California software developer and publisher, has designers interact with customers in its laboratory and visit them at home to observe them in action. And in the Ritz-Carlton Hotel chain, which won the Baldrige Award for its world-class service, all employees are asked to record and report customer requests and comments on "guest preference" forms which are input into a data base that is accessible to all of its properties worldwide. For its preferred customers, British Airways keeps a similar data base available to all of its agents.

Continuous dialog with customers is an essential prerequisite for building and maintaining relationships with them that make them feel understood and appreciated. World-class service is impossible without closed-loop communications which facilitate the delivery of exceptional value to customers.

Complaints Provide Valuable Feedback

Research indicates that for every dissatisfied customer who complains to an organization, there are 26 other customers who are equally dissatisfied but do not complain to the organization. But they tell others—in fact, about 10 others on average. This negative word of mouth discourages potential customers from ever giving the organization a chance. So for every complaining customer, there are possibly 260 others who have either had a bad experience or heard about one and thus will not/ no longer do business with the organization. But the organization never gets a chance to hear about it and take corrective action.

So it is essential to encourage and welcome complaints instead of treating them as unjustified nagging or evil nuisances. A customer who complains offers an organization a chance to correct an alleged faulty performance or set the record straight by educating the customer about the true nature of the situation. Most customers whose complaints are resolved will continue to do business with an organization. If complaints are resolved promptly, they may even become loyal customers.

It helps to ask complaining customers what would make the situation right for them and then go beyond what they requested to surprise them. Correcting perceived performance problems is known as *recovery*. Recovery requires an appropriate process that enables quick action. It is both an art and a skill. As an art, it involves sensitivity, judgment, and flair. As a skill, it can and must be taught because it is an invaluable means of gaining critical insight and recapturing the goodwill of customers ready to defect.

The Harvey Hotel in Plano, Texas, uses a video entitled "Exceeding Guest Expectations" to encourage this spirit in its employees. The video stars actual colleagues recounting "moments of truth" which represent encounters between employees and actual or potential customers. In those moments, in the eyes of the customers, the employees *are* the organization. Whatever they say or do will reflect on the organization as a whole. If the situations are mishandled, bitter feelings can result, and the customers may defect. But if the employees shine, the organization shines. At the point and moment of contact, the employee personifies the organization. This is why proper selection, training, and motivation of employees are essential ingredients in the success of any organization.

Systems as Barriers

But many impediments can get in the way of providing excellent service to customers. Ever since Alfred P. Sloan created functional specialization at General Motors, American organizations have been characterized by vertical structures. Functions such as marketing, purchasing, and finance are distinct and separate from each other, have their own hierarchies, and protect their respective turfs from intrusion by others. Some have referred to these breakdowns as "silos" to highlight the insular, self-contained nature of traditional functional specialization. Others talk about throwing things "over a wall" to indicate that accountability ("the buck") passes from one function to the next with little cooperation. In fact, such interactions are often characterized by hostility, finger pointing, and rejection.

Experience indicates that customers often become the unwitting victims in such internecine wars. The individual functions suboptimize because their own performances are more important to them than the success of the organization as a whole. Marketing may make promises that the operations function cannot keep. Purchasing may follow standard procedures instead of making a special effort to meet customer needs. And customer requests or inquiries may be bounced around all over the place because nobody cares to assume responsibility for a problem.

Most systems have indeed been designed to suit the convenience of the organization, not that of its customers. Patients who are brought to emergency rooms of the nation's hospitals in acute distress are typically forced to undergo thorough examination of their medical coverage and wait extensively before they are seen and perhaps treated by a caregiver. This apparent lack of concern for their condition in fact tends to aggravate it further and is thus clearly counterproductive.

People as Barriers

Ultimately, its employees make or break an organization. Unmotivated employees provide at best indifferent service. This fact is perfectly evident in many civil service settings. All too many government workers interacting with the public treat the recipients of their "service" with a strange mixture of arrogance, lack of concern, and even disdain. They can get away with this kind of behavior as long as the public does not have any alternative to their "service."

No private sector organization could survive treating its customers this way unless it faced no competition. In fact, the quasi-private United States Postal Service has seen its business eroded by more nimble competitors. Federal Express and others offer overnight small package delivery service that the USPS has tried to match with its Express Mail service. This kind of vigorous competition has done wonders to transform the USPS into a more responsive organization with more service-minded employees.

It is also evident that inadequately trained employees simply cannot excel. New employees are all too often merely shown "how we do things around here." After this perfunctory introduction to the organization and its practices, employees are usually left to their own devices, learning on the job as they go along. If employees have not been taught how to identify customers and understand their expectations, it will be all but impossible for them to meet these expectations, far less exceed them.

And employees simply cannot excel without the proper support systems and tools. They need fingertip access to computerized data bases and the capability to enter and update information instantaneously. State-of-the-art information technology is an essential prerequisite for excellent performance. In a broader sense, the latest equipment, properly serviced and maintained, enables professional service delivery. Federal Express can track packages continuously because its couriers carry scanners that they insert into on-board computers in their delivery vans. This information is, in turn, transmitted to a central station to monitor package movement and delivery. The company equips major customers with terminals that facilitate shipping and tracking, including electronic transmission of receipt signatures.

Creating Customer Passion

To create customers for life, management must instill and continually reinforce a genuine passion for delighting customers throughout the entire organization. Toward this end, it must present a vision of excellence, champion it, and provide appropriate rewards.

A *vision* is a powerful image of what an organization intends to *become*. In contrast, its *mission* describes its *current* state. A mission statement outlines the uniqueness of the organization or *what* it proposes to be to *whom*. By painting an inspiring picture of its future condition, a vision statement enables an organization to transition to an improved, more advanced level of performance.

Delivering world-class service requires a powerful, exciting vision that moves people to act in concert to delight the customer. This vision must be based on a set of values that are easy to understand and widely practiced. Just below is a list of customer service values that can form the foundation of this vision.

- Honesty and trustworthiness
- Innovation and creativity
- Openness and flexibility
- Customer concern and passion
- Proactive service improvement

To be effective, a vision of world-class service must focus on employees and customers. In fact, it is important to do so in this order. To put it simply: happy employees make for happy customers. Happiness is contagious. It spreads quickly. The cornerstone of the success of the Marriott hospitality organization is the motto advanced by its founder, J. Willard Marriott: "Take care of the employees and they'll take care of the customers." His son, the current chairman, makes it his business to talk to dishwashers, housekeepers, and other staff members as he visits the company's properties to find out whether they are being treated fairly and their concerns are being addressed.

Hal Rosenbluth, CEO of the Philadelphia-based international travel organization that bears his family's name, entitled his book *The Customer Comes Second (and Other Secrets of Exceptional Service)*. In this book, he describes the transformation of a small, local travel agency into a significant international operation based on the careful selection and development of his "associates." Their commitment and excitement translate into many loyal "clients."

Rewarding World-Class Service

Excellent performance cannot and should not be expected to be its own reward. Rather, world-class service needs to be rewarded. If an organization truly wants to encourage world-class performance, it must provide appropriate rewards.

Recognition involves public praise in front of one's colleagues, usually in an appropriate ceremony. Winning an award for exceptional performance has a great deal of meaning for employees because it publicizes their accomplishments and holds them up as examples for others. Some organizations attach monetary benefits or prizes to an award; others grant temporary or lasting privileges.

Recognition for outstanding performance has greater meaning if the criteria for selection are clear and if the recipients are nominated or even chosen by their peers. Many hotels recognize the "employee of the month" in this manner, post his or her picture in the lobby, and award the winner a reserved parking space for a month. There is considerable controversy as to whether recognition should be given to individuals or only to teams. While the answer to this question will depend on the circumstances, one thing is quite clear: recognition is an effective and efficient way to spur outstanding performance.

A number of leading organizations have gone so far as to pattern their internal award systems after the Baldrige Award. Westinghouse and AT&T are among the companies that use this approach to promote aggressive internal competition for excellence. Reflecting Olympic medals, AT&T has bronze, silver, and gold categories for its teams. In a somewhat ironic twist, its Universal card unit won an internal Chairman's bronze award in the same year that it received the Baldrige Award for world-class quality in services. This attests to the high standards imposed by AT&T and others in their recognition programs.

Celebration, finally, adds an element of fun to the never-ending quest for world-class service. Having a good time with colleagues at a picnic, golf outing, show, or similar event to celebrate joint efforts to achieve excellence for customers is a neat way to say "thank you" to all and keep up the good spirit.

Conclusion

For organizations to survive and prosper, creating competitive advantage through customer loyalty is *the* strategic imperative. Substantial customer churn is expensive and risky for any organization. It is said that it costs five times as much to gain a new customer than to hold on to an existing one. And it may be not only expensive but quite difficult to replace departing customers. So it is essential to stem defections by satisfying, if not delighting, customers. It is also worthwhile to attempt to regain lost customers who may well be ready to return.

It is worthwhile and exciting to turn one-time customer transactions into long-term relationships by rendering world-class service. Delighting customers is psychologically and financially rewarding. Loyal customers will not be swayed by competitive offers but will instead bring more business to the organization. Delighting customers through world-class service is not a luxury but an investment in an organization's future success.

About the Author

Eberhard E. Scheuing, Ph.D., C.P.M., A.P.P., is Professor of Marketing and the NAPM Professor of Purchasing and Supply Leadership at St. John's University in New York. Born and educated in Germany, he received his M.B.A. in management and his Ph.D. in marketing from the University of Munich. The author of 26 books and more than 500 articles, Eb is the founder and president of the International Service Quality Association, co-chair of international service quality conferences, and a frequent seminar leader, conference speaker, and consultant.

5

CUSTOMER RETENTION AND THE STAGES OF SERVICE AFTER THE SALE

Terry G. Vavra and Douglas R. Pruden

Businesses too often tend to treat the customer as an angler treats a fish: once you've located it and hooked it, you put it away and forget about it, turning your attention to catching another. This article explores the concept of aftermarketing and describes the stages of service and meeting the expectations of customers after you've sold them something. Each stage requires that the company deal with the customer in different ways. And if you do this well, you're far more likely to retain those customers.

The Philosophy of Aftermarketing

"Aftermarketing" is the term we use to refer to any marketing activity directed at current customers with the express purpose of increasing those customers' likelihood of repurchasing a product or service in the future, or of increasing their share of requirements in the category from the represented supplier.[1]

As we've written in *Aftermarketing: How to Keep Customers for Life Through Relationship Marketing*, the entire process of relationship marketing depends upon the quality of the after-sale servicing customers receive. Aftermarketing requires that businesses not abandon consumers immediately after the purchase has been made. Rather, a sale should hopefully be the start of a long-term, respectful relationship between the business and the customer.

Unfortunately, even though relationship marketing has become a mid-'90s management buzzword, most firms have not made the commitment necessary, nor have they undertaken the cultural transformation that is a critical part of the process. They even more visibly still lack the show of commitment that could be demonstrated through the creation of an "Office of the Customer," a "Department of Customer Retention," or a "Loyalty Management Team." Without such areas dedicated to relationships, one can ask the question, "Who is looking after *current* customers?"

1. Terry G. Vavra, *Aftermarketing: How to Keep Customers for Life Through Relationship Marketing* (Burr Ridge, IL: Irwin Professional Publishing, 1992, 1995).

Unfortunately, in far too many cases, *no one* is focused on current customers. Instead, attention is aimed at potential customers, and conquest marketing is still the rule of the day. As more and more new customers are enticed to buy, current customers not receiving much attention become disillusioned and silently leave, succumbing to the conquest efforts of competitors. This silent exodus has become recognized as business's worst nightmare. Companies, without much understanding of their current misallocation of effort, are nevertheless rallying to reduce "customer churn"!

Yet while more and more executives are rewarded for and evaluated on their effectiveness in reducing churn, far too few know anything about how to achieve this worthwhile goal. In many cases they'll spend more time discussing definitions of churn and trying to count the numbers defecting than actually working on remedies—not a surprise given their lack of training in the use of retention marketing tools. This is because most successful business leaders today have risen to their current positions based on their ability to conquer new customers, to build sales, and to increase market share. Few if any have had to think about maintaining the customers they have won or increasing their share of current customers' spending.

This leads us to an inescapable conclusion: while retention may be the current talk of the marketplace, the mindset of the marketplace is still firmly rooted in conquest marketing!

But currents in business are shifting. Middle managers (those closer to customers) are beginning to understand the futility of a solitary focus on conquest marketing. And these individuals are leading a "grass-roots rebellion" against upper management's misdirection. More and more quality action teams and retention task forces are earnestly discussing the need to develop tools and programs to retain current customers.

Components of After-Sale Servicing

When an organization decides that aftermarketing makes sense, it needs to develop a toolbox of effective retention tactics. To use these tactics strategically, managers need to identify areas of opportunity. After-sale servicing is a good place to start. We believe after-sale servicing can be thought of in at least three components:

1. **Initiating dialogue with current customers**—what we call "formal communications." Formal communications include dialogue initiated by the business with its current customers. These are the structured programs most organizations consider to be part of their retention process. They benefit from being driven by an intelligent customer database that allows them to address the needs and tenure of each individual customer.
2. **Responding to customer-initiated dialogue**—what we call "informal communications." Informal communications involve response to customer-initiated dialogue. Properly conducted, they are even more work than one might imagine and are considerably more structured than they might appear. Informal communications not only involve being prepared for contact and responding to customer questions, compliments, and complaints in a timely fashion, but also require that the business encourage dialogue and provide

an easy avenue through which customers can transmit their questions, compliments, and complaints.

3. **Managing** *moments of truth.* These are the points at which customers "test" a business to see if it really responds the way it promised or acts the way it should. Managing these important events requires a business to think through the entire "customer experience," identifying all of the points (possible interactions with the business, product use occasions, etc.) customers will use to judge the value of the product or service they've selected. Once they've identified these points, managers should proactively prepare for each. Moments of truth vary by business category, but they generally include such things as receiving the first bill, contacting the business for after-sale service, submitting a claim, receiving a competitive offer, etc.

The trick to successfully exploiting these opportunities is to develop tactics according to what customers want and need in that specific instance, depending upon their tenure with the business. These components ought to be conceived and managed based upon the individual customer's status, in the customer's own, personal purchase cycle.

How Tactics Are Frequently Misdeveloped and Mispracticed

More times than not, when managers pay attention to customer retention, their activities on this front are designed and offered on the organization's timetable—not the customer's. This means that, for example, although a cable TV customer may already subscribe to premium channels, if it's September and September is Premium Channel Promotion Month, the customer is likely to receive a solicitation to subscribe to a premium channel—perhaps one he or she already receives!

When tactics are developed and delivered on the organization's timetable, they tend to be less relevant, less valuable, and less sought by customers. They are, therefore, less effective. But beyond being less effective, they show the business's indifference toward the individual customer—making it clear no personal relationship exists.

Of course, to allow the customer's timetable to govern outreach, organizations need to maintain a database of their customers that is complete and current. This database (we refer to it as a "customerbase") needs to identify dates of transactions, what the customer purchased, and other details about the customer (household composition, facts about the customer's industry, and so on). Doing this is consistent with the trend in basic marketing of moving from treating the marketplace as a mass market to treating it as a collection of individual consumers whose individual wants and needs we can know, monitor, and satisfy.

A New Timetable: The Aftermarketing Purchase Cycle

It has long been accepted that in making a purchase decision, consumers pass through a series of stages of varying investigation and commitment to a selected brand. This process is often referred to as a buying decision process. In an advertising context, the process has been referred to as a *hierarchy of effects*. And it is often defined by the stages of awareness, interest, desire, and action (purchase).

There is also an equal if not more important process customers pass through upon purchasing a product or service. We call this second process a *hierarchy of experience*. It's represented by the stages customers pass through in their actual interaction with the product or service they've purchased and its vendor, provider, or manufacturer. This hierarchy is the summation of what the customer experiences. The stages are **commitment**, **learning/evaluation**, **appreciation/reconciliation**, and **reevaluation**. Figure 5-1 shows how this hierarchy of experience takes over from the hierarchy of effects, once customers have experience with the product or service. In the same way that *brand equity* is the result of the hierarchy of effects, the hierarchy of experience creates *customer equity*—the value of a committed, loyal customerbase.

Advertising agencies (and some businesses) attempt to explain repeat purchase and customer loyalty solely as a function of advertising. They downplay the role of customers' personal experiences with a product or service, suggesting it is advertising alone that continues to influence consumers' repurchases, even after they experience the product, brand, or service. Organizations that overlook the existence of an after-purchase hierarchy are the same businesses that refuse to allocate any funds to retention marketing activities, while squandering unreasonably large budgets on advertising.

Surveys we've conducted reinforce the notion of the after-purchase hierarchy. These surveys show customers reject the influence of advertising after they've had a "hands-on" opportunity to personally experience a product or service.

Table 5-1 shows the results from one such survey. Prior to purchase, reputation and advertising account for 31% of the sources of information, with anticipated quality of the product/service and anticipated level of servicing and support accounting for 44%. After purchase, customers shift much more importance to the experienced levels of product/service quality and servicing and support; word-of-mouth also becomes far less important.

Some intuitively astute businesses may indirectly address some aspects of a hierarchy of experience, but rarely does any organization appear to totally understand, believe in, or act upon the process. The stages in the hierarchy of experience can be represented by stages in what we call the Aftermarketing Purchase Cycle.^{SM}

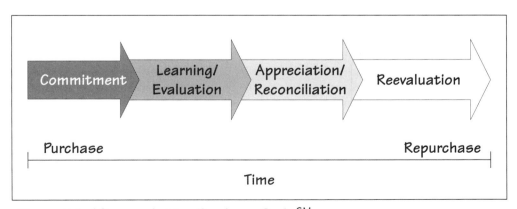

Figure 5-1. Aftermarketing Purchase Cycle.^{SM}

The Source of Information	Before Purchasing a Product/Service		After Purchasing a Product/Service	
• The reputation of the company	20%		11%	
• What friends and associates say about the product or brand	25%	45%	9%	20%
• Claims and promises made in advertising	11%		6%	
• The imagined/experienced*quality of the product or brand	30%		54%	
• The imagined/experienced* level of the company's servicing and support	14%	44%	19%	73%

* imagined was used in the before purchasing scenario; experienced in the after purchasing scenario.

Table 5-1. Survey results: The importance of sources of information to customers. (Source: Marketing Metrics survey, 1995.)

Figure 5-2 describes the Purchase Cycle, with each stage identified by the predominating need the customer is experiencing. We believe an appreciation and understanding of this after-purchase hierarchy is absolutely necessary for the creation of successful retention marketing tactics.

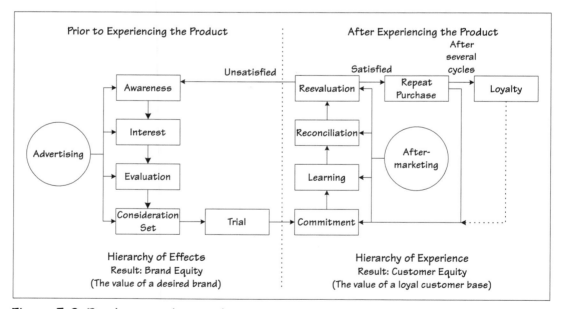

Figure 5-2. Purchase and repurchase sequence.

Stages of the Aftermarketing Purchase Cycle

1. Commitment. As consumers become a business's customers, they outwardly commit to the brand, product, or service. This commitment is very often accompanied by considerable internal questioning or doubt. Their desire for consistency—to have purchased the *right product* for a fair price—means their outward appearance of resolve may be deceiving. Some businesses may totally overlook both the opportunities as well as the obligations at this stage. But others do recognize this uneasy state of the new buyer. The automobile industry acknowledges "buyer's remorse," clothing stores experience the second thoughts of customers attempting to return purchases, and even colleges and universities experience students transferring to "better" schools.

The fact is, early in their stage of commitment, customers are often quite uncertain about the wisdom of the decision they've made and are usually eager for reinforcement. Unfortunately, they often feel cast adrift by a sales force eager to move on to other potential customers. Exacerbating this customer uncertainty is the likelihood of their decision being scrutinized by friends and associates. Left on their own, their attempts to explain or defend their purchasing decisions may be frail, which only amplifies their uneasiness.

The commitment stage is terribly important in establishing a long-term relationship with customers. If the business revisits the customer and offers information or evidence to reinforce the buyer's decision and shows it will be around for future support, the buyer's anxiety will be considerably relieved.

The primary actions of the business at this stage should be continued accessibility and commitment to its customers, and should supply ample confirmatory information to validate the purchase as a wise and thoughtful one.

2. Learning/Evaluation. As customers resign themselves to the brand, product, or service they've selected, social psychology tells us they'll continue to seek as much confirmatory information as possible. Studies show that most of the readers or viewers of advertisements are actually new customers searching for information about the brand they've already chosen that reinforces their selection and purchase. The Learning/Evaluation stage represents one of the biggest opportunities for organizations to provide after-sale servicing. In this stage customers are motivated learners—they want to learn as much about the product or brand as possible.

Businesses can capitalize on their understanding of this stage by remaining accessible to new customers and by offering training and support. Key tactics are providing easy access and following up with customers to determine their level of comfort in using the product or service.

3. Appreciation/Reconciliation. During this, the longest phase of the Aftermarketing Purchase Cycle, customers have resigned themselves to their product or service choice. In "living with their decision" they've accepted all of the benefits and/or annoyances and inconveniences that come with it. Remember the last pair of shoes you purchased that looked great but always caused a blister whenever you wore them? Too often customers are suffering with a "blister" but simply forbear, waiting until the next repurchase opportunity, when they can remedy the situation by switching to another brand, supplier, or company.

Customers at this stage are eager to become "masters of the product or service." They're likely to become very active and invest considerable effort in learning as much as possible about their acquisition. They hope to become power users, knowledgeable owners, and satisfied customers. This, too, is where the business stands to gain the most in benefits from stimulating positive word-of-mouth. Satisfied, happy customers will go out of their way to urge others to adopt the product or brand.

4. Reevaluation. As customers recognize their need to replace the now worn-out, used-up, or obsolete product with a new one, they enter into a reevaluation stage. In this phase they reassess their satisfaction with the current brand and organization. They compare their experiences with what they believe their satisfaction might have been with alternatives. Though they look to numerous sources for information at this stage, their own experiences as well as the word of mouth they receive from others become primary influences on whether they change brands or remain loyal.

Businesses at this stage should attempt to minimize customers' search efforts, heading off exploration of competitive options. Since the business should know the value of different customers, it should be clear how much energy and resources to expend on each customer. Because skilled relationship marketers will also have developed a comprehensive customerbase, they will know much more about their customers' needs, uses, and approximate timing for replacement purchase. The advantages accruing to such a business are numerous. Depending upon the situation, the knowledge in the customerbase may suggest:

1. A special promotion to encourage repurchase even before the customer spends any time considering a competitive offering;
2. A strategically timed on-site visit to strengthen the relationship; or
3. A carefully crafted guide comparing the current brand with competitors' offerings, with the intention of influencing an inevitable shopping-comparison exercise.

Gridding the Aftermarketing Components Against the Purchase Cycle

Creating retention tactics is not that difficult—in the abstract. Everyone can think of at least one or two activities that will probably help save customers. Even the process itself, like the venerable "Hawthorne effect," creates positive value. (That is, simply talking about the value of current customers in and of itself creates an environment more sensitive to retaining customers.) But the fact is that retention tactics, like anything else, are more effective if they're created with specific objectives in mind and with a better understanding of the mindset of their intended target.

The Aftermarketing Purchase Cycle helps us better understand the state of mind of customers relative to their feelings about the brand or organization. As we've described above, different needs and concerns are relevant in certain stages. Table 5-2 briefly reviews the most important needs at each stage of the Purchase Cycle.

If organizations use the Purchase Cycle as a way of understanding their customers' most salient needs, we believe they can better plan retention tactics that will be relevant and therefore successful. This means that tactics will be strategically aligned to answering customers' needs at their respective stages of the Aftermarketing Purchase Cycle. Table 5-3 identifies some tactics created using the combination of the after-sale components and the Aftermarketing Purchase Cycle.

Stage	Most Salient Needs
Commitment	Validation of Choice
Learning	Access, Proficiency
Appreciation/Reconciliation	Continuing Access, Assistance
Reevaluation	Information about Alternatives

Table 5-2. Needs relevant to each stage of the Aftermarket Purchase Cycle.[SM]

After-Sale Servicing Component

Stage of the Purchase Cycle	Formal Communications	Informal Communications	Managing Moments of Truth
Commitment	Welcome Kit	Notice of customer support phone number	Aids to reinforcing information to help customers respond to challenges from friends/associates/others
Learning/ Evaluation	Contact based on experience level (customer base)	Reminder of customer support desk	Ensure a satisfactory outcome to early requests for service and support
Appreciation/ Reconciliation	Conduct customer satisfaction assessment responding to both aggregate findings and individual cases	Listen to most valuable customers through preferential access channels	Extend preferential access to maintain customers' feeling of a relationship
Reevaluation	Contact reconfirming differentiating benefits	Dialogue to incorporate customer needs into future products and services	Facilitate product repurchase by simplifying the process, e.g., negative option

Table 5-3. Retention tactics organized by component and purchase cycle stage (illustrated with hypothetical tactics).

A Practical Example

We can produce an even stronger case for the contribution of the Aftermarketing Purchase Cycle and Planning Grid in building retention tactics by considering a real-life example in today's marketplace. While we believe the Purchase Cycle applies equally well to both consumer and business-to-business products, let's use an example most of us are familiar with, the purchase of a new automobile.

Commitment. Typical American new car buyers today plunk down more than $20,000 for a new car. They drive their new purchase home and the next morning they come out the front door feeling pretty good. Then on their first drive to work they discover a considerable blind spot they didn't notice in the excitement of their test drive. However, still seduced by the new car aroma, they're feeling pretty good, until a co-worker announces, "Isn't your new car the model that was panned by *Consumer Reports*?" By the second trip to the gas pump, they discover that their new car's mileage isn't quite what the EPA sticker rating led them to expect.

At the same time, the salesperson who seemed to have become their newest best friend only a few days earlier, and who phoned several times in the week preceding the purchase, somehow now can't remember the customer's name or how to return their calls. To confound matters, the manufacturer has ceded ownership of the customer to the dealer, fearing dealer reciprocity. Besides, the manufacturer believes it has already communicated *everything* that a customer could ever want to know in the owner's manual it's packed in the glove compartment of the car.

Slowly buyer's remorse sets in. The customer urgently needs facts to support (to friends, spouse, and self) the big decision just made, and he or she needs the comfort of knowing the dealer and the manufacturer not only guarantee their products but also support them.

While there are exceptions, buyers typically get scant support during those critical early days of the commitment stage. Searching for support, they become the most ardent readers and viewers of their brand's advertising. But despite the high production values and great photography, they quickly realize that there's little in those ads to support their $20,000 + decision.

This is a golden opportunity for the salesperson or other customer support person who understands the critical points that made the sale and can therefore remind the customer of these points and reinforce the intelligence of the purchase decision. Unfortunately, in most situations, the salesperson will claim to be too busy to provide this after-sale reassurance, and there usually isn't another person who has this responsibility. Besides, the salesperson now views the customer as a *past* customer—someone with a mathematically minute probability of buying another new car. Hence, the customer is now of little interest to the salesperson.

The manufacturer may reach out to the customer to reinforce the wisdom of the purchase and to "manage the expectations" it built during the advertising and sales process. Unfortunately, its "welcome kit" may not get to the owner within those crucial early weeks. And then, nine weeks into the period of ownership, when the kit finally arrives, its objective clearly is not to help the customer resolve his or her questions of the commitment phase. Instead, the kit typically is focused on trying to sell an extended warranty or proclaiming the benefits of factory authorized service and parts. Disregarding the customer's need to know where to turn if a question or a problem arises, there's no corporate toll-free number or, if so, it has been conspicuously omitted from the manual. And, much to the owner's consternation, this telephone number isn't easily available from #800 Directory Assistance.

Learning/Evaluation. About the time the new car aroma is fading and dust is being allowed to settle on the hood, the customer moves into the learning/evaluation stage. Customers all know the basics of driving a car, but the pesky questions start to arise, like how to adjust the passenger seat, how to switch the clock to daylight savings time, how to release the kid locks, etc. The answers are somewhere in the owner's manual, but the typical owner doesn't have the time or perhaps the patience to find them. The dealer should have noted on its customer database whether the customer had children under the age of 10. The salesperson could have sent a postcard a few weeks after the sale with a few tips to match the customer's individual lifestyle. But instead he or she made do with a 10-minute tour of the car at delivery.

The implication is that the customer should have paid better attention; now the customer is on his or her own. However, the dealer and salesperson could send a helpful postcard the first time that the car's clock needs to be set backward or forward for daylight or standard time. They could call or write to remind the customer that he or she can always contact them with any questions or concerns. But these contacts rarely happen. After all, the customer's not likely to buy again in the near future, and the dealer and manufacturer apparently have more important things to do than talk to customers who've already bought something from them.

The time arrives for the first service visit—a *moment of truth* for any business. It's another opportunity for the manufacturer to be sure the customer fully understands the features of the new car. It's also a critical chance to demonstrate that the manufacturer is standing behind its product and will provide the kind of relationship that its advertising and sales representatives promise.

In this first service experience, the customer is back again in a face-to-face situation with the dealership to whom they wrote that big check only a few months earlier. This could be an excellent opportunity to help the customer become a more experienced and comfortable owner of that new car. It could be an opportunity to remind him or her where to call with any questions or problems. It could also be the time to showcase the manufacturer's guiding principles of safety or good citizenship or the work the manufacturer is doing to protect the environment. Instead, it's often only a poorly executed service experience with a big price tag and little communication.

The manufacturer will rationalize the inadequate first service experience of any one customer by acknowledging that problems sometimes occur, but that it has a quality process in place and it is continually surveying customers to identify problems and the key drivers of satisfaction. Still, its customer satisfaction measurement process, if executed on a sample basis, may reach only one in every 100 customers. That may be sufficient to gather research statistics, but it doesn't do much for the unhappy customers who aren't surveyed or whose concerns are not captured.

When customers who have had a problem are interviewed, the manufacturer should consider itself fortunate to have been alerted to the problem while it has the opportunity to correct it, overcome any bad feelings, and limit the negative word of mouth that would result. Unfortunately, most customers who indicate they're experiencing a problem or who express a less than satisfactory service experience are often considered by the survey researchers as outliers—their reactions lie beyond the majority of responses, so the researchers ignore or at least fail to examine their more in-depth comments.

The customer may have welcomed the satisfaction survey as an invitation to a one-to-one dialogue with company. But sadly, the company may only have wanted to hear what its average customer had to say. Rather than enhancing relationships with individual customers, the satisfaction survey may actually disappoint some customers, alienating them still further.

Appreciation/Reconciliation. The longest part of the Aftermarketing Purchase Cycle is the Appreciation/Reconciliation Stage. Once again at this stage there are opportunities for formal and informal communication and a need to manage the moments of truth. Formal communications have less to do now with fostering an understanding of basic operations than with establishing an enjoyable driving experience and helping the customer keep his or her car in good operating condition.

For example, Jeep Jamborees™—where owners have fun and learn how to push their vehicles to the limit safely—are a great example of working to improve the Appreciation/Reconciliation Stage. However, they could be more strategically implemented if they were targeted at customers with one to three years of ownership experience. (Customers in their first six months of ownership would be better served with educational activities for basic functionality, while owners of four or more years would be better served with activities tied to new capabilities and benefits of new models.)

The Appreciation/Reconciliation Stage is also a time to again encourage the customer to phone, fax, or e-mail (with addresses clearly provided and a setting of expectations for response time) with any questions, concerns, or problems that might arise. Instead, all owners are typically lumped together in a single list. Anything the manufacturer or dealer learns about a customer in the sales process is lost, and all future interactions with the customer are embarrassingly conducted on a one-size-fits-all basis. No matter when customers purchased, they all receive the same promotional mailings as new models are announced. When the new models come out in August, the brochure and the invitation to come in for a test drive go out to customers who purchased new cars in June!

The negative impact of this disregard is twofold. First, since those customers are unlikely to be ready to buy another new car after only two months, the mailing is inefficient and wasteful. But the biggest problem is not the sales that don't happen; it's the impact on those customers. Customers who just got over their buyer's remorse are suddenly told by the dealer that they are correct to question their buying decision, since their new car is now outdated! The newer models have newer features, which may make the customers feel sadly stuck with an inferior product. Instead of helping their customers feel good about the brand and positive about their experience, the manufacturer has made them feel trapped and foolish. It's likely to be a lesson that the customer won't easily forget.

Formal communications during the Appreciation/Reconciliation Stage should be developed with the long-term customer value in mind at all times.

For example, a recall notice can be written like a legal notice (to keep the manufacturer out of court) or it can be written to help keep the relationship with the customer. If it takes the "we are being forced to do this so more of you don't take us to court" tone, the true intention of the communication will be obvious to the customer. But there's an alternative. A recall notice can also:

1. Explain that the company is always seeking customer feedback, which is how it identified this problem,
2. Establish that the manufacturer is always working to improve its products, and
3. Provide several options for scheduling, to make the repair service easy and convenient for the customer.

Reevaluation. Timing may not be quite everything, but it's very important in managing relationships and in selling. The business that has taken the opportunity to learn about its customers as individuals and has stored that information in a customerbase should have major advantages over its competitors in the Reevaluation Stage. At the minimum, the business will know when its customer last purchased and therefore have a good chance of being able to anticipate, in a very timely way, the customer's next purchase. The business should at the very least get its message to the customer before the purchase reevaluation is fully under way. In the best of cases, the business may even know about each customer's *individual* usage requirements and the points of satisfaction or dissatisfaction with the brand, and have captured the customer's evaluation criteria for the next purchase. This knowledge, when properly leveraged, should give the incumbent an "unfair advantage" in retaining the customer.

As we all know from personal experience, however, businesses either haven't maintained those customer databases or haven't yet built the processes that would allow them to capitalize on the information. The process, on the customer's part, becomes one of evaluation (rather than reevaluation)—and the incumbent brand sometimes is not even among the options. The manufacturers' gross oversight of the importance of interacting with customers during the Reevaluation Stage translates into an average customer retention rate of only 25%–40% in the automobile industry.

With some 30% of new automobiles now being leased rather than purchased, the understanding of customer repurchases should be moving from uncertainty to the realm of certainty. But the number of lease customers who report little or no contact throughout the term of their lease, and too little contact too late in their Reevaluation Stage, remains significant.

The purchase of a car or truck, whether new or previously owned, should provide manufacturers and dealers with an opportunity to begin to prepare for the timing of the next Reevaluation Stage as well. During the selling "courtship," the dealer generally learns the year of the trade-in and frequently talks with the potential customer about other vehicles he or she has owned. But often neither piece of information is retained in the customerbase, though this information could certainly provide valuable insights regarding the timing of each customer's next reevaluation.

Still, some businesses are making admirable attempts to learn from their customers when they plan to purchase next. They're asking for this information from people who respond to their ads and promotions, they're asking for it in their credit card mailings, and they're asking for it from the customers with whom they maintain an ongoing dialogue. Unfortunately, they're not asking the questions with the benefit of the customer in mind. So, their questions are likely to be interpreted by the customers as, "Tell us when to have one of our salespeople start chasing you," rather than as concern shown as part of an ongoing relationship, "When might you find information about our new models useful and relevant?"

Businesses that have continually shown that they're open to informal communication throughout the first three stages of the purchase cycle can benefit during the Reevaluation Stage. The customer who knows where and how to contact the company and has enjoyed the benefits of an open dialogue and timely response won't need to be told how to receive new information. In this happy case, the customer will call asking for comparative information or details on the new year's models: that call will signal the time when the customer is entering the Reevaluation Stage. The manufacturer or the dealer won't have to guess. If businesses provide a little encouragement (e.g., reminders of how to contact the business, invitations to contact the business, well-posted hours of operation), it will help get their customers to identify when they're moving into the Reevaluation Stage.

Conclusion

Discussions of retention marketing seem to be dominated by frequent flyer points and customer discounts. But research shows that what really drives repurchase is high-quality customer service and well-managed, strategically delivered formal and informal communications that are in synch with the purchase cycles of individual customers.

This suggests an opportunity for service professionals to take the lead in devising and supervising customer retention programs. All too often customer service is viewed as a cost center. However, when service activities are directly related to customer retention, customer service takes on the role of revenue generator. In this capacity, CS staff are extending the lifetimes of individual customers and thereby increasing the lifetime value of customers. This suggests possibly renaming the service center the Department of Customer Retention or the Division of Customer Relationship Management.

About the Authors

Terry G. Vavra, Ph.D., is president of Marketing Metrics, Inc. in Paramus, New Jersey, a firm specializing in customer retention programs and strategic marketing planning. He is the author of two books related to customer care: *Aftermarketing: How to Keep Customers for Life Through Relationship Marketing* (Irwin Professional Publishers, 1992 and 1995) and *Improving Your Measurement of Customer Satisfaction* (American Society for Quality, 1997). Terry is also Associate Professor of Marketing in the Lubin School of Business, Pace University (White Plains, New York), where he teaches courses in Strategic Marketing, Consumer Behavior, and Financial Services Marketing.

Douglas R. Pruden is Senior Vice President, Director of Retention Practices, at Marketing Metrics, Inc., Paramus, New Jersey. He has a multi-faceted background in direct marketing, database marketing, and public relations. Prior to joining Marketing Metrics, Doug worked in New York at JWT Direct, BBDO Direct, and in Connecticut with Mason: Madison Advertising and the American Cancer Society. Doug is a frequent speaker at industry seminars and professional meetings on the topics of customer care and customer retention.

PART TWO

Practical Models for Managing Customer Service

6

How to Create a Plan to Deliver Great Customer Service

Susan Smith

Now more than ever, customers are rewarding the companies that meet their needs and expectations and avoiding or even attacking those that do not. This article will take you through the process of setting up a customer service initiative, from assessing your current customer service approach and determining your customers' requirements to creating a customer service vision with customer-friendly policies. It suggests methods for dealing effectively with your customers and offers advice for educating the rest of your organization to focus on customer service.

What Is Customer Service?

Customer service is meeting the needs and expectations of the customer as defined by the customer. "Meeting the needs and expectations of the customer" means you know what your customers want and what they expect, and you provide that to them on a consistent basis. And to know what your customers want, you've got to ask them!

As obvious as that may sound, many companies establish customer service initiatives without ever talking to their customers. "As defined by the customer" is a very important point to get because it says that if the customer doesn't perceive you as offering good customer service, then you aren't. The customer is the judge here. No matter how good your internal records claim you are, the customer is the only voice worth listening to. So in order to have an effective customer service initiative, you must know what your customers want, provide it to them consistently, and ask them how you're doing.

Benefits of an Effective Customer Service Initiative

You and your organization can benefit from a customer service plan in the following ways:

○ **Less stress**. If you're dealing with customers directly, especially unhappy ones, there will be a certain amount of stress with each episode. You can reduce it if you have a systematic way of dealing with your customers.

○ **Higher efficiencies**. When you focus your efforts on the areas that directly affect customer satisfaction, you can use your resources more efficiently. An effective customer service program provides a plan for working on those areas most important to your customers and lowers the "noise" level that may distract you and your organization from focusing on these areas.

○ **Better morale and greater satisfaction**. When you're working on those areas that mean the most to your customers and to the success of your organization, then you'll share a common vision and meaning with your entire organization.

○ **Survival**. Effective customer service has become a given for staying in business. With increasing globalization and the reducing of trade barriers, competition is fierce. There are plenty of suppliers eager for business and the opportunity to satisfy customers. If you're not one of them, you may not be around for long.

○ **Increased profits**. According to the U.S. Consumer Affairs Department, it costs five times more to gain a new customer than to keep a current customer. With just a 5% increase in customer retention, a firm can raise its profitability by 25% and in some cases as much as 85%. Similar studies also show that the longer a company keeps a customer, the more money it will make. This happens because consumers spend slowly at first, but as time passes with good experiences, they will spend increasingly more.

Customer Service as a Competitive Advantage

Fierce competition means that firms need more and more innovations to differentiate themselves. With technology available to virtually all organizations today, traditional advantages of features and costs no longer provide for a sustainable competitive advantage. More and more companies are turning to quality of service as a way to distinguish themselves from the rest. They're talking to their customers to determine what's most important to them and how they can further add value for them. Smart companies are positioning themselves to be an extension of their customers, thereby making it very inconvenient for the customer to frequently change vendors.

Steps to a Customer Service Initiative

Each organization's customer service plan must be customized to suit its own needs. But, more important, it must satisfy the needs of its customers. There is no "specification" for an effective customer service program. Each one will have its own distinct differences. Nevertheless, there are some common steps that you'll need to consider when setting up your program:

○ Assessing your customer service quotient
○ Understanding your customers' requirements
○ Creating your customer vision and service policies
○ Recognizing the skills needed to deal effectively with your customers
○ Educating your organization on your customer focus

Step 1. Assessing Your Customer Service Quotient

In order to establish an effective plan to focus on customer service, you need to know where you're starting from. The following is a self-assessment that, when completed honestly, will begin to point out opportunities for improving your customer service efforts. For each statement, rate how well your office or your organization satisfies the condition. Use the following scale:

1. Are you kidding?
2. Hardly ever
3. Sometimes
4. Usually
5. It's our way of life!

Note: If you're a one-person office, answer it from your own perspective. If you're an organization with several employees, answer it from an organizational perspective.

Our Culture

____ 1. We're committed to do whatever it takes to create satisfied customers.
____ 2. We try to do things "right the first time."
____ 3. The owner provides the leadership philosophically and by example that customer service is important.
____ 4. Serving our customers' needs takes priority over meeting our internal needs.
____   Total Score, divided by 20 = ____%

Customer Alignment

____ 1. When we sell, we aim for a partnership approach.
____ 2. In our collateral materials, we don't promise what we can't deliver.
____ 3. We know the features and benefits that are most important to our customers.
____ 4. We design new products/services based on info provided by our customers.
____   Total Score, divided by 20 = ____%

Error Reduction

____ 1. We review customer complaints.
____ 2. We constantly ask our customers for feedback.
____ 3. We regularly look for ways to eliminate errors based on customer input.
____   Total Score, divided by 15 = ____%

Using Customer Info

___ 1. We've determined what our customers expect from us.
___ 2. We frequently interact with our customers.
___ 3. The entire organization knows what is important to our customers.
___   Total Score, divided by 15 = ___%

Customer Outreach

___ 1. We make it easy for our customers to deal with us.
___ 2. We aim to resolve all customer complaints.
___ 3. We encourage "wowing the customer."
___   Total Score, divided by 15 = ___%

Qualified and Empowered Staff (answer only if you have a staff)

___ 1. Employees are respected.
___ 2. All employees have a good understanding of our product/service.
___ 3. All employees have the right tools and skills to perform their jobs well.
___ 4. All employees are encouraged to resolve customer issues.
___ 5. All employees feel that customer satisfaction is a responsibility of their job.
___   Total Score, divided by 25 = ___%

Improving Products/Services and Processes

___ 1. We constantly work to improve our processes and products.
___ 2. We network with other groups to learn from their strengths and weaknesses.
___ 3. When problems are identified, we quickly try to resolve them.
___   Total Score, divided by 15 = ___%

(Source: Adapted from Forum Corporation's Self-Test for a Customer-Driven Company)

Now evaluate how well your organization focuses on customer satisfaction. Note the areas where you score high and those where you are low. The low scores will suggest opportunities for improvement. List three areas you need to improve:

1. _____

2. _____

3. _____

Step 2. Understanding Your Customers' Requirements

Often organizations claim to know their customers' requirements, yet they've never taken the time to do a really thorough analysis. Sure, they probably know their customers' general requirements. But do they know what's really important to their customers, how they measure up relative to the important factors, and how they compare with the competition in the areas most important to the customers? In most cases they don't—and they won't unless they collect this information in a formal, systematic manner.

Sources of Customer Information

Your own organization. Without looking too far, you'll be able to uncover potential areas of customer dissatisfaction by reviewing your key operational data. Check on the status of backlogs or stockouts. If these are significant, chances are you may have some customers who are not happy with your delivery cycle time. Review your "Returns and Allowances." If they're high, then your customers may be unhappy with the product they purchase—either the quality is inferior or they felt the product was misrepresented and not what they expected. Another place to look is your internal reject or yield rates. If your rejects are high or your yields low, you can bet that some bad product is leaking out to your customer. Even if you inspect the product before shipping it to the customer, tests have shown that inspection isn't 100% reliable—some bad product will sneak out.

A service company. Perhaps you could even get information from your local telephone company. Customers are typically concerned with the turnaround time (from time of request to completion of service) for performance of service. The telephone company could review its internal records for the average turnaround time. If it's excessive, they probably have some unhappy customers. Another measurement to look for is the number of times the company must redo a service. Customers expect you "to do it right the first time." If you don't, they become unhappy.

Your employees. Don't forget your employees as a valuable source of information on customer requirements. They interact with customers constantly and probably know a great deal about their likes and dislikes. If you're a one-person organization, then you're the one dealing with customers. You know what's going well, what needs fine-tuning, and what needs a major overhaul. Begin your search for customer data in-house. Most likely you'll uncover some things that you can fix immediately, which will make your customers happy and get you started on the right track.

Internal data. Review your internal data to pinpoint potential problem areas for customers. Also, gather your employees together and get their inputs on your customers' satisfaction level. Assemble a list of strengths and weaknesses, but don't get bogged down in the details. You're looking for a few areas where you can begin making improvements.

Customers. You should start with a review of customer complaints and inquiries. If you don't have a systematic way of collecting these, you should develop one. Both are good indicators of opportunity areas. However, don't limit yourself to just complaints and inquiries. Studies show that only 2%–4% of dissatisfied customers ever complain. If you're only looking at complaints, you're missing the other 96%–98% who have problems with you.

Surveys and focus groups are two of the most popular methods for gathering information on customer needs. Surveys are written questions given to individual customers; focus groups are oral questions administered to groups of customers.

Both must have clear and specific goals up front in order to be successful. A broad questionnaire or focus group session provides you with a lot of information, but it's usually too general to be of any value. Your objectives must be clear and your questions must be specific to provide results that you can act upon. Although focus groups and surveys are similar in what they can help you accomplish, one may be more suitable than the other, depending on the application.

Surveys are relatively simple and economical to administer and can reach large numbers of customers, but the information can sometimes be limited, since it is a one-way exchange of information. On the other hand, focus groups take more time and effort, are often more expensive to administer, and may not be as far-reaching as surveys, but their interactive nature may produce clearer feedback. The best results are found when combinations of both techniques are used to identify customer requirements and expectations.

Review customer complaints and inquiries. Identify the top three requests and compare them with the list you created from your internal data and employee inputs. Do you find any overlap? Any surprises?

The Best Kind of Customer Data

More is not necessarily better when it comes to customer data. Getting the right kind of data is critical. The following are the key characteristics of good customer data:

○ **Ongoing**. One thing is certain—change. Your customers may change, their needs may change, the environment may change (e.g., the competition gets tougher, regulations change), and most certainly you too will change. As you improve, your customers' expectations will likely rise, too. To respond to these changing needs, you'll need to constantly assess your customers. How often you assess your customers will depend on your business, its sales volume, and the relative value of its product or service. For instance, a fast-food restaurant that sells thousands of hamburgers a week may survey its customers continuously, while a large equipment manufacturer that sells only a few pieces of equipment each month may survey customers once a year.

○ **Specific**. In order to make the kind of improvements your customers will appreciate, you'll need specific feedback. While general inputs may give you an overall tone of the customer, you can only respond to specific feedback. Shape your surveys for specific information. For instance, rather than having customers answer yes or no to the statement "The length of time that I have to wait in line is satisfactory," try instead asking the question, "How much time is satisfactory to wait in line?"

○ **Timely**. If you're working with old data, it may no longer reflect customer sentiments.

○ **Focused**. Organizations have limited resources. While the problems can be overwhelming, you can realistically work on just a few. If you try to do too much, you might not do anything well.

○ **Weighted**. Assess your data in terms of relative importance. This will help you narrow down the list of opportunities to just the few on which you should concentrate. You can rate the relative importance, but it will be much better if your customer does it.

○ **Competitive comparison**. You should always know where you stand in comparison with your competition. If your customers are willing to provide you with feedback on competitors, take it. And you won't need a separate survey, either. When you ask your customers to rate your performance, ask them to rate your competition as well.

Step 3. Creating Your Customer Vision and Service Policies

In order to transform your company into one that values customer satisfaction, you must establish a customer-centered vision for your company. So what is a vision, exactly? According to Richard Whiteley of the Forum Corporation, a vision is a vivid picture of an ambitious, desirable future state that is connected to the customer and better in some important way than the current state.

In other words, your vision is what you want your organization to become, what you want it "to grow up to be." And a client-centered vision is one that takes its direction from the customer. A vision performs two critical functions:

○ It serves as a source of inspiration that rallies the organization around a single unifying purpose, which in this case is the customer.
○ It guides decision making and aligns an organization so that all functions work toward a single goal.

In the business world, there are rarely black-and-white decisions to make, but there's an awful lot of gray. A vision that spells out what the organization wants to become provides direction needed to make better decisions. After all, an employee who knows where the business wants to head is more likely to make decisions that help it move toward that goal.

So how do you create a vision? It's really quite easy. Vision statements need not be elaborate. For instance, Ray Kroc's vision for McDonald's was "Quality, Service, Cleanliness, Value." Keep your vision short and concise so that your organization is clear on the meaning. Many companies make the mistake of trying to create literary masterpieces. The problem is that such a vision statement tends to be so long that no one in the organization really knows what it means. The hard part in creating a vision is deciding what you want your organization to be in the future.

Establishing Customer-Friendly Policies

There isn't anything that makes a customer angrier than someone saying, "I'm sorry, but that's our policy." In many cases policies exist because "that's the way we've always done it before." There may be no reason behind them, just tradition.

Take an inventory of your organization's policies. Do they facilitate customer satisfaction? Or do they only erect barriers and cause customer frustration? If you're having difficulty identifying these "unfriendly" policies, review your customer complaints and assessments. A quick scan of the feedback is sure to direct you to some of these "unfriendly" policies. Now segregate your "friendly" and "unfriendly" policies into "necessary" and "unnecessary" groups.

Now, throw out your *unnecessary* "unfriendly" policies immediately. You don't need them and they're most likely frustrating the heck out of your customers. For example, if you own a commercial cleaning service and "you don't do windows," get rid of that policy immediately. Businesses hire you to clean their premises, so if there isn't a health or legal reason for not cleaning windows, you better think about cleaning them. Otherwise, they'll find someone else who will.

It's certain that you will have some *necessary* "unfriendly" policies that your customers may not like, but that you're legally bound to have. You can't do much about these except make them as "friendly" as possible. For instance, if you're cleaning healthcare facilities and your insurance company restricts you from disposing of certain medical wastes, inform your customers of that restriction and the reasoning behind it, but then investigate if there's some sort of compromise you can make, such as disposing of wastes if they've been properly contained.

Keep your *necessary* "friendly" policies. These policies make sense and are good for your customers, so strengthen them even more if you can.

Finally, create more *unnecessary* "friendly" policies wherever possible. This type of policy might be, for example, offering your "extra special clean-ups" on a 24-hour basis. Use customer-friendly policies as a competitive edge and keep your customers coming back for more.

Now, take a few moments and, together with your customer complaint and feedback data, revise your policies so that they are customer-friendly. Are there any additional "policies" that you can institute that would further differentiate you from your competition?

Step 4. Dealing Effectively With Your Customers

Once you've established your customer-centered vision and created customer-friendly policies, you're ready to sharpen the skills necessary to deal effectively with your customers. These skills can be segregated into two areas—communication skills and problem-solving skills.

Communication Skills

How you communicate to your customers is just as important as *what* you communicate. Here are six behavioral skills that will communicate to your customer that you are an organization that values their business. (This list is adapted from *Hey, I'm the Customer—Frontline Tips for Providing Superior Customer Service* by Ron Willingham, Prentice Hall, 1992.)

○ **Greet your customers**. "Put them at ease and make them feel comfortable!" When your customer or prospective customer first walks in or telephones you with an inquiry or order, make him or her feel welcome. This sets the tone for the rest of the transaction. If this is the first time with this customer, remember that first impressions can help or hurt, depending on how you make your customer feel within those first critical moments. If the impression is favorable, that person will continue talking, browsing, or ordering. If it's unfavorable, you may have lost a customer forever.

○ **Value your customers**. "Let me know that you think I'm important!" Customers want to feel special; to make them feel special, your attitude and behavior must say, "You're the customer—you pay my salary, you make my job possible." When you value customers, your sincerity makes them feel good about you and your organization. A customer-focused organization is not in business to deliver a product or service, but instead to enable people to enjoy the benefits of its product or service. What's the difference? Compare two temporary agencies, one that's in business to fill job vacancies with temporary personnel and the other that tries to help its customers enjoy the benefits that it provides—immediate placement of highly skilled individuals. The difference is subtle, but the effect is not!

○ **Ask how to help your customers**. "Find out what I want!" You've already gotten a head start on that by reviewing customer complaints and other feedback, but it's important that each customer encounter make that customer feel special. You do that by trying to understand your customers' needs each time you deal with them—not just their overall needs, but their needs at that particular moment. A desire to genuinely understand your customers' needs or wants will give you an edge. Now, how do you do that? Simply find out why they came in or contacted you: "So what can I do for you today, Mr. Jones?" Then ask open-ended questions to further understand their needs: "Are you looking for any special features in a briefcase? How often will you be using it?"

○ **Listen to your customers**. "Please listen to me and understand me!" Listen totally—to your customers' words, their tone, their body language. According to a UCLA study, 7% of our communication is verbal, 38% is tone of voice, and 55% is nonverbal. Listening totally will enhance your understanding of what your customer really needs as well as make him or her feel valued.

○ **Help your customers**. "Help me get what I want!" Customers don't buy products and services for what they are, but instead for the benefits that the products and services offer. That's why you must be customer-focused rather than product- or service-focused. Don't waste your time explaining your product or service features. Explain how your product or service benefits them—how it satisfies a need, solves their problems, or gives them extra value. Instead of "Super Duper Carpet Cleaner offers the latest in stain-resistant technology," you should try "Super Duper's newest technology continuously repels stains for up to 20 years so you'll never have to clean your carpets!"

○ **Invite your customers back**. "Let me know that I'm welcome back anytime!" This is about last impressions. Thank your customers for coming in or contacting you. Tell them you'd like to see them or hear from them again. Then, try to do something that makes them want to come back or refer you to a friend or colleague—maybe a discount off their next appointment for referring a friend. Last impressions are important because that's how your customers will feel about you until you have a chance to interact with them again. If you do it right, your business will surely reap the benefits.

Now, make two columns. List each of the communication skills in the left-hand column. Think about how you can improve each in your business. In the right-hand column, write down what you are going to do.

Communication Skills	*What We Can Do*
1. Greet your customers	
2. Value your customers	
3. Ask how to help your customers	
4. Listen to your customers	
5. Help your customers	
6. Invite your customers back	

Now, post these two lists where you and others in your organization can see them—and begin doing those things immediately.

Problem-Solving Skills

Problems will always occur. But taking responsibility for these problems can turn a negative customer into a positive one. Studies show that if a problem is resolved quickly, 98% of your customers will buy again—and even tell colleagues that they had a positive experience! However, the longer the problem drags on, the more frustrated a customer becomes and the less likely he or she is to be satisfied. So how do you resolve problems quickly? Read on for a four-step process to help you do just that! (This process is adapted from *Hey, I'm the Customer* by Ron Willingham.)

- ○ **Understand the problem**. "Try to understand my problem from my viewpoint!" First, "get the facts, Jack!" Listen nondefensively. Then, repeat your understanding of the problem back to make sure it's accurate. For example, your customer is having a problem with the juicer that you sold him. You listen to his problem nondefensively, probing him for more information, then say, "As I understand the problem, the juice that is extracted does not have any pulp."

- ○ **Identify the cause of the problem**. "Take enough time to understand what caused my problem!" After you understand the problem, you're ready to identify possible causes of the problem. First, you should find out what happened. ("I made the orange juice according to the enclosed instructions.") Next, you need to find out what should have happened. ("There should have been pulp in the pulp reservoir.") Then, find out what went wrong. ("There wasn't any pulp in the reservoir, or anyplace else that I could see!")

○ **Discuss possible solutions**. "Explore possible solutions with me!" At this time you should suggest possible options. ("You may not have the model that removes the pulp from the juice, perhaps the wrong instructions were enclosed, or maybe the juicer has malfunctioned.") Next, you should ask your customer for ideas. ("Do you think it is a malfunction? Is it the wrong model? Are the wrong instructions enclosed? Do you have any other ideas?") Finally, agree on a course of action. ("Let's first check the model numbers to make sure that the instructions are for your juicer.")

○ **Solve the problem**. "Solve my problems, and you'll enjoy my loyalty forever!" Now it's time to remove the cause or take corrective action. ("Ah ha! The model numbers don't match. The instructions are for our higher-end model that doesn't extract the pulp separately, but feeds it into the juice automatically. Do you want to keep this model and I can send you the appropriate instructions? Or would you prefer the lower-end model with a cash refund for the difference?") Now, ask your customer if he is satisfied with the resolution. ("Have we solved your problem satisfactorily? Is there anything else we can do?") Finally, the kicker—offer something to the customer to compensate him for his troubles. ("And for your troubles, we'll be sending you a bushel of fresh Florida oranges that should arrive at your home next week. Again, I'm sorry for the problem this has caused you, but thanks for letting us resolve it.")

Write down this four-step problem-solving process. Commit it to memory and post it so that you can use it the next time you run into problems.

Step 5. Educating Your Staff

Now that you've learned to assess your current customer service condition, to understand your customers' requirements, to create a customer-centered vision and establish customer-friendly policies, and to deal with your customers more effectively, you need to educate your staff (if you have one) on how to carry out your customer service focus. This will involve two steps, *communicate* and *train*.

○ **Communicate your focus**. Schedule a meeting to roll out your vision for your organization and to explain the reasoning behind your customer service focus. Make this meeting mandatory. For successful implementation, you need to get your staff's full cooperation and buy-in. After all, the vision and policies must become theirs, not just yours. At the end of the meeting, determine the next course of action, noting responsibilities and timing. Important: This should not be the only time that you talk to your staff about the importance of a customer focus. You must work it into your daily routine, your regular meetings. It must become the basis for your entire business. And you must demonstrate by example—"Walk the talk!"—to reinforce the fact that things are going to be different from now on.

○ **Train your people**. In order to achieve your customer-centered vision, your staff must be properly trained to do so. As mentioned earlier, you can incorporate some of this training into your usual meetings. In fact, it's important that you include some training in your regular meetings so it becomes a part of your normal operations. However, you'll find you'll need to schedule an incremental amount of time to train personnel in problem-solving and communication skills. Again, so your staff don't doesn't consider this the "boss's program," suggest that a team of volunteers determine the organization's training needs and outline a suitable approach. Then, have the team present it to the rest of the organization in an upcoming meeting.

Now you're off to transforming your organization into one that's customer-centered! Good luck and have fun in the process!

About the Author

Susan Smith was Vice President of Operations for Entrepreneurial Edge, a Philadelphia-based research and training organization for entrepreneurs. She is President of Discovery Group, Inc., a training and consulting firm specializing in high-performance management.

Excerpted with permission from Entrepreneurial Edge, a service of the Edward Lowe Foundation. For more information call (215) 619-4660 or visit their Web site at http://www.edgeonline.com. © 1997 Edward Lowe Foundation.

7

BUILDING A PICTURE OF PERFECT SERVICE

Michael Vandergriff

How can companies use the Ishikawa diagram to achieve "perfect service"—and establish a good foundation for "exceptional service"? The author maintains that most American companies use this tool less effectively than Japanese companies. He explains the difference in perspectives and offers advice on maximizing the benefits of this approach.

Our large jet was put through "bush pilot" maneuvers as we powered away from the airport in Juneau, Alaska. My business associate and I grinned nervously at the hard banking the pilot employed to avoid mountains around the city. We told jokes to relieve the tension. When we reached high altitude, the flight attendant began the drink service and quickly reached our row. Efficient and fast, she talked as she served us, telling us about the wonders of Alaska. Across the aisle, a passenger became increasingly agitated; he fidgeted and glowered at the attendant. Finally, in a spew of verbal venom (with expletives), he accused her of being incompetent, uncaring, and related to canines. Unfortunately, she turned to him and asked, "Do you have a problem, sir?" which was, in effect, like asking, "Could you repeat that, please?"

With the second round of obscenities, I attempted to rise to my feet. Sensing danger, my associate grabbed my shoulder and held me to the seat. My effort still had a positive impact in quieting the situation; as I am an ex-collegiate shot putter, the irate customer noted I was both largely unhappy and large.

Later, finding the attendant crying in the galley, I offered my business card and mentioned that I was available to discuss with her bosses the angry man's demeanor. As we left the plane, I noticed that the malcontent had cornered the pilot to further his case against the unfortunate attendant.

In recent years, stories of bad customers have . . . ahem . . . fallen from the skies. In the above example, the irate traveler apparently felt that the attendant could serve faster if she kept her mouth shut. His expectation of a fast-but-mute slave was rude and wrong and would have deprived me of the excellent service I was receiving. Perhaps one of the most rabid forms of "bad customers" is the individual who is both wildly irrational and aggressive with his expectations. Barely tolerable in a store or restaurant, these customer behaviors are insane at 30,000 feet.

Extremes in customer behavior aside, it's productive to analyze the elements necessary to provide quality service to "normal" folks. A structure that delivers a clear picture of perfect service would give a tremendous boost to organizations attempting to design or improve their customer service operation. Such a model would, of necessity, begin with generic quality but allow customization to address specific organizational needs. This article introduces such a model.

Building a Model

Models develop insights into management topics. Graphics have the potential to communicate information quickly and thoroughly, delivering panoramic views of complex situations. Prescriptively, they can help us choose appropriate courses of action in leadership (Situational Leadership), management (Managerial Grid), and psychological preferences and their resulting behaviors (Myers-Briggs).

While most models present choices, few deliver a picture of perfection. Perhaps this is because, culturally, we assume that everything is situational: there cannot be one correct answer and the best we can achieve is a range of alternatives.

The Japanese don't seem to limit themselves to the same extent as Americans. They use the structure of the Ishikawa diagram to lead them to perfect outcomes. This tool is also known as a "fishbone" diagram, because of its appearance, and a "cause-and-effect" diagram, because of its function. People use the tool on both sides of the Pacific, but in different ways.

In learning the tool, the Japanese most often use the positive outcome of "A Perfect Plate of Rice," which they enter into the Perfect Rice box to the right of the diagram (see Figure 7-1). By continually developing the "cause" categories of People, Materials, Methods, and Machines, they pursue the goal of perfect rice.

Americans, on the other hand, embrace the tool differently. The contrast in the teaching is profound. The "effect" used for instructional purposes is "A Bitter Cup of Coffee" (see Figure 7-2). The full development of the generic cause categories constitutes an after-crisis investigation. In other words, we use the tool only after we have experienced grief. The implications for our use of this tool are:

- ○ The tool is used *infrequently* rather than *continuously*.
- ○ The tool is used *diagnostically* rather than *prescriptively*.
- ○ There are greater *failure* costs rather than lower *prevention* costs.
- ○ We are myopic to the inherent *flexibility* of this wonderful tool.

The flexibility of the fishbone allows us to easily modify cause categories to contribute to alternative perfect outcomes. Whether the goal is great rice or perfect service, the cause-and-effect diagram can serve well in delivering a schematic of

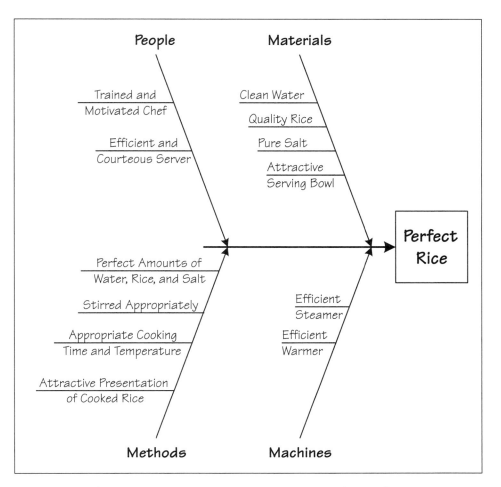

Figure 7-1. A fishbone diagram showing how to make perfect rice.

success. In pursuit of a picture of perfect service using the fishbone, we can develop a tool that:

- Presents a comprehensive one-page picture of what is required to achieve excellent customer service,
- Is infinitely adjustable and can be tailored to the organization and its environment,
- Graphically establishes ownership of elements of the customer service formula,
- Can be used to present "before-and-after" pictures of improvement efforts,
- Is unique in ways that may score points in award competitions (Baldrige, etc.).
- Can be used to lobby senior management for additional resources, and
- Reduces stress by providing reassurance (through the structure of the tool) to individuals responsible for only a piece of the customer service model, potentially reinforcing that they have given their best effort.

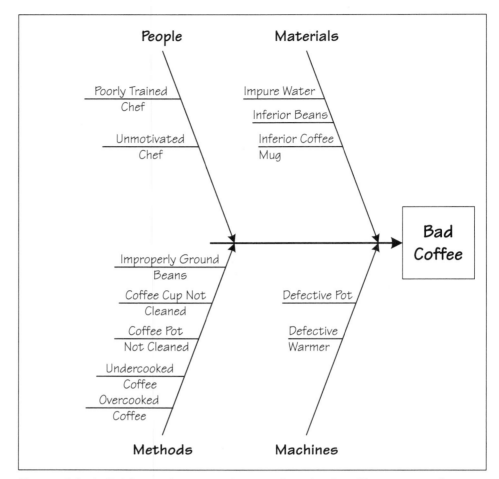

Figure 7-2. A fishbone diagram showing how bad coffee comes about.

The Categories

As stated earlier, the generic categories used for cause-and-effect diagrams are People, Materials, Methods, and Machines. In seeking perfect service, seven "cause" categories apply:

- Processes,
- Contact Person(s),
- Systems,
- Printed Materials,
- Environment,
- Contingency Plans, and
- Expectations.

Plugging relevant elements into the branches of the model creates a very powerful and useful tool (Figure 7-3).

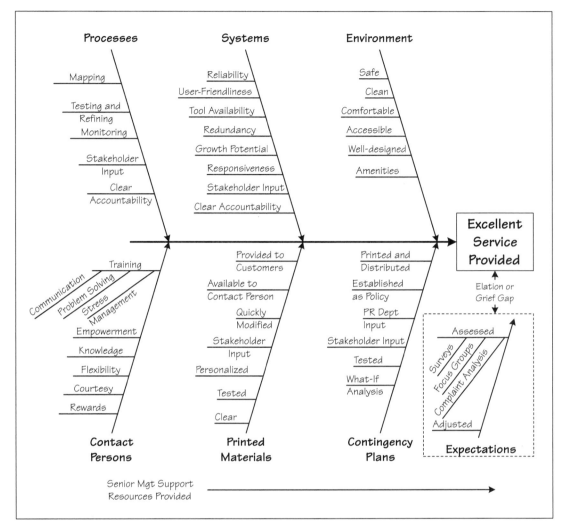

Figure 7-3. Perfect customer service "fishbone".

Each of the seven categories will be explained and its elements defined, so that any organization can work toward the picture of perfect service depicted in the centerpiece graphic. Each category section includes examples that demonstrate the customer grief that's predictable when components are missing or poorly addressed.

Processes

All work is process and, as such, can be mapped, measured, and refined. The following elements contribute to ensuring that the processes supporting service efforts run smoothly. (See Figure 7-4.)

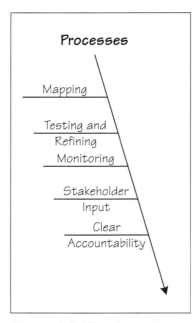

Figure 7-4. The elements.

Mapping. Fundamentally, this is flow charting for the purpose of data collection and process refinement. The finished process map delivers a true and accurate picture of the action steps, decision points, and wait sequences that constitute the overall job to be done. This graphic helps the process owners communicate the flow of work to others and identify data collection points through which process refinement can be accomplished.

Testing and Refining. This element represents the actual collection, analysis, and interpretation of the data. Action plans for improvements are developed and implemented and their impacts are measured. Delays and rework are eliminated.

Monitoring. Processes, when not being refined, are periodically checked for compliance with the latest, *accepted-as-best* practice.

Stakeholder Input. Affected parties are included in process improvement efforts. Otherwise, energy is siphoned from the implementation of changes and redirected to "selling" the stakeholders that the changes are necessary and proper.

Clear Accountability. Jurisdictional and functional responsibilities are clearly established. All parties understand who is responsible for all components of the customer service system.

Case Example: Nice Map, No Destination

Last year, the top bosses decided we should have "process maps" of all major processes in our customer service department. We all were trained on how to flow-chart, collect and analyze data, and use tools to guide us toward process improvement. Our intense work sessions filled the conference rooms with flip-chart paper

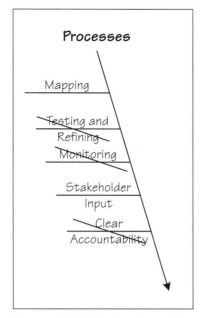

Figure 7-5. Missing in action.

and sticky notes. All of the completed maps (we now call them "pretty pictures") are on the wall under sheet plastic—where they have been for ten months. Once in a while they get used; someone writes birthday wishes on the top of one with a grease pencil. (See Figure 7-5.)

Contact Person(s)

Some of the critical factors in this category are psychological characteristics that the contact person should, to some extent, innately possess. Courtesy, for example, could be seen to depend on patience and interpersonal skill. The fact that interpersonal communication is widely taught at the college and university level attests to the belief that people skills are teachable. Patience, on the other hand, seems to be embraced as primarily a genetically fixed trait; it appears unlikely that Patience 101 will be taught soon on a campus near you. Although anger management training programs are being conducted with greater frequency, this is not the same as extending patience.

The other factors listed involve actions management should take on behalf of the employee. Providing rewards, removing stumbling blocks to flexibility, empowering the employee to make decisions, providing training in essential skills—these concerns are the responsibility of senior management. (See Figure 7-6.)

Rewards. Employees must be appreciated if they are expected to care about customers. Research is necessary to determine what workers consider to be a reward. Efforts must be expended to ensure that good workers are acknowledged and benefit from their good work.

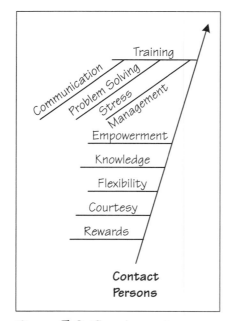

Figure 7-6. The elements.

Courtesy. The contact person should be cordial and polite. He or she should show patience.

Flexibility. If there are alternate means of reaching the same destination without incurring excessive additional costs or risks, they should be accommodated, if not encouraged.

Knowledge. The contact person must possess sufficient knowledge to effectively address the needs of the customer.

Empowerment. The contact person should have a level of authority commensurate with the amount of responsibility imposed.

Training. The contact person must be provided with training necessary to help him or her manage customers needs. Related topics include communication, problem-solving, and stress management.

Case Example: The Service "Sinkhole"

You would think that our best people would be placed at the customer service desks. This is not true in our organization. Last year two workers, Bert and Ernie, were shunted off into our Customer Service Department, where they truly don't belong. Very low in communication skills and not very competent, they are an embarrassment to our company. Especially Bert, who I think is a classic "passive-aggressive" type. They were both dropped into Customer Service during a transition in management and the manager of that department has no power to do anything about the assignments. The problem is that, with downsizing, lateral movement of any employee is virtually impossible. I doubt anyone would take Bert or Ernie now, anyway.

Can these two be trained? I say no. Medicated, maybe.

I, and all of my fellow salespersons, pray that any customer service problems miss B&E's desks and find a sympathetic ear. The manager of the customer service department is hoping to get downsized by two more positions. (See Figure 7-7.)

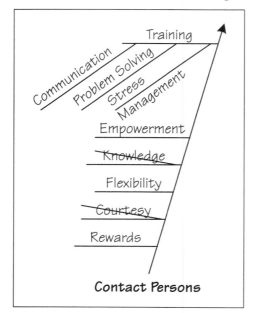

Figure 7-7. Missing in action.

Systems

Computers and telecommunication systems are indispensable when attending to customers' wants and needs. Appropriate technology, well maintained, allows customer service employees to do more, faster, and better. Conversely, an absence of the following elements creates a technological albatross that few customer service teams can survive. (See Figure 7-8.)

Reliability. Equipment supporting the customer service activities must operate well, with a minimum of maintenance or, worse, down-time.

User-Friendliness. Computers, software, and telephone systems should be easily mastered by the average employee. Learning curves should be short, shallow, and relatively grief-free.

Tool Availability. Tools and equipment necessary for all foreseeable system needs (as well as customer needs) should be available and in good working condition.

Redundancy. Systems should have built-in capability to compensate for failures, however rare they may be. This ability complements the "contingency plan" leg of the perfect service diagram.

Growth Potential. As the customer base grows in size or if the needs of the customers increase through change, the system should possess the potential for growth. Examples would include telephone lines and hardware, hard drive storage, and computer CPU upgrades.

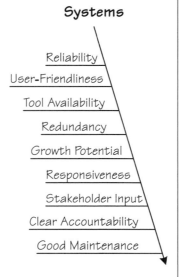

Figure 7-8. The elements.

Responsiveness. System capabilities should deliver, whenever possible, immediate feedback. An example would be the creation of a computerized fax-back system.

Stakeholder Input. Employees who manage systems or system elements should be encouraged to contribute to system modifications or changes. This input improves morale and increases commitment while decreasing mistakes and their resulting costs.

Clear Accountability. Ownership of systems and system elements should be clearly established. The consequence of a lack of accountability is finger-pointing in the midst of a customer service crisis. Perhaps a universal truth in customer service is that *placing blame does nothing to resolve the immediate problem.* Worse still, the customer may be exposed to the acrimony, which further hurts his or her impression of the organization as a whole.

Good Maintenance. Maintenance should be performed on all system hardware at regular intervals, based on manufacturer's recommendations. System administrators should be well trained on maintenance issues.

Case Example: New and Abused

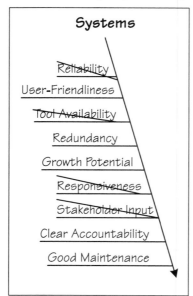

Our company recently "reengineered" our customer service department. As part of the change, senior management purchased a "cutting edge" computer server for our area. The problems are: 1) the server still has no uninterruptible power supply (UPS) and 2) the network cards for each of our PCs are not installed—and it appears that they might never be.

Making things worse, the tape backup is on the server and the interim policy requires everyone to hand-carry floppies to the system administrator at the end of every day. Furthermore, we are very worried that the new server might crash without a UPS, so we keep multiple disk backups as well. We are awash in a sea of floppies. Supply can't keep pace with demand and we will soon be short on disks. I also suspect that hoarding has begun.

In similar fashion, senior management also purchased a "high end" photocopier. Maybe someday they'll get us another toner cartridge for it.

Figure 7-9. Missing in action.

Only occasionally do we actually respond to customer concerns. But at least we've been reengineered! (See Figure 7-9.)

Printed Materials

Often, printed materials represent a "safety blanket" when a customer requires reassurance that his or her needs are being addressed. The printed content can either reinforce or undermine the spoken words of the customer contact employee, so great care should be taken when composing supporting materials. (See Figure 7-10.)

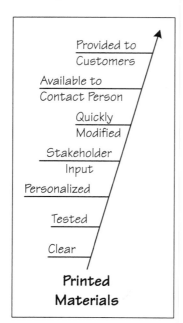

Figure 7-10. The elements.

Clear. The content is well-written. The language is clear and straightforward, effectively communicating information and options to the customer. The layout of the materials is logical and facilitates understanding.

Concise. The materials convey all of the essential information succinctly. Designers of the printed materials are sensitive to the fact that receivers of the information (potentially disgruntled customers) may not be receptive to lengthy content.

Tested. A review team has analyzed the materials for clarity and appropriateness. A "pilot" study is performed in which a location is chosen and materials are put to use in actual customer service situations. Problems are logged, solutions are generated and implemented, and the documentation is ''fine-tuned'' for effectiveness.

Personalized. Rather than placing ''Dear Customer'' greetings on correspondence, letters or cards are personalized through the use of customer contact software.

Stakeholder Input. Customer contact workers, their managers, the Public Relations Department, the Graphic Design Department—all stakeholders should be consulted in the effort to produce perfect printed materials.

Quickly Modified. Printed material content is modified whenever there are changes in the environment, customer expectations or needs, or the goods or services your company provides.

Available to Contact Persons. The printed materials must be distributed to all customer contact personnel and their managers.

Provided to Customers. The customer contact person must deliver the printed materials to the customer. Otherwise, all of the effort expended to create the printed resources is wasted.

Case Example: Passing Bad Paper

An airline lost my baggage during a recent trip. The service representative in ''Baggage Handling Services'' took my report in about 30 seconds, then jammed a piece of paper in my hand. He said, ''Call the number on the form if you have any questions'' and turned to the next sad traveler.

Bluntly, the paper looks like it was printed on a one-pin dot matrix using toilet paper as the medium. Maybe the FBI crime lab can pull a message off this paper, but I can't. (See Figure 7-11.)

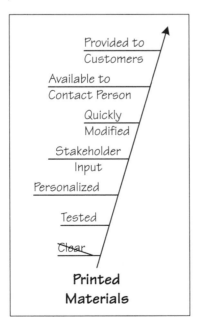

Figure 7-11. Missing in action.

Environment

Note: This category of concerns exists if the organization has an onsite facility for addressing customer concerns. For telephone service operations and the like, some of these areas might still be addressed for the benefit of the employees. (See Figure 7-12.)

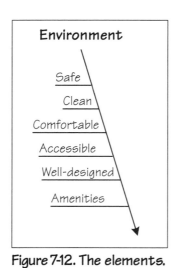

Figure 7-12. The elements.

Safe. The environment should be designed to provide employees a measure of protection from angry customers. If necessary, the layout should physically and/or psychologically deter such customers from making contact with any employee. The challenge, in this age of workplace violence, is to provide maximum customer access while ensuring employee safety.

Clean. Waiting areas, rest rooms, and office areas should be clean and well organized.

Comfortable. Heating and cooling should be effective. The chairs should be comfortable. Square footage of the waiting area should be adequate for the number of customers served.

Accessible. The onsite facility should be convenient to the customer, allowing easy accessibility for customers with disabilities.

Well-designed. The onsite facility should be designed with adequate lighting and appropriate furniture. The layout provides for isolating the customer from other individuals, if necessary.

Amenities. Items should be provided for the customer if it has been determined they will influence the customer's impressions of the quality of service. These items might include telephones, magazines, background music, and coffee and soft drinks.

Case Example: Inviting Harassment

Our Customer Service Department was just redesigned. It now boasts a long front counter, which keeps upset customers from walking right up to our desks. However, it also presents a problem for one of my co-workers, Darlene.

Darlene seats herself at the counter, rather than at her desk. This is commendable, in a way, but the frequency of customer visits does not warrant it. The problem is that Darlene sits in a "hole" below the relatively high counter, so customers virtually look down on the top of her head. Darlene is also something of a "lightning rod martyr." She has the kind of accommodating personality which allows angry customers (we get some really irate visitors) to escalate their venting. The customer will start with complaints about our products and services, then ultimately end up screaming about world hunger or something like it. It is a remarkable sight to see Darlene's head showered with the spray of a customer's expletives and saliva.

This is dangerous. I recommended to Darlene that she stay at her desk until

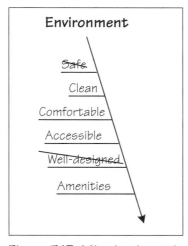

Figure 7-13. Missing in action.

needed and then move over to stand behind the counter. I have asked management to build an elevated platform if she insists on working at the counter. I have contacted the union to push for a safety glass shield, because our customers are getting nastier and I am worried about workplace violence. I have nominated Darlene for sainthood. It will probably be awarded posthumously. (See Figure 7-13.)

Case Example: Some Really Sick Customers

(Some solutions can be truly easy.) I work in an Air Force Hospital Emergency Room. In our ER we had a huge volume of complaints, which were evenly distributed across a wide range of predictable areas: the doctors were rude, the nurses were rude, the paperwork was too lengthy, etc. As a team, we took a look at all of the complaint forms and made a "stretch" in our intuitive reasoning: we hung a television set on the wall and the number of complaints dropped 93%. None of the complaint forms stated, "I am bored, therefore I hate the doctor." They just said, "I hate the doctor."

The beauty of our solution is that it accomplished the following: 1) it was a zero-cost solution, because a local appliance store donated both the TV and the plaque giving recognition to his store, 2) it knocked out 93% of the complaints attributable to boredom, leaving us the true 7% on which to focus our scarce resources, and 3) it spared us from the actions of a disgruntled senior manager who was about to make massive changes in ER people, policies, and procedures, which would have either had no effect or made the problem worse.

Actually, our first cure for the boredom wasn't the TV solution. We initially purchased $200 of magazines, but after a week every publication was missing

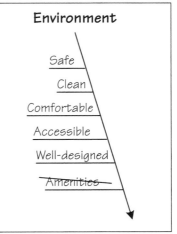

Figure 7-14. Missing in action.

except for a couple of *Bible Stories*. It appears TVs are much harder to remove from the premises. . . . (See Figure 7-14.)

Contingency Plans

The intuitive skills of key members of the organization should be tapped in efforts to avoid customer service mishaps. Plans should be developed and distributed so

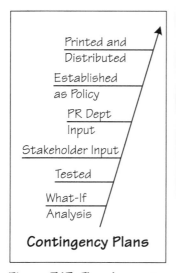

Figure 7-15. The elements.

that, should an event occur that is even remotely possibly negative, customer contact personnel will know what to do. (See Figure 7-15.)

What-if Analysis. A thorough analysis of foreseeable problems should be performed.

Stakeholder Input. All concerned or affected parties should be consulted on the development of action plans to address predictable problems. This facilitates ownership of the plans, fostering ownership of the problems should they arise.

PR Department Input. The final plans should be reviewed once more by the Public Relations Department, if deemed appropriate. Preparations should be made for all foreseeable outcomes.

Tested. The plans should be tested, if possible, through the use of "mock" or "dry" runs, with difficulties recorded, addressed, and resolved.

Established as Policy. After successful testing, the plans should be formalized as policies.

Printed and Distributed. The end products are printed and distributed to all stakeholders. Confirmations of the receipt of the documents may be warranted.

Case Example: 20-20 Hindsight

I work for the Customer Service Department of an Internet service provider. Our company markets so aggressively it is an industry joke that we "carpet bomb" the public with our free software disks. Recently we offered a lower access rate that was so attractive that new signups swamped our system, damaging our service to our customer base. "Logging on" took forever, if you could get on at all, and data transfer rates were painfully slow.

Senior management was bathed in negative publicity for the situation; in the Customer Service Department, we got nuked. It's one thing for an unhappy customer to return a widget for repair; it's a whole new level of grief to disappoint millions of customers several times each day.

I'm just a customer service rep. I wonder what communication transpired prior to the crisis. Did anyone ask what might happen if response was too strong? Were the system engineers consulted on this possibility? Did PR have a plan if service was disrupted? Was this "deer-in-the-headlights" look the best we could do? (See Figure 7-16.)

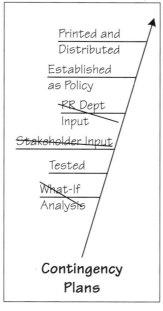

Figure 7-16. Missing in action.

Expectations

Perhaps a good definition of the word "grief" is the distance between expectations and reality. On the other hand, if the reality of the service exceeds the expectations of the customer, then excitement or even elation can occur. This range of possible outcomes is represented on the model by a gap or a break. In "real life" the gap must be measured to assess the success of the customer service operation. This assessment must also consider the appropriateness of the customer's expectation. (See Figure 7-17.)

Assessed. Using surveys, focus groups, and complaint analysis, customer feedback is collected, analyzed, and interpreted in the effort to gain an accurate picture of what the customer expects in terms of service. Special attention is given to any gaps between what the customer expects and what the company delivers.

Adjusted. If the customer's expectations are unreasonable or cannot be met, a plan is developed to adjust or "educate" the customer into adopting a new, more reasonable expectation.

Case Example: All Signs Point to Rudeness, or Ugly Americans Will Be Served in Turn

I recently became a manager at a State Department consulate in a foreign country. We process visas and other related documents. American citizens, although only a part of our customer base, often demand instant service before all others, especially

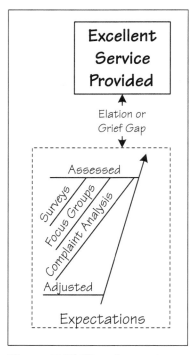

Figure 7-17. The elements.

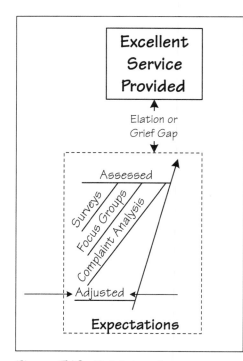

Figure 7-18. Put into play.

foreign citizens. One of my employees, Grace, is masterful at informing the Americans that we are all human beings and all customers will be served in turn. She is truly amazing. In fact, Grace is successful about 98 times out of 100 in adjusting the expectations of the customer. The problems are: 1) the two individuals with whom she is unsuccessful will contact their congressmen and then I get "flame-broiled" for not providing the special treatment demanded, and 2) Grace spends a lot of valuable work time educating these unhappy Americans.

Recently, I commissioned a large, clearly printed sign which states that all customers, regardless of national origin, will be served in turn. I placed the sign behind Grace's desk. Now, she is rarely challenged on the queuing of customers and I have reclaimed her lost productivity. We still get the occasional jerk and I still take the congressional heat, but I guess that's my job. After all, I am the manager. (See Figure 7-18.)

Case Example: Breakfast at the "Bait and Switch" Buffet

My problem is with my favorite motel chain. The words "continental breakfast" are emblazoned on their motel signs, but the food provided differs greatly from location to location.

An experienced traveler, I would expect a continental breakfast to include cereal or yogurt, toast, and milk or juice. I recently hit bottom at one of their motels in Texas. The breakfast consisted of a tray of six round brown things (they called them donuts). A posted sign read, "If you want orange juice, you must ask the clerk at the counter." When I requested juice, a frowning clerk (obviously bothered) emerged, shaking a gallon jug in my face. She splashed my cup with some very thin liquid and then disappeared. I got some juice; the family after me did not.

This is not an isolated incident. No bread, no milk, no cereal: at all locations, things are always missing.

It's funny. The cost of lodging is so reasonable at this chain, I would stay there without a continental breakfast. But because they promise and don't deliver, I'll be staying elsewhere— and I'll eat breakfast at Denny's or the International House of Pancakes. (See Figure 7-19.)

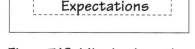

Figure 7-19. Missing in action.

Management Support and Creativity

Across the lower half of the model, an arrow is displayed to represent senior management support. It is inherent in this broad approach that resources be provided to further the pursuit of perfect service. Glaring deficiencies in the model cannot be addressed with denial, lip service, or a cavalier attitude. Providing appropriate resources is a management responsibility.

Case Example: What to Do at the Zoo?

As a zoo director, I manage the oldest zoo in the Southwest and the worst politicians anywhere. The zoo is the oldest because a cowboy put a fence around a longhorn steer in 1898 and called it a zoo. The politicians are the worst because, if common sense is dead, it expired here first. (See Figure 7-20.)

Our zoo, now with over 300 animals in its collection, has a loyal and dedicated customer base. I serve as the zoo director, construction manager, fund-raising chairperson, volunteer coordinator, etc.

A recent customer satisfaction survey identified numerous problems, many of which we were painfully aware of. Most significant was the lack of concrete walk-

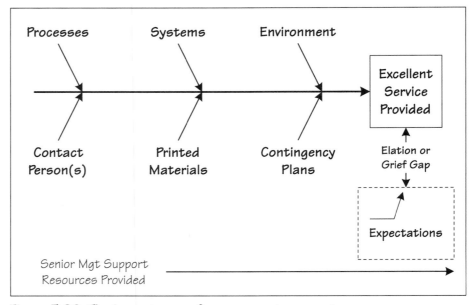

Figure 7-20. The importance of managment support.

ways throughout sections of the facility. I approached my team with the challenge to change this situation.

My team, hard-working and committed, developed a proposal. Entitled "Concrete Walkways for the Anderson City Zoo," it was presented to the city commissioners as a very polished package, making use of grant funds which were in a *must use* situation, volunteer labor, and donated materials.

In canvassing the commissioners to assess their support for the project, we discovered that the proposal was going to be defeated. A majority of the commissioners were against it, but for unclear reasons. It seemed the commissioners had no problem with the swamps that formed after a downpour, and the commissioners would not explain themselves further. All lines of communication were closed. My team and I were despondent. The city commission would vote in one week.

At our weekly meeting, we brainstormed for ideas. Our ultimate solution was to rename the project "Handicapped Access at Anderson Zoo." Since this was an election year, the project was unanimously approved. I also think we scored points with the commissioners for our ingenuity.

The bigger problem is the lack of senior management support in dealing with customer service needs. Not every year is an election year, and we cannot co-opt such a sensitive issue at every impasse.

I have recently applied for jobs elsewhere.

Benefits of This Model

Now that we have developed and defined the perfect service model, we can consider its benefits, as outlined above. This approach presents seven potential advantages:

1. **The tool presents a comprehensive one-page picture of what is required to achieve excellent customer service.** The completed graphic shows, in detail, those areas which must be addressed to provide quality customer service. Intuitive types or experienced managers will benefit from seeing the "forest" (all factors present) when, in the past, they may have struggled primarily with the "trees" (individual factors) with crisis-mode responses. The entire organization will benefit as the employees understand that there is a "bigger picture" and they own a role in it.

2. **The tool is infinitely adjustable and can be tailored to the organization and its environment.** Product or service, high- or low-tech, small business or large corporation—any organization can modify the tool to reflect the dynamics required to provide quality service to its customers and accommodate its idiosyncrasies quite easily.

3. **The approach graphically establishes ownership of elements of the customer service formula.** Individual functions or groupings of functions can be clustered, with jurisdictional responsibilities noted directly on the graphic. Ownership is clearly established and reinforced through distribution of the completed fishbone. Fingerpointing is reduced, because of the document and because of senior management's efforts to eliminate role ambiguities.

4. **The finished graphic can be used to present "before-and-after" pictures of improvement efforts.** The completed model can guide survey and improvement efforts. Data can be collected and placed on the graphic, then augmented with color to indicate problem areas. Solutions can then be generated, improvement plans implemented, and data collected again to measure the outcome. The "after" picture data can similarly be displayed on the model, quickly and effectively communicating results to others. Interim "data pictures" can be provided to stakeholder employees, providing them with more immediate (possibly real-time) feedback.

5. **The approach is unique in ways that may score points in award competitions (Baldrige, etc.).** With points for customer service figuring prominently in computations for awards, organizations must discover ways to package their awards submissions effectively. A clear and concise "before-and-after" sandwich, with a well-designed improvement strategy in the middle, should boost the point values earned. At least, the clarity of your submission should earn your organization all of the points it deserves for its efforts.

6. **The graphic can be used to lobby senior management for additional resources.** The linearity of the model is compelling when lobbying for resources. After identifying deficiencies or problems in the customer service model, the argument for additional resources can be effectively made in a single page. Causality can be more effectively established, even when senior management might prefer to pretend that a factor within the overall customer service picture is unrelated. The lobbyist can point at the model and state (diplomatically, of course), "If you want this over here (pointing to the 'satisfied customer' end of the model), I need this over here (pointing to deficiencies)."

7. **Reduces stress by providing reassurance (through the structure of the tool)**

to individuals responsible for only a piece of the customer service model, reinforcing that they have given their best effort. Too often, senior management attempts to improve customer service by "cheerleading" employees toward better performance. But in the complexity of customer service, as shown by the model, exhorting the employees to "try harder" or "have a better attitude" while leaving significant pieces of the model unaddressed may yield no significant improvement. Worse, the employees may intuitively know that the deficiencies in the customer service formula are not under their direct control, thereby undermining their morale. Conversely, this knowledge may actually reduce stress, as the employee understands he or she has done the best job possible. The model has the potential to communicate to conscientious stakeholders, "Relax. It wasn't your fault."

Case Example: Dealing With Red-Hot Customers

I manage a lodging facility at a military site in the desert Southwest. A good number of our customers are active-duty military personnel who travel here to attend a special school. This commitment requires a lengthy stay. The soldiers go to school all day, then return to their accommodations to study for most of the night.

When the soldiers return to our facility, though, they sometimes discover the temperature in their rooms to be above 100 degrees. This is due to a less-than-reliable air conditioning system. Making the situation worse is that repairs must be arranged through our Public Works Department, which then, due to government cutbacks, must contract with a private firm to perform the repairs.

The Public Works folks are dedicated and conscientious workers and I respect them for doing everything they can do. Despite this, I feel much removed from a quick solution. My customers are often unhappy, but I have done everything humanly possible to provide excellent customer service. In other words, I am able to sleep at night. But, then, I have an air conditioner in my home.

From Perfect Service to Exceptional Service

The model, when you tailor it to your organization's environment and needs, presents a panoramic view of the essential elements necessary to provide perfect customer service. It also establishes, in graphic form, that your customers' expectations and perceptions are the key criteria for judging your service.

Unfortunately, even with all of the "building blocks" in place, you may still lose business rather than grow it. A Xerox study reported in a 1995 *Harvard Business Review* article by Thomas Jones and W. Earl Sasser noted that "satisfied" customers (4 on a 1-to-5 scale) are six times more likely to take their business elsewhere than those who award a 5 ("completely satisfied"). Your organization's completed model may not readily show customer service activities that generate joy, elation, thrill, memorable experiences, and—most important—"fives" on the surveys. In other words, you can push the perfect service model for all it's worth, but crucial factors still exist outside the structure that may require considerable intuitive effort to address.

This distinction may best be reflected in the transition from "perfect service" to "exceptional service." A serious and thorough development of the model can give you "perfect service" and you may still lose customers. But a zany and creative brainstorming session built around the model might earn you the label "exceptional service" for your efforts—and you'll retain your customers and attract others.

The model also graphically establishes that an organization must invest a tremendous amount of effort in the essentials before it can focus on action plans that deliver customer excitement. Perhaps this observation represents an eighth benefit to the user, in that the model presents to senior management a case for being patient in turning around a dysfunctional customer service operation. Before you can *ice* a cake, you have to *build* the cake.

About the Author

Michael Vandergriff is president of The Vandergriff Consulting Group, "The Conflict Experts," a division of Vandergriff & Vandergriff, in Plano, Texas. He has been handling conflicts and providing conflict resolution training since 1979, for 14 years as head of Skill Trainers, then for the last six years with The Vandergriff Consulting Group. He is a dynamic speaker and often addresses regional, national and international groups. You can learn more about Michael at his Web site (http://www.vand ergriffgroup.com).

8

STANDARDS FOR SERVICE: FROM COUNTABILITY TO ACCOUNTABILITY

Kristin Anderson

Service standards are the way an organization can meet or exceed customer expectations consistently. This article discusses three types of service standards: outcome, status, and transactional. The first two are generally relatively easy to define and achieve—and usually not enough. The third is often the key to customer satisfaction. The author outlines a five-phase approach to creating transactional service standards, the competitive edge for "organizations that wow their customers, that knock their socks off and keep them coming back again and again."

Several years ago I found myself in Raleigh-Durham, conducting a full-day workshop for front-line customer service professionals. During the first break I was approached by a participant. I'll call her Nancy.

"I really *don't* need to be here," she insisted, "but my boss *made* me come."

"Oh?" I asked, inviting her to say more. Nancy's demeanor made it clear that she'd been "sentenced to training" and very much resented her "prisoner" status.

"My boss told me I *had* to come because I'm not nice enough, but I *know* that I am perfectly nice," she declared, daring me to contradict her.

"And where are you originally from?" I asked.

"Chicago," she stated proudly. "I just moved here four months ago."

Suddenly, everything was clear to me.

Nancy and her boss were both right. Nancy *was* nice, by Chicago standards. "Nice" in Chicago can mean that you don't waste my time chitchatting about things that are, frankly, none of your business.

And, just as surely, Nancy was failing the Raleigh-Durham test, where niceness often implies taking a personal interest, even if that takes a little more time.

Nancy and her boss were both following the Golden Rule of Customer Service—"Treat others as you would have them treat you"—and that gold was returning as only lead. The Golden Rule is a good place to start in service, because it helps you put yourself in your customer's shoes and to look at the world from the customer's point of view. But it's a poor place to stop, because it tells you only half the story.

In the end, customers want to be treated the way *they* want to be treated. It's as simple as that—and as difficult.

The Role of Service Standards

Service standards are essentially "the rules you write for getting work done." They're a tool for designing and delivering a service experience that's what the customer wants, even when—perhaps especially when—what the customer wants is different from what the service provider's personal preference might be.

Our research suggests that all organizations operate with three types of service standards—whether those standards are codified into policy or simply accepted as informal norms. The three forms are transactional, outcome, and status.

Transactional standards are about the human-to-human dimensions of customer contact. They're often expressed in terms that are warm and fuzzy: be nice to customers, be friendly, wear a warm smile. *Outcome* standards communicate about the completed service: "The guest has been satisfactorily checked into the hotel when . . ." or "The repair ticket will be considered closed when. . . ." *Status* standards cover those conditions that affect (directly or indirectly) the customer's experience, but that do not involve a personal exchange: "Clothing will be neatly displayed on racks or shelves at all times," or "Coffee break areas will be fully set up 20 minutes prior to the meeting start time."

Outcome and status standards are objective and measurable. Their countability makes them comfortable and easy to communicate. Think for a moment about the outcome and status standards in effect in your organization. Would you have any difficulty explaining them to someone from outside your region of the country? Or your part of the world? Probably not.

More difficult to form and communicate are transactional standards. Yet, in our work with service professionals in all types of business—from theme park employees to truck drivers, from hospital RNs to hotel desk clerks, from bankers to ballpark concessionaires—the transactional standards are equally, if not more, important in garnering great marks from customers.

Organizations where transactional service standards are clearly defined and commonly understood, and where those standards reflect actual customer needs and expectations, are organizations that wow their customers, that knock their socks off and keep them coming back again and again.

Organizations where transactional service standards are assumed—"I hire them to be nice"—or where transactional standards are fuzzy—"Show that you care"—are ripe for miscues and poor communication. Managers are bound to be caught, as was Nancy's manager, in an uncomfortable discussion of employee attitude—"What do you mean I'm not *enthusiastic*?" or "I did so show *empathy* to that customer!"—in their efforts to shape the behavior that customers respond to best.

From Countability . . .

It's small wonder, then, that many managers focus their training and coaching efforts on outcome and status service standards. And certainly there's a need for those types of standards.

Outcome and status service standards do provide important countability in the customer service delivery process. As formal, written instructions, they allow consistent service performance in those encounters where consistency is a virtue. The need for consistency is key. In a manufacturing or data processing setting, consistency often means little or no variation. In customer service interactions, customers eschew "Thank-you-for-shopping . . . Next!" robotics in favor of "It-happens-similarly-each-time" predictability.

In writing or reviewing your own outcome and status service standards, one format we've found helpful is as follows:

Who delivers? What does it look like? When is it done?

For example, a courier service might have the following outcome and status standards:

Package Delivery Attempt (Outcome)
The courier rings/knocks four times and waits a full two minutes when delivering a package, before leaving an attempted delivery notice.

Truck Appearance (Status)
The courier will examine the external and internal cleanliness of his/her truck and see that it is washed if needed, each morning before beginning his/her route.

To the extent that these standards are tied to actual customer needs and expectations, they're appropriate. Stated in an objective manner, they're also countable: the courier either did or did not wait two minutes and did or did not clean the exterior of the truck.

. . . To Accountability

Unfortunately, outcome and status alone won't ensure success in the eyes of your customers. Customers evaluate service success based on their perception—their perception of the reality of the service delivery process (how long I waited, for example) and their perception of the quality of the human-to-human encounter (they treated me as a valued customer, for example).

Consider the experience of a major telephone company in the Midwest. The company was required by the public utilities commission always to advise residential customers who reported a phone problem that, if an on-site inspection revealed the problem was with the telephone unit or the wires in the wall, the customer would be charged a visit repair fee. So, the company instituted an "appropriate" outcome service standard:

Visit Repair Fee Notification
All customer-inquiry center telephone operators will read the legal notification script before scheduling a repair visit.

The utilities commission and the company lawyers were satisfied. Through call process monitoring, they could prove that the outcome of every repair inquiry call was a properly informed customer.

Not surprisingly, customers were less positively impressed. Focus group interviews revealed that many customers felt "Mirandized" by the cue-card reading of the notification script. It was as if needing service were a crime and the repair police were notifying them of their rights.

Telephone operators needed a way to maintain the countability standard while taking accountability for creating a more positive service transaction as measured by the customer's perception of the human-to-human element of the encounter. In short, they needed an appropriate transactional service standard.

To create the appropriate standard, management went back to the original intent of the rules—to ensure that the customer was informed about the possibility of a repair fee before the repair was scheduled or completed. A team of telephone operators was asked to work on alternative wordings of the notification script, wordings that met the legal criteria but sounded like real people talking to real people. The team created four alternative scripts, each carefully worded to both meet the legal test and convey to the customer a sense of "working together."

Now, employees could be held accountable to an appropriate and effective transactional service standard:

Visit Repair Fee Notification
All customer-inquiry center telephone operators will read the legal notification script that is most comfortable for them, before scheduling a repair visit.

Vital Signs of Service

Most organizations find the move from countability to accountability to be difficult. Managers and front-line employees alike resist setting or formalizing standards of human interaction:

- ○ "You can't codify a smile," they protest, imagining a service standard such as "Employees will show a smile 2.75 inches in length at all times."
- ○ "The needs of our customers are too diverse. Each interaction has to be unique."
- ○ "You'll end up with too many standards. It will get ridiculous."

Each concern has validity and should be addressed.

Transactional service standards are not about "a smile 2.75 inches in length." Rather, they are about the *manner* in which the customer service provider and the customer interact. They are created to ensure that customers perceive the human-to-human interaction as meeting, or better yet exceeding, their expectations.

Transactional standards, like outcome and status standards, are most appropriate where consistency is valued. The goal is predictability, not robotics. A term we like to use is "consistent uniqueness," meaning that appropriate transactional standards allow employees to creatively respond to the unique needs of individual customers, while remaining consistent with the service strategy of the organization.

Finally, most organizations need only a few transactional standards—between eight and twenty. These core transactional standards inform the manner in which all outcome and status standards are met or exceeded.

To address these concerns, we now refer to transactional service standards as "Vital Signs of Service." Just as temperature and heart rate indicate physical health, these Vital Signs of Service will indicate the health of the service relationship between employees and customers, as measured by the customer's perception and evaluation of the interaction.

Each Vital Sign (transactional service standard) is a clearly understood statement, written from the customer's point of view, that describes a measurable transaction standard. Most Vital Signs are "house-wide"—that is, they're appropriate measures for employees in a wide variety of job functions, including those who serve internal customers rather than external ones. To ensure that Vital Signs are clearly understood and appropriately implemented, individual departments or areas may create unit specific Best Practices—customer-focused actions—that describe in greater detail how the Vital Sign is to be achieved.

Consider, for example, how a Vital Sign of Service and the accompanying Best Practice improve on a traditional hotel check-in service standard:

Old Model for Check-In: Process each guest check-in accurately, explaining check-out and room charge practices.

Vital Sign of Service: All hotel employees will treat each guest in a manner that makes the guest feel expected, welcome, and catered to.

Best Practice: Front Desk Clerks will use the guest data base to welcome repeat guests *back* to the hotel, mentioning past stay preferences and asking how we might make this stay even better, before completing the check-in process.

Discovering Your Own Vital Signs: A Process

We've developed a five-phase approach to creating transactional service standards. While the details and timing of each phase necessarily vary from organization to organization, this process provides a useful framework.

Critical to the success of this process is grounding in the actual needs and expectations of your own customers. Resist the temptation to "guess" based on personal experience or what seems to have worked in the past.

For example, in conducting patient and family member focus groups for a large Midwestern hospital, it became clear that many customers felt lost and ignored as they tried to navigate through the hospital campus. This was no great surprise—except when we realized that in many, many years of satisfaction studies, nobody had ever asked customers about the ease with which they were able to find their way or their satisfaction with the efforts of hospital staff to help them to their destination. Subsequent research confirmed that a key factor in overall satisfaction was "I never felt lost. Employees valued my time and helped me find my way."

Phase I. Overview for Managers

One measure of the success of any service standard is the extent to which employees value it and adhere to it. And a key predictor of that is management buy-in. If management does not see the importance of the service standards, neither will front-line employees.

For this reason, it makes sense to begin the service standards process with senior management and their reports. Key information to be shared in this phase includes:

○ What service standards are in general and how Vital Signs of Service and Best Practices are defined.
○ Why setting service standards is an important step for the organization. Included here is the link between customer perception of the transactional elements of service and customer satisfaction with the overall organization and its service offerings.
○ How Vital Signs of Service and Best Practices will be created. This is a preview of the next three steps.
○ How Vital Signs of Service and Best Practices will be sustained. This is a preview of the final step.
○ The role of management in the effort.

Phase II. Identify Service Standard Teams

A cross-functional service standard team (or teams) should be created to draft the initial house-wide standards. In some organizations we've worked with where the total number of employees was smaller (such as at a restaurant) or where the employees had a good understanding of how other employees interacted with customers (such as in a department store), a single team of 12–15 members has completed this task. In larger and more complex organizations (such as a hospital with 3,000-plus employees), four or six teams may be needed to ensure that all employees feel represented in the process.

Team members are "service champions," nominated by their managers based on demonstrated exceptional service performance, commitment to service quality improvement, respect from peers, and general savvy about customer service issues.

Phase III. Service Standard Teams: Discovering the Vital Signs

Teams participate in a four-hour session on discovering the Vital Signs. Like the managers' session, this process begins with a discussion of what service standards are and how Vital Signs and Best Practices are defined. Examples from other industries are extremely helpful.

Key to the success is ensuring that employees understand why setting standards is an important step. Real examples from customer focus groups and satisfaction surveys have the greatest impact. They demonstrate what Nancy and her boss needed to learn—that the key measure is customer perception and that the purpose of the standard is to help us manage that perception in a positive way.

It's also important to discuss how Vital Signs will be used now and in the future. Vital Signs are focused on identifying and celebrating service strengths, as well as on clarifying areas for improvement. Explain how your organization plans to incorporate them into programs for employee recognition and performance evaluation.

Team members will be asked to work in small groups, to brainstorm possible Vital Signs of Service and Best Practices. We find it works well to have the team write each Vital Sign or Best Practice on a separate 5 x 8 card. Use one color of card for Vital Signs and another for Best Practices. The facilitator should ensure that Vital Signs are written from the customer's point of view.

After 20 minutes of brainstorming, post the Vital Signs and their accompanying Best Practices around the room. Give the participants about 10 minutes to walk around and review them. The facilitator should then lead the group in a process of moving the cards so that similar Vital Signs are together with their related Best Practices.

Then, give each sub-group a different Vital Sign and related Best Practices to refine and revise. Give the groups about 30 minutes for this. Remember: the goal of this phase is a draft, not a final product. You may need to remind participants that Best Practices are frequently unit-specific. For example, in a retail store the associate staffing the fine jewelry area may not be able to escort a customer to another area of the store, while that practice may be expected of general floor associates.

Phase IV. Finalize the Vital Signs of Service

Collate and review the ideas. Give yourself and the team members several days to consider and comment on the draft. It is also appropriate to involve management in this review process, though our experience suggests that you should wait until after your second draft.

As you go through the review and revision process, keep three things in mind:

- ○ Vital Signs are about the customer's *perception* of the quality of the human interaction. They should be stated in a way that makes them measurable through customer satisfaction measurement surveys and focus groups.
- ○ Respect the work of the Service Standards Team. They are the people who'll have to live these standards each and every day. Resist the temptation to rework their draft to the point where they no longer recognize it. Otherwise, you'll lose the valuable perspective and expertise they bring to the process— and lose their buy-in to the implementation of Vital Signs and Best Practices.
- ○ Keep it simple. Ask yourself if any of the Vital Signs are overlapping or if any should be Best Practices instead. While some organizations have as many as 20 Vital Signs, you should press hard to simplify if the review and revision process leaves you with more than 12.

Phase V. Communicating the Vital Signs of Service

The final phase of the process is communicating the Vital Signs of Service. Begin with a presentation to the Service Standard Team(s), celebrating their efforts and enlisting them in communicating the Vital Signs. Include senior management in this, both to inform them and to convey the importance and the value of this effort.

The Vital Signs should then be presented to the larger management group. We find that a three-hour session allows adequate time for helping managers know how they can communicate commitment to the service standards and understand their role in facilitating unit efforts to create Best Practices where needed, grounded in the Vital Signs. Managers also need to be clear on the appropriate and inappropriate links between Vital Signs and performance review and evaluation. Vital Signs and Best Practices are powerful tools for coaching and counseling employee performance.

Summing Up

Standards of all kinds are an everyday part of our lives and relationships. They help ensure the consistency and predictability that give relationships order and stability. In the delivery of high-quality service, we communicate our service performance expectations through outcome, status, and transactional standards.

If we, like Nancy's boss, are to hold employees accountable for customers' perceptions of the quality of the service we provide, we must also provide employees with a clear understanding of how to achieve excellence. The rule for service today is clear: treat customers as they would like to be treated. Vital Signs of Service, accompanied by unit-specific Best Practices, allow savvy service professionals to do that—and to do it well.

About the Author

Kristin Anderson is a Principal with Performance Research Associates, Inc., in Minneapolis, a firm that specializes in needs assessment, service research, service management programs, and evaluation research. Kristin coordinates efforts on consulting and joint venture projects, as well as new product development. In client consulting, she specializes in focus groups and survey research. She's worked with a wide variety of clients, including Aurora HealthCare, Motorola, Kinko's, M-Care, PaineWebber, West Publishing, Merchant's Home Delivery, Star Tribune Newspaper, American Water Works Association, Bell Canada, and Cincinnati Bell Information Systems.

Kristin is the author of *Great Customer Service on the Telephone* (AMACOM Books, 1992). She also wrote (with co-editor Ron Zemke) the books *Coaching Knock Your Socks Off Service* (AMACOM, 1996), *Delivering Knock Your Socks Off Service* (AMACOM, 1991), *Knock Your Socks Off Answers: Solving Customer Nightmares and Soothing Nightmare Customers* (AMACOM, 1996), and *Tales of Knock Your Socks Off Service: Inspiring Stories of Outstanding Customer Service* (AMACOM, 1997).

In addition to writing articles for *Training, Mobius* (now *Customer Relationship Management*), and *Boardroom Reports*, Kristin hosts the six-part "On the Phone" video training series produced by Mentor Media. She's also worked with Lily Tomlin, Ron Zemke, and Mentor Media to create a series of "Socks Off Service" training videos.

9

WHAT CUSTOMERS REALLY WANT: HOW THAT AFFECTS WHAT SERVICE TO DELIVER

Georgette M. Zifko-Baliga

You can't effectively improve customer service until you know what your customers think about your products or services. But, the author of this article maintains, you can't accurately measure how they feel until you've determined why they feel that way. Do you know the difference between satisfaction with current offerings and perceived ideal quality? This article will help you answer that question and use the answer to better evaluate and improve your service.

"Hey, Mom! We're *really* hungry for a hamburger. Can we *pleeease* stop at McDonald's on the way home?"

Oh, how to answer? Just how do I manage these "customers" of mine? Is it "yes" because it's easier for me? After all, we're returning from five days in Florida, where we "relaxed" by visiting Magic Kingdom and doing the cycling, swimming, paddle boating, swimming routine. Or is it "yes" because there's no question in my mind that they *will* eat the hamburgers—as they've done before? And yet, there's another angle to consider. Is a McDonald's hamburger *good* for them? Is it really nutritious? My perception on the last question is "no."

So, then, what is my criterion for answering the kids? Do I want to feed them so they're satisfied ("predictable," "always-exactly-alike" McD's burgers)? Or do I want to feed them quality food (balanced, low-fat, tasty)? So, satisfy them or give them quality food?

Satisfaction and Perceived Quality

Hmmm. . . . Satisfaction or perceived quality. Wait a minute! Aren't they the same thing? Or, at the very least, doesn't one measure the other? It's a legitimate question. But it's a dual question, because it's a question of satisfaction and it's also a question of perceived quality. It's a question that we need to ask ourselves concerning our customers, so that we can offer better customer service.

The answer to this question will be given from three perspectives:

1. **Definition**. Exactly how are the satisfaction and perceived quality constructs defined? What are their differences and similarities? How does this affect the customer service manager in the short term and long term?
2. **Industry**. Where does your industry and company fit into the EI (Expectation/Industry) Matrix and how might it use these two constructs? What exactly do your customers care about? How can customer service managers utilize this information in the long term?
3. **Research**. When your customer service department conducts consumer research, there are five points to keep in mind. What exactly should you measure for short-term information as well as long-term?

Definition

The two constructs—satisfaction and perceived quality—are not the same. While it's important to note their similarities, these similarities do not make them the same. They're similar because both constructs compare expectations with actual events. They're different because each construct compares a different type of expectation. Consumers clearly distinguish between the two; thus, as a customer service manager, your response to a customer should be based on that customer's expectation at the time.

Satisfaction

Satisfaction is based on *predictive expectations*. Satisfaction measures the perception of what actually happened in a service or product encounter compared with what the consumer thought *would* happen in the situation. *A satisfaction measure is a comparison of a perception of an event to predictive expectations.* Thus, satisfaction is a measure of how well consumers predicted the product or service level they received and were satisfied by it.

Therefore, eating McDonald's hamburgers would have resulted in two very satisfied kids. Why? Because they know exactly what to expect in a hamburger from McDonald's because they are the same every time! A company that can close the gap between predictive expectations and the product or service it delivers can achieve high satisfaction levels.

How does this affect the customer service manager? How do you know that the customers are comparing the product or service they buy with their *predictive* expectations? By *listening* to customers and developing your response from the cues they're giving you. For example, you may hear the following phrases:

- "It's not the same as last time . . . "
- "It shrank more than I thought it would . . . "
- "It didn't last as long as I expected . . . "
- "But the last time I was here, it was _____ (warm, tasty, smooth—whatever the adjective). Why wouldn't it be the same?"

All these words and phrases (such as, "same," "last time," "would") are cues from the customer to you, the customer service manager, that your customers' perception of your product or service did not meet the customers' *predictive* expectations. In other words, they were not satisfied because their purchase did not live up to their expectations in some way.

So what should you do? Your immediate response *should not* be to explain why your product or service is superior, wonderful, and so on, and that the customer just doesn't "see it." Your immediate response *should* be to understand the exact predictive expectation that was not met (size, taste, defect, etc.) and then adjust the event to at least meet that expectation. You could replace the defective part, give another product that meets their expectation for taste or color or whatever, or ask for a chance to redo the service. All of these responses allow the customers' perception of the event to match their predictive expectation and to achieve satisfaction. All organizations have this same opportunity—to recover. Consumers are basically a forgiving group, and more organizations should use this "recovery dimension," as Christian Grönroos named it.[1] But a discussion of dimensions is best saved for another time.

Thus, for the short term, managing customer expectations for a product or service is the correct approach for the customer service manager. And it's important to note that, over time, the customer service department can impact both customer expectations and perceptions of the products and services offered.

Perceived Quality

Perceived quality is based on *ideal expectations*. Perceived quality measures the perception of what actually happened in a service or product encounter compared with what *should* happen in the situation from the perspective of the consumer. *A perceived quality measure is a comparison of a perception of an event to ideal expectations.* Thus, perceived quality is a measure of how closely the product or service levels provided came to the *ideal*, to what *should* be offered. In other words, customer expectations for a particular purchase may be correct, but the quality of that purchase may be lower than what they would consider to be ideal.

Therefore, a McDonald's hamburger for my kids would most likely have gotten different ratings for perceived quality from my kids and from me because our ideal expectations are probably different. I would venture to say my ideal expectations for a hamburger (nutritious, low-fat, fresh, not frozen) are not the same as my kids' ideal expectations (tastes good). In this situation, it's easy to see that perceived quality depends on whose perspective is being considered. (In this case, I determined my perspective to be more important. I realize *you* would *never* think you know what's best for your consumer.) Again, it's the gap between the expectation and the situation that measures the construct.

As in the prior situation about satisfaction, a customer service manager should *listen* to the customers and hear the cues they're giving about which type of expectation they're using. Examples of words used by customers with *ideal* expectations are:

1. Christian Grönroos, "A Service Quality Model and Its Marketing Implications," *European Journal of Marketing,* 18:4 (1984), 36–44)

○ "What you should do . . ."
○ "For what you charge, you should . . ."
○ "Ideally, we should not have to wait like this . . ."
○ "You told me this product was ideal for my skin type, and . . ."

These cue words demonstrate that the customers' perceptions of your product or service did not meet the ideal expectations of them. Your customers did not perceive that they'd received a quality product or service.

Your immediate response, as a customer service manager, is to determine the exact ideal expectation that has not been met and attempt to close the gap by altering the product or service for your customer, that is, changing his or her perception of it. Again, for the short term, working within the "recovery dimension" and managing the perception of the event is the correct approach for the customer service manager.

For the long term as well, it's the altering of product or service that is the focus for the customer service manager. This is because ideal expectations are more difficult to change; in fact, you need to baseline a customer's ideal expectations only occasionally, as they're usually more deeply rooted than predictive expectations and difficult to change.

Finally, it should be noted that satisfaction has been researched and studied for many years, while perceived quality has only achieved prominence more recently. The emphasis on service quality came into being in the mid-'80s, primarily due to the research of A. Parasuraman, Valarie A. Zeithaml, and Leonard L. Berry with their focus on *perceived* quality of services and their resulting instrument.[2]

Though a relationship exists between satisfaction and perceived quality, the exact nature of it is unclear. There are three questions about the satisfaction-perceived quality relationship that The Institute for Quality Center (IQC) is researching:

○ Does one construct's measurement go up as the other construct's measurement level does? In our research, one answer we've seen is that a firm's perceived quality measures decline while satisfaction levels remain constant.
○ Which of the two constructs' measurement is the global measurement? That is, do satisfaction measures "collapse" into an overall perceived quality measure? Or vice versa? We feel that the impact on value is important to this question.
○ What is the impact of "certainty" on satisfaction or perceived quality measures? At IQC, we've determined that certainty impacts what dimension of perceived quality is important to consumers. (The topic of dimensionality is best saved for another time.)

To summarize, *satisfaction* and *perceived quality* are different constructs. They measure a comparison with *predictive* expectations and *ideal* expectations, respectively. Consumers can and do clearly distinguish between the two.

2. A. Parasuraman, Valarie A. Zeithaml, and Leonard L. Berry, "SERVQUAL: A Multiple-Item Scale for Measuring Consumer Perceptions of Service Quality," *Journal of Retailing*, 64:1, Spring 1988, 12–40.

Industry

The constructs of perceived quality or satisfaction have been defined and explained in terms of their impact on customer service in the short and long terms. It's also important to management, however, to know how these two constructs fit into a framework that incorporates both constructs and to identify the type of industry your firm is in.

It's crucial for customer service managers to ask which construct they should monitor. In other words, wouldn't it be nice if you knew about the type of expectation your customers were using to evaluate your performance?

Which construct your firm should monitor—perceived quality or satisfaction—depends on two issues:

○ Where does your organization fit into the Expectation/Industry (EI) Matrix (Figure 9-1)?
○ Do your customers most typically use their *predictive* expectations or their *ideal* expectations when measuring the product or service they're receiving from you?

These questions can be answered by utilizing the EI Matrix and your knowledge of your customers' "cues" as explained in the previous section.

The "Type of Industry Continuum" shows how an organization's output can be characterized as a product, a service, or a product/service combination. At the "product" end of the continuum are the manufacturers of products sold to different types of consumers. At the "service" end of the continuum are the providers of services, such as utilities, healthcare, cable TV, hair salons, etc. Between "products"

Expectations of Consumers	Product	Product/ Service	Service
Predictive	Manufacturers	Fast Food Restaurants	Salons
Ideal	Innovators/ Leaders	Five-Star Hotels Five-Star Restaurants	Utilities Healthcare

Type of Industry Continuum

Figure 9-1. The expectation/industry matrix.

and "services" are those organizations that provide a product and a service, such as distributors, restaurants, and hotels. Where does your firm fit on the continuum?

Additionally, each of the three groups along the product-service continuum is further divided vertically, with each sub-group being shown as typically being within the ideal or predictive expectations measure of the consumers (as noted). What type of expectations does the matrix suggest for your customers? And a question of far greater importance: What type of expectations do your customers actually have, according to how you understand them? The EI Matrix can demonstrate where customers typically use current satisfaction expectations and where they use perceived ideal quality constructs, but only customer service managers who truly hear the voice of the consumer can be sure of the type of expectation their customers actually use.

If you know which construct your customers generally use for your products or services, you know how they're evaluating your firm. This knowledge can guide you in determining what type of research you need to do for the long term. Consider the following examples.

A manufacturer of industrial gloves can measure the satisfaction levels of its customers to discover if its gloves are meeting their *predictive* expectations. In addition, if that manufacturer is the industry innovator, it would also want to measure what the customers think the firm *should* be doing for them, their *ideal* expectations. In that case, the manufacturer would measure perceived quality levels as well.

A fast-food restaurant would probably be content with measuring satisfaction, as its goal is to make burgers, fries, and shakes that meet the *predictive* expectations of its customers. The five-star restaurant across the street, in contrast, aims to meet the *ideal* expectations of its customers and so it measures perceived quality.

Organizations that attempt to offer "quality" services should always be measuring levels of perceived quality. Healthcare organizations are an example of this—though they often make the mistake of only measuring satisfaction levels of their patients.

It should be noted that the EI Matrix is a generalized view of complex issues. Because ideal expectations are "over" the predictive expectations does not mean that perceived quality measures are higher or better. Also, it's sometimes difficult to place a particular firm exactly along the product-service continuum; however, a more critical question for that firm is its placement within the expectations levels.

In sum, there are three steps involved in using the ideas in this article:

1. **Focus on your firm.** Answer the following questions: Where are you on the continuum between current satisfaction and delivering the ideal? What are your objectives? Are you content where you are? Should you be content? Be realistic (e.g., don't try to move a fast-food restaurant into a five-star location).
2. **Focus on your customers.** Understand how they perceive your organization and which expectations they most likely use to measure your product or service level.
3. **Measure appropriately** when conducting your research.

Researching Customers' Perceptions and Expectations

When you're gathering data on your customers' perceptions of your firm, *what are you really measuring*? That's a crucial question. As discussed above, satisfaction and perceived quality are not the same constructs, they do not measure the same thing, and consumers clearly distinguish between the two. A common mistake companies make is to conduct *satisfaction* studies and think they're measuring *perceived quality*. Another common mistake is to use the *satisfaction* construct as the way to measure *perceived quality*.

As you develop your research questionnaire to assess your consumers' perceptions, keep in mind the following areas of caution:

○ **Decide what you want to measure.** Do you want to measure *satisfaction* or *perceived quality*—or both?

○ **Understand the underlying foundation of both constructs.** While both constructs are measuring expectations, they are measuring different expectations! A *satisfaction* measure is a comparison with *predictive* expectations, so it measures how well consumers can predict the level of service they receive. A *perceived quality* measure is a comparison with *ideal* expectations, so it measures the services provided as compared with the ideal, or what the consumer believes *should* be provided.

○ **Decide how the criteria used in the questions are to be determined.** First, be sure the consumers have input into those criteria. Too often we feel, as administrators or researchers, that we can speak for our consumers and construct questionnaires without their input. However, that bias alone could seriously distort the results of the study. Second, it's important to think about or ask the vendor how "expectations" were defined for the consumers. Were they defined as 'ideal' or as 'predictive'? This determines whether data will be collected on *perceived quality* or on *satisfaction*.

○ **Determine what set of dimensions is being used as the framework for the questionnaire.** Consumers evaluate providers of services along dimensions, which are groupings of criteria. Parasuraman, Zeithaml, and Berry delineated first ten, then five dimensions of service quality.[3] They proposed that their dimensions fit all services. However, research conducted in healthcare at The Institute for Quality Center found those dimensions did not represent patient care. There are 12 dimensions of perceived quality of care that are grouped along structure, process, and outcome. Also, further research is being conducted that will address the issue of differences of dimensionality between perceived quality and satisfaction.

○ **Review the scale being used in the questionnaire.** Be sure that it represents the construct you want to measure. For example, the scale of ''Very Satisfied

3. Valarie A. Zeithaml, A. Parasuraman, and Leonard L. Berry, *Delivering Quality Service: Balancing Customer Perceptions and Expectations* (New York: The Free Press, 1990).

. . . Very Dissatisfied" is appropriate for a measure of *satisfaction*, but it does not represent the construct of *perceived quality*.

To summarize, define your own objectives of research and choose the correct measurement process and tool appropriate to meet your objectives. In essence, know *what* you are measuring and *why*!

Conclusion

It's important to understand there's a difference between the measurement of *satisfaction* and the measurement of *perceived quality*. Both are effective measures when used appropriately (knowledge of the definitions). Understanding your consumers and your firm's objectives is paramount in deciding which measure to use (knowledge of the EI Matrix). Once that decision is made, conduct the research correctly, so you get scientifically valid and reliable results. Remember: the link to the bottom line is through the study of the perceived quality construct and its input into perceived value—which is a topic for another time.

Oh, to finish the story. . . . Did I stop at McDonald's for my kids or not? I drove right past as I made the executive decision that my "consumers" wanted quality food and not just quick satisfaction. No, I didn't conduct research: this was a case of really knowing and understanding the consumer.

About the Author

Georgette M. Zifko-Baliga, Ph.D. is a founding member and senior partner with The Institute for Quality Center. She has held management positions in both healthcare and consumer products manufacturing. She also possesses academic experience, having been on the faculty and received excellence in teaching awards at The Ohio State University and Kent State University. She conducts market research, workshops, and keynote addresses on perception, self-image, expectations, and quality. You can learn more about her activities at her Web site: http://www.ne-ohio.net/iqc/index.html.

10

CUSTOMERS CARE WHEN THEY SHARE: HOW TO NURTURE LOYALTY THROUGH INCLUSION

Chip R. Bell

When customers understand your business and understand how they can help you serve them, they'll take on some of your work, and this can even result in improved loyalty. How do you create such partnerships and how can this result in more satisfied customers? This is what Chip Bell explains in this article.

"How 'bout goin' and gettin' the tractor and parkin' it in the barn?" These sweet words were music to my ears when I was a 10-year-old growing up on a farm in south Georgia. It was my dad's way of nudging along my maturity. To get the very special privilege of starting, driving, and parking a large, expensive tractor communicated trust and respect. His gesture also left me feeling thrilled . . . and tall.

I have recently reflected a lot on that childhood experience. In part because my dad passed away not too long ago at age 84. The death of a parent is typically a passage that prompts nostalgia and reflection. But there's another reason.

There is a magic that inclusion adds to all relationships—especially customer relationships. The tractor-parking incident was more than a badge of being "grown up." It was a symbol of partnership—I obviously relied on my dad, but at that moment, he trusted me enough to return that dependence. Customers who feel like partners reward service providers with long-term loyalty.

The word "partnership" suggests a variety of qualities—trust, respect, mutual goals, and open communications. Partnership also means give-and-take—some level of mutuality or reciprocity. If you only serve and customers only take, there is a risk of feeling like a slave to customers. If customers feel they only give, they go elsewhere for their next purchase or service.

The Magic of Inclusion

A few years ago Hurricane Hugo caused an unexpected crowd at Myers Park Hardware in Charlotte, North Carolina, as customers rushed to purchase candles, propane gas, camping stoves, flashlight batteries, and other emergency supplies. The store turned to its patrons for help. As three frequent customers were recruited by the store manager to help bag merchandise and ring up sales, the crowd of formerly frustrated customers suddenly broke out in applause. These "volunteers" also registered their pleasure with the scene by offering to give up their "helper" slots to the highest bidder. It became a bit like Tom Sawyer convincing his skeptical onlookers that whitewashing a fence was an honor only for the carefully chosen and lucky few!

Sound like a good idea? It is. However, note this warning: inclusion must be clearly grounded in an attitude of partnership, not exploitation. Inclusion as a clever tool to "use" or take advantage of customers is obviously a no-no and will backfire. Likewise, partnership inclusion is far from a fancy version of "serve yourself" service. The familiar fast-food concept of "you fix your own salad while I fry your burger" can work, but that approach is more about *productivity* than *partnership*.

Partnership inclusion is collective exploration into role-reversal. This means the service provider invites the customer to perform a role normally performed by the service provider—and expected by the customer. Since this type of role-reversal is generally unfamiliar territory for the customer, such a request must be managed with great sensitivity.

Customer inclusion begins by being comfortable enough to ask the customer for assistance. It also means being willing at times to sacrifice a bit on efficiency or effectiveness for the commitment gained by inclusion. It would have been safer and perhaps faster for my dad to have parked the tractor in the garage himself. But he opted for *partnership* over *perfection*. When you invite customers to assist you, the path they take may not be identical to the one you would take or expect. It's like delegation: the delegator must exchange some control for cooperation. But, also as with delegation, inclusion can produce great benefits.

The Key Principles of Customer Inclusion

1. **Only ask for what is reasonable—a request appropriate to a loyal customer**. Avoid any request of a customer that puts the organization or customer at any liability or risk if things go wrong. While the goal is to help the customer feel like a partner, it's important to remember that the customer is always the guest of the organization.

2. **Make the request with the manners your mother taught you, the "May I?" and "Please" courtesies we learned growing up**. Preface your request with a simple statement—"I need your help"—or a simple question—"May I ask of you a small favor?" Simplicity and sincerity are important tunes and tones to help the customer want to get into the rhythm of partnership. My dad never barked a "Go get the . . ." type order; rather, his "How 'bout . . . ?" request always carried the tone of a partner inviting a partner.

3. **Find a way to remind the customer that your request is based on your belief that you enjoy a special relationship with the customer**. However, steer very clear of communicating that this special relationship carries any obligation or potential burden. Communicate your request with an obvious tone of admiration.

It's important for the customer to experience that you are proud of your relationship and would never do anything to jeopardize losing it.

Cox Cleaners in Dallas takes meticulous care of my dry cleaning needs and sends me a bill at the end of the month. Sam Cox is the epitome of the old-fashioned "know all your regulars" neighborhood merchant. And he helps me feel proud to be "a regular"!

Late one afternoon, when I stopped by Cox's to pick up my clothes, Sam was shorthanded and swamped. I patiently waited in the back of the crowd as he struggled at the counter to take orders and retrieve clothes as fast as he could.

At some point he looked and saw me waiting. He smilingly said, "Hey, Mr. Bell. You know the drill here and where everything is. If you want to, you can go on back and get your stuff off the rack. Just leave your tickets in the box." As I proudly worked my way past the crowd into the bowels of this cleaning establishment, some customers seemed clearly curious (and envious) of my privileged position. Sam told me later that two of the waiting customers shifted the next week from "cash and carry" to "monthly account" regulars.

4. **Provide customers a brief background when making a request for assistance**. Avoid complaining or whining. Simply and positively describe your reason for inviting them to help. And, be clear and specific about how the customer can assist. It might be as simple as "We're a bit swamped today and I could really use your assistance. If you could complete your own paperwork on this order while I get the part, I can get you processed and on your way a whole lot quicker. What do you think?"

I was enjoying a three-day stay at a Courtyard by Marriott Hotel in San Antonio. Shortly after lunch on my second day, the hotel manager placed a hand-printed sign in the lobby:

> *Dear guests: We need your help. The aunt of one of our housekeepers passed away and her funeral is this afternoon. Since the aunt was a special person in our housekeeper's life, we all felt we should be at the funeral. There will only be one employee on site . . . at the front desk . . . between 2 and 3:30 p.m. We appreciate your understanding. Thanks!*

The Courtyard customers immediately shifted into a mode of helping each other. Customers served other customers coffee in the lobby café. Customers greeted arriving guests and personally explained what was on the lobby sign. Customers demonstrated great patience and tolerance. There was a tone of camaraderie that even carried over to the following day.

5. **Requests for customer participation must contain the element of choice**. The customer must clearly have an option to pass on involvement. Make a demand on a customer and you're asking for resistance. Avoid managing the encounter so the customer feels "guilted" into meeting your request. A customer made to feel guilty may comply and respond today, but will quietly disappear tomorrow.

6. **Make certain the customer sees participation as a collective effort**. The customer must experience you sharing in the effort or he or she will feel duped, set up, and unfairly used. Customer participation is a powerful tool for customer commitment. However, remember that the pronoun in "po**we**r" is "we."

7. **Give the customer plenty of breathing room**. This means being selective in how and when you invite customers to participate. Too little participation and the customer never gets to feel the glow of inclusion. But too much can be worse—the customer will feel crowded and leave feeling "They knew me too well" or "They took me for granted." Smother customers and they will fly away; take them for granted and they will steal away in the night without warning.

Several years I was working three to four days every month in Miami on a long-term consulting project. I chose a comfortable chain hotel within walking distance of the client's headquarters office. I got to know everyone in this "home away from home" hotel. They would do small favors for me; I would sing their praises and encourage my client and others to use the hotel for major meetings.

After a year, however, the "shine" wore off, and they began to treat me with too much familiarity. Employees told me their hard luck stories like I was a fellow employee; one even gave me his résumé to help him find another job and leave the hotel. They once gave me a poor room when a key group of executives came in. Their explanation: "We knew *you* would understand and not mind!" They never bothered to ask me ahead of time! The punch line? I plotted my escape and switched hotels for the final 36 months of my Miami work.

8. **Never forget to express your gratitude**. The organization (*aka* managers, associates, owners) may ask us to do things all day long. To say "thanks" all the time, every time, is unrealistic. However, asking a customer to assist should be as unique as it is special. Customers will remember it that way if you remember to always communicate appreciation for their efforts. Remember: customer requests should be seen as an option to the customer. Reward their caring enough to accept that option by letting them hear, and feel, your thanks.

Partnership Is About Fairness, Not Perfect Balance

Good partnerships are about fairness, not keeping score. Some people make the mistake of wanting all the customer relationships to be 50–50—giving only as much as is received. But, healthy partnership are fair . . . over time, not with every transaction. Most solid relationships are balanced 60–40 today and 40–60 tomorrow—a kind of floating reciprocity. Such fairness is created by giving the customer an opportunity to be fairly served. It is also created by giving the customer an opportunity to fairly serve. Read those last two lines again! Give and take means serving others and helping customers return the service to the organization or unit.

My partners and I have written a few articles and books together. We have also developed a number of products—training programs, surveys, films, and so on. An obvious issue would be how to split up the royalties and recognition. Since we all have healthy egos, you might imagine there would be some concern over whose name went first on a book or how to fairly split royalties. Many business partners would decide that issue up front. But we always decide it after the fact! We trust that after the dust settles on each effort we can fairly decide based on contribution. Since 1986, there has never been a credit problem. And revenues are rarely split exactly evenly; books and articles have my name first about as often as one of the other partners.

The Path to Partnership

A secret to customer loyalty is the magic of inclusion. The wise organization makes the path to customer contribution comfortable and obvious. As you find opportunities for customer inclusion, remember: some customers want to be *pampered*, not *partnered*. They would be insulted if you suggested they do more than give you their money.

For customers who would enjoy participation, the trick is finding and maintaining the balance between using the customer and ignoring the customer. Look for your special version of "How 'bout goin' and gettin' the tractor and parkin' it in the barn?" Your customer will feel trusted, respected, . . . and maybe even a little taller!

About the Author

Chip R. Bell manages the Dallas, Texas, office of Performance Research Associates, a consulting firm that specializes in helping organizations improve customer loyalty. He is the author or co-author of ten books, including three best-sellers—*Customers as Partners: Building Relationships That Last* (Berrett-Koehler, 1994), *Managing Knock Your Socks Off Service* (AMACOM, 1992), and *Managers as Mentors* (Berrett-Koehler, 1996). Look for his newest book, *Dance Lessons*.

11

TRAINING FOR SUCCESS THROUGH SERVICE: HOW DELTA AIR LINES DOES IT

Nora Weaver and Tom Atkinson

This article describes how Delta Air Lines achieved a competitive advantage through its Success Through Service *training. Whether you operate a huge commercial airline or you sell widgets, the management challenges Delta faced will seem familiar—and the management practices will help you address those challenges and encourage a culture of customer service.*

How do you manage customer service in a company with 67,000 employees, spread among 191 cities in 26 countries around the globe, one-third of whom at any given time are 30,000 feet in the air? This is the challenge faced by Delta Air Lines, one of the world's largest commercial carriers.

Delta-Style Service

In the seven decades since its origin as a small crop-dusting company, Delta built a legendary reputation for family-friendly, "Delta-style" customer service, reflecting the "southern hospitality" of its home base in Atlanta. Delta's long-term profitability allowed it to lead the industry in compensation to employees, who tended to be loyal and contented members of the "Delta family." Delta also led the industry in customer satisfaction ratings, providing passengers with a consistent, high-quality flying experience.

Turbulence in the Airline Industry

And then turbulence set in. In the early 1990s, airlines began to compete by simplifying and lowering fares, resulting in dramatic increases in passenger loads. The ride became especially bumpy for Delta's business passengers, its most profitable customer segment. Business passengers had to wait longer to board and exit the aircraft and could no longer count on such amenities as an open center seat. Not surprisingly, their ratings of the overall travel experience began to decline steeply and their loyalty to Delta began to erode. At the same time, war in the Persian Gulf made transatlantic passengers reluctant to fly and boosted fuel prices, one of the largest components of an airline's operating costs.

These industry dynamics placed a heavy burden on Delta. By 1994, faced with financial losses, Delta began a dramatic cost-cutting initiative, including laying off personnel and reducing pay and benefits. Many of Delta's most experienced employees took advantage of a generous severance package and left the airline. As in other companies experiencing similar turmoil, employee morale began to drop substantially.

Competing Through Customer Service

In 1995 Delta's management launched a comprehensive strategy to regain its competitive edge by reducing operating costs through process and technology improvements, while restoring its reputation for customer service. Rather than provide the same quality of service to everyone, Delta began a more differentiated approach, focusing particularly on business travelers. A task force interviewed 1,200 business customers to identify specifically what they valued most in a travel experience (seat comfort, on-time performance, leg room, reliability of baggage delivery, and so on) and asked over 7,000 Delta employees around the world what must be done to improve service. Among the task force's recommendations was providing training in customer service to all Delta employees.

Success Through Service Training

Delta determined that, for its customer service strategy to succeed, every employee must understand his or her role and how what he or she does affects the customer's flight experience. But delivering customer satisfaction consistently takes more than individual effort. It also requires providing people with a "big picture" view of the whole process and the skills and tools to do the job. Most important, it takes leadership: managers at all levels of the organization must continuously model and reinforce customer service and motivate employees to "go the extra mile" in serving customers. To help provide employees with knowledge, skills, and tools for delivering customer service, Delta created a training program called *Success Through Service*.

The goals of *Success Through Service* are to help Delta employees:

○ Understand what "Delta-style" customer service is,
○ Learn skills and tools for improving service individually and as a team, and
○ Improve the management skills critical to achieving Delta's vision.

There are three versions of *Success Through Service*: one for front-line service providers (such as flight attendants and ticket agents), one for internal service providers (such as mechanics and baggage handlers), and one for managers and supervisors. All seminars represent people from different functions and divisions of the company. In the first year and a half since its launch, approximately 30,000 Delta employees have participated in the program.

Management Challenges

Success Through Service provides Delta with a way to identify the kinds of challenges managers face in helping their people deliver "Delta-style" service day to day, in a demanding environment. Managers and supervisors have an opportunity during the program to share these challenges, to learn a coaching process, and to practice handling difficult situations.

When we asked a sample of typical managers and supervisors to describe the most difficult challenges they face, among the most frequently mentioned were:

○ Working in an environment of constant change.
○ Building trust with employees. Overcoming the distrust of management.
○ Trying to motivate the work force. Motivating team members with diverse experience and commitment levels to provide customer service.
○ Getting caught in the middle with demands being placed on you by superiors and the people you supervise.
○ Being willing to stick up for the underdog. Remembering what it's like to work on the front line face-to-face with our customers.
○ Being a good coach. Giving good feedback and encouraging people to grow and improve.

Management Practices

The following are some of the concepts and practices that Delta managers and supervisors have found effective in addressing these challenges and in creating and sustaining a culture of customer service.

Focus on the Customer

Competing through customer service requires a relentless, organization-wide focus on creating delighted customers. Delta defines "customer" in terms of three groups:

○ **External customers:** People outside the organization who purchase Delta's products, services, or information. These include cargo shippers and leisure and business passengers, each of whom has different needs and expectations;
○ **Intermediate customers:** Individuals or organizations, such as travel agencies or freight forwarders, who provide Delta products or services to external customers; and
○ **Internal customers:** People within Delta to whom products, services, or information are provided.

Treating passengers and intermediaries such as travel agents is not new to Delta. However, the concept of "internal customer," which is broad enough to include essentially any Delta employee, is a new idea to some. Why identify personnel as "customers"? The idea of internal customers reinforces the concept that everyone at Delta serves an external customer or serves someone who does, it encourages teamwork and smooth "handoffs" between groups, and it helps the whole company remain customer-focused by communicating a "common language" of customer service.

In some companies, managers are considered the "customer" by front-line employees. At Delta, the internal customer is most often the team member; management's job is to provide employees with the direction, skills, information, tools, and support to serve external customers well. In serving employees, the managers' role is to model and reinforce the customer service skills that front-line employees use with *their* customers.

Application Story 1

One of my team members seemed to make excessive personal phone calls rather than consistently answering calls from our SkyMiles™ members. I had spoken to her once before but the personal phone calls did not diminish. After I attended Success Through Service, I talked to her again. I advised her up front of the purpose and benefit of our discussion and then asked for her ideas on how we might solve this problem. Together we came up with an agreement on how she would remain available for customer calls. We set up a follow-up date to see if our talk had resolved the problem. I believe that the level of agent frustration was lowered because we came up with a plan together.

Treat Coaching as a Process

An airline is a highly operational environment, where great attention is paid to the hundreds of work processes involved in moving passengers and cargo from point A to point B. Delta is improving customer service by applying its process discipline to the way that it *serves customers* and *manages people*. For example, the process of coaching people is defined as a continuous cycle that involves four steps:

- *Receiving/Initiating*: Setting a positive tone and clear purpose for the interaction. ("Let's take a minute and discuss how you handled that situation. I've got some ideas that might help you next time.")
- *Understanding*: Concentrating completely on what the service provider is saying and asking questions to ensure accurate understanding of both facts and feelings. ("What do you think is the root cause of the problem?")
- *Helping*: Involving the team member in a discussion of options, so that he or she has the confidence and ability to serve customers well. ("What are our best options for dealing with that problem if it arises again?")
- *Sustaining*: Closing the interaction in a way that makes the provider feel valued and supported in his or her role. ("You've done a great job handling

a very stressful situation. Let's see how we can make it less stressful next time.")

Each step includes specific substeps (such as restating feelings and facts) that managers apply in coaching situations (see Figure 11-1).

The Coaching Interaction Cycle helps take the "mystery" out of coaching; rather than a random or haphazard event, coaching is a well-defined process in which all managers can learn and improve and which yields predictable, positive results. Also, since the Coaching Interaction Cycle is very similar to the Customer Interaction Cycle, a process that all employees use in serving customers, managers coach people in a way that reinforces good customer service skills.

Application Story 2

During a Success Through Service *class, I role-played a challenging situation with a team member who had a history of frequent need for time off for personal situations. Although the time off was to be paid back to the company, the 81 hours of time owed diminished individual and team performance. The next morning I called the team member into my office and opened the conversation on a personal note, knowing his area of interest. I asked if he had been doing much fishing lately and he replied that he had not been able to because of several personal situations*

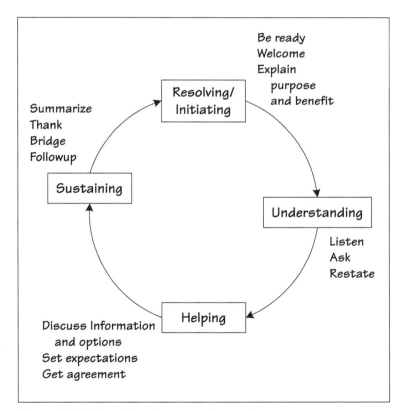

Figure 11-1. Coaching interaction cycle.

requiring his time. I asked if that was why he had been absent from work so much lately and he replied that it was. As we discussed the circumstances, I restated his feelings and took an empathetic approach. I used a series of questions we had developed in class to gain agreement to a time repayment schedule.

Provide Effective Feedback

One of the most powerful tools at a manager's disposal is the use of feedback. When given with care, feedback has two positive effects: it *motivates* people to continue doing what they are doing well and it provides *information* about what they can do differently to be more effective. When not given well, however, feedback can demoralize employees without giving much guidance about how to improve.

Below are guidelines that Delta managers use in giving feedback to service providers:

- **Separate motivational feedback from corrective feedback.**
  The first reason for separating feedback is *setting. Motivational* feedback can be powerful when it is given publicly. *Corrective* feedback is most effective when given privately, to help focus the person's attention on the problem rather than on his or her embarrassment or resentment.

  The second reason for separating feedback is *timing. Motivational* feedback is most effective when given as soon *after* the performance as possible. *Corrective* feedback is most effective when given right *before* the service provider is ready to perform again.

  The third reason for separating feedback is *effect.* Combining the two types of feedback often results in one being overshadowed by the other. Separating them improves the chance that both will be equally effective.

- **Do not underestimate the power of motivational feedback.**
  Most managers find they give little, if any, motivational feedback to their employees. They *assume* their service providers know what they've done well. But even if a provider knows he or she has done a good job, it means much more to hear it from a manager. In fact, if you tell a provider that he or she is good at something, the provider is much more likely to focus on improving that skill than to be satisfied with his or her present level of performance.

- **Make your corrective feedback future-oriented.**
  Service providers cannot correct something they did wrong in an interaction, but they can work on improving that skill for the next interaction. Therefore, it's important to direct corrective feedback to a future event. For example, phrasing your corrective feedback as "Next time, you would be more effective if you would establish eye contact with the customer," rather than "Your eye contact with that last customer wasn't very good," is more likely to encourage the provider to plan for actions to take next time.

- **Make your feedback specific and clear.**
  Make sure the service provider understands what needs to be changed and what was effective. For example, saying, "Great job, Frank!" is not as effec-

tive as ''Frank, you restated the customer's feelings very well, and I think that turned the situation around.''

○ **Avoid feedback overload.**
When giving feedback, concentrate on one thing at a time and make it simple. Feedback that covers too many performance areas tends to overwhelm the provider and blurs the message you are trying to communicate.

Application Story 3

When monitoring a Reservations Sales Representative for quality control, I noted that she exhibited only three of the five critical steps required in a call. Rather than calling her in for a conference to tell her what she had missed, I used the rules of good feedback. I called her in immediately, welcomed her, and told her that the purpose of our talk was to increase her future effectiveness on sales calls. I engaged her by asking what she thought she did well and what she might do to be more effective. We then talked about the specific behaviors noted on the call and discussed specifically what had been done and what was missed. I mentioned that if she added these two missing steps dependably, she would have complete, high-quality calls consistently. By taking a positive, future-oriented approach in which the representative participated in finding solutions, there was much more buy-in on her part. She said our session seemed more like helpful advice than criticism and made a commitment to focus on completing all five required steps in the future.

Results

Since Delta began its customer service initiative, it has received a higher percentage of compliments and a lower percentage of complaints about service for every 1,000 passengers. Beyond the statistics, however, are the thousands of ''moments of truth'' that occur every day. For example:

○ A couple arrived at the airport to pick up the husband's 82-year-old mother. The mother's connecting flight was canceled due to bad weather, and her whereabouts were unknown. The ticket agent expressed empathy for the couple, then contacted other airports to locate the mother and arrange for her to fly home on the next flight. The couple expressed relief and gratitude to the persistent agent.
○ An air cargo customer was angry when the Delta agent told him that company policy prevented the agent from accepting his shipment. After listening to the customer and acknowledging his anger, the agent found a way for the cargo to be shipped. The customer felt that the agent understood and cared and he intends to continue using Delta for his shipping needs.
○ A passenger was frustrated that the seat assignment and special meal she had ordered through her travel agent were not recorded in Delta's computer. The flight attendant listened sympathetically and found a way to accommodate her needs. The passenger said she had intended to write a letter of

complaint, but now would write a letter of compliment. The passenger's job is to book travel arrangements for a large government agency.

- A manager noticed an employee's performance was slipping. Rather than get angry or confrontational, the manager sat down with the employee and listened to his explanation. Then they agreed to a specific plan of action.
- An employee from the marketing department was negotiating a corporate travel contract with a major client. As negotiations became heated, the employee applied the skills for handling angry customers that he learned in training and was able to rescue a million-dollar deal.

"Thank You for Flying With Us"

If you've been a passenger on a commercial airliner lately, you've probably heard a cabin announcement like this: "We recognize you've got a choice and appreciate your flying _____ Airways." Delta people know that a major influence on that choice is the service the passengers receive. The management practices outlined here enable Delta to keep a continuous, company-wide focus on customer service and to strive to achieve its vision to become the "worldwide airline of choice."

About the Authors

Nora Weaver is system manager of Integrated Customer Service and a master facilitator of Success Through Service Training, Delta Air Lines, Atlanta.

Tom Atkinson is Vice President of The Forum Corporation, Boston. A senior consultant, he is skilled in research, development, and training. He consults with client companies to develop programs and systems for improving individual and organizational performance. His experience includes assessments, competency studies, program development, and evaluation.

PART THREE

Practical Methods for Leading Customer Service

12

AUTHENTIC COACHING: GETTING THE BEST FROM CUSTOMER SERVICE PROVIDERS

Anne Bruce and
James S. Pepitone

In customer service, your only competitive advantage may be your people. And the most formidable task faced by customer service managers may be to help their workers make the most of their potential. Research shows that most managers are incompetent when it comes to organizing, leading, and supporting the people they supervise. This article shows how managers can be more effective through coaching.

The greatest single challenge managers have today is in engaging their workforce to produce high levels of human-work performance. Particularly true in customer serving functions, managers have been unable to generate and deploy their workers' unique human qualities into the work of serving customers.

Savvy executives already know that only by successfully meeting this challenge can their companies achieve sustainable competitive advantage in customer service. Customer service managers are realizing only gradually that their most formidable task is not in controlling their assigned workers. Their greatest challenge is in engaging their workers in ways that yield continual learning, competence, flexibility, innovation, discretionary effort, added value, and worker satisfaction—which altogether generates high-quality work and high productivity.

In addressing this challenge, more and more companies are experimenting with alternatives to the traditional role of manager. Much of this effort is focusing on new ways of organizing, leading, and supporting workers. Rightly so, because most managers are incompetent in this area. Research conducted by Lominger Limited, Inc. ranked the competency "understanding people" in the top 10 of the 67 competencies linked by research to successful performance. This same research showed that North American managers are rated poorest—67th out of the same 67 competencies—in this crucial capability.

Companies taking the initiative to improve the performance of managers are generally following one or more of three basic strategies:

○ Emphasizing the coaching aspects of the managers' roles,
○ Renaming and redefining the role of managers to make them more like coaches, and/or
○ Dividing the current management role and shifting the human side of the job to designated coaches.

It's too early to draw any conclusions about the strengths and weaknesses of any of these approaches, though our experience with all three provides insight on their common element of coaching. Recently we have honed this experience into a new role-concept that can help managers meet today's customer service challenge. We think authentic coaching may well be the answer to the problems faced by customer service managers.

For perspective, we should remember that traditional management methods were first adopted by businesses beginning in the late 18th century. Copied from the successful organization of the Prussian army centuries before, these methods particularly suited the transition that people were having to make from independent farming and trades to the very large factories that were employing more and more of the population.

As you might imagine, emphasis then was placed on keeping track of people and on controlling their work to best suit the uncompromising machinery. This was in accordance with the dominant organizing principle of the industrial age: if workers would only do exactly what the machines required, the machines themselves would ensure a quality performance. This concept of management has served enterprise well.

Today the mix of issues that define work quality are considerably different from the issues in the late 1700s. There is substantially more emphasis on having workers perform in ways that are uniquely human and not machinelike—particularly in areas of customer service. For quality customer service today, workers must project empathy, concern, understanding, appreciation, knowledge, perspective, and spirit. And they must instinctively integrate and genuinely express these behaviors effectively just when and as the situation dictates. Consider too the fact that not one of these behaviors can be produced by machine . . . not even by computers. They also cannot be produced effectively by people who are treated like machines.

Service by the Numbers

Most customer service functions are managed like production lines. Generally gratuitous talk about service quality aside, these operations are managed to operate with machine efficiency so as to incur the least possible expense. The negative impacts of this approach are frequently overshadowed by positive business trends. As a result, managers grow accustomed to operating problems like marginal performance, absenteeism, excessive turnover, and others. In industries for which the customer service function is a sales channel, slightly more consideration is given to the effectiveness of the service process.

Industry is so accustomed to the production-line approach to service that management is virtually unaware of its costly impact—on workers, on management, on customers, and on the business. The financial impact of this approach, in our estimation, is worker productivity at 30%–70% below potential and unproductive turnover and hiring and training costs 100%–500% above the necessary. That estimate holds for customer service in virtually every line of business. This does not include the financial impact attributable to customers who are left ambivalent or displeased with the machinelike service they've received.

Our culture has become so indoctrinated in this approach to service that managers often struggle with the fact that there is a problem, and struggle even more to develop an alternative. In many areas of life, each of us is reduced to a mechanistic image, whether by a number (e.g., Social Security, wait list, table, address, account, etc.) or industry jargon (e.g., customer, be-back, complaint, double-cheeseburger, line-on-hold, etc.). Influenced by this mechanistic reduction, we don't think twice before treating someone else the very same way. Managers do it to their employees; employees do it to their customers. And the problem isn't that this treatment is unpleasant or inhumane, although this may be true. The problem for industry is the millions (or billions) in excess service costs, unnecessary and costly customer ambivalence and dissatisfaction, and needless worker turnover costs.

If a customer service manager cannot grasp this reasoning, we might suggest a role reversal—for the manager to work as a customer service representative. Most managers can't stand it for more than a couple hours. They typically get frustrated with restrictions against taking action and insulted by the rules and other measures by which their performance is now evaluated. It's not the work that gets to them; it's the treatment—being treated like a machine. When asked what impact this treatment has on their attitude toward serving customers, they finally feel the frustration and resignation felt by many customer service providers. It's a fact that performance is directly impacted by how people are treated; machinelike treatment, however well intended, will generally result in the worst of human behavior.

Think about what we tell our customer service providers:

- Customers talk to *you*, not to a *company*.
- Customers think of themselves as *people*, not as just *customers*.
- It's not enough to *service* customers; you have to *care* about them.

We ask our customer service providers to make the company human and to treat customers as people. But how can they do this if we don't treat them as people?

Though customer service providers are admittedly a business tool used to provide certain kinds of customer service, treating them as not much more than a tool diminishes the real potential inherent in their human nature. We can see this same human nature at work in children. It takes recognizing and appreciating them for their uniqueness to develop their self-esteem, ignite their spirit, and fuel their discretionary effort. We also feel it as adults.

Single out a time or two in which someone recognized and acknowledged you as an individual and treated you like somebody special. How did that make you feel? How did that affect your attitude, your feeling toward that person, how you treated him or her, how you felt about yourself, and what you did in response? It lit a spark, didn't it? That's the spark you want to light in your customer service providers, if you want them to really put themselves into their work for you.

A Better Way to Manage

The term "authentic coaching" describes an approach to working with direct reports—a management concept that promises big potential for managers of customer service providers. During the past 20 years, we've studied the manager's role in most industries, researched the vast human and social sciences, and worked with clients experimenting with numerous alternative approaches to management's traditional controlling methods. More and more often today, we see the authentic coaching approach adopted for the human side of managing. We have seen it provide better results in more situations and in more industries than all other supervisory approaches combined.

"Coaching" is a term everyone is familiar with from school and sports in particular, and maybe less familiar with in the contexts of singing, dancing, acting, painting, work trades, and numerous other human pursuits. Of course, the meaning is similar—helping people prepare to do their very best. Yet the methods and effort vary widely according to the student's goal. In a management context, the emphasis of coaching is placed on providing individualized support to achieve high performance and productivity.

"Authentic" is also a familiar term to most of us, though at times we may have to look hard to find anything that is authentic in today's culture. Western society has become so focused on achieving end results that it has sacrificed concern for the means by which the end is achieved. As a result, it seems as if the behavior of most people, as they attempt to attain their objective, is frequently contrived and artificial. This creates a problem, however, because such behavior distances people from their true values and beliefs, qualities that are, after all, the root of their human nature and the source of those attributes that create high performance in customer service.

If we combine these two words—"authentic coaching"—and their meaning, we describe a manager who is focused both on providing appropriate support to his or her workers, and on doing so in ways that accept their human nature and allow them to more genuinely express themselves. What?! And give up tight-fisted control? Give up the privilege to treat people any legal way you want to just because they report to you? Our best answer to these frequent first responses of resistance is . . . let's compare performance.

Customer service managers who fully adopt the authentic coaching approach to managing routinely improve the performance of their operations by 20%, 60%, or even 200% and more, and in every important measure. And, they consistently outperform their peer-group managers who are unwilling to try it. In fact, we have seen authentic coaching work in enough customer service settings now that we rarely hesitate to recommend it as an obvious solution to many of the typical performance problems. It's the closest thing to a universal management approach that befits today's workers and the challenges faced by managers in today's customer service function. It presents managers with the ultimate question: Which is more important, to have your way with workers or to have their best performance?

The Human Side of Managing

Authentic coaching is not hard to like. For people who are managing a large number of customer service providers, one of the strong appeals of authentic coaching is that it's grounded in natural human behavior. Both customer service providers and managers win, because they're able to be more of themselves without pretense or role-playing. It also guides the manager to experience and act toward his or her employees as real, individual people.

For many managers, authentic coaching is a refreshing change. It guides them to act out of their real selves, to not abandon personal values and style to adopt some false persona as a manager. For others, though, this can be uncomfortable at first. They're not accustomed to behaving genuinely. Like many people, they are well practiced at adapting to situations by adopting behaviors that they think will be approved. So to accept and express themselves genuinely carries with it many apprehensions. Fortunately, these long-avoided fears will diminish as the managers witness the acceptance and successful impact of their more natural behavior.

For workers, a strong appeal of authentic coaching is its emphasis on integrity, honesty and sincerity. People are more and more getting tired of never getting an honest answer to their questions . . . if they get any answer at all . . . and of having to contrive different artificial behaviors for every situation. Authentic coaching guides a manager to accept others as they are and to work with each as a real person—not treat him or her as a machine (number, desk, territory, etc.).

Authentic coaching, as an alternative to traditional, control-based management, is grounded in a set of guiding principles. These are 10 of the guiding principles explained in *Authentic Coaching: Real Guidance for the Human Side of Performance*. These principles are easy to understand, remember, and apply. More important, perhaps, these principles are based on science, validated in research, and proven through experience. They are not simply myths, feel-good beliefs, or conjecture.

1. Human nature provides all of the technology necessary for leading people to do their best. Authentic coaches know that nature has "wired" people to act in ways that support their own safety and self-satisfaction. So when they coach in ways that respect these natural behaviors, the objectives are achieved and often surpassed with minimal support. When workers are in situations aligned with their human nature, they can be fast learners and powerful achievers. Typically, company-imposed barriers and constraints get in the way of high-performance work, often simply because they ignore natural human behavior.

2. Workers respond and adapt to the whole system that defines their roles and responsibilities. Authentic coaches think in terms of the whole system—the many interacting elements of enterprise, organization, and work design that potentially impact workers—in order to provide effective support for higher performance. The causes that undermine performance are generally not obvious or direct, such as an old policy, workers in another department, the wrong resources, weaknesses in the organization structure, lack of feedback, and so on. Nor are the solutions obvious or direct. When dealing with complex human behavior in an inherently complex work system, authentic coaches know to avoid snap decisions and jumping to the first solution considered—the managerial behaviors that allow many workplace problems to persist year after year.

3. People are different, not broken; they do not need fixing. Authentic coaches respect human nature and accept that people are OK just the way they are. Some people will be open to learning in the coach's ways and meeting the coach's standards, yet many won't. Coaches know to focus on selecting people whose human nature is consistent with the real challenges inherent in the work to be performed. People can be trained on equipment and procedures, but training will not change their natural behavior. Authentic coaches carefully define what is acceptable, and then let workers decide if this is something they want to do. Certainly people can learn and change; however, adults will do so only if they strongly feel a need.

4. Caring is essential to coaching. Authentic coaches care about the people they coach, and coach only people they care about. If put in a situation to supervise anyone they don't care about, authentic coaches find reasons to care about that person. They are honest with themselves. Only through caring can they hope to connect with people and influence them. This is particularly true when seeking cooperation and change. Most often, authentic coaches can develop a caring spirit for anyone just by knowing more about them: their kids, childhood, joys, challenges, and dreams are all pathways to caring.

5. Attitude defines working relationships and determines the influence achieved. Authentic coaches know that their attitude largely determines the success of their coaching. The coach's attitude toward workers sets the boundaries for the workers' attitude toward him or her. If the coach wants to receive respect, trust, and support, then he or she must first approach workers with respect, trust, and support. Likewise, if workers sense disrespect, mistrust, and weak support, then the source is probably the coach's attitude toward the workers. This truth of human nature is the basis of the Golden Rule that has been passed from generation to generation for centuries—Do unto others as you would have them do unto you. It works.

6. Vulnerabilities create the opportunity for influence and relationships. Authentic coaches know that relationships are rooted in compensating vulnerabilities. That's equally true in both personal and professional relationships, because it's inherent in human nature. If people appear perfect or like they think they're perfect, and they do not expose their natural opportunities for growth, then they will not be in a position to form genuinely supportive relationships. Those who relate to the perfect persona will soon be disillusioned, and all others will be unable to feel the human vulnerability that is necessary for a relationship to form. Managers who appear perfect to their workers seem inhuman and unapproachable, so they'll be unable to coach them effectively. Authentic coaches make the effort to seem very human to their workers.

7. Honest and considerate communication is more likely to get an honest and considerate response. Authentic coaching requires that you say what you mean to workers. All too often workers are left in the dark and simply don't know what they need to know in order to do their work. Authentic coaching demands straightforward talk, although with consideration for the esteem of the worker. (Honesty is no excuse for disrespect.) If coaches are not honest with their workers, then it's virtually assured that their workers will not be honest with them. Because managers characteristically have been less than open and honest with workers, distrust and cynicism dominate the typical workplace. Authentic coaching can begin to reverse this pattern.

8. For improved performance, trust clear expectations, accurate feedback, and aligned support. Authentic coaching is grounded in a clear understanding of human behavior, which is not the mystery it once was. Today, human work-performance technology—humaneering[1]—is nearly as advanced as engineering, pharmacology, and other major technologies. Because of this, we know the essential ingredients for high levels of human performance include, at a minimum, (a) clear objectives for acceptable performance, (b) methods for workers to measure their own performance and thus receive instant feedback, and (c) support needed for performance improvement objectives. Since these essential elements are often missing, authentic coaching often begins the performance-improvement process by putting these elements in place.

9. Replace most training with self-directed learning. Authentic coaching requires the effective application of all sorts of technology, including instructional technology. Training was first introduced into the workplace by Frederick Taylor to standardize workers to their assigned machinery. This is considerably different from the challenge of preparing customer service providers to produce high-performance work. At best, training teaches workers how to use equipment, the current best practices, and essential policies they must follow—the basics. For achieving higher levels of human work-performance, however, authentic coaching stresses self-directed learning. It's also important to provide workers with effective tools for learning and skill development, targeting the competencies important for their brand of customer service.

10. Know what you don't know about human nature and identify knowledgeable support. Authentic coaches use authoritative information when determining workforce needs and don't play psychologist. Coaches keep in mind that everyone is different; what works for one person will likely not work for others. For example, it's generally true that whatever would work best for the coach if in the same role is not what will work best for most of his or her workers. Authentic coaches use the available professional tools (e.g., validated surveys, instruments, etc.) to detect individual and organizational needs and diagnose performance problems. And, though coaches can expect workers to know when something is not working, they don't make the mistake of expecting the workers to (a) accurately recognize all of the contributing causes, (b) create an alternative that will work permanently, and (c) convince the people in charge to try something different. Coaches need to know their limits—to know what they don't know—and engage objective professionals to work with their workers for permanent solutions to problems.

---

1. Humaneering is a term coined by James Pepitone in his book, *Humaneering: Technology for Improving Human Performance at Work.*

Switching to Authentic Coaching

These guiding principles do work, if applied in earnest. The greater challenge, we find, is for managers who are making the switch to authentic coaching to persist in this effort in the face of doubting workers. Unfortunately, years of a machinelike working environment have engendered skepticism and cynicism regarding management. It will take time for some people to give up this impression. However, the current high turnover prevalent in poorly managed customer service functions can accelerate this process by more quickly bringing in new workers, who can begin with an impression of management as cooperative.

The hard part of authentic coaching, if there is one, is dropping the control-oriented behavior to which many managers have grown accustomed. Before making the switch, it can be helpful for managers to consider their current style of managing people and how they learned it. Very few ever learn their style from a truly effective manager. And they don't teach this in school. So most managers are left to trust their instincts, which in the case of managing people are most often very misleading.

In the hundreds of customer service operations that we've examined professionally, we've most often found in popular use the approach we named the "lazy-parent" style of managing. Our professional work further indicates that this style is a significant cause of endless workforce problems that waste the potential for extraordinary customer service and employee satisfaction. Furthermore, the lazy-parent style not only fails to improve and maximize workforce performance and productivity, it actually creates problems. When this all-too-popular management style is used, it seems the only possible winner is the manager who adopts the style. The win for the manager is hollow, however, because of the additional problems he or she encounters and the relatively poor business performance that results.

When dealing with the lazy-parent manager, employees are naturally motivated to do the minimum that is tolerated. This paternalistic management approach just seems to bring out the childhood rebellion inside all people, and it wreaks havoc in the workplace.

But, you ask, if this approach is so devastating to business, why is it so common? This is an important question. Our research indicates that the prevalence of this style is substantially due to insufficient, ineffective, or inappropriate training for new managers—or no training at all. As a result, many new managers resort to the dominant image they have for the exercising of authority—their parents, and in particular the one who was more controlling. The result is a fascistic behavior that emphasizes control, guarded communication, artificial motivation, and other dysfunctional behavior that virtually destroy the human spirit and the will to achieve. And in a largely unconscious exchange for this treatment, the workers respond about as well as children do—with minimal compliance, active rule testing, minimal tolerance, passive aggressiveness, and so on.

The Results Speak for Themselves

Positive results with authentic coaching are not always immediate or dramatic. For workers who haven't received much respect or consideration throughout their lives, trusting and responding to this new treatment may take time. But don't be surprised when those workers who are full of life but have learned to park their human nature at the door start to enjoy serving and delighting customers.

Eventually, the results are generally profound. Managers who adopt the more natural authentic coaching approach to management—after employees sense that the change is genuine—realize improvements in work performance and productivity that they cannot explain to other managers, except by attributing them to their change in approach. Problems that seemed unsolvable can cease to be issues, particularly as the manager makes policy changes consistent with this approach. Turnover, absenteeism, poor attitude, marginal performance quality, slack follow-through, slumping sales promotion, and low productivity—problems generally accepted or attributed to inferior employees—are attributable to the lazy-parent managerial style.

In our book, *Authentic Coaching: Real Guidance for the Human Side of Performance*, we outline an alternative approach to management that treats your people and you as the real people you are. It's based on mutual respect and appreciation and on an honest and sincere dialogue. And, perhaps most important, it will bring out the best performance your people can provide. In most cases, managers do not know just how good customer service performance can get until they try the authentic coaching approach. It makes all the difference.

This article is based on the book, *Authentic Coaching: Real Guidance for the Human Side of Performance*, by James S. Pepitone and Anne Bruce (AddVantage Learning Press, 1997, (214) 503–6800).

About the Authors

Anne Bruce is a principal and senior consultant for AddVantage Learning, Inc., based in Dallas, Texas. She is a nationally recognized keynote presenter, conducting her programs for major organizations, such as Baylor University Medical Center, Continental Airlines, the Georgia Power Company, and the American Management Association. Anne has taught at Harvard and Stanford Law Schools and frequently contributes to national training and human resource publications. Between 1995 and 1997, Anne served as lead designer, writer, and developer of more than 40 leadership, customer care, communications, and train-the-trainer programs, launching the curriculum nationwide for Southwest Airlines' University for People, which now serves more than 27,000 Southwest Airlines employees and is considered an industry benchmark.

James S. Pepitone is a 20-year veteran management consultant often praised as "the architect of high-performance work." In addition to client engagements, Jim is chair and CEO of Pepitone Worldwide, and a pioneer in the field of human performance improvement. In recent years, he has developed breakthrough strategies for reducing the time and cost of corporate training programs by one-half while increasing the results, and has counseled numerous companies on the launch or re-launch of corporate universities. He is the author of *Future Training: A Roadmap for Restructuring the Training Function* (AddVantage Learning Press, 1996) and *Humaneering: Technology for Improving Human Performance at Work* (AddVantage Learning Press, 1998).

13

Unleashing the Power of Customer CARE in Your Organization

JoAnna Brandi

What do you need to have more excited customers and more committed, enthusiastic employees? The secret to that competitive edge is as basic as human nature: you need to foster an environment that promotes caring and healthy relationships. That's natural—but certainly not easy! How can a manager create an environment where caring is the culture, the force behind a high-quality service effort? This article offers ideas, questions, and suggestions that provide a great start.

What is it that forward-thinking companies want these days? Customers who are loyal advocates and employees who are excited, enthusiastic, energetic, and empowered to make decisions that benefit both the customer and the company. They want commitment. They want people who love and take pride in their work and will represent the organization in the best possible light.

Companies that will move skillfully, successfully, and gracefully into the next century want people who *care*—people who care about who they are, what they do, and what kind of contribution they're making to the world. These companies—like Starbucks, Rosenbluth Travel, and L.L. Bean—know that people who care will deliver a quality level of service in a heartfelt and even effortless manner and require very little "managing" from the organization.

Every organization has a few of these people. But we all need more of them. What percentage of your workers are people who resemble that description? About 3%, 10%, maybe 50%? Can you increase the number of people who care? What can a manager or supervisor do to create an environment where caring is the culture, where caring is the norm, where caring is the driving force of a high-quality service effort that flows with seamless agility?

How Can Managers Encourage Caring?

The answer is no secret: create an environment where people feel cared about, where people feel valued, where their personal growth is encouraged and nourished, and where every effort is made to build self-esteem and self-worth—and you've got an environment where customer caring will abound.

How ludicrous has it been to believe that we can deprive people of those basic human needs and then expect that they will care for customers? *And,* **caring** *is what customers are looking for.* Study after study tells us that the majority (68%) of the customers who quit doing business with us quit because they perceive we don't care about them. Customers buy with their heads *and* their hearts; and all things being equal (price, quality, availability), customers prefer to buy from people they like and trust.

Every customer is seeking value. Some find it in the lowest price and shop at warehouse clubs. Some find it in the most convenient access and, like me, phone catalog companies at 1 a.m. Some find value in a particular *combination* of features and benefits, like breadth of product line, availability, product quality, security, reliability, courtesy, money-back guarantee, and potentially dozens of other reasons, both rational and emotional. Value is an equation. We weigh the price we pay against the things and *feelings* we get for our money.

Make no mistake about it: there's a high emotional content to value. And while many customers would have a difficult time enumerating precisely which factors influence their buying decisions, what they do know is how they *feel*. Good, bad, or indifferent, they have an emotional opinion about the exchange. In studies done on customer loyalty, when customers are asked why they've stayed loyal to a particular company, they state simply, "Because they cared about me." Of course, what goes unsaid here is that the customers also, therefore, care about the company.

How can we give our customers this experience of caring that will keep them happy and keep them coming back? There are two ways:

- ○ By creating an environment where it naturally happens, where employees (internal customers) are treated as well as we want them to treat external customers.
- ○ By reframing the notion of what it is we are here to do.

What Does "Customer Service" Mean?

Companies keep telling their people they are here "to do customer service." But most companies don't take the time to understand what service means specifically in terms of both belief and behavior. Many companies don't take the time to think about the specific "brand" of service they want to be known for and can't define for their people what that service should look like. So, the service delivered is the service defined in the mind of the service-giver. And much of the service delivered today is mediocre at best.

I don't believe we can get past the mediocre service, partly because of the number of negative definitions of "service" that reside in the minds of those who deliver it.

Language structures our experience; it forms our reality. It is how we define ourselves and our jobs that determines how we will perform in them. Disney has been brilliant in the use of the word "Guest" to describe a customer and "Cast Member" to describe an employee. Today companies often use the words "associate" and "partner" to describe the worker's new role in an organization. So let's look at the term "service" and see what that conjures up.

We bring our cars in for *service*. We often have strong opinions of those who work in public *service*. Many people were drafted into the *service*. Getting my point? The word "service" is related to the words "servant" and "servitude." If you had to learn Latin as I did, you know its root word, "*servus,*" means "*slave.*" In my opinion, these are pretty loaded words—loaded with previous associations and beliefs. It's entirely possible that the *definitions* we carry of service are not conducive to the type of performance we really need to deliver.

I believe, by and large, that "service" is often defined in such a way that it actually *prevents* people from delivering the customer-caring experience.

For the past five years I've been asking my audiences this question, "When do you go to the customer service department?" The answers are always the same: "When I have a problem" or "When I have a complaint." My next question is, "Where do you find that customer service department?" Again, consistent answers: "In the basement" or "In the back."

My next challenge to the audience is this, "How many of you have children getting ready to go to college next year?" Invariably a few people raise their hands. "How many of you are counseling them to go into the venerable career of customer service?" My points then are easily made. First, we define service as *reactive*, something that happens after something else goes *wrong*. There is a distinct possibility that there is a negative connection in the mind with the word "service." And second, we don't think of the delivery of that service as a career worth even mentioning to our kids. There's food for thought there.

Reframing Our Concept of "Service"

If, in fact, we define "service" as associated with negative events and as a reactive response, we will never be able to provide the "proactive customer service" managers are clamoring for. So, our first attempt to change old, negative associations with the word "service" is to reframe what it is we are here to do. Will "servicing" the customer get us where we want to go? Will it engender the kind of emotional bonding that will keep the customer coming back and bringing friends? I think not.

Imagine this scenario. You've just accepted a position with a "customer-caring" company. During your extensive orientation process, learning about the company's vision, mission, and values, you hear something you have never heard before:

> Here at the C-C company we don't have a customer service department. In fact, here at the C-C company we don't do customer service! We see the customer as the reason for our existence—our one and only focus is to create happy customers. In order to do that, we don't want you to do customer service. We would like you to see your job as customer **CARE**[3SM]. Let's look at that as an acronym and you will know what you are here to

do: Create **A R**elationship *Enthusiastically, Energetically,* with *Everyone* with whom we do business!

Do you think this introduction to a company might set the stage differently for delivering a high quality of customer caring? I do. And so do companies that are experiencing the distinction of having high rates of customer retention and loyalty. They are deeply committed to building relationships with workers, customers, and community. They don't "close sales"—they "open relationships." They've moved from being transaction-based businesses to being relationship-based businesses.

They've found the secret to *thriving:* nourishing relationships, honing interpersonal as well as technical skills, and slowing down long enough to listen to what customers and staff members are saying. And, honoring their contributions by putting many of them into practice.

Three Working Relationships

Let me engage your imagination once again. I will share with you my view of business. Imagine, if you will, that business sits atop a tripod. Each of the three legs of the tripod represents a different set of relationships. One represents the *external* relationships a company has, one the *internal* relationships, and the third the *inner* relationship of the individual. I call this the Working Relationships Tripod℠.

Company leaders must be at all times aware of and working to improve all the relationships in the tripod. The *external* relationships are those you have with your customers, your suppliers, your community, your stockholders, the families of those who work for you, and yes, even your competitors. The *internal* relationships are those inside the company, among staff members and their management. The *inner* relationship—the one companies have been denying existed for so long—is that all-important relationship an individual has with herself or himself.

Responsibility of Leaders and Managers

It is in the care and feeding of the interaction of these three relationships that we have the opportunity to create an environment that breeds success in all measures—*physically,* through providing an ample living and good working conditions; then *emotionally* and *intellectually,* by providing challenge and opportunity; and finally *spiritually,* by providing the means to make a significant contribution.

It's a considerable leadership feat to balance all these relationships, delicately yet powerfully, at the same time. It takes commitment on the part of the leader to dig down deep and examine her or his own personal feelings about relating to other human beings. Any management role at all in today's world—team leader, supervisor, or vice president—requires a higher level of human insight than ever before.

The world is becoming more competitive: we now compete with the sophisticated and unsophisticated and unconventional at the same time. Our range of available responses to a rapidly changing marketplace is directly related to the amount of intelligence and creativity we unleash in the hearts and minds of those we work with. Caring is the seed of the passion needed to move us forward in the quantum leaps that become increasingly necessary in today's fast-forward world.

Managers can play a transformational role in the "culture-crafting"SM of an organization if they choose to play in the emotional soup of relationships. While there are parts of the business community that have openly embraced the new thinking on leadership and management, most companies are stuck straddling a fence between old, deeply ingrained management beliefs and suspicion of many of the "new age" approaches.

What Do People Need?

Without a doubt we are living in a time of deep transition, and no one has *the* answers.

As the nature of work continues to change, knowledge workers will increasingly insist on environments that suit their particular lifestyle. While many younger workers are driven by the traditional pursuit of upward mobility, many are also driven by the values of a more balanced, more honest life. They will be the ones who wholeheartedly support a company and its customers when the company provides them the opportunity to meet their physical, emotional/intellectual, and spiritual needs.

In the quid pro quo balance that many of the maturing baby boom generation as well as the young knowledge workers are seeking, companies will have to examine their fundamental beliefs about people. It's no longer acceptable to just *say*, "People are our most important assets." If you are not living it, you will not get back in return the energy produced by *both* the hearts and the minds of those who work for you. And one without the other will not get you the maximum effectiveness of each person you are paying to help you grow your business.

Even if you manage a department of only three people, you are in control of how much the emotional energy gets focused and on what. To meet the challenges of the future, leadership is required in every individual. As the structure of work changes, what will remain the same is the need for inspiration, motivation, and management skills that view the whole Working Relationships TripodSM.

Looking briefly at the relationships, we can begin to ask ourselves insightful questions to get an honest view of our current state of reality.

External Relationships

Do we know who our customers really are? Do we really know why they buy from us? Do we know what their needs and desires are? Do we know what keeps them up at night? Do we have customer care standards that everyone understands—including the customer? Do we have a way of measuring our success in the areas that count?

As you can see, the questions could go on and on—and these are the kinds of questions a consultant will ask and you will pay money to discuss. And that's great—I'm an external consultant and make part of my living by asking these very questions. But my big question is, "Why won't companies go through the process, the discipline of asking these kinds of questions of themselves?"

Many claim that they don't know what questions to ask. I always suggest they find a way to ask the people who work there, "What questions should we be asking ourselves in order to continuously improve?" You should get *lots* of answers, if people know you're sincere in requesting their help and participation.

Internal Relationships

What about relationships you have with your suppliers? Are you working together with them toward a common, win-win goal? Are you using them as part of your consulting team, as they should be doing with you? Do you learn things from them? If not, why not? Have you considered that your key suppliers are really your business partners? How does that consideration alter your thinking?

I'm sure you're getting the gist of my questioning. You might even think it's fun to keep the list of questions going on each of these relationships—and bring the play out to your team for some input. I collect lists of questions I've come up with, and I'm learning to ask empowering questions that build my know-how and self-confidence at the same time.

If you're working with a team, it's crucial for you to look at the interactions in the internal relationship leg—how people work together as a team. Everyone in an organization has the responsibility to serve and care about customers, even when those customers are each other.

All together, internal suppliers and internal customers form a chain of value that reaches out to the external customer. It's important for us all to deal with each other with trust and respect and strive to communicate clearly and honestly with each other, because we all have the same goals: each supporting the other to provide an exquisite level of customer care.

While all teams inside a company support an overall vision, it's critical to the success of the team to create a vision for itself and to live its own purpose in alignment with the company's vision and purpose. A vision provides focus. What links your team to the other teams and to the customers? Do people know what they can expect from each other? Do they trust each other? Do we all tell the truth? Do we really pay attention to each other? Do we listen with empathy and concern? Do we have common goals? Do we celebrate? Are we, as a team, dedicated to providing a high quality of experience for ourselves and the customer? Are we committed to learning from each other's ideas and creating new possibilities together? Co-create a vision that can be personalized so it has meaning for each and every one of the people in your system.

Inner Relationships

The third leg of the Tripod is the one I label "Inner." It is the personal relationship each individual has with himself or herself and with the company. I believe it is the health and nourishment of this relationship that is the real secret to creating an enthusiastic, energetic, and motivated work force.

The questions in this area should first be asked and answered personally before asking them of anybody else. In an ideal world, every person would take personal responsibility for monitoring this internal relationship. Questions to help do this might include: How do I feel when I'm getting ready to go to work? Do I want to be there? Do I like what I do? Is my sense of self-worth growing? Do I feel like I make a difference? How is my sense of self-esteem? Am I supporting it? Is the company supporting it? Does what I do count? Is this a place where I can learn something? Is this a place where I can feel important? Is this a place where I can do good work?

For far too long, managers have believed that they are supposed to tell employees to leave their emotions at home. Of course, this is an impossible expectation. And we are still dealing with the consequences of a business model that encouraged people to leave their hearts, as well as their heads, at home and just bring their bodies to work.

When we tell people to leave their emotions at home, we're asking them to detach themselves from their passion. Yet, passion is exactly the emotion we need to fuel the change efforts that will keep us globally competitive in the future. In the end, it is human emotion that drives success in business. We are just recently acknowledging with data what intuitive managers have known all along. There is a direct correlation between employee happiness and loyalty, customer happiness and loyalty, and investor happiness and loyalty. Score one for common sense.

Unfortunately, while many managers may have the training necessary to manage tasks, fewer have the skills necessary to lead people. Yet good managers have always known that they influence more by modeling their values than by just mouthing them. They will ask themselves: What am I doing (saying, training, being) on a daily basis that provides a model for people on how to build healthy relationships? How can I build on what's already working? Do I embody what I ask of others? Am I positive and optimistic about the future? Do I like what I do? Do I bring all of myself to work every day? Do I walk the walk, not just talk the talk?

Everything Starts From Within

The real energy in the tripod of relationships comes from the individual. *The inner relationship is what drives the dynamic of all the other relationships.* Positive, knowledgeable, optimistic workers who clearly know what they are there to do and are motivated by the caring they feel from the organization, from its culture, and from its people will take it upon themselves to take good care of the customer—and even go out of their way to delight them! In companies where nourishment and growth of the individual are integral to the culture, where strong values are articulated in word and deed, and where people are truly valued as assets, we regularly see extraordinary innovation and accomplishment along with higher levels of customer loyalty.

In the end, in the interaction with the customer and in the delivery of the service and care, it is the commitment on the part of the individual to use each moment of truth to create and add value. It is a conscious decision to make a choice—in the moment—to build and affirm the relationship or to treat it with indifference and negate it.

What Managers and Leaders Must Do

There are millions of moments of opportunity every day in business. It is up to our managers/leaders to inspire individuals to make the choice to make a difference. The process of shifting from a business built on transactions to one built on relationships is a challenging process for all those involved. It takes patience and persistence and passion on the part of the manager/leader.

To create a customer-caring culture, it's your job and the job of your management to create an environment where people gravitate in the direction of caring. Where people participate because they know they will be heard. Where people are rewarded for their positive changes and not punished for their learning experiences.

To create a truly customer-focused company, one where people are encouraged and rewarded for pleasing the customer before pleasing the boss, for doing the "right" thing (even if it means occasionally they misjudge what that thing is while they are learning), we need to create a safe, emotional environment where people can feel free to share, to learn, and to experiment. Remember: "responsive to the customer" means having a wide range of responses to his or her needs, and that means drawing on the individuality and creativity of all those smart people working for you.

We need the courage to look at things differently. We need to move out of our own comfort zones before we can ask our employees to move out of theirs. We need to be willing to be vulnerable as we learn. And we need to sacrifice our old ideas about customer service and wholeheartedly embrace the idea of customer *caring*.

About the Author

JoAnna Brandi is the founder of Working Relationships, Inc., a Customer Care company committed to helping companies build better relationships with their customers through the strategic use of marketing, research, and training.

JoAnna has spoken before many industry groups, such as the American Marketing Association, the Direct Marketing Association, and the American Telemarketing Association. She regularly contributes to trade magazines, and her work has appeared in publications such as *Direct*, *Database Advisor*, *Impact Advertising*, and *DM News*. Her work in customer care has been cited in *The Libey Letter*, *The Van Vechten Report*, *Direct*, *The Retail Advantage*, *The Competitive Advantage*, and *Communications Briefings*. She is frequently interviewed for magazines such as *Inc.*, *Entrepreneur*, and *Home Office Computing*.

JoAnna has developed seminars on customer care, teamwork, and customer-focused vision and culture. She publishes a semi-annual newsletter, *Dare to Care*, and a newsbrief, the *Customer Care Bulletin*. She is author of *Winning at Customer Retention: 101 Ways to Keep 'em Happy, Keep 'em Loyal, and Keep 'em Coming Back* (Lakewood Publications, 1995) and *54 Ways to Stay Positive in a Changing, Challenging and Sometimes Negative World* (Lakewood Publications, 1998). Her Web site address is http://www.customerretention.com.

14

HOW TO LET CUSTOMER VALUE DRIVE CUSTOMER PROBLEM SOLVING

R. Eric Reidenbach, Gordon W. McClung, and Reginald W. Goeke

When your customers tell you a product or service is not worth it, that means that their value proposition is out of alignment with their perceptions of value. So, how do you fix those problems? This article recommends value mapping—a process measure designed to improve value delivery by identifying opportunities to enhance benefits to the customer while reducing the price the customer pays for those benefits.

There are probably no more fearful words that a seller can hear from a customer about his or her product or service than "It's not worth it!" And unfortunately for many companies, the "not worth it" cry is being heard more and more. Just ask McDonald's, American Express, Kmart, and Mercedes. And let's not forget Procter & Gamble. These companies, among many, have been faced with eroding market value.

What are customers telling sellers when they say that their product or service is not worth it? Simply put, customers are telling sellers that their value proposition is out of alignment with customer perceptions of value. In other words, there's not enough bang for the buck.

Value

The concept of value clearly is nothing new. However, its resurgence as the prominent driver in the purchase decision process is getting a lot more attention. Most definitions of value relate quality to price in the following conceptual configuration:

$$\text{Value} = \text{Quality} \div \text{Price}$$

Price is something most sellers understand relatively well. It's the cost that the customer incurs in exchange for something he or she is trying to acquire.

Quality in the value equation is somewhat more complex. It may be measurable, objective, such as when we use "quality" to define the nature of a physical product, like a tensile strength, weight, length, wattage, horsepower, etc. But the notion of quality is somewhat more problematic when it's applied to less tangible products or services. In these cases, the assessment of quality becomes more perceptual and subjective. It's often defined in broad conceptual terms such as responsiveness, concern, communication, reliability, etc.

Clearly, these elements of quality apply just as well to an organization that manufactures and sells a product as to an organization that provides a service. Is quality defined in terms of responsiveness and reliability less meaningful when applied to a dry cleaner or the post office than when it is applied to a manufacturer of heavy equipment? Hardly. Service is a critical portion of any quality calculus, regardless of whether or not the organization offers a product.

From Product Quality to Customer Service

Many manufacturers are beginning to understand that they have a new role in the creation and delivery of value. Traditionally, manufacturers have borne the primary responsibility for quality. However, to a much greater extent, quality is now being pushed to a point where it's no longer the critical differentiating factor that it once was. As more and more manufacturers subscribe to ISO 9000 standards and more and more competitors become quality-oriented, product quality, created in the manufacturing process, has less differentiating capability. This can lead to a false sense of security and to reliance on a consistent level of conformance product quality. As a result, across many industries the competitive product quality gap is shrinking.

As the product quality gap diminishes, so too does the role that product quality plays in the creation of customer value. Many manufacturers are coming to grips with the reality that product quality is a qualifying need, something that they provide that keeps their dealers in the game, but that does little to differentiate them from their competitors. The burden of competitive differentiation is being taken up by customer service, delivered by the dealer. In other words, a significant part of the battle for a differential value advantage is being waged on the customer service front!

Handling Complaints

Arguably, nothing is more telling about an organization's commitment to customer service delivery than how that organization solves customer service problems. Many organizations—from supermarkets and factories to the dry cleaner, hospital, or IRS office—display signs proclaiming the importance of the customer, mission statements extolling the preeminence of the customer and the organization's commitment to service, and clever little slogans about customer service. Such pronouncements may momentarily impress and reassure the naïve customer, but there's probably no better proof of the organization's commitment to the idea and concept of customer service than in its treatment of customers when there's a problem.

Consider the case of a prominent truck manufacturer with a strong and well-developed dealer network. Competitive pressures accelerated product life cycles and new product introductions to such an extent that new product quality was declining. The result was an increasing amount of new equipment being introduced with early hour transmission failure rates. Moreover, models of the customer value delivery process indicated that a key value driver for customers was the ability of the dealer to fix product problems right the first time. In the face of heightened customer demand for equipment availability and minimum downtime, dealers felt increasing pressure to solve customer problems. In fact, it was widely recognized that any real differential value advantage that the original equipment manufacturer (OEM) had was being produced at the level of the dealership, not at the level of the factory. If the dealers were inattentive to problem resolution, it would surely erode any customer value advantage enjoyed by the OEM.

Problems with early hour failure rates were beginning to show up in a number of key performance measures. Models linking customer value to such critical concerns as customer loyalty, retention, willingness to recommend to others, satisfaction, market share, and profitability signaled areas of vulnerability. For example, customers who had been loyal purchasers of this OEM's equipment were shopping around to a much greater extent, spending more and more time looking elsewhere. Margins on sales were also declining. Customers were negotiating to a much greater extent, attempting to better align the company's value proposition with their expectations of performance and price.

It was not necessarily that the dealers were inattentive to customer problems—at least not this specific dealer. But survey after survey of customers showed a significant inconsistency in the service that customers experienced when they tried to get a problem resolved. The fact was that the dealership was unprepared for the service demands that were increasing as the quality of the product declined. Moreover, the dealer found that this current approach to customer problem solution was increasingly expensive. His people were working harder, not smarter.

When a customer encounters a problem with an organization, it's very probable that the value the customer experienced or expected has declined. In the case of the truck dealer, the customer expected that his newly purchased truck would operate properly without significant downtime. Not an unreasonable expectation. When the dealer can't take care of his problem to his satisfaction, his perception of the quality he expected in the transaction declines, while the monetary price remains constant. This results in a lower value. This relationship is depicted in what we call the Service-Value Chain (Figure 14-1).

Restoring Value Through Better Service

The value relationship can be restored only through effective problem resolution. Thus service becomes a key ingredient in the creation and delivery of value.

A customer problem situation can exert a double whammy with respect to value. First, as just discussed, the occurrence of the problem typically reduces value, because it disconfirms the customer's original perception of value. Second, problems with service in getting the problem resolved further undermine that perception of value.

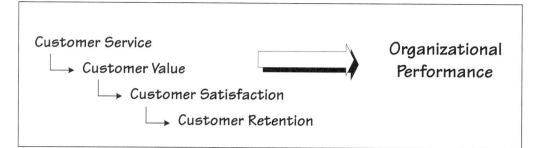

Figure 14-1. The service-value chain.

However, a quick and satisfactory resolution to the problem can restore the original value perception—and in some cases maybe even enhance it. How you handle a customer problem will determine whether you *disconfirm* your value proposition, creating a dissatisfied customer with a lower probability of repurchase, or you *confirm* your value proposition, creating satisfaction and increasing the likelihood of further business.

Identifying the Hidden Pitfalls of Problem Resolution

In our experience, many customer problem resolution processes are ineffective and therefore value-disconfirming, not because the organization does not want to address the problem, but rather because it doesn't understand how to address it, it thinks it has addressed it, or the process itself is a black hole.

That was the case with this truck dealership. It was not addressing many customer problems. When it did address problems, it did so slowly and, as it turned out, incompletely. Product support personnel in the dealership who did not have an immediate answer for the customer were following a convoluted process of filling out forms, sending those forms to product support counterparts at the manufacturer, attempting to contact technical consultants, leaving messages with the wrong people, and engaging in many other types of activities that were part of the "process." Typically, once the problem had been passed on to the next step in the "process," the service manager felt the problem was being taken care of. Inordinate amounts of time would pass. Customers were forced to take the initiative to find out the status of their problems. This gave the perception that problem were not being resolved. As a result, customer value was declining significantly.

This issue is exacerbated when a multi-level distribution system is involved in the problem resolution "process." When a problem solution requires coordination and communication, not only across functional boundaries but also over vertical distribution levels or even multi-institutional gaps, it's more likely that the process will not operate seamlessly.

How then can you improve your ability to solve customer problems in a manner that restores the customer's original perception of transactional or relationship value?

You Can't Improve What You Don't Understand

You can't improve what you don't understand. This may sound trite, but there's nothing that says trite cannot be true. As we indicated earlier, many glitches in problem resolution result from a poor understanding of how the process actually works and how it should work. This lack of understanding results from a phenomenon we call "process creep."

The best way to understand "process creep" is to understand how sidewalks on college campuses are built. The original architectural rendering shows the campus with wide, sweeping lawns and crisscrossing sidewalks cutting throughout the campus. This is the way the architect sees traffic flows. These sidewalks are laid out to provide effective and efficient flows throughout the campus. Enter the students. One year after construction, you can visit the campus and find worn paths indicating where students actually walk. These paths represent their different understanding of efficient and effective flows.

In a similar fashion, organizations design processes that are subsequently changed and modified by actual users in a manner that they consider more efficient or effective. For example, a service manager might bypass several stages in the process in order to expedite a request for information. Over time, this becomes an alternative process: "process creep" becomes institutionalized. When this occurs on an ongoing basis, the original process becomes corrupted and confusing. This is why very few people in the organization can accurately explain how the process works.

Sometimes "process creep" result in a more responsive process in the short run. Unfortunately, modifying the process on an ad hoc basis often thwarts the original function of the process. For example, problem resolution processes should capture information about product problems that can be useful in design and product modification. When people bypass the process, this information is often lost. The short-run effect may be a speedier response, but the long-term effects may be that product design problems may not be corrected appropriately. This perpetuates the product/service problem resolution cycle.

Mapping the Process

To understand how the problem resolution process (or any process) works, we use a technique called "value mapping." Value mapping is a flowcharting technique enabling a cross-functional and multi-level analysis of a process, in this case the problem-resolution process. The analysis has two specific purposes: 1) to identify and quantify activity-based costs and 2) to identify opportunities for making the process more effective.

By identifying and quantifying activity-based costs, then eliminating all of those costs not associated with enhanced service delivery, the dealer can either pass on price reductions to the customer or enjoy greater margins. By identifying and capitalizing on opportunities for improving service delivery, the dealer is improving the quality of his service. The interaction of the two activities enhances the overall value proposition of the dealer. This value enhancement can be leveraged for superior performance.

A value map provides four important benefits to management. First, it helps management to build a shared and consistent understanding of the customer's experience of the process and the business as a whole. In the case of problem resolution, a value map enables the dealer's employees to understand what the customer must endure to have a problem fixed. Second, mapping the process enables the dealership, in this case, to identify critical interfaces with the customer. These critical interfaces are often referred to as "moments of truth" in which the customer truly understands an organization's commitment to customer service. Third, mapping a process such as problem resolution provides dealer management the opportunity to increase and enhance the value proposition it's delivering to the customers. Enhancing value is important because it affects such critical performance outcomes such as loyalty, willingness to repurchase, willingness to recommend the dealer to other customers, market share, and profitability. Finally, the mapping process provides insight into how strategic measures and controls of quality and cost can be built into the new process. Without incorporating these measures into the redesigned process, management cannot accurately gauge the incremental improvements the redesign has produced.

Building the Value Map

There are eight basic steps in developing a value map:

1. Identify key customer interfaces.
2. Identify "back room" activities related to these critical customer interfaces.
3. Identify information system requirements.
4. Identify related management reporting systems.
5. Determine the flows among system levels.
6. Assess the need and opportunity for changing the system.
7. Implement the changes.
8. Monitor the results.

The first step in constructing a value map is to identify the key customer interfaces. These are those pesky "moments of truth" to which Jan Carlzon first alerted many organizations in his book, *Moments of Truth* (Ballinger, 1987). For problem resolution, this means understanding how a customer contacts the organization, how employees pass that customer off to other employees, how the customer gets news about his or her situation, and how the organization ultimately deals with the customer. This is the first step in the mapping process, because everything else is done in response to these critical interfaces.

The next step is to identify "back room" activities related to these critical customer interfaces. Each customer interface is typically supported by some kind of activity that the customer does not see or knows nothing about. In many unsuccessful problem resolution situations, these activities are blamed for the problem. The P word (*policy*, as in "It's against our company policy to . . .") is often used to globally categorize these back room activities. A major source of problem resolution process failure is snafus in these back room activities. They also represent a major potential source of process improvement and customer value enhancement.

Information systems and management report levels are next, steps 3 and 4. These levels represent the nervous system and the memory of most organization processes. Understanding how they work and why they do not work is critical for process improvement. Not having adequate information or generating useless reports, never to be used again, guarantees poor service and unnecessary costs.

Once these levels have been mapped, the flows between the levels can be laid in. How are the back room activities facilitated by having adequate information where and when needed? Are the activities streamlined so that the customer gets service that's appropriately responsive and accurate? These are a few of the margins that must be managed in order to provide the kind of service that will enhance the value proposition you deliver to your customers.

Once you understand how the system works or does not work, you can begin to identify the areas where improvement is possible, step 6. This improvement process is guided by twin concerns: 1) identify and fix those areas in the process that will provide better customer service and 2) drive out all costs not associated with delivering top-notch value-based service. Then, the final two steps in developing a value map: implement and monitor the changes.

Mapping the Problem Resolution Process

The dealership and the manufacturer formed a cross-functional team to map the process for handling customer problems. The resultant map is too large to reproduce here. However, we'll use portions of the map to illustrate the process and how it can enhance the value of the problem resolution process.

Figure 14-2 provides detail of the initial customer contact and job authorization portions of the problem resolution process. As the map will indicate, there are value-enhancing opportunities from the moment the customer makes contact with the dealership concerning a problem.

Typically, the dealership is made aware of a customer problem through a phone call to the receptionist. The receptionist then contacts the workshop supervisor, who alerts a branch manager about the customer and his problem and at the same time authorizes a field inspection. Since the problem in this case occurred on the road and the customer cannot bring his truck in for inspection, the branch manager must inspect the truck out where the problem occurred. The branch manager then reports back to the supervisor, who authorizes the branch manager to fix the problem, either under conventional warranty, extended warranty, or any other provision. The customer is apprised of the situation and is offered one of three options: 1) field service, if possible, 2) workshop service, or 3) a parts exchange. Depending on the option chosen by the customer, a job quote is developed. In the case mapped here, the quote is based on the workshop repair option. It's composed of a parts quote and a labor quote. The customer reviews the job quote, then either accepts the problem resolution or chooses to go elsewhere.

Right at the start, the dealership's mapping team identified a problem—or an opportunity for enhancing the value it provides its customers. When a customer calls in a repair request, the team found it could take as long as five minutes to reach the workshop supervisor. Often, it was impossible to reach the supervisor, so the receptionist took a message and promised to get back to the customer as soon as

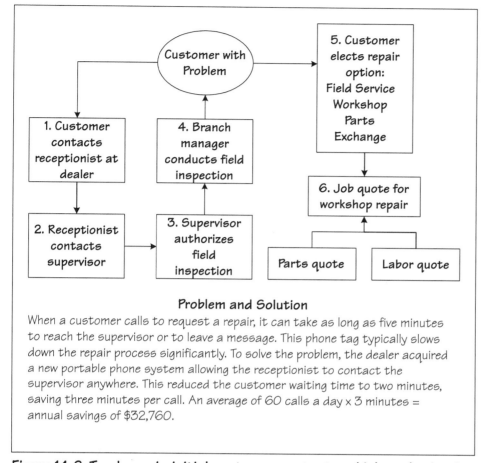

Problem and Solution

When a customer calls to request a repair, it can take as long as five minutes to reach the supervisor or to leave a message. This phone tag typically slows down the repair process significantly. To solve the problem, the dealer acquired a new portable phone system allowing the receptionist to contact the supervisor anywhere. This reduced the customer waiting time to two minutes, saving three minutes per call. An average of 60 calls a day x 3 minutes = annual savings of $32,760.

Figure 14-2. Truck repair: initial customer contact and job authorization.

possible. In many cases this was not acceptable, since the customer was calling from the side of the road and had a delivery schedule to meet.

The result was a delay in the repair process and the creation of an additional customer service problem. The map led the team to a plausible solution. Since the supervisor was usually busy on the workshop floor and often unaware of the call, the team suggested that the dealership acquire a mobile phone system so the receptionist could communicate with the supervisor regardless of his location. This eliminated wasted time and put the customer in direct contact with the one person who could initiate the problem resolution process. The dealership saved an average of three minutes per phone call and provided better customer service.

This concern for initiating the process keyed the team to focus on another problem, lost revenue due to inability to respond to customer calls. The team asked a fundamental question: "How much revenue are we losing when there is insufficient personnel available to accommodate customer need?" Their solution was to set up a log to record calls and reasons for lost revenues. The log contains a brief explanation of the work that was to be carried out and an estimate of revenue lost from that job. The information from this log is used in planning and scheduling.

Another example of the value mapping process can be seen in Figure 14-3, a map of the dealership's parts ordering process. The availability of needed parts is an important point on the critical path for repair.

When the parts department activates the quote (see Figure 14-2), it generates a document detailing the part. Someone in the parts department then selects the part, if it's available. If it's not, a demand for the part is generated and sent to the regional parts distribution center. A back order report is simultaneously generated. If the part is not available from the regional distribution center, the order is then sent to the manufacturer. When the part is received from the manufacturer, a back order receipt is generated and the part is then made available. The availability is recorded on the DTS (Dealer Tracking System). When the part is demanded, this order is recorded on the DBS (Dealer Business System), and it's noted when the order finally arrives. The DBS generates a weekly report detailing parts, revenues, and documents processed.

The team found a glitch in the ordering process that could be removed to increase the value delivered to the customer. The team noted that when a parts order is placed, the DTS shows that it's available, but does not indicate where it's located,

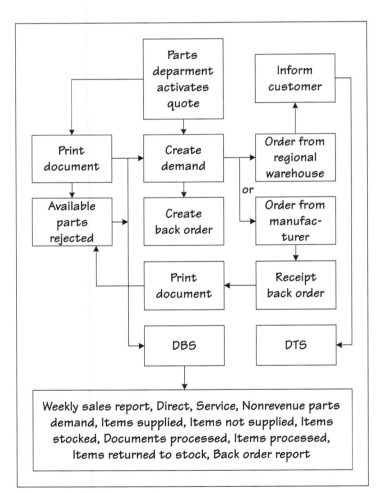

Figure 14-3. Parts orders.

whether at the regional warehouse or at the manufacturer's warehouse. When an estimated time of arrival (ETA) is given for the part, it's based on availability at the regional warehouse. If the part is at the manufacturer's warehouse, that ETA will be different. This, of course, affects back order availability and customer service.

The team suggested two options for improving this part of the process. First, it suggested changing the DTS screen to include manufacturer warehouse location as well as the regional distribution center. This would tell the dealership that, if a part were not available from the regional location, it could immediately be obtained from the manufacturer. A second option would be to immediately inform dealership personnel that a part was not available from the regional location, automatically order the part from the manufacturer, and provide an ETA based on receiving the part from that source. Both solutions would speed up response time to the customer and expedite part movement.

A secondary concern focused on the reports generated from the DBS. No one on the team had ever reviewed the reports, and team members questioned their utility. Questions were raised as to how the reports could be used. How could they provide more real-time information on parts availability? This question is still being examined.

The analysis of the value map revealed several other ways in which problem resolution could be expedited from a customer's standpoint. For example, the map indicated that, after a sale, the customer was not contacted by the dealership. All contact with the customer was through the OEM via a survey. So the dealership decided to place a flag on the customer's file that would alert the service department to call the customer one month after the sale. The purpose of the contact was to alert the service department to any early hour problems the customer might be experiencing and to schedule a routine maintenance service visit within the next month. In addition, the contact would make the customer feel that it would deal with any problems as quickly and efficiently as possible.

The team also improved the problem resolution process by changing how service manuals were ordered. Usually, the dealership didn't order service manuals from the OEM until it had sold a new-model truck. If a customer bought a new-model truck from another dealership and then brought his truck in for repairs, often the dealership did not have the updated service manual. This resulted in repair delays, which meant downtime and loss of revenue for the owner. By ordering service manuals as soon as they're available, the dealership is able to move faster on repairs and less likely to incur the unnecessary cost of rework.

Finally, the map helps the dealer identify an embarrassing problem that had occurred several times in the past. When a new customer purchases a truck from the dealer, the customer presumes that the dealer has set up a credit account. But that isn't part of the process. When the customer later brought his truck in for repairs and a work order was opened or parts were being purchased, the repairs were delayed while the dealer contacted the customer and ran a credit check. This angered customers. The dealer solved the problem by providing the customer with a credit application when he purchased his truck and making him aware at that point that accounts were not opened automatically. This avoided embarrassing confrontations and unnecessary delays in the repair process.

Value Mapping

Value mapping is an important tool for optimizing the service value relationship. In our example, we've shown how it can be used to sharpen the customer problem resolution process. To increase customer perceptions of value, it's essential to evaluate your entire value delivery system for a specific product or service. In doing so, it's critical to pay particular attention to those dimensions of value regarded as important by the customer. This process of evaluation begins with the customer's perspective of the entire service experience. Then, all activities relating to critical customer interfaces with a specific product are mapped or charted. We call this adding value for the customer; the purpose is to improve perceived quality on important dimensions of value and/or reduce the perceived price.

A comprehensive map of the value delivery system will identify all activities and activity interfaces relating to the delivery of value. Specifically, a value map will allow you to identify all activity-based service costs, which you can then evaluate relative to the benefits (quality) they're meant to provide. This evaluation can help you identify opportunities for making the value delivery system more effective, either by improving the quality delivered or by reducing the costs of providing benefits, which can then be translated into price reductions.

Development of the entire value delivery map requires extensive interviewing of employees. Simply designing the map on the basis of "how things are supposed to work" frequently obfuscates the reality of the workplace. Employees frequently develop shortcuts, information is lost along the way, and different departments each assume that the other is monitoring the task.

The detailed map of the value delivery system enabled the truck dealer to evaluate all delivery processes in terms of important dimensions of value. The dealer's value team identified specific steps in the value delivery process where unnecessary costs were incurred or where opportunities existed for enhancing important benefits to the customer. Analysis of these steps led to a redesign of the entire delivery system.

Value mapping is a process measure designed to improve value delivery by identifying opportunities to enhance benefits to the customer while reducing the price for those benefits. Developing value maps for each product and market helps ensure that you focus on important dimensions of value when evaluating your delivery system. Value mapping enables a cross-functional analysis of the entire delivery process, focusing employee attention on the customer's perspective of the process. Value mapping enables you to identify and quantify activity-based costs and identify opportunities for making the delivery system more effective. Finally, value mapping provides a blueprint for developing strategic measures and controls of quality and cost.

About the Authors

R. Eric Reidenbach, Ph.D., is a founding principal of the VALTec Group, Inc., Morgantown, West Virginia. He has consulted with the Pentagon, the Naval Research Laboratories, Walt Disney World, Benetton Spa (Italy), and McDonald's. Work for these clients ran the gamut from the development of values-based instrumentation to the deployment of value-driven systems to improve organizational productivity. He is the author or co-author of 12 books on marketing and marketing research techniques.

Gordon W. McClung, Ph.D., another founding principal of the VALTec Group, Inc., served as marketing manager and marketing director at Investors Mortgage Insurance and AT&T Long Lines. As a consultant, Gordon worked with such companies as Holiday Inns of America, Silver Springs Sportwear, Caterpillar, Dow Chemical, and Kmart. He has pioneered work in value analysis and value management. He has contributed more than 100 articles to professional and academic publications.

Reginald W. Goeke, Ph.D, is also a founding principal of the VALTec Group, Inc., with a background in marketing research and data analysis. He has been involved in the development of unique and proprietary instrumentation for such companies as Caterpillar, Caterpillar of Australia, Gough, Gough & Hamer (New Zealand), Westrac Equipment (Australia), and Elphinstone Underground Mining Equipment (Tasmania).

PART FOUR

Customer Service on the Front Line

15

Six Tools for Improving How You Deliver Service to Customers

Rebecca L. Morgan

If you want specific ideas you can use immediately, this is the article. The author offers a tool for assessing customer service skills, six ways to retain your customers, top 10 mistakes employees make with customers and how to prevent them, 14 tips for calming upset customers, six common questions about customer relationships, and four ways to rebound from customer annoyances.

As a manager of a customer contact department, I bet you're reading this book for specific, immediately usable ideas. This article is written for you with this need in mind.

First, you'll get a tool to help you assess the customer service skills of your staff. It's an instrument that you, members of your staff, and the customers they serve can all complete. By comparing the results, you'll be able to see where you need to coach each of your team members.

Then you'll learn six ways to manage so you'll retain your customers, top 10 common mistakes employees make with customers—and what you can do to prevent them, 14 tips for calming upset customers, six frequently asked questions about customer relationships, and four ways to rebound from customer annoyances. I'll share with you answers to questions I've received in my speeches and seminars and from articles I've written on customer service.

Customer Service Assessment

Have you ever wondered how your staff stacks up in the customer service area? Here's a quick assessment to help rate them. Make copies of the survey on page 153. Then ask each of your customer contact employees to complete it on themselves. (That's why it's written in the first person.) You should also complete a copy on each of them. Then compare your answers.

Of course, the real test is to photocopy this and give it to five or ten of their customers. Ask them for their candid feedback, so you know where your people can do better.

Here's a scoring tool to help you see how you rate.
Score: 61–75 = Excellent! Doing an outstanding job.
        46–60 = Very Good. Focus on the few things to work on.
        31–45 = Good. Got some good skills.
        16–30 = Need Improvement. Get guidance from supervisor.
         0–15 = Help! If you want to keep your job, run to the boss.

Six Tips for Managers on Retaining Customers

Sam, your normally considerate subordinate, has had a hard day. He didn't sleep well last night because his young daughter was up with the flu. And today, nothing seems to be going right. At 3:30 he answers a call.

> **Sam:** Hello. Sam Short here.
> **Customer:** Hello. I'm inquiring about the availability of your XT23P. Do you have any in stock?
> **Sam:** I don't know. The computer doesn't show any in stock.
> **Customer:** When do you think you might have it in?
> **Sam:** How should I know? Your crystal ball is as clear as mine.
> **Customer:** I need it soon.
> **Sam:** Well, you should have called earlier. Those items go quickly. Call back in a few weeks.
> **Customer:** I guess I'll have to.

Scenarios like the above happen all too frequently in organizations without managers being aware of them. When we aren't around, how do we really know how our people are responding to our customers? We don't. We can only rely on how we communicate about customer service and hope that our examples will live on through our staff's communication with customers.

What can managers do to create an environment conducive to continual customer satisfaction? Here are six tips.

1. Remember that you are a role model. Your model can be either positive or negative. You must give more than lip service to the concept—you must practice it visibly and frequently. The concepts of customer satisfaction must be created internally and reinforced internally. Sending staff to outside courses on customer satisfaction is sometimes a waste of money if the manager does not reinforce good service.

2. Establish the attitude of treating customers with respect and dignity. If there's a problem, assume your organization has made the mistake until you have evidence otherwise. For example, "We don't have a record of receiving your payment. Would you be kind enough to see if your check cleared the bank?" is certainly better than "You didn't pay us." Work to eliminate your staff's suspicious or aggres-

ACTION	Always	Usually	Some-times	Rarely	Never
When a customer calls, I am cheerful.	5	4	3	2	1
When a customer has a complaint, I handle it quickly and professionally.	5	4	3	2	1
After dealing with an upset customer, I don't waste time telling my co-workers about it.	5	4	3	2	1
I answer the phone professionally.	5	4	3	2	1
I take responsibility for my own calls and work.	5	4	3	2	1
I tackle unpleasant work diligently.	5	4	3	2	1
I can explain complex policies/procedures without jargon to my customers.	5	4	3	2	1
I pride myself on finding little ways to go the extra mile for my customers.	5	4	3	2	1
I come to work dressed and groomed so the CEO would be proud to show any prospective customer my work area.	5	4	3	2	1
I handle my work effectively and pride myself on having very few errors.	5	4	3	2	1
My positive attitude is demonstrated to all those who interact with me.	5	4	3	2	1
I prioritize my work so the most important tasks are done first.	5	4	3	2	1
I handle inappropriate or excessive interruptions tactfully and speedily.	5	4	3	2	1
I feel comfortable suggesting additional products or quantities if I believe it will benefit the customer.	5	4	3	2	1
I follow up all promises and requests within the promised time frame.	5	4	3	2	1
TOTALS					

sive behavior—body language, voice tone, eye contact. Some employees project an "us vs. them" attitude about customers through their nonverbal communication.

3. Initiate a policy to be proactive in letting customers know if there is a problem with their order. Don't wait until the last minute.

4. Discuss customer satisfaction at staff meetings. Give examples of good customer service behavior as well as problems that may need to be corrected. (Don't embarrass anyone.) Make your concerns and philosophy about customer service known regularly.

5. Solicit customer feedback. There are several inexpensive ways to get feedback. One is providing customers with postage-paid return cards or surveys. Make sure the surveys are short and to the point. Have a place for the customer to write his/her name and phone number so you can call to clarify any questions. Another way to gather feedback is for you to personally call customers (e.g., five to ten each week) to check on service. Make sure not to call only customers who you know love your company. Call some who haven't bought from you in a while as well. Then use the information you receive to improve operations.

6. Make customer satisfaction a part of the staff member's performance evaluation. Be clear on expectations and minimum levels of customer service. Be specific—e.g., phone answered within two rings, walk-in visitors greeted within 30 seconds, phone calls returned within four hours, upbeat and helpful behavior. Let them know their performance in these areas will be included in their performance evaluations.

Customer satisfaction is essential to a successful organization. Instill the value of this with your staff, recognize their commendable behavior, and teach them to think on behalf of the customer, and you'll have an organization that will keep your customers coming back.

Top 10 Common Mistakes Employees Make With Customers—and What You Can Do to Prevent Them

Having conducted customer service training since 1980, I've observed many "sins" of customer contact personnel. Most of the time the problems I've seen are easily corrected, once the staff member is aware he or she is doing something wrong. However, managers or owners may not even be aware of what their employees are saying to the customers, so they don't know what needs to be corrected.

Allow me to be your ears and eyes and report on 10 of the common mistakes I've noticed and offer some suggestions on how you can correct them.

1. Taking the customer for granted. I've noticed it's common for employees to forget the expected niceties: "Good morning," "How can I help you?" "Let me check for you," "Thank you," "We appreciate your business." Customers have come to expect these phrases, delivered sincerely, when they are purchasing something. A quick way to make customers go away is to take them for granted and stop showing you appreciate them. Make sure your staff knows that you expect them to show politeness and appreciation toward customers. Give them some leeway on how to express that, so they don't sound like robots. But if they go a bit too far—"Hiya, dude!"—reel them in by telling them what you'd rather they say.

2. Using jargon, expecting the customer to understand your lingo. Even when the customers are highly trained professionals, they may not be familiar with your company's acronyms or buzz words. If your company deals with consumers, don't assume they understand industry talk. For example, the insurance professional who says "binder" means something entirely different from the image the consumer conjures up, which is usually a vision of a three-ring binder! Listen closely to what your people are saying. Or ask someone who doesn't know your business to call and talk to your people. Get them to tell you how they were treated and what words your people used that were confusing.

3. Speaking so fast that the customer has to ask the employee to repeat. When you hear a customer repeatedly asking your staff member to repeat himself, this is a sign he's speaking too quickly. When he slows down, he needs to make sure his tone won't be interpreted as condescending. The reason the customer is asking for the information again is not because she's dumb; she just may be unfamiliar with what your employee is saying and just needs him to slow down.

4. Giving short, clipped answers. When staff say, "Yes" instead of "Yes, let me look that up for you," or "Yes, we do have that in stock," it can come across as unfriendly and curt. Adding a few additional words to amplify the point conveys a friendly demeanor. When you hear your employees giving short answers, pull them aside afterwards and help them understand how clipped answers can be interpreted negatively by customers. Suggest they add a few more words to their answers to show they're friendly and interested in making the customer feel appreciated.

5. Not being proactive when a problem arises. When a customer initiates a call about a problem, he's even more angry when he finds out your company knew about the problem but didn't notify him immediately. Train your people to call customers as soon as they're aware of a problem. It may not be a pleasant call to make, but it's less difficult than the situation can get when the customer calls first.

6. Not appearing like they care about the customer's complaint. Often customer contact staff don't show that they care about a customer's concern, or they may even get defensive when a customer complains. Perhaps it's a common complaint, one they've heard so often that they've become callused. Or perhaps there's nothing they can do about this issue. If they would even just act like they cared, many problems would be resolved more quickly and the customer would feel that your business was concerned about their issue.

7. Being preoccupied with other tasks (talking with co-workers, doing paperwork, stocking shelves). Train your staff to notice what's going on around them. Teach them to look up often from what they're doing and approach customers who may look puzzled or lost. This not only improves the customer's impression of your service, but also cuts down on shoplifting.

8. Interrupting the customer or no longer listening, believing they know what the customer is asking or saying. After working in a customer contact position for a while, you can begin to predict what customers are going to ask or complain about. But it makes matters much worse when the employee cuts the customer off in mid-sentence. Remind your people that each customer wants to be heard out and not cut off. It will help build a positive relationship with the customer, which will encourage him or her to come back again.

9. Making judgments about the buying power of a customer based upon his or her appearance, language skills, or company's reputation. Buyers come in all levels of dress and education, so it's unwise to assume buying ability by these aspects. Sometimes employees make these judgments because the customer's company has never bought much, so the employee doesn't think this order will be large and neglects the customer. Help your employees see that these assessments hurt your company and are unfair to the customer.

10. Arguing with the customer. You can't win an argument with a customer. Even if you win the disagreement, you lose the customer. When the customer is wrong, there are ways to help him understand without throwing it in his face. Role-play with your staff common scenarios where the customer may be wrong, but is trying to blame your company. Help them work out how to phrase it so the customer leaves with her dignity intact and stays your customer, rather than becoming embarrassed and more angry.

Heading off these 10 common customer contact mistakes is not easy. It takes vigilance, caring, and time on the manager's part. You need to help your staff see new ways to interact with customers, yet you need to do so in ways that spare their self-esteem. It is easy to yell and berate your staff. It's harder to coach them in ways so they want to improve.

14 Tips for Calming Upset Customers

Unfortunately, unhappy customers are part of every business, even businesses that are renowned for their customer service. Just because a customer is unhappy doesn't mean she has to become upset.

As the author of *Calming Upset Customers*, I'm often asked to give some general guidelines for handling these stress-producing encounters. The following offers some general thoughts for you and your staff.

General Philosophy

○ **Don't take the rantings and ravings of upset customers personally.** Don't get emotionally hooked. When you let him or her "push your buttons," you lose. When you respond emotionally—with anger, sarcasm, tears—you can't respond rationally. He wants to upset you because he thinks you'll give him what he wants just to get rid of him.

○ **Make it a game or challenge to see how many upset customers you can turn around.** See if you can get them to be reasonable.

○ **Look for the "gifts" upset customers offer you.** These gifts are what they can teach you about dealing with ugly human behavior. The better you deal with them, the fewer upset people you'll have in your life. They'll see through your body language and composure that you're confident you can find a solution without getting rattled.

○ **Understand that obnoxious customers are often embarrassed** because they made a mistake and want to blame it on you.

○ **Respond by being reasonable, firm, pleasant, mature, and professional** to show them that you're going to do what you think is right, no matter how obnoxious they get. They think that being rude is the only way to get action.

○ **Don't give away the store to shut her up.** That rewards her behavior and teaches her—and others—that acting belligerently is the way to get what she wants.

○ **Remind yourself that this abusive person must really have problems** if this is how he treats others. He doesn't respect himself, so he doesn't show respect for others. He doesn't know what you know about how to get people to do what you want—happily.

Specific Behaviors

○ **Listen fully—don't interrupt.** If you do, it will escalate her anger. Take notes, looking up often to maintain eye contact. Assume body language that shows you're interested and concerned.

○ **Maintain a respectful tone**, even though you don't respect his behavior. Your voice should show that you're calm but concerned. Don't get distracted.

○ **Remove the upset customer from the main customer area**, if possible. She rants and raves to get attention and knows that many people will give her what she wants to shut her up quickly.

○ **Let him cool off** when on the phone by saying that you need to research the situation and possible solutions. Ask if you may call him back, then do so at the appointed time. He probably will have calmed down by the time you call him back.

○ **Talk about what you *can* do,** not what you *can't* do. Put it positively. Don't talk about the "policy." This will anger her more.

○ **Use the "broken record" technique**, firmly, yet politely repeating what you can do for him.

○ **Ignore her impoliteness and cursing.** She's really lashing out at your organization, even though she may find various ways to say, "You're incompetent." If you allow the cursing to offend you, you've lost your objectivity and control, and she's won. Edit her comments in your head so you can make sense of her words without getting upset. For example, the statement "You're a fool. Why did you do this wrong? Who would ever hire an incompetent worker like you?" translates for you into "She's really upset. Something is wrong. What can I do to help set it right?"

An important point to remember is that you won't please all people. You should do the best you can, but there are some customers your organization can do better without. It is management's responsibility to determine if this customer is one that should be encouraged to patronize another organization.

Upset customers can be unnerving. But with the right attitude and techniques, many of these people can be turned into satisfied, loyal customers. It's not always easy, but it's worth it.

Six Frequently Asked Questions About Customer Relationships

Q: My customers are from all over the world. Sometimes I have a hard time understanding them. I don't want to be rude, but I need to understand what they want. How can I do this?

A: Most people appreciate it if you calmly and politely explain that you're having a hard time understanding their request. You must be certain you don't sound annoyed. Try something like, "Sir, I really want to help you. I'm sorry, but I can't understand what you're asking. Would you mind slowing down for me? That way I can get you the information you want." If there is someone else in your business who speaks the customer's language, don't be afraid to ask them to help. You may also request that the customer e-mail or fax the request so you can help him or her more effectively. The most important thing is to be patient and respectful.

Q: I've been told you should always call customers by name. I have customers around the world, so some of their names are difficult to pronounce. What would you suggest?

A: People appreciate it when you work to call them by name. If you don't want to butcher their name, simply ask, "Sir, would you say your last name for me?" Then repeat it to them until you get it right. Make an effort to remember it for the next time. I log the phonetic spelling in their record in my database. Remember also that sometimes it may not always be appropriate to call a customer by name. A bookstore owner shared with me that many customers in her store like to be anonymous so they don't feel uncomfortable about their book purchases—for example, if they're buying books that reveal a personal trait or may be considered risqué.

Q: How can I keep my customers buying from me?

A: They have to like your products, prices, and service. If you have the same products and prices as your competitors, you have to focus on service. Find out what kind of service your customers expect, then see if you can beat it. Sometimes it's simple things. If they expect you to answer your phone within three rings, see if you can do it in two. If they expect their shipment in a week, see if you can get it to them in four days.

Don't just decide what you think they want—ask them. Frankly, you'll be wrong more often than you think. For example, maybe you think they'd like a remodeled store. But they would just like you to sweep up the mess on the floor more often. You can get information through customer surveys, but many people are reluctant to fill these out. You can lead focus groups, which often yield good, specific suggestions. You can also make it a practice to periodically ask your customers, "What could we do to serve you better?"

Q: I've heard from my customers that sometimes my employees are brusk and curt. Yet when I'm around, they sound fine. How can I get them to be that way all the time?

A: You need to spend time around them and coach them when you hear them saying something that could be improved. Hang out in their area more often. Make sure you "catch them doing something right" and praise them for the good stuff you hear. And when you hear something you don't like, break it to them gently—don't pounce on them. Often it works to take the blame: "I bet I never told you that I want us all to thank each customer for her business." "I know we talked about this a long time ago, but it's easy to forget." "I know it's hard to juggle in-person customers with the phone, but I'd really prefer we all stay focused on the person in front of us and let someone else get the phone."

Q: I have a couple of abusive, manipulative customers. Nothing I've done seems to work with them. They're always yelling, complaining, and trying to get me to lower my prices. What can I do?

A: You may have to "fire" these customers. No matter how much business they're bringing you, it's not enough to compensate for the headaches they're causing. Not only are they putting you in a bad mood and adding to your stress, but they're probably causing your staff untold grief as well. You can fire them politely by saying something like "Ms. Difficult, it seems that we've been unable to provide what you want. Our business isn't set up to be able to satisfy every need. I think it would be best for everyone if you found another supplier."

Q: Because of circumstances beyond our control, we sometimes can't deliver our customers' orders on time. They get really mad. I'm not sure how to best handle them.

A: Upset customers are part of every business. We all make mistakes. It's how we deal with mistakes that makes a difference. In my presentations on this topic, I always suggest that the first thing you do is apologize for their inconvenience. Then empathize and finally focus on positive actions. "Mr. Customer, I'm sorry for your late shipment. I know how hard it is for you to keep the production line going if you don't have parts. I just checked on the computer and saw that the reason for the delay was that big snow storm between our plant and yours. The dispatcher isn't sure when the highways will be clear, so I'll check to see if we could truck parts through a different route. If that doesn't look good, then I'll check with some of our other customers in your area and see if they have any extra stock that they could spare to get your line back in production. Again, I'm sorry this happened. Please trust that I'm doing everything possible to get you those parts."

Four Ways to Rebound From Customer Annoyances

Most customers are cordial when things are going well. But when things go awry, it's easy for the killer instinct to come out. When things go wrong with a customer, you not only risk their wrath, but jeopardize their willingness to continue to do business with you. Sometimes there's not much you can do to prevent the cause of their upset, but there are always ways you can try to appease them, thus winning back their loyalty.

Here are six common customer annoyances and how to handle them if you're responsible for creating a solution to the problem.

RUDE SERVICE
Problem: A bride becomes furious with a curt saleswoman.
Solution: Acknowledge the bride's complaint, apologize, and assign another salesperson to the customer. If you feel her business warrants it, offer her a 5% discount on her purchase or some small gift to go with her purchase (e.g., hose or a hair ornament). Give the customer a reason to return. In order to keep a good customer, you must be prepared to go that extra mile by showing you truly value his or her business. Giving lip service and making excuses are not enough.

SHODDY OR DEFECTIVE MERCHANDISE
Problem: A customer storms in to return a "defective" calculator that she or he apparently misused.
Solution: It's always a touchy situation if a customer misuses the product. Having a "No Returns" policy is not a good idea: you need to show you are flexible and you stand by what you sell. Whatever happened, be gracious and don't make a customer feel stupid for being careless or misusing the product. If you can, replace the product and absorb the cost—you'll make up for your loss in their future purchases and positive word of mouth. If you can't exchange the product (if it's a one-of-a-kind item, for instance), try to de-escalate the customer's anger and frustration with an alternative solution. Apologize for not being able to replace the merchandise. Offer to repair it for free. Then give a 10%–20% discount on the customer's next purchase.

LATE DELIVERY
Problem: A print shop has to stop operations because the paper mill's delivery truck is stuck in a blizzard.
Solution: Always be proactive in informing your customers of any problems. You might call them and say, "I'm calling to tell you that our trucks had to be rerouted because of a blizzard in the Midwest." In emergency situations where you fear losing customers because of late deliveries, it's best to over-communicate. It shows not only that you're on top of the situation, but also that you care. Even though the late delivery is no fault of yours, take responsibility and give your client free delivery or a discount on the next shipment. Plan now to create contingency policies to avoid future late deliveries. But don't make promises you don't plan to keep. Good customers don't forget a promise.

SCREW-UPS
Problem: A travel agent forgets to make a car rental reservation. When the customer arrives at the rental firm, there are no more cars.
Solution: Acknowledge the mistake, apologize, and then make good on it. If the client had to rent a car from another firm at a higher rate, reimburse her the difference. See what else you could do to show her you appreciate her business. Perhaps

you could arrange an upgrade on her next travel plans. Also, a handwritten apology note will help ease the sting.

Satisfied?

So there you have it, as promised: a tool for assessing customer service skills, six ways to retain your customers, top 10 common mistakes employees make with customers and how to prevent them, 14 tips for calming upset customers, six frequent questions about customer relationships, and four ways to rebound from customer annoyances. If you're reading this book for specific, immediately usable ideas, I hope that you're now a satisfied customer.

About the Author

Rebecca L. Morgan, CSP, is Managing Partner of Morgan Seminar Group in San Jose, California. She works with organizations that want their people to work smarter and with people who want to get more done. Rebecca travels nationally to share her research and experience to help make people and organizations more productive and profitable. Her hundreds of clients include Hyatt Hotels, Royal Cruise Lines, Meeting World, Outrigger Hotels Hawaii, and the Internal Revenue Service.

Rebecca has written four books—*TurboTime: Maximizing Your Results Through Technology* (Morgan Seminar Group, 1996), *Professional Selling: Practical Secrets for Successful Sales* (Crisp Publications, 1988), *Making Time For Excellence*, and *Calming Upset Customers* (Crisp Publications, 1989 and 1996). She has also produced six audio cassette programs and has been featured on Nightingale-Conant's audio sales magazine, "Sound Selling." She's appeared in *Home Office Computing, Sales and Marketing Management*, and *Business Ethics*, as well as on National Public Radio and *The Oprah Winfrey Show*. Visit her Web site at http://www.rebeccamorgan.com/.

16

MAINTAINING SUPERIOR CUSTOMER SERVICE DURING PERIODS OF PEAK DEMAND

Janelle M. Barlow and Dianna Maul

Every industry faces peak-volume periods—times when employees tend to get overworked and stressed out, when customers may become upset and turn elsewhere. How well do you handle your periods of peak demand? How would your customers and employees answer that question? This article offers 13 strategies to help you better manage to make the most of your peak challenges.

The flashing signal board indicates your customers are waiting in a telephone queue over 15 minutes long. And every single member of your team has a call-back list that rides like a monkey on their already burdened shoulders. By the time your customer service team is able to pick up a waiting call, many of the customers are already frustrated by the long wait they've endured. Welcome to your peak-demand period!

Dealing With Demand

Every industry has its peak-volume times—in some cases on the telephone, in others in person. For some companies, this period stretches over several months. For others, it ebbs and flows depending on marketing campaigns, public relations events, and the vagaries of the marketplace.

Airlines face peak volumes during the summer months, over the big year-end holiday season, in lesser holiday periods, and during spring break. Call centers incur high volumes during billing cycles, promotions for new products, or crisis situations. Hotels also experience peak traffic: their reservations staff can be tested preceding conventions, vacation periods, and special events, such as the Olympics or a national political convention.

One thing is for certain. Practically every business faces the impact of high volume at one time or another. Many companies hire additional staff for these times, with little opportunity to train this temporary staff, particularly in the "soft skills" side of customer service. You can give your new hires a script to read when they answer the phone and teach them how to place an order, answer simple customer queries, or make a reservation, but there's little time to train them in how best to relate to a customer. Likewise, your permanent staff may be inadequately trained to cope with the pressures of this peak-volume period. And, no matter what their training and experience may be, many of their relationship skills are sorely tested under the demands of intense and extra work.

Most jobs in the American market today are service-related—76% of them to be exact. Yet fewer than 10% of these service staff have received formal training in how to deliver quality service. Workers in the retail industry, for example, who spend an enormous amount of time with customers, receive an average of seven hours of training, the lowest of 14 industries. Many companies feel forced to hire just about anybody to get a "warm body" in place. Most front-line staff do their best, but often that's not good enough, particularly if they're young and inexperienced.

How Well Do You Handle Complaints?

Perhaps the biggest challenge to staff during peak-demand periods is handling complaints. Not only are there more customers to serve, but more of those customers are frustrated because they have to wait longer to speak with someone and because their needs mean more to them at special times of the year. For example, parents who can't figure out how to operate that new computer they just purchased and who sit with an impatient child screaming to get at the latest software game are understandably under greater pressure.

Customer complaints statistics, under normal-demand periods, are not encouraging. First, very few people complain. The most widely quoted customer research group, the Technical Assistance Research Programs (TARP), found that 26 out of 27 customers with service complaints will not bother to say anything—to their service providers. Because of the hassles and confrontation involved with complaining, many people allow themselves to get upset before they complain. Second, of the 4% of customers who do speak up, over half state that the way their complaints are handled actually increases their negative feelings. This represents a lot of room for improvement, under normal circumstances. But it becomes even more difficult to handle complaints effectively during peak-demand periods.

Complaint handling is something that very few people do well naturally. As a result, staff need training in this critical area of customer communication.

We have found that as little as a half day of complaint handling training can significantly improve customer retention rates, staff retention rates, and customer satisfaction. Such training needs to:

○ Encourage staff to view complaints as gifts (a concept based on the book *A Complaint Is a Gift*, by Janelle Barlow and Claus Moller),
○ Provide staff with adaptable, easy-to-use formulas,
○ Allow practice of specific strategies for handling upset customers, and
○ Create opportunities for staff to view complaints from the customer's point of view.

According to a 1997 customer survey, 90% of customers feel they pay enough to receive the highest level of service, yet 64% say the service representatives they deal with do not care about their needs. The American Customer Satisfaction Index has dropped steadily from 1994 to 1997. Customers cite such poor examples of service as calling in to see if a flight is on time, only to be put on hold for seven minutes, all the while hearing a recording every 30 seconds, "Please continue to hold. We value your business." They talk about staff who don't know their company's products, its procedures, or the names of their co-workers. Customers often know more about the organization than staff who are supposed to provide service.

When the customers deal face to face with front-line staff, they frequently report that service staff are so busy they don't have time to look at them. When there's no eye contact, many customers feel that the service providers wish they would just go away; they certainly don't get the impression that the staff are delighted to serve them and have their business.

If this is the norm, what happens when companies face high-volume traffic? The reality, unfortunately, is that staff are unprepared and, regrettably, managers and supervisors are equally unprepared. If companies deliberately plan for and correctly manage this peak-demand period, they have a golden opportunity to win over customers by showing their best service. Remember: your customers are frustrated and pressed for time during your periods of peak demand, and they deeply appreciate the attention and care they receive at these times.

Strategies for Surviving the Peaks

We suggest a baker's dozen (13) strategies you can use to better manage these periods. You may already be using some of these approaches; others may be new for you. We encourage you to continue with the approaches you're already using and experiment with two or three of the ones you haven't yet tried. Our experience shows us that each strategy can have a dramatic impact on staff attitudes and performance. When combined, they're even more powerful.

1. Visible Management. At a time when companies are asking staff to go the extra mile, managers and supervisors have to be willing to do this as well. This is the time for managers to get out of their offices and appear on the front line. If managers "carry water" for their customer service staff, this supports those workers and underscores the value of the work they do.

In many organizations, managers become invisible during high-volume periods. Remember: managers are coaches, mentors, and cheerleaders, so staff under pressure need them to be visible. Even if managers merely listen to staff vent, give them a pat on the back for a job well done, or are available for answering questions, staff will not forget these validating efforts.

One airline blocked out all vacations for managers over the year-end holiday period—as they had also done for front-line employees. This same airline required all managers, at both senior and mid levels, to work at specific airport locations or to get on the phones and help with reservations—in short, to get down in the trenches with their staff. The managers were trained to assist in any way they could. Rather than sitting in their offices, the managers handled excess baggage, helped travelers board the aircraft, and greeted travelers as they arrived at their destinations.

These behaviors created a win/win feeling inside this airline. Employees felt supported. Managers felt the value of what they were doing from the feedback of their employees. Customers raved about the quality service they received during a period that most travelers describe as the toughest time to be flying.

At the reservations center, where the volume of calls doubled over the holiday season, managers helped on the phones or wandered among their staff, helping in whatever way they could. Three times a day the management team went through the reservations center with gourmet coffee carts, cookies, and ice cream sundaes. Try it: it really works—especially those ice cream sundaes.

2. Prepare People for What They Are About to Face. Let your staff know they're approaching a high-volume period. Staff will have an easier time coping with extraordinary demands if they know what's coming. Help your staff take on the work ahead of them as a *challenge*, rather than as a *burden*. In your meetings, talk about the high-demand period before it starts. Your staff shouldn't have to face any surprises. Our experience is that if staff know they're facing greater pressures, they later report that it wasn't as bad as they thought it would be—once they make it through the period.

Here are some suggestions you can use in your meetings to prepare your staff:

- Alert them to the heightened emotional state of their customers. Get them to look at this increased energy from the customers' point of view. Remember: your customers are also pressured for time, especially during the holiday season.
- Ask them about experiences they've had as customers when dealing with other companies during peak-volume periods. How were they treated? What did they like? What didn't they like?
- Be available to answer all their questions. Even if they don't have any at the moment, knowing you're available to them will make a big difference.
- Teach them simple stress management techniques. For example, encourage them to take a deep breath of air after every telephone call. Remind them to stretch their shoulders and hands. Encourage them to drink lots of water. It's very easy to get dehydrated while talking a lot.
- Encourage them to be friendly and use humor when appropriate with stressed customers. You might develop lines for them to use, such as "Congratulations—you got through at our highest-demand time. The customer service angels must really like you."
- Talk about how to handle customers when they are upset. This topic is another book in itself, but the most important thing is to show genuine concern.
- Let your staff know how important this period is for the economic success of your company. This is the time when your organization can prove itself to its highest volume of customers and keep them coming back.

3. Set Realistic Goals. Many organizations set measurable standards for determining whether they are delivering quality service. For example, they may set the demanding standard that all calls must be answered within 20 seconds. During peak periods, this goal may need to be adjusted to reflect the reality of higher volumes.

There's nothing worse than to feel defeated before you even start. And if in the early days of your peak volume, they fail to meet any of your performance standards, your staff may feel like a football team that's down by two touchdowns just five minutes into the game. Unfortunately, this feeling is not uncommon among employees who are trying to achieve unattainable goals. This feeling, in turn, gets communicated to the customer in subtle ways through, for example, a depressed tone of voice. When we're honest with both our customers and employees, we set up realistic expectations and maintain a winning edge.

4. Practice Ongoing Coaching. Above all, don't stop your coaching efforts, even in your busy periods. You may need to reduce the amount of time you spend on coaching, but don't eliminate coaching altogether. That sends the wrong signal about continuous quality improvement. And besides, what better time to coach your staff than while they're in the midst of the action? You can be sure that football coaches don't stop coaching while the team is playing—even in the Super Bowl.

You may need to work with small groups of people at a time, so the remaining phone personnel aren't overwhelmed. And keep your coaching sessions short, but regular. One effective way to do this, especially with staff who are on the phones, is to have them listen to tape-recorded telephone calls of staff talking with customers. (It may be better not to use calls involving current staff, to avoid embarrassing anybody.)

Give your staff the opportunity to listen to good examples of customer service. Let them also hear some bad examples, especially calls where the staff person sounded short, arrogant, or irritated with customers. Many call center staff have no idea how they sound on the phone. Encourage your staff to evaluate the calls along the standards that are important to you. For example:

- Were we helpful?
- Did we sound rushed?
- Did we suggest additional products for sale to the customer?
- How was the upset customer handled?

Choose the standards of behavior you wish to promote, underscore them, and point out how an interaction could have been handled better.

5. Give Employees Rewards and Recognition. Show your staff you care and that you value their extra efforts during these critical periods. When the peak period has subsided, have a celebration party and sincerely thank them for their support. Let them know you're planning a celebration, so they can look forward to it. If it's not possible to host this kind of party, give each employee a sincere thank-you letter with a small gift or token of your appreciation. You can bet they'll deliver for you again in the next crunch period.

A celebration party at the end of the peak period is exciting, but that shouldn't stop you from holding "mini" celebrations during the heavy time. Here are some types of things you can celebrate:

○ *Volume of response.* Bring attention to record-setting events. In the TMI office, when we're sending out huge volumes of Time Manager materials over our busy season, we play a special celebration song on a tape recorder when the package volume reaches a certain level or when new records have been set.

○ *"Quarter way," "halfway," and "almost there" marks.* If you know how long your peak period runs, celebrate milestones when you reach them. You can do this with small giveaways, such as candy kisses or specially engraved pencils ("We're halfway there!").

○ *Numbers of days with no absenteeism, no mistakes, or whatever quality you would like to emphasize.*

6. Allow Small Breaks After Dealing With Upset Customers. Some customers are truly demanding, even vicious in their attacks on your staff. Allow your staff to take a two- or three-minute "walking" break after such an encounter. Encourage them to get up and move around, get a drink of water, make some noise, and let go of that conversation. Develop a ritual for them to perform after a tough call. Teach them to not let the residue of a negative conversation affect their next telephone call or other interaction.

It's unrealistic to expect young people (as are many call center staff) to deal with high degrees of negativity and then behave as if nothing has happened. These small breaks will reduce staff turnover by keeping your staff happier—and will also help them treat your customers better.

7. Encourage Appropriate Customer Descriptions. In short, don't call your customers names—and we don't mean just to their faces. Most staff are sophisticated enough to know they should never call customers names—directly. However, almost every organization we've worked with allows name-calling to go on behind the customers' backs. These names include "turkey," "idiot," "dimwit," and many others that we don't feel comfortable repeating here. But everybody reading this article knows what they are. Some companies even have special code names for their difficult customers.

Let your staff know this name-calling will not be tolerated. Remind them that your organization doesn't exist without these customers. They are the reason you're in business, and they may be behaving the way they are for some pretty legitimate reasons. Who knows? In their situation, you might be behaving even worse. Perhaps your customers were disconnected three times in a row. Perhaps they've waited 20 minutes when they thought it would be 10, so it's affected their entire day's schedule. We really have no idea why certain people are in the mental state they're displaying to us.

In the TMI office we make it a practice to never call our customers names. The worst thing we will ever say—even after a vicious attack by a customer—is "That was a challenging telephone call." It helps to create a spirit in our office that values our customers—which we do!

If you allow your staff to describe your customers in negative terms, you encourage a mood suggesting we are in a battle with our customers. And the more people call their customers negative names, the worse this battle gets. Furthermore, we believe that customers—at some level—know they're being treated disrespectfully.

8. Pep Talks From Experienced Staff. Your experienced workers can become cheerleaders for your front-line customer response staff. They've "been there, done that." They can relate to specific situations or the stress new hires are dealing with and can share their observations in ways that will be more meaningful, precisely because of their previous hands-on experience.

As a bonus, your experienced staff will have a greater feeling of being needed and valued, a feeling that their tenure means something. Your new staff will be motivated and feel they are part of a larger effort.

9. Allow for "Steam Blowers." Let's face it. Everyone needs to vent from time to time, to blow off some steam. Allow your staff the opportunity to talk about their frustrations, their stress, and the reasons for it.

The key to managing steam blowers is to keep the negativity enclosed, within limits. If everyone is constantly venting, no work will ever get done and staff can easily talk themselves into a negative mood. But periodic interludes for discussions about stress and the pressure of work are a real gift for your staff.

Hold an open forum to discuss customer interactions. Ask each member of your staff to describe situations that were particularly difficult for him or her to handle, particular customer behaviors that were annoying. Ask how others would have managed these kinds of situations or customers. Let your staff share with each other communication strategies that helped them manage difficult interactions. If you manage the negativity, it will be less likely to spread during work hours into the hallways and the lunch room.

10. Share Staff Successes. There isn't a better feeling in the world than when you know you've turned a situation around with a customer or handled a frustration so well it never escalated. Staff need to talk about their wins as well as their frustrations.

This type of sharing can create a strong sense of commitment toward the delivery of quality, as well as allow people the chance to toot their own horns. This feeling can become contagious, especially when staff realize that it's a lot more fun to have these positive experiences rather than negative ones. So, staff become inspired to create more and more of these successes.

If a customer sends a warm thank-you letter, enlarge it and post it in a prominent place. Broadcast it in as many ways as possible. If you get a lot of these letters, start your morning off by reading one of them. If you receive such a letter by fax in the middle of the day, take a moment and read it during the lunch period, if your staff eat together in a lunch room. All too often we only give people bad news, when a little good news goes a long way toward recommitting attitudes.

11. Career Path Planning. Managers need to describe to new hires the genuine parameters of the work they will be doing. Too often, after they've been on the job for only a short time, new employees at call centers will say, "This isn't at all what I expected. No one told me I was going to have to do this." During the hiring interview, let potential staff know the challenges of the position—especially those that will come during the peak-volume periods. Let them also know that your managerial staff will support them in their work.

Recent studies show that many new hires arrive at work with low or at least shaky self-confidence. You can help your new employees by being honest and direct about what they may face, so the challenges don't further undermine their confidence. We're asking mostly young, inexperienced people to do difficult jobs, and we owe it to them to make sure they grow from this test, rather than being demeaned or shaken by it.

Sell the job as a critical business skill that will create great value to them in their career path. If you speak openly and honestly when hiring, your new hires are more likely to stick it out during the tough times and build a long-term career with your organization. Many people take jobs in call centers primarily because they see this job as a way into your company, perhaps the best way to get into another position. Over the years, such a person may be a genuine asset to your organization, and you do not want to lose him or her because you did not describe realistically what that first position would involve.

12. Keep Your Staff as Well Informed as Your Customers. Nothing is more frustrating to customers than to reach someone on the phone who hasn't been informed of a special sale the company is advertising in newspapers or on television. Staff are equally embarrassed to be asked about something that is known to everybody in the world but them.

Teach your staff how to handle situations when the customer asks about something that they don't know about. Provide them with responses they can use, such as "Gosh. That sounds wonderful. Thank you for bringing that to my attention. I'm afraid I don't know too much about that. But I can get the information I need to assist you."

Encourage your staff to never pretend they know about something when they don't. Also, coach your staff to not treat customers with suspicion if they're better informed than the service provider. That sometimes happens—and everyone needs to be gracious in those uncomfortable situations.

13. Manage Your Feedback. Use what you learn in your peak-volume period to ensure that your next high-volume time runs even more smoothly. Gather your staff together and ask them what they learned. You'll learn from them, you'll make them feel more valued, and they'll learn from the process as well. Too many times, we have a wealth of experience we never fully use.

After you've done your analysis, summarize the main learning points into a plan for the next busy season. You can post these on the wall, or bring them out for the next high-demand period, so you continue your improvement.

So, there's your baker's dozen!

Any one of these strategies can help you greatly improve customer service during peak-volume periods. Combining several can create an exponential effect that is truly staggering. The key is to deliberately prepare for what you want to achieve. Maintaining superior customer service during periods of high volume demands advance preparation and continuous nurturing. The results are well worth it in terms of happier staff, satisfied customers, and regenerated managers!

About the Authors

Janelle M. Barlow, Ph.D., is President of TMI, USA, a partner with the Danish-based multinational training and consulting group. She's the author with Claus Moller of

A Complaint Is a Gift: Using Customer Feedback as a Strategic Tool (Berrett-Koehler, 1996). She's also a speaker and seminar leader who has personally experienced the frustrations of managing a company that experiences a high-volume period five months in length! (TMI sells its popular Time Manager product, and thousands of customers order calendar products at year's end.) Visit TMI's Web site at http://www.tmius.com/.

Dianna Maul manages TMI's Pacific Northwest office. Dee Dee brings years of experience in customer service and call centers while working for Nordstrom, Horizon Airlines, and AT&T Wireless Call Center. She was one of the founding directors of Horizon Airlines, where she conceptualized the Horizon Air Training Academy. She honed her ability to handle peak demands while raising five children, including a set of triplets.

17

CREATING THE SOUNDS OF QUALITY: DELIVERING GREAT SERVICE ON THE TELEPHONE

Kathleen Brown

The telephone is a necessity and a convenience for almost any business. But it can also be a handicap. In most communications, we benefit from facial expressions, gestures, and other body language. But, as the author notes, because we're so accustomed to using phones, it's easy to forget how fundamentally handicapped we are on the phone, particularly when dealing with complex and/or stressful matters, such as customer service issues. Here are some ways you can help your customer service personnel compensate.

"What's the matter, Sally? You sounded like you were about to slam down the phone on whoever you were just talking to."

"Oh, I just get so frustrated trying to deal with that class schedule problem at Johnny's school over the phone. I'm going to drive over there tomorrow and talk to them face to face. I've got to see who I'm talking to when I try to solve something this complicated."

Sally has just experienced the single biggest handicap for people trying to communicate over the telephone. That handicap is the lack of visual clues about what's really going on with the other person.

Nonverbal language—visual clues such as facial expressions, gestures, and other body language—provides enormous advantages to most human communications. Unfortunately, your telephone customer service personnel don't have the benefit of those advantages.

Telephone customer service professionals can neither send nor receive the kinds of visual signals that most of us rely upon heavily in our work. Since the use of phones is so common, it's easy to forget how fundamentally handicapped our phone reps are when they try to serve customers on the phone, particularly regarding complex and/or stressful matters.

Training for Excellence in Telephone Customer Service Communication

The lack of specific telephone skills is one of the main reasons why poor telephone customer service is so common and so commonly joked about. The results, of course, are no joke: lost customers, lost profits, and lost reputations—all precious organizational assets that are extremely difficult, often impossible, to recover.

That's why it's so important to give the people who must satisfy your customers over the telephone the skills they need to communicate effectively using this blind medium. They must know how to use every other skill at their disposal to compensate for their lack of visual contact. (Unfortunately, specialized, *skill-building* training is too often overlooked for these employees.)

To achieve consistent excellence, our experience indicates that telephone customer service professionals need to be well trained in at least three broad areas. They need to know the answers to the following questions and be able to act upon that information:

- What do our customers really want?
- What challenges do we face when supporting customers on the telephone?
- What tools and skills can we use to manage those challenges and produce high levels of customer satisfaction?

This article will focus on answering these three questions and illustrating some of the training necessary to help representatives deliver extraordinary telephone customer service.

It's important that the training for these professionals not be just informational; it needs to be behavior-based training, training that develops demonstrable skills—skills that can be seen and heard on the job. That means those employees need to practice each new skill during their training, get feedback on those practices, and practice again until they master the new skill sets. Then, they need to demonstrate the new skills back on the job in the presence of a trainer, who can provide real-time coaching to solidify the skills. As with other professionals, such as musicians, dancers, or athletes, knowing the theory is important, but it's the practice that develops excellence.

Here's a bit more detail about each of the three training areas.

What Do Our Customers Really Want?

The basis for your customers' opinion about the quality of your telephone service goes far beyond the technical aspects of the conversation. Customer surveys indicate that technical knowledge, although important, is not the key factor in overall customer satisfaction. Call center managers often find that the customer support representatives with the highest customer satisfaction scores are the ones who have the interpersonal skills to leave their customers feeling that somebody has listened to them, *heard* them, and given them appropriate care.

U.S. News & World Report, in a recent study, reported that 68% of all customers who quit doing business with an organization do so because of "bad attitudes" on the part of customer service personnel. Your professionals need to know how they can be perceived as having "good attitudes" when they deal with your customers. Fortunately, that's a set of skills that can be taught, learned, and demonstrated.

> *Dan is an account executive with a Silicon Valley consulting firm and, by his own admission, gets pretty frustrated by "computer stuff." Recently, however, he had a surprisingly positive experience with the technical support engineer of the company that provided his new database software. Jeff, the software engineer, walked Dan through a complicated installation process on the phone, step by step, without sounding condescending or impatient (even though he had probably done this a hundred times before). His tone was friendly and interested, he checked for Dan's understanding throughout the process, and when Jeff needed to get additional information, he explained to Dan what was happening and why. Jeff had the necessary technical knowledge and, more important, his skillful management of the interaction left Dan feeling appreciated, understood, and well-supported.*

What Challenges Do We Face?

When they provide customer service on the phone, your representatives encounter several unique challenges that they must overcome, or those challenges will drag the whole operation down. Fortunately, training can help your employees meet each of those challenges.

No Body Language to Read! Voice Is Everything!

The customer's voice is the only clue a telephone representative has about the customer's attitude, and the rep's voice is all the customer has by which to judge him or her. Yet people often are totally unaware of the message their voice is communicating to their customers.

> *Meredith, a customer service rep in a telecommunications company, found out her use of voice was working against her. In one of our training sessions, when Meredith listened to a tape of her telephone work, she was amazed at how fast she was speaking as she answered her calls. The perception created for the customer was that she was distracted and in a hurry. That didn't happen to be true about Meredith, since she is a very dedicated and caring person. But how would the customers know that? That's not how she sounded to them. Through training, Meredith learned how to use her voice to communicate a positive, caring attitude.*

The visual anonymity in a telephone call often results in a caller being much more aggressive and verbally hostile than he or she might be in a face-to-face encounter.

> *Henry, who serves customers for a large medical insurance plan, experiences a high number of irate customers who vent their frustration freely to him over the*

telephone. He knew some of that came from financial and health worries that the customers had, but he took it personally a lot of the time. He's had to learn the skills to keep himself calm in those situations, calm the customer, and manage the interaction toward a positive conclusion.

High-Stress Environment

It's a hot box. Inherent in telephone support is the pressure of the constantly ringing phones and the feeling that there are never enough people to answer the ringing! It takes skill to give 100% of our attention to a customer call when phones are ringing non-stop and calls are stacking up in the queue. Although most departments within organizations are running "leaner and meaner," it seems that call centers are always particularly shorthanded.

Before training, Linda would try to save time in customer calls by making assumptions. Her tendency was to interrupt customers before they were finished talking, and she was perceived as "stepping on toes" far too often. Through her tone of voice and rate of speech, she transferred to her customers the tension and stress she felt from her call load. When she became aware in training of that pattern and its negative impact on her customers, she was very open to learning some new skills that would produce better results—and save time too.

Inadequate Product Knowledge

Because of the competitive rush to get new products into the marketplace faster, call center staff members often have inadequate training (or no training) on a product before it is shipped.

James felt very frustrated in his work because he would receive calls from customers about updates to their software or new releases before he had a chance to learn about them himself. In our telephone skills training program, he learned how to stop inadvertently communicating his frustration over the phone to his customers and, as a result, making his job even harder.

Everybody Calls the Call Center!

Call centers are often toll-free and well-publicized numbers, and customers often will make that call because it's easy to do. When you answer a call center phone, you can't be sure what awaits you!

Barbara found it very difficult to maintain a friendly, helpful tone of voice when customers called her by mistake. They seemed to constantly dial her very overloaded software support hotline to ask questions about hooking up a modem, to solve a billing problem, or to discuss some other issue totally unrelated to software. At first it took her a while to realize that she was the whole company to every customer calling, even those who called her department in error and had to be routed elsewhere for help. When she was taught that her job's big picture was to impress every customer with the quality of her service, she developed a new level of skill—and even started to like her job a bit more!

What Tools and Skills Can We Can Use?

Our goal when conducting training for call center professionals is to develop skills that will meet two needs: 1) to better serve customers and 2) to make doing that job easier for the call center professionals. We've learned that there are three on-the-phone behavioral skill sets that can be developed to make significant progress toward meeting both of these needs:

- *Delivery:* Establishing Customer Perceptions
- *Managing the Interaction:* Listening and Alignment
- *Focusing the Call:* Position/Action/Benefit

The rest of this article will provide an overview of each of these skill sets.

Delivery: Establishing Customer Perceptions

How your telephone customer service personnel sound on the telephone is pivotal to establishing trust and credibility with your customers. Research indicates that, when there's an inconsistency between *what* is said (the words) and *how* it is said (tone of voice), 84% of customers will make their judgment based on vocal quality, as opposed to the actual words. This is where customers make the decisions about "bad attitudes" that were reported in the *U.S. News & World Report* study—the decisions cited by 68% of lost customers as their reason for going elsewhere.

Few people get up in the morning determined to sound cranky on the telephone all day long! Nevertheless, the pressures of answering so many calls, dealing with irate customers, trying to sort out confusing conversations, rarely getting a break—all add up to constant stress. And when people are stressed, it takes a great deal of skill to keep customers from hearing it in their voices.

Learning how we sound to others is the first step in improving the quality of our voice and improving the customers' perception of quality service. Through tape-recorded exercises, we help people understand how they come across on the phone and how they can be more effective.

Breathing and Relaxation

As in singing, proper breathing is the foundation for good telephone vocal quality. Talk about starting by teaching the basics! It might seem unnecessary to suggest to your representatives, "Remember to breathe," until you observe how shallow many people's breathing becomes when they're under job stress, particularly on the phone. Shallow breathing causes the body, including the vocal passages, to become even more tense, and that tension affects their tone. Learning to breathe deeply and naturally, even when under the pressure of serving customers on the phone, works to the benefit of the customers and to the customer service representatives as well.

In coaching sessions with call center professionals, we regularly notice the tendency to carry over the stress from one call to the next. If you've just completed a tough call, give yourself a few seconds to relax and recuperate before answering the next call in the queue.

In training we provide several techniques for quick refreshers on the job. There are a number of extremely useful techniques that can provide a quick, yet powerful break between calls.

We recommend, for example, the simple 3-3-6 Breathing Exercise. Representatives learn to sit up straight and comfortably in their chairs, feet on the floor, arms relaxed with their hands in their laps. They inhale deeply through the nose for a slow count of three, hold their breath for a slow count of three, and then exhale slowly through the mouth for a slow count of six. Repeating this one or two times after a stressful call can make a huge difference. Try it yourself. People are surprised what noticeable, positive results such simple techniques can produce in high-stress situations.

Most of us carry stress in our neck, shoulders, and face—the "Bermuda Triangle of Tension." Deep breathing and movement can help enormously. The key is to recognize tension and stress as they start to build. Know that when representatives are uptight, customers hear it in their tone of voice. If they take better care of themselves on the job, they can take better care of their customers.

To relax, reps should try shoulder rolls, neck rolls, stretches, isometric exercises, and standing and walking around in their office area. One of the best stress relievers, if time allows, is for reps to physically leave the call area. They might walk to the break room for a glass of water or go outside for some sunshine. Also, they should try to avoid eating lunch at their desk. Instead, they should take that opportunity to get out, if possible. When they're refreshed and relaxed, their voices convey that message.

Some big-name, yet high-pressure call centers have a variety of "fun stuff" to play with at various break times during the day: stress balls, Koosh™ balls, wooden foot rollers, Nerf™ balls, yo-yo's. Don't be fooled by those toys: this isn't child's play. By taking a break and having some fun, people in such stressful settings can shake off some of the physical tension and re-energize themselves. Their customers will hear it in their voices. The customer service representatives in the Returned Materials Department of a high-tech company even invested in the services of an on-site massage therapist. She would provide a 15-minute neck and shoulder massage at breaks to help relieve the tension that would otherwise be communicated on the phone to customers.

Vocal Variety

Since the customers on the phone can't see your reps' smiling faces, vocal variety is a tool that they can use to manage your customers' perceptions of their concern and competency. Using taped telephone conversations and individualized coaching, we train telephone professionals how to improve their use of vocal variety along several dimensions—pitch, volume, articulation, pausing, and body language.

Pitch. Monotone talk is boring, yes, but it also may be perceived as a lack of concern or attentiveness. We help participants in our training to cultivate a variety in pitch, with high and low tones. The deeper tones convey a sense of confidence. High tones add enthusiasm, warmth, and friendliness.

Does a rep's voice sound a little too high? This may be perceived as too youthful, hesitant, or lacking knowledge.

Beware of a tendency to end non-question sentences with a question mark (called "upspeak"). This can sound too young, tentative, unsure. Even if you're unsure of an answer, you want the customer to feel he or she is in good hands. Make sure your voice sounds confident as you say, "I'll check on that for you."

Rate. Have you ever been on the phone with someone who spoke exceptionally fast? It probably wasn't a very comfortable conversation; the speed probably made you feel rushed. Unfortunately, a common tendency when we have other calls waiting is to hurry through each call. That, of course, creates more problems than it solves. Rushed calls do not build trust or confidence, and they often create misunderstandings that take even more time to clear up.

> *Paula was aware that she spoke very rapidly, but she didn't think it was a problem until our training. She's a very high-energy person who does everything quickly. When she listened to a tape of her voice as she gave technical instructions to a customer on how to reboot a system, she was surprised at how difficult it was to follow the steps. She recognized that a customer, especially one with limited technical knowledge, would have been lost and annoyed.*

Speaking too slowly doesn't work well either. The customer may perceive a lack of dedication or enthusiasm. Even worse, the customer may feel you're being condescending. In group discussions of "what constitutes poor customer service," one of the pet peeves is having someone "talk down" to us. Talking too slowly can give customers that impression.

Volume. Over the telephone, volume (high or low) is not as great a concern as it can be in face-to-face communications, but it's still important. Telephones amplify the voice, but people need to speak directly into the mouthpiece. If a person speaks too softly, the perception can be that he or she lacks confidence. On the other hand, too loud a voice can be overbearing. It may also affect other workers. Since many call centers are open areas, with customer service professionals seated in cubicles, voices that are too strong may interfere with other reps' calls.

Articulation. People need practice pronouncing their consonants and being careful not to drop word endings, as in "How ya doin'?" Mumbling and running words together creates the perception of being unconcerned and/or uninformed. Have you noticed how clearly people tend to pronounce each word when they're speaking with a friend or family member whom they like but who's a little hard of hearing? In our training, we help people pronounce their words clearly and precisely in a natural way.

Pausing. In our everyday speech patterns, many people have developed the poor communications habit of filling in all of their "air space." When they're thinking or searching for the right piece of information, they plug in what are commonly called "filler words"—"You know what I mean," "uh, um," "you know," "well," "basically," "like" . . . You've heard these and more. Why do we use such fillers? We're thinking or we're afraid to stop talking for a moment. What value do these words add? Not much—and they can be distracting, even annoying for our customers.

When we tape voices in our training, the biggest "Wow!" often comes to people as they realize how many common filler words are muddying up their conversation. Most of us don't even hear those useless words slip out as we speak. The second "Ah ha!" comes when people realize how valuable a pause (just plain silence) of two to three seconds can be in place of the filler word.

Without filler words, people speak more directly and with greater clarity and impact; they sound more knowledgeable and confident. The pauses give them a chance to think of what they want to say next. A pause also gives your phone customers a chance to digest what you've told them, which is especially important when you're giving instructions to them on how to correct a problem.

Remember the example of Paula, who spoke very rapidly? When she worked with pausing, she found that she could still keep her high energy and enthusiasm, which the customers loved. When she simply added a pause at the end of her sentences, her customers were able to follow her directions without asking her to repeat steps. It saved time and frustration for the customers—and for Paula.

Body Language. Pacific Bell, for years, has trained telephone professionals to "smile while you dial." One of the challenges we identified earlier in this article is our inability to see our customers and the fact that they can't see us. That does not mean, however, that our body language is not important. Have you noticed what happens to your voice when you're tired and slumping in the chair? Notice also what happens negatively to voice quality when you tilt your head to hold a traditional handset.

When you're tense, your voice will tend to be tense. If you're relaxed, your voice will also be relaxed. People can better manage their voice quality by keeping their posture relaxed and balanced.

Language

Certain phrasings and word choices dramatically affect a customer's perception of the quality of service they receive. We sometimes pick words and phrases out of habit, without actually recognizing the impact those words may have on the listener. Here are some of the language choice techniques we believe important to teach to telephone customer service professionals.

Assume, Don't Ask. Whenever possible, we suggest that reps assume permission rather than ask for it. For example, when Sarah says, "I need to ask you a few questions to determine the exact nature of the problem," she sounds confident and self-assured. If the sentence is turned into a question—"Is it OK if I ask you a few questions to determine the nature of the problem?"—Sarah begins to sound a little tentative or unsure. She may even sound a little phony to the customer, who knows she's going to ask the questions no matter what.

We often ask permission because we think it sounds polite, but then we go ahead and do whatever we've asked without waiting for the customer's reply. If you're really requesting permission, such as "May I put you on hold?," then for goodness sakes, wait until the customer replies. Don't just push the hold button! (How maddening for the customer.) Most will say, "OK," but be prepared for some customers to say, "No, it's not OK!" In that case, the representative will need to take care of that customer right away. If there's no choice, say something like, "I must put you on hold for a moment, but I will return. Please do not hang up because I don't want you to lose your place in line."

If you need to put someone on hold to gather additional information, try this: "I'll need to put you on hold for about 30 seconds while I access this code in my database" or "I'll need to search for that information for a couple of minutes. Would you like to hold, or would you like me to call you back?"

Avoid Tentative Language. Tentative language creeps in because we think it sounds polite or because we truly aren't sure of an answer. The problem with what I call "mushy" words is that the customer then perceives that we're unsure. This does not inspire customer confidence!

Instead of:	"I might be able to get that information possibly this afternoon."
Try:	"I'll call you by 4 this afternoon with that information."
Instead of:	"Do you think it's possible for you to answer a few questions?"
Try:	"I need to ask you just a few questions."

Avoid Negatives. It's amazing the difference this one little change can make in managing a customer's perception of the quality of service he or she receives. There are many times when we need to tell a customer what may seem like "negative" information. Reframe the sentence in a positive way and create a different perception. For example . . .

Instead of:	"I can't get back to you until Friday."
Try:	"I will give you a call Friday morning with that information."
Instead of:	"I won't be able to get in touch with engineering until late today."
Try:	"I'll speak with engineering this afternoon and give you a call tomorrow."

Avoid Jargon. When we talk about the challenges of providing customer service on the telephone, one of the issues that sometimes comes up is how to deal with people who speak a different language. We generally think of a different language as perhaps being German, French, Spanish, Mandarin, or Japanese. There is yet another type of "foreign tongue," however—the jargon you use within your own organization.

Buzz words and "in-group" phrases that you use among colleagues may sound completely foreign to customers. If you must use jargon, make sure you define each term for the customer the first time you use it. Don't assume the customer will know what you're talking about. Without a definition, it can be confusing. Also, some customers may conclude that you're using jargon to put them down in some way. That's obviously not a perception you want to encourage.

Avoid Killer Phrases. There are certain phrases that are guaranteed to put a customer over the edge. They slip out when we aren't paying attention or when we lose track of the fact that we *are* the company to this customer at this moment. Avoid phases such as these like the plague:

- ○ "It's not my job."
- ○ "You must be mistaken."
- ○ "That's so simple; I can't see how you could have missed that."

Be careful also with what you say about other departments within your organization. Sometimes a customer service representative will try to create an alliance with the customer, such as this representative in a major brokerage, by saying something that sounds like:

"Oh, you know those salespeople. They'll do anything to get a new account. Then we have to take care of all the problems. But you've got the right person now! I'll help you."

This customer service person thought he was being reassuring by telling the customer he was there to help. But what did he really do? He shot the organization in the foot by criticizing another department and undermining the customer's confidence in it! Representatives need to see the bigger picture and represent the *whole* company by saying something like this instead:

"We have many excellent products on the market. The salespeople really do a great job of matching products to customer needs. I'm sorry you're having a problem, and we'll work together to make sure it gets resolved."

Managing the Interaction

Listen

To effectively manage the interaction, an important communication skill your representatives must master is listening. Then they can move to use the information they acquire to quickly solve the problem in a mutually beneficial manner.

Listening is not just waiting for a split second of silence so the "listener" can interject his or her opinion into the conversation. Listening really means gathering information, and that's critically important when you're trying to solve customer problems.

There are three skills that can help people dramatically improve the quality of their listening: focus, explore, and reflect.

Focus. Representatives must give the customer their undivided attention. They need to work at eliminating distractions. They might turn away from the computer for a moment if it's distracting them, stop the multi-tasking (trying to do two things at once), and/or physically change their position. Some people find it helpful to take notes. If something distracts them and they miss a part of the conversation, they should stop, then let the customer know they missed something and ask him or her to repeat the information. They should not assume they can figure it out from context or by making an assumption. Rather, they need to hang on to every word like a super detective. They should not assume they know what's coming next, even if they think they've heard this problem a hundred times before.

Explore. You're probably familiar with the concept of open-ended and closed-ended questions. In the Explore step of listening, representatives should ask the appropriate type of questions to uncover information. If a caller is confused or unsure, the rep may need to use closed questions that require a yes/no response to guide the customer through a series of steps. If reps need more data, they should ask open-ended questions: what? when? where? why? who? Then they should be interested—or at least act interested. They'll learn (often to their surprise) a great deal from their questions that can suggest the appropriate action.

Reflect. Reflecting means that the rep summarizes or paraphrases back to the customer what he or she has heard, for verification. It does *not* mean parroting back word for word, nor does it mean offering *an* opinion. It's giving the speaker the benefit of hearing from the rep, in the rep's words, what he or she believed to hear. The speaker's response to those reflections gives the rep the benefit of being sure he or she heard the customer correctly. If not, the representative can ask for further clarification. For example . . .

> *"I want to check my understanding of what you've said. You looked into all the shipping crates and part number 397 seemed to be missing. There was a part there, however, that looked like the 397 drawing, but it didn't have a number. You installed that part and that's when the problem began. Am I correct so far?"*

When we work with this skill in a training setting, many participants find that, instead of reflecting, they're actually offering solutions—and far too early. To really please customers, check to make sure you understand before you offer solutions or advice. Assuming you know what the problem is and giving the customer the wrong solution, or missing their point entirely, does not result in customer delight!

Align

As you do your logical detective work to get the problem well-defined, don't forget that a feeling human being is on the other end of the line. Customers with problems often feel alone and at the mercy of *your system*. Some can stay fairly rational about it all, but others get confused, frustrated, and/or angry.

In the customer's perception, it's *your company's* product or service that's at the root of his or her problem. So representatives need to accept responsibility! Then they should align themselves with resolving the customer's concerns. They should let the customer know they're on the same team and they'll be working together to get at a solution. Here are three examples:

○ "I know how difficult it can be to have a system down for so long. Your business is important to us and I'm as anxious as you are to get this fixed."

○ "You have helped me understand the problem, and I think we can get to a solution quickly. Thanks for such a clear description of the situation."

○ "I'm going to do everything I can to get you out of this spot and up and running again. I really sorry we've put you in this situation."

Alignment goes a step beyond empathy. It communicates that the company understands and cares about the customer's concern or problem *and* you will work with them to resolve this. It says: "When you win, Mr. or Ms. Customer, I win."

In the concept of alignment lies the secret of providing consistently excellent customer service on the telephone. When people really care about helping others, it comes through even over the phone. Customers appreciate such caring as a rare gift in this rushed world of "customer care" slogans with little substance.

Focusing the Call: Position/Action/Benefit

Learning how to use Position/Action/Benefit (P/A/B) statements is often a highlight of telephone customer service training for the participants. This simple technique can keep the conversation moving in the right direction and keep the customer engaged, responsive, and feeling heard.

Here's the P/A/B model that we teach, with a few examples.

Position: Representatives should state their attitude, opinion, feeling, or belief about the issue.
"I want to resolve this problem for you as soon as possible."
"You are a very important customer to us."
"Our product is the best on the market."

Action: Representatives should tell the customer what they need the customer to do or what the company will do for the customer. Include a time frame if at all possible.
"I will call you Friday before noon with that information."
"Please go to the 'Tools' pull-down menu and select the 'Format' option."
"I'll need you to answer a couple of questions about your machine."

Benefit: What's in it for me? The old WIIFM. Let the customer know the advantage *to him or her* of the action plan you've just proposed.
"With that information, we can get your system back up."
"It will save you a great deal of time."
"We'll be able to access the information in your database."

P/A/B statements can help to set the customer's expectations and build rapport right from the start. They also are useful in the middle of a long call, if the rep or the customer gets a bit lost or if a new issue comes up. Finally, they're a powerfully positive way to wrap up a call. They help ensure that you and the customer are in agreement; not only is the problem being resolved, but you both have a clear understanding of any other needs or next steps.

Opening a Call

Getting off to a good start helps greatly. The P/A/B statement is a sound bridge between your greeting and the main body of the call, and it's a good way to build rapport.

While working with the customer service representatives at a major telecommunications company, we heard a typical greeting:

"Good morning, this is Customer Service. Is this a new or existing location?"

While this is a quick, efficient greeting, when we listened to a tape of the conversation, the class agreed that a customer might perceive a lack of sincere concern and a sense that his or her call was not too important—that the customer service representative was in a rush. We practiced a P/A/B statement as a tool to establish rapport before asking the customer our questions:

"Good morning, Customer Service. How may I help you?"

When the customer responds with, "My system is down," the new P/A/B statement was:

"We need to get that one solved right away! (Position) I'll need to ask you a few questions (Action) so that I can direct your call immediately to the right technician." (Benefit.)

It takes just a few seconds to set a clear expectation for the customer and to give him or her the sense that this call is important to you.

Closing a Call

It's important to close a call solidly, leaving the customer with a sense of completion. The P/A/B model can be useful here as well:

Position:	*"I'm very glad that we were able to resolve the problem.*
Action:	*"I'll overnight that software to you today.*
Benefit:	*"You'll be able to install it first thing tomorrow morning, and you'll be up and running!"*

Voice Mail/E-Mail

Many of my customers tell me that a good part of their call volume is returning customer calls, so they often have to leave voice mail messages. Some customer service representatives also communicate via e-mail. As you probably have experienced, many voice mails and e-mails are unorganized, much too long, and difficult to follow.

A good way to practice the P/A/B process is to formulate in your mind, or on Post-it notes, your P/A/B statement anytime you need to do a call back to a customer. If you get their voice mail, you can use your P/A/B to leave a focused, concise message. If you get a real live person, you can use it to set expectations for the call.

Recently, I needed to contact a client on the East Coast regarding the details of a customer service training I was preparing to do for them. After a rough day with a lot of hassles, I called late from California and, of course, got a voice mail. I started my conversation with,

> *"Oh, gosh, that's right—you are gone for the day. Let's see, this is Kathleen. Uh, I need to talk to you tomorrow, if you could call me. . . . Uh, let's see. . . ."*

Fortunately, the voice mail system had a delete button! I used it, then I reframed my message with a Position/Action/Benefit:

Position:	*"Hi, this is Kathleen. It's important that we talk live sometime tomorrow morning.*
Action:	*"Please call me at this number anytime between 9 and 12 noon your time, or have someone leave me a time when I can reach you.*
Benefit:	*"We'll be able to agree on the final details for next week's training in time to have a smooth and well-customized program for your people."*

The same model is useful in focusing an e-mail communication. At the beginning of your message, let the customer know your position on the issue, what you will be asking of them or doing for them, and what the ultimate benefit will be for them. People are much more likely to read a lengthy e-mail message if they know where it's headed and the payoff for them.

Putting It All Together

The information and skills overviewed in this article can improve your telephone customer service meaningfully and measurably. It's not just a matter of knowing *what* to do, however; it's knowing *how* to do it and doing it consistently under pressure! That's why the training for your key customer contact professionals needs to be based on behavior and centered on *practice, practice, practice.*

In my work with telephone customer service professionals, I've been struck by their dedication to quality and their willingness to work hard to deliver quality for their customers and for their own organizations. To capitalize on that willingness and effort, however, they need to acquire the tools and skills to succeed. Otherwise, willingness eventually turns to cynicism and effort turns to just getting by. Your organization, your customers, and your telephone customer service professionals deserve better than that.

About the Author

Kathleen Brown is Senior Training Consultant with Mandel Communications in Soquel, California. For the past 10 years, she has trained thousands of people in communicating more effectively and providing the best in customer service. She's worked with corporations such as Bank of America, Xerox, National Semiconductor, Nikon, and AirTouch Cellular.

18

Problem-Solving Tips for Telephone Representatives

Donna Hall

The people who handle your telephones are ambassadors for your company, providing information and generating good will. Are they making the best impression and maximizing on opportunities? That largely depends on the managers who train, monitor, and coach them so they can properly represent your company. This article provides guidance for managers who care about their ambassadors—and about making a good impression for the company.

This article reviews some techniques that managers can use to help improve the skills of their telephone representatives. The main objective of telephone representatives is to communicate and to serve customers—to be ambassadors for your company, if you will. They generate good will and provide information to your visitors and/or customers. They greet your customers by answering telephone inquiries, they lead your customers on company tours by describing your products and services, and they sell your customers on your company by taking orders for those products and services.

Managing Customer Service

My aim is to provide telephone call center managers with some helpful insights into training and motivating their employees to handle their jobs more effectively, to be better ambassadors. It goes without saying that providing service to a wide variety of individuals can be challenging at times. It's the job of telephone representatives to positively represent their company. They are expected to consistently be courteous, knowledgeable, and efficient.

Who helps train them and ensure that they're doing this on a regular basis? Management, that's who. Since management implements the procedures that the telephone representatives will be following, it's also the manager who will be monitoring and coaching those reps on a regular schedule. I'm a firm believer in training employees to become an effective and self-directed team. And, with the proper training and leadership, you too can build a *team* that is self-confident and self-assured.

This allows their creative minds to work in synch with the processes and procedures you've established.

Silence Is Golden

The first rule of thumb is to emphasize the importance and the art of good listening skills. This is one of the best skills customer service telephone representatives can have. When I was managing a large telephone customer service call center, I found out rather quickly that listening does *not* come easily to many customer service reps. Most reps usually want to get their point across as quickly as possible. This is normal and natural, yet it can get in the way of really hearing what's on the customer's mind. So, just how do you discourage this natural behavior and get your telephone reps to understand that they should be patient and listen as the customer expresses his or her point of view?

Trust me: you can get your employees to understand that saying less and listening more is actually better! You can help them learn that pausing and listening to the customer actually helps them to gain control. Not only does it help eliminate repetition, but it also helps reduce the chances of creating a combative situation with the customer. Customers want and need to be heard. The job of a telephone representative is to listen.

But how does good listening allow the rep to gain control of the situation? By not losing the chance to establish good communication. As the old saying goes, "We can all sing together, but we can't all talk together!" When two people try to talk at the same time, both are likely to miss something. So, when emphasizing the importance of good listening skills with your employees, remind them that, if they try to speak at the same time as the customer, communication will suffer, and it will take more time and energy to remedy the situation.

I'm sure some of you are saying, "My reps are good listeners." But be honest. Haven't you ever talked with a customer, heard a few words, and immediately believed you knew exactly where the customer was going—only to be surprised when the call took a turn you didn't anticipate? It's happened to me. When it did, the customer was not very pleased that my mind-reading skills were not working so well that day. So, stress to your telephone representatives that it's best for them to wait for the customer to complete his or her thought before they attempt to respond.

Interrogatives, not Interrogation

In dealing with customers, think of reps as "ambassadors" who are taking your customers on a metaphorical "guided tour" of your company. Are the "visitors" enjoying all that your company has to offer? For your telephone reps to show your customers what a wonderful company they're dealing with, they must realize how very important it is to find out what the customer really wants. Therefore, it's essential that telephone representatives understand how to probe and ask questions to obtain the information needed to better help the customer.

Telephone representatives will tell you that each call is different. That's true, of course. But they can all be handled with the same kind, courteous, and helpful attitude. I mention these characteristics now because, if your reps remain focused and friendly, and they seek permission from the customer to ask questions, it will be easier for them to obtain the information they need from the customer to best handle the problem or query. So representatives should remember to courteously probe customers' concerns and listen to the responses. In that way, the representative is more likely to solve the problem on the first call, saving the company and the customer time and grief.

How May I Help You?

Make sure that your telephone representatives are fully prepared to answer just about any type of question that might come up. This is extremely important. Remember: they are your ambassadors—the representatives of your company.

When a consumer encounters an ill-informed representative, the results can be time-consuming at best—and perhaps even disastrous. Experience has taught me that a customer's encounter with other customer service departments can determine the level of service that he or she expects from the next contact with the company.

If the first representative was not helpful or did not meet the customer's expectations, this experience will play a pivotal role in how the customer expects to be treated overall by your telephone representatives. It will influence whether this individual will continue to do business with your company.

On the other hand, if your reps are prepared to provide the type of service your customers expect, they can easily impress customers who have had bad experiences, either with reps from your company or with other companies. A well-trained representative will help heighten the expectations of the caller who needs assistance. Consumers will appreciate the time that the well-trained representative will invest in taking care of their concerns. With so many companies competing with their products and services, the companies that treat their customers the best have a significant competitive edge.

There are a wide variety of situations that customer service representatives may encounter—situations that require proper and thorough training. If your reps are not trained to fully address a multitude of concerns and personalities on a daily basis, you're working with a ticking time bomb. Any complication can hinder your efforts to provide the type of service that will keep your customers satisfied.

The Benefits of Confidence

Good training enables your reps to treat your customers better. But there's a substantial bonus that I should mention here. When you properly train your staff to work with customers, they project confidence and are less likely to view customer contacts as problems. In other words, they'll view these encounters as opportunities to serve and build better relationships between the company and its customers. This results in happier customers and happier reps.

While an untrained phone rep may enjoy the job initially, the honeymoon will end soon. Before you know it, you'll have a fearful, unenthusiastic, and resentful representative, someone who will most likely expect the majority of customer contacts to be frustrating and problematic—and whose attitude might be contagious. Then what kind of ambassadors would be representing your company?

With thorough training and preparation, your phone reps are less likely to have problems with customers and are more likely to enjoy their jobs. Good training helps create a confident telephone rep who will not feel intimidated in a situation that might baffle a less informed rep. Knowing the correct steps and procedures for managing difficult situations helps your employees use their creativity in resolving possible problem situations. That's self-management in progress: oh, how I do love that!

An Example of Outstanding Customer Service

Once, during a seminar I was conducting, there was a trainee who was extremely confident in expressing her opinions. My initial reaction was that she was obviously very knowledgeable on current issues and events. As the seminar progressed, I found out quite a bit about this trainee. She seemed to stay focused and interested, even into day three of training. She sparked my interest, and I wanted to know what she was like on her job. (During the seminar, I refrained from talking to her about it, because I'm careful not to show any favoritism for any of my workshop participants.)

When we approached the question-and-answer phase of the workshop, I was looking forward to seeing how, or if, she would participate. Well, I started out asking fact-based questions on information that had been covered earlier. Without any hesitation, her hand would shoot up at every one of my questions. I tried to be fair and give all participants an opportunity to answer the questions. But, I have to tell you, each of her answers was correct. Was she superhuman when it came to customer service?

During a role-playing exercise, I listened to her play the role of the customer. I noticed that she was courteous but firm in her demands. She was able to persuade others into giving her what she wanted.

Now, when the group reversed roles and she was the customer service representative, she worked her magic again. Her role-playing customer was a man who was trying to "stick to his guns." He demanded that his tractor be fixed by the day's end. But she succeeded in providing him another option—and he left satisfied with the agreement that had been made. She was charming, courteous, confident, and willing to help.

After the seminar, I asked her to join me for a cup of coffee to find out more about her. I learned that she had been working in customer service for about six years and she really loved it. As she put it, "I never thought this type of work would be good for me, but I have been trained to be customer-focused." That investment was surely paying off for her company. She was a perfect ambassador.

The moral of this story: With the right people, training, and company orientation toward serving customers, you too can have representatives who are consistently satisfying customers and building win-win relationships with them.

The Importance of a Positive Attitude

Another point that you need to discuss with your telephone representatives is their voices. After all, in their contact with your customers, your reps' voices are as important as the telephone system. The following are the major aspects of voice and a few basic suggestions:

- ○ **Speed.** Remind your reps to speak slowly, especially when giving names and numbers or when speaking with people who are having problems understanding. They should also pause occasionally, to allow the customer time to process the information and to reply.
- ○ **Quality.** Stress the importance of proper pronunciation and careful enunciation. We often tend to be lazy with our language, but that forces others to ask us to repeat or they simply guess at what we mean. That's sloppy communication.
- ○ **Intonation.** Reps should speak with natural inflections, that is, they should emphasize key words, and their voices should fall when ending a statement or rise when asking a question. Keeping the voice alive may be difficult when a rep is tired, but every call should be treated as carefully as if it were the only call—which it is for that customer.
- ○ **Tone.** Emphasize that your reps should smile through their voices. This helps convey a positive message, communicating that your company is ready to serve the customer.

Do Procedures Really Help?

Yes! Procedures provide consistency, direction, and guidelines that can help simplify the task of providing quality customer satisfaction. Good procedures allow your telephone staff to quickly identify the guidelines that they should follow. How should they handle the task? Why should they do it? When do they do it? Who should do it? Well-outlined procedures will cover all of these things.

As a manager, it's your job to help guide your telephone reps through the maze of activities in which they will routinely be engaged. You can do that by creating procedures that are logical, simple, complete, and flexible.

For example, should you answer the telephone by the third ring every time? Some would say that it doesn't matter. Others would say no, not as long as you apologize for allowing it to ring so long before picking it up—especially if it rang at least 15 times or more.

I disagree with both of these answers. You should absolutely require that your telephone personnel answer calls in a timely and friendly manner. I'm sure you would agree that it's very frustrating and unsettling when we make a call and then wait while the phone rings and rings and rings. Is that an experience you want for your customers? Imagine them sitting there, wondering if anyone is ever going to pick up, if anyone cares. In fact, they will begin to wonder why they are sitting there listening to it ring, why they care about getting through to you. With every ring, their mood gets worse. With every ring, you risk losing those customers. Sounds bad, doesn't it? I can't imagine wanting to be the person who finally has to deal with this individual, can you? (Of course, that person may be one of your competitors, called in frustration.)

If you're open for business, then someone should be available to pick up the phone and be ready to do business. If you let the phones ring, that irritating noise sends the message that you don't care enough about your customers. Your callers get that message—and so do your competitors: it's the sound of opportunity knocking.

That is just one example of the need for procedures. If you establish that every call must be answered by the third ring, your reps know what's expected of them, and you serve your customers better. It's just that simple—and it makes more sense than leaving such matters up to individual preferences, moods, or whatever.

Getting your staff to do what it takes efficiently and effectively requires that you pay close attention to the procedures you're requiring them to follow. Generally, the simpler they are, the better. The procedures should provide solutions, not cause problems. Simplifying your procedures can help eliminate difficulties that can occur when handling telephone complaints or inquiries. If you make the procedures too complex, you can cause your reps unnecessary frustration, which might lead them to abandon the procedures altogether. If this occurs, your reps may possibly make mistakes that will take a lot of time and effort to correct.

Now, after stressing the need for procedures, let's not forget about being flexible in your processes. I highly recommend that you allow for some leeway within the procedures, so your employees can use some sensible discretion. Such decisions will be based on the individual and unique situations that will occur in your workplace. A rigid and inflexible system of procedures will frustrate and anger both employees and customers. After all, what's more important to you—your procedures or your customers?

Help your reps by letting them know that your goal, as a manager, is to allow them to provide superior service and that, when the occasion calls for it, they may have to go beyond the normal procedures to better serve the customer. In fact, encourage them to do so in these cases. This will help build trust and loyalty between management and employees. It will also show your commitment to service to your customers.

Avoiding Identity Problems

Do your telephone reps identify themselves, every time? They should. The job of an ambassador begins with the first impression. Your reps should greet each customer with a pleasant smile in the voice and a welcoming, "Good morning, this is Jane Doe. How may I help you?" This will help the caller relax and feel confident and ready to state his or her reason for calling, with respect and an attitude open to what your rep might say.

As I stressed above, listening is essential to customer service. Help your phone reps develop their listening skills. Hearing it right the first time can help reduce the possibility of a problem down the road. Teach your employees to get all the necessary information that will help you better serve the customer. Remember: it's easier to prevent problems than to solve them. When reps can listen to the customer and then relay the customer's wishes or concerns, your company makes fewer mistakes and your customers have greater confidence that you care about serving them.

Some communication problems are inevitable. So, you want to train your staff to clarify any possible confusion promptly. This allows your reps to be more effective and efficient. It also lets your customers know that you fully understand their concerns and you'll work to resolve the problems.

Advising your staff on proper telephone etiquette is very necessary. The reps should know that it's appropriate to ask their customers to please wait when it's necessary to leave the line to obtain more information. They should always give the customer an opportunity to decide if he or she wants to wait while they step away for any reason. Insist that your reps tell the customer why they need to step away from the phone and to estimate how long they expect to take. If the customer agrees to wait, they may then ask the customer to hold. When they come back to the phone, they need only explain the situation. Your reps should offer to call back, if the customer does not wish to hold any longer. However, in that case, they should offer the customer an expected call-back time. Most customers will have no problem with this. After all, it's better to wait a short time for the correct information than to get wrong or evasive answers immediately.

Of course, your reps must honor their commitments. They must remember to do what they say they will do. Allowing representatives to follow through on commitments made to the customer can help eliminate problems in the future.

If policies prevent a rep from following through on a problem from beginning to end, it can be disastrous. What can be worse than to have a rep take an irate call, then offer the caller a solution, only to find that, due to a lack of follow-up, the customer fails to get what was promised? What credibility does the rep have then with the customer? *None.* The customer certainly does not trust the company—and for good reason. Maybe the customer blames the rep. Maybe the customer blames the system. But whatever the source of the problem, he or she is disappointed, at the very least. And that's not good customer service.

Now, if the rep had the authority or flexibility to follow up on what he or she committed to, this problem would be less likely to occur. By allowing your reps to commit to your customers, you give your customers more options and show them how much you value their time and business. Spare them the need to make another call, to find out what is going on. Untie your telephone reps' hands so they can do the job right. Your ambassadors need to be free to serve your customers.

Nothing Teaches Better Than a Good Example

Don't be afraid to show your staff that you understand what it's like to be on the front line. I've seen many a rep's eyes light up with excitement when they see the "magic" that their managers can work with challenging customers.

I don't recommend that you do their jobs for them. But if one of your reps is struggling to handle a problem, I urge you not to force him or her to pull through it alone. We learn through experience, but often what we learn through failure is frustration and resentment. Your reps should feel free to ask you to intervene—and you should be ready and willing to show them how to handle the problems.

Many managers have heard the horror stories of working in environments where assisting the rep is considered a no-no. "Leave them alone, they can handle it. They have to learn from it!" Yikes!! Who actually learns anything from being frightened and frustrated to the point that they're no longer able to think straight?

The only thing that something like that might teach someone is "Uh-oh! I've got to get my résumé out there—and *fast*!!!"

As managers, you should work and communicate with your employees. If need be, help them on the follow-up commitments that they have made. Set the example. Instill in them this aspect of service. It's extremely important.

Monitoring

After you've designed and implemented the procedures that will help your staff provide the kind of service that customers will expect and rave about, the next step is to ensure that this exceptional service continues. How can you ensure that your staff is always providing an optimum level of service? Monitoring.

This vital process, often overlooked, is crucial to your company's success. You may be asking yourself, "Why?" After all, most people don't feel comfortable monitoring others. But the reason is simple. If your company normally provides exceptional service, this shows your obvious commitment to quality. Congratulations! Yet if you develop a pattern of providing less than the desired/expected level of service, you will definitely have serious problems. And a bad pattern can develop gradually, almost imperceptibly.

Diligently monitor your employees' interactions with customers, to determine if they're following procedures and meeting both your company's and your customers' expectations. Also, you must assess your standards of service, to ensure that procedures are not only followed properly, but are adequate to allow you to meet your customers' expectations. Monitoring should go both ways, covering both people and procedures.

Remember to be consistent with your staff. Nothing can discourage and burn out a phone rep more than not knowing what to expect from management from day to day. Before you begin to monitor, make certain that the employees know exactly what's expected of them. One of the main benefits of monitoring is that it's a teaching tool for both you and your employees. It's extremely important that monitoring not be perceived as a form of reward or punishment, but for what it is—a way to ensure the best possible customer service.

With the proper support and guidance from you, your reps will not fear or run from the next challenging situation. In fact, they may well hope that this is a time when you'll be monitoring their activity, so they can show you how skillful they've become.

Identify where you are, in terms of procedures, and where you can and want to go. If your employees are meeting the standards you've put in place, then it may be time to consider raising that level a little higher. It's never a bad idea to look ahead and raise your service perception and standards.

One last word on monitoring: you're not the only one. That's right: your employees are monitoring you. As with any relationship, you as the manager have to lead your reps by example. Practice what you preach. Show them how it's done. Show them how you appreciate your customers. Not only will they respect you, but they'll look forward to the opportunity to imitate your expertise. Be proud to show them why you're the manager of the customer service department.

When you have a group of well-informed and thoroughly trained individuals, who clearly understand what good customer service means to you and who can count on your support and direction, you've created a good team. Your employees will have no problem using their creativity and their ability to think on their feet, in dealing with situations that might baffle other phone reps.

Gaining trust and loyalty from your service staff is the key to getting the most from them. Being prepared to handle customer interactions effectively will minimize possible problems. But, should problems arise, you can feel confident that your reps will be able to resolve them. Then you can be proud of having ambassadors to properly represent your company.

About the Author

Donna Hall earned a degree in medical technology from Trinity College in Washington, D.C. She began her career working in customer service at the Children's National Hospital Medical Center. Working very closely with the emergency room staff and patients, she realized she had an ability for calming and diffusing feelings in chaotic and stressful situations. After working for *The Washington Post* and *The Wall Street Journal,* Donna joined *USA Today* as it was being launched as a recruitment customer service/sales representative, where she later created a department to handle all outbound serve communications. In 1993, she started her own company, The Right Answer, Inc. (Web site: http://www.therightanswer.com). She works with companies to develop and improve their service operations and publishes a monthly newsletter for The Right Answer Society, which she founded.

19

Customer-Sensitive Automated Response Systems

Marlene Yanovsky

Automated Response Systems have been a blessing and a curse for businesses. There are considerable advantages—but not if customers react negatively, finding them difficult to use or just preferring a human contact. This article explains how to make the most of technology, based on research findings, and how to better serve your customers.

When many companies first introduced Automated Response Systems (ARS),[1] they met with two types of reaction from consumers. Some were excited and intrigued by the idea of participating in the delivery of their own service. Others were dissatisfied and irritated, because they felt that this impersonal intervention would prevent them from reaching a live representative. Much of this negative response can be attributed to three major factors:

- A lack of understanding of the evolving definition of service and the support role of the call center of the future,
- Little knowledge of the critical success factors in the design and implementation of ARS, and
- An absence of good data and experience to allow companies to understand the impact of ARS on workload and customer satisfaction.

Acceptance of ARS has increased as companies have developed strategies to deal with these factors. Yet, both the positive and negative feelings about ARS may still be valid today, depending on the purpose and design of the application.

To understand how to develop ARS that work, we'll explore the evolving defini-

---

1. Automated Response Systems (ARS) is used as a generic reference to Automated Response Unit (ARU), Voice Response Unit (VRU), Interactive Voice Response (IVR), and other systems that perform an automated or interactive routing function or transaction processing function, or that operate in response to speech recognition.

tion of service and the role of the call center, as well as the reasons for installing ARS applications, successful and unsuccessful uses, and the steps and criteria that should be considered in the design of a proposed application.

Information to support the findings and recommendations is based on the results of the 1995 and 1996 benchmarking surveys on Automated Response System technology conducted by Technical Assistance Research Programs (TARP). The studies were conducted in North America, Australia, and New Zealand; they represent the responses of 92 companies that primarily serve national or international markets and report an average of approximately one million calls per month into the ARS.

The Evolving Definition of Service and the Need to Use High Tech to Create High Touch

The definition of service has changed. It used to be that personal service meant that you always spoke to the same person every time you called. That person knew your personal history, knew your family, your cat, your kids, and your dog. It was your warm social experience of the day and he or she always promised to check on your question or problem and get back to you.

Today service has become a fast in-and-out experience. You can talk to someone any time you need to. It may be a different person each time you call, but that person understands your value as a customer and handles your questions on the first contact. Additionally, you can now have access to the company, your information, and your account whenever you want it and determine if and when you want to speak to a representative to verify information. It has become service on demand.

The call center that supports this service has three primary objectives:

- To respond on first contact,
- To gather data for preventive analysis, and
- To cross-sell when appropriate.

In order to achieve these objectives, it's necessary to offload simple, repetitive calls to automated systems, thus freeing the customer service representative to respond to more complex calls. Call centers also have become more complex as they've moved from servicing single products and simple transactions to providing information on a multitude of products, assisting in technical support, and explaining complicated financial transactions.

Successful ARS applications that support the modern call center allow the call center to use technology to provide high-touch service. It's important to understand what has made some applications successful while others miss the mark by locking the customer in an automated jail.

Why Do Companies Implement ARS?

The common justifications that companies give for implementing ARS are as follows:

- **Ability to Handle More Calls.** About half of the respondents in the benchmarking survey reported an increase in total call volume as a result of the ARS, with most reporting an increase of between 11% and 25%. Financial services companies—i.e., credit cards, mutual funds, and banks—have often cited the benefits of ARS in contributing to their ability to provide access 7x24 (7 days a week, 24 hours a day).
- **Reduced Staff Requirements.** It's questionable whether ARS applications truly reduce staff requirements. Nearly 60% of the companies in the study reported a decrease in calls handled by CSRs with the introduction of the ARS; however, call length increased between 10% and 25%. With the ARS, many routine calls are offloaded, leaving the CSRs to handle longer, more complex calls. Additionally, callers opting out of the ARS may require that the CSRs gather the same information as was entered into the ARS, e.g., account information or Social Security number. Companies that have implemented CTI screen pops migrate the customer information with the call and potentially increase productivity and customer satisfaction.
- **Lower Cost per Call.** The median cost per minute for ARS calls is about a quarter of the cost of a CSR call. This finding is widespread across a variety of industries.
- **Increased Customer Satisfaction.** Although companies cited customer satisfaction as a reason for implementing ARS, very few companies can actually tie the measurement of satisfaction to the customer's experience with the ARS. TARP's baseline satisfaction research contains questions on satisfaction with the use of the ARS. More and more companies are beginning to measure customer satisfaction and acceptance of their applications. A recent survey by American Express measured utilization, satisfaction, and reason for the opt-out to a CSR. The short survey included questions about how the customers felt about transferring their information with screen pops and whether the CSR addressed them by name.

How Do You Define a Successful ARS Application?

If companies are implementing ARS to handle more calls and increase customer satisfaction, then it stands to reason that these should be measures of success for ARS applications. World-class applications have utilization rates of at least 80%, completion rates of more than 50%, and customer satisfaction scores of 90% or higher. Further, a low rate—fewer than 20%—of users opt out of the application prematurely and need to speak to a CSR to complete the transaction.

While this may be an accurate measure of success for simple applications, for more complex usages we may need to set our goals lower and use customer education to reach those goals. In setting usage goals, it's important to estimate the actual number of contacts that can be finalized in the ARS. This can be done by developing an understanding of when and why customers opt out. If the application does not include all the information to finalize the transaction or respond to questions or if customers have additional questions, they will realistically need to speak to a representative. Therefore, these measures represent very general guidelines and should not be seen as standards, as they may not be relevant to all applications.

What Are the Most and Least Successful Applications?

The most successful uses of ARS are fairly simple. They include

- **Creating Access by Routing,** where callers are routed to the proper group for assistance.
- **Provision of Basic Information**, such as balance inquiry and rate quotes where the caller decision burden is light. These simple requests can be offloaded, allowing the CSRs to handle more complex calls.
- **Simple Transactions**, such as funds transfers and credit card payment arrangements. These applications provide for 7x24 access and allow customers to take control of their own service, which may increase privacy and be less threatening.

More complex transactions, such as bank by phone (i.e., paying bills) and collections applications used by utilities to automatically make payment arrangements, are highly successful, if the companies give proper attention to customer education.

The least successful uses of ARS are not related to complexity but rather to a variety of issues, including:

- **Inquiries Requiring Timely Data**. This data may not be available or will require information from a computer database using less than state-of-the-art integration and response systems.
- **Provision of Information That May Disappoint the Customer**. For example, batch system updates are unacceptable to savvy customers who expect "live on-line systems" with up-to-the-minute information.
- **Technical Assistance for Complex Issues Varying by Customer.** Companies using ARS on their technical assistance help lines should do so for routing purposes only. The more high tech the reason for the call (e.g., installing a hard drive or resolving a computer hardware or software problem), the more high touch the service needs to be. A customer calling for technical assistance should not be forced through an ARS that's not likely to provide the assistance needed.

    For example, some companies attempt to provide technical assistance to their customers with an ARS loaded with answers to frequently asked questions. To make matters worse, some of these companies do not provide an option to escape the ARS and be routed to a CSR. Figure 19-1 shows an example of a successful high-tech routing option.

What Are the Critical Success Factors?

Luckily for companies looking to structure successful ARS applications, there are some tactics that have helped some companies succeed with ARS. The following six practices will increase your chances of success.

1. **Clear Definition of Market and Customer Needs.** Before designing your system, conduct customer research and analyze current call types to identify

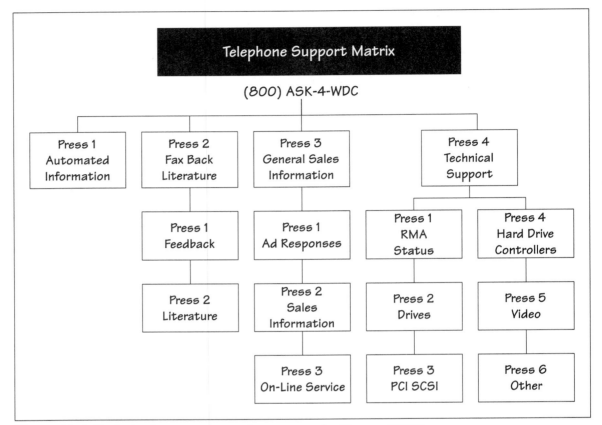

Figure 19-1. Technical support services example. (Source: TARP.)

which calls are more likely to be satisfied in an ARS application. For example, a mail order pharmaceutical company servicing many older customers recently conducted a series of focus groups to understand which transactions their customers were willing to conduct using the ARS. This allowed the company to avoid creating low-usage applications. Another factor related to market needs is the trade-off with cross-sell opportunities. One company in the benchmarking study reported that revenue gains from cross-selling by trained live CSRs far exceeded the efficiencies gained by having the customer complete the transaction in the ARS. A financial services company reported that it has overcome the cross-sell issue by identifying which prompts on the ARS present the best cross-sell options and directing those prompts to default to a CSR.

2. **Human Factors Experts.** Companies that have invested in involving human factors experts in the design of more complex ARS have achieved a higher utilization and finalization rate. The higher success rate, coupled with an increase in customer satisfaction, can justify the investment in a design expert.

3. **System Testing.** Better a small success than a large failure. Companies have learned that implementing ARS can be as complicated as implementing com-

puter systems. Even small changes should have a test phase, so companies can understand how consumers use them and where they have difficulty and opt out. An innovative approach is the use of system and live monitoring of customers using the ARS. Additionally, companies in the design phase often incorporate usability testing in a focus group setting. At the very least, the new script of design should be shared with CSRs who can point out pitfalls that customers may encounter.

4. **Clear and Pointed Scripting.** The system script must be crisp, clear, and to the point by indicating what information is available through the ARS and how to get it. Companies with successful applications have experimented with voice tone, inflection, gender, and word-smithing to keep customers satisfied and increase utilization and finalization in the ARS. Most ARS applications use a female voice. One company found, after extensive testing, that its application achieved the highest completion rate by using a female voice for normal scripting and a male voice if a second prompt was needed for the same activity or entry. Some ARS applications have experimented with conversational-like scripting, giving the ARS a persona such as George, and using the customer's name in the response. The results have suggested that a computer should act like a computer.

5. **Number of First Menu Options.** Defaults and user errors go up and customer satisfaction goes down as the number of menu options increases. Four appears to be the ideal number for options (with one of these, usually the last option, being an opt-out to a live representative). Figures 19-2 and 19-3 illustrate the impact of the number of menu options on satisfaction and finalization. Higher numbers of menu options are possible with frequently used systems (e.g., financial service systems that might be used multiple times a week) and with customer education.

Number of Options on First Menu Affects Customer Satisfaction	
# of Options	Mean % Satisfied
3	94
4	91
5	62
6+	50

Figure 19-2. Key success factor: number of menu/options. (Source: TARP.)

Number of Options Also Affects Opt Out Rate		
# of Options	% Opt Out Before Choosing	% Opt Out After Choosing
3	18	10
4	30	20
5	40	43

Figure 19-3. Key success factor: Structure of menu/options. (Source: TARP.)

6. **Customer Education.** Companies that educate customers on how to use the ARS report a higher percentage of customers entering the ARS and completing transactions and a higher level of customer satisfaction. Customer education takes two forms: (1) education prior to use, in the form of brochures, wallet cards, and statement stuffers, and (2) education during use. Several companies have trained their CSRs to identify when a customer is calling with a request that could easily be completed through the ARS. The CSR responds to the customer's question or problem, but then guides him or her through the system so that the customer will be able to use it next time. While this increases talk time on a short-term basis, it is offset by the long-term increase in ARS use. If this becomes part of the ARS strategy, CSRs are often monitored and compensated for the training opportunities. Figure 19-4 shows a chart to help educate customers and support their informed use of a financial service ARS application.

Create the Basics Before You Innovate

When new technologies are introduced, it's best to understand the basics and do them well. The goal is to establish a solid base for growth and innovation. Two innovations that are meeting with success are the increased use of technology in speech recognition and text-to-speech to make systems more efficient and more customer-friendly. For example, some mutual fund companies are using speech recognition to allow customers to "speak" the fund name instead of entering digits. A good example of text-to-speech technology is a tourism department that's matching addresses to send information based on customer-spoken phone numbers, while a help desk provides computer-spoken status reports on dispatch and repairs.

Additional innovations involve ARS reporting that will allow companies that capture and analyze data on ARS usage and opt-out location (i.e., last menu item picked) to realize increased efficiencies from being able to constantly make the system more usable.

Finally, a limited number of companies are using Computer Telephony Integration (CTI) to drive data about the caller's ARS experience to the CSR workstation, along with a screen pop of the customer account. This allows the CSR to provide high-touch, customer-friendly service—and to identify customer education opportunities on the ARS.

Summary

There are opportunities to use high-tech ARS applications to create high-touch service. By applying the basic principles for creating ARS as outlined in this article, you can provide cost-effective customer service while increasing the number of calls handled, reducing costs, and at the same time better satisfying your customers. As you design your ARS applications, keep in mind the following points from the findings of the benchmarking study:

- Clearly define market and customer needs.
- Consider involving a human factors expert if the application is complicated.

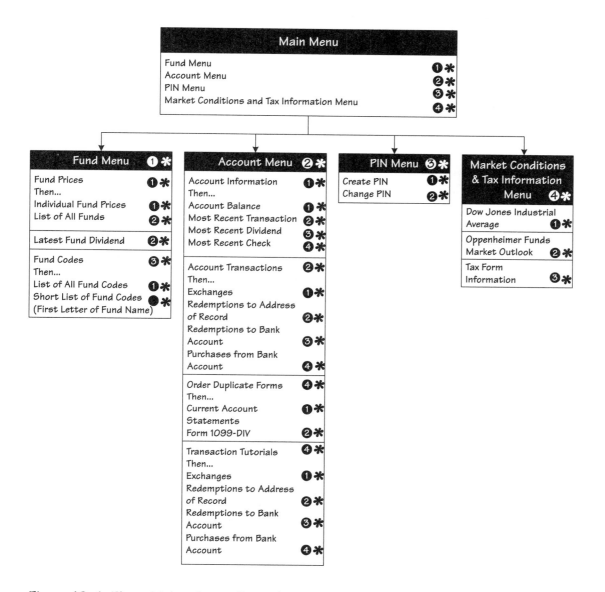

Figure 19-4. PhoneLink takes callers through the touch tone selections indicated. For each selection the caller presses a number and the star key. (Source: TARP.)

- Develop a testing plan prior to deployment.
- Devise clear and pointed scripting.
- Limit the number of first menu options.
- Develop education materials for customers, to increase usage of the system.

About the Author

Marlene Yanovsky is Vice President of Technical Assistance Research Programs (TARP), an Arlington, Virginia–based research and consulting firm specializing in customer service management and measurement. Marlene has helped clients across a wide range of industries evaluate and improve their service processes, assessing and implementing 800 numbers for customer response, telemarketing and teleservicing call centers, and measuring and tracking customer satisfaction. Her clients include Chase Manhattan Bank, Chemical Bank, CIGNA, Aetna Health Plans, Wawa Convenience Stores, Associates Financial Services Corporation, Henry Ford Health Systems, Metropolitan Life, McGraw-Hill, and Panasonic.

Before joining TARP, she was the Chief Quality Officer for Service Quality at Aetna Health Plans, where she was responsible for defining and rolling out TQM. As part of her responsibility, she led the re-engineering of the call centers; this included redesign, pilot, and implementation of all facets of the organization, employee development and training, and processes management and measurement.

Marlene is a member of ASQ, AQP, SOCAP, and ASTD. She is an examiner for the Malcolm Baldrige National Quality Award and the New York State Excelsior Award. She is a frequent speaker on customer-focused quality and service management and measurement.

PART FIVE

Improving Customer Service: Strategies and Techniques

20

THE TEN PRACTICES OF EXCEPTIONAL SERVICE

Mark Sanborn

Exceptional customer service can make your company more competitive. As the author notes, "People are so accustomed to mediocre service that when they experience exceptional service . . . they come back—and they tell other people. It's still easy to be exceptional in serving customers." Do you know the 10 practices that make the best service providers exceptional? At least some of them may surprise you. Learn about them here—before you learn about them from your competitors.

The airline had set a new standard for incompetence: they damaged my carry-on luggage. How?

Flying from Atlanta to Hilton Head, I was forced to "gate check" my garment bag and flight bag because the commuter aircraft was so small. When I picked them up in Hilton Head, the garment bag's spine was broken.

It took an airline representative 20 minutes to fill out my claim form. After I'd signed the form, she said, "Now, if you'll just leave your garment bag with me, I'll send it to a repair service and have it back for you in two weeks."

This posed a small (and, I thought, obvious) dilemma. I told her that I really needed the items in the damaged bag for the rest of my trip.

She offered me a "loaner" garment bag, which wasn't anything close to the quality or convenience of my own bag.

"Doesn't it strike you as odd," I inquired, "that first you damage my luggage and then you want to further inconvenience me by sending it off for two weeks to be repaired?"

Her response was classic: "Sir, if we paid for all the luggage we damage at this airline, we'd be out of business!"

The Problem

For almost two decades, American businesses have been preoccupied with customer service. We've been aware of, focused on, and sensitized about delivering superior service to our customers. However, although many have preached it, few have actually reached it.

In fact, according to a joint study by the University of Michigan and the American Society for Quality, service levels have declined nearly 3% over the past two years. While this number may not seem dramatic to you, it's atrocious in light of the time and money American businesses have invested in raising service levels. Sadly, service has declined, despite the resources we've thrown at efforts to improve it.

Of course, that's good news for you and me. How is it good news? Because people are so accustomed to mediocre service that when they experience exceptional service, that is, when they do business with an individual or a company that goes beyond mere talk to actually deliver it, they come back—and they tell other people. It's still easy to be exceptional in serving customers.

You can read best-selling books, watch hours of videos, listen to content-packed audio tapes, and attend the latest training sessions on customer service. But none of the ideas you get, no matter how great they are, will help your business until you've implemented them. In other words, knowing what to do isn't enough. Execution is everything.

The difference between mediocre service providers and great service providers is the difference between good ideas and great implementation. Great service providers practice the art of exceptional service. Excellent service sprouts with good ideas, but it comes to full bloom only with persistent practice.

10 Practices of Best Service Providers

My research and my work with the very best service providers demonstrates that they all do a lot of things right. However, I've found that there are at least 10 practices that they have in common.

1. Eliminate Irritants

Customer service is as much what you don't do to customers as it is what you do for them. For example, in most hotels today, it's not uncommon for a local phone call or an 800-number call to cost from 75 cents to one dollar. As a frequent hotel guest, I find it irritating to pay $100+ for a room and be charged for local and 800-number calls. When will hotels learn to quit alienating guests with such surcharges?

Obviously, they don't want to lose the revenue from these surcharges. But it costs them in customer good will. It would be better if hotels determined the revenue amount generated by access surcharges, divided that amount by the average number of guest stays each year, added that figure to the basic room rate, and then told guests that local phone calls and access to 800- and credit-card numbers are free!

The scary thing about customer irritants and aggravations is that they often make perfect sense to the service provider. For example, have you ever tried to get a small cup of coffee served in a large cup? This would seem like a reasonable request from someone who doesn't want to be scalded by opening the spring-loaded lid on a cup filled to the top. Yet the average fast-food establishment is dumbfounded by that simple request. Why? Because restaurants often track coffee sales on the basis of cup size. Give a customer a small, $1.00 cup of coffee in a large, $1.25 cup and—heaven forbid!—you throw the system off by a whole quarter!

A solution to this problem is as simple as keeping a roll of quarters on hand. If a customer wants a small cup of coffee in a large cup, provide it. Then just toss a quarter into the cash drawer to make up the difference. The system is intact and, more important, the customer leaves happy.

What are you doing to—or not doing for—customers that makes perfect sense to you but irritates and alienates them? Conduct a search-and-destroy mission to eliminate customer irritants.

2. Perform as Promised

A vendor tells a client he'll send him one of the embroidered polo shirts that the client admired. It never arrives.

An account executive promises a prospective customer that she'll call back next Wednesday to discuss a potential order. The call never comes.

A long-distance company begs a business owner to consider using its services. However, he must call and request a quote several times before the company finally gives him one.

Consider your own experience. In the past two weeks, how many organizations or individuals have told you that they were going to do something—and then didn't do it? And what have you told others you would do for them, but haven't done?

Follow-through is abysmal today. Excellent service providers always deliver what they promise. When they commit, it happens.

Don't make promises you can't keep. If you think you can have something for a customer by the end of the day, but you're sure you can have it by noon tomorrow, commit to noon tomorrow. Then if you're able to have it by the end of the day, your customer will be ecstatic that you performed even better than promised.

Most service complaints evolve from poorly managed expectations. Don't waste your time trying to exceed customer expectations or provide added value to your product or service if you don't have a fool-proof system for the basics: delivering *what* you promise, *when* you promise it.

Make it an unforgivable sin in your organization to make promises that you don't keep.

3. Manage the Customer's Experience

The Palm Desert Marriott is a beautiful resort near Palm Springs, California. This past March, I was at the resort to speak to the American Hardware Manufacturing Association. The night before my breakfast presentation, I dined in one of the resort's fine restaurants, the Tuscany. While the food and ambiance were very good, the standout of my dining experience was my waitperson. She was prompt, attentive, and pleasant. But what I remember most happened at the end of the meal.

"Thank you for dining with us," she said as she shook my hand. Each year, because of my business travel and love of fine food, I eat at least 300 meals outside my home. And yet, this was the first time anyone had thanked me and shaken my hand! While such a move on the part of a restaurant employee might strike most customers as odd, this waitperson extended her hand in a manner that I found to be classy and natural.

Then she added, "And don't miss the comet, Hale-Bopp, tonight. The sky is especially clear. Also, at 7 p.m. you'll want to watch for the lunar eclipse."

In those two closing gestures, a handshake and a suggestion to view the night sky, my waitperson added immensely to my enjoyment of the evening. In fact, the real treat of my dining experience had nothing to do with northern Italian cuisine! It was about courtesy and astronomy. She managed my dining experience so that it was particularly enjoyable, personal, and memorable.

No matter what business you're in, it's critical that you manage your customer's experience. Customer experience is a broader canvas for the service artist to paint on. It's those seemingly little touches and comments that often have nothing to do with your specific business but will make your customers remember doing business with you as personal and enjoyable.

Your competitors are managing product or service delivery. You can leapfrog them all by focusing on managing the customer's total experience.

4. Make Customers Insiders

Flight 675 had been slowly taxiing, waiting its turn to take off, for nearly 30 minutes. It was Friday night and travelers were anxious to get home or arrive at their destination for some weekend recreation. I was seated in 3B of the first-class cabin. The door was open to the cockpit, where the captain and first officer were pointing out to two flight attendants something outside, to the right of the plane. One of the flight attendants came back to the first row to share her find with some friends who were on board. She pointed out the window toward a hangar, and soon her friends joined her in fascinated attention. Then I overheard her laughingly say, "Everyone will wonder what we're looking at!"

As a matter of fact, yes, the rest of us in the first-class cabin were at least mildly curious about what the crew and a few favored flyers were observing. And we felt like outsiders. Since we weren't part of the "inner circle," we had to just sit there and wonder what was of such interest.

More important, we wondered how long it would be before we took off. But there were no announcements forthcoming from the crew, who were obviously too preoccupied to worry about such customer concerns.

Airlines claim to be competing for customer loyalty. Most are losing the battle. They just don't get it. Customers want to be treated like insiders, not outsiders. They want to feel that the flight crew is interested in letting them in on information that affects their travel plans, allays their anxieties, and enhances their enjoyment. Typically, however, the norm is silence from the cockpit and flight attendants, who often seem incapable of empathy.

Today's leading-edge companies make their customers insiders. FedEx, for example, has a Web site that receives 108,000 hits every day. That's because their site allows customers to track their own packages. You can't get much more "insider" than that!

What are you doing to make your customers feel like insiders?

5. Create Ownership

On January 15, 1997, Barnett Banks, the 22nd largest bank in the United States, made owners of all 22,000 of its employees by granting them stock options. The program is a terrific effort to create ownership in the hearts and minds of employees who work in this premier financial institution.

When I spoke at Barnett Banks' CFO conference later in the year, each participant was wearing a badge with his or her name printed on it. Underneath was the word "owner." The enthusiasm of the participants was palpable, and their commitment to helping Barnett reach the next level of success was apparent.

But employee ownership is not always such a rousing success. I recall one major airline's ill-fated attempt to make such a move and then advertise it. Their posters and television spots featured the friendly faces of employee owners. Ground crew, gate agents, pilots—all were identified as the airline's "proud owners." However, my experience, and apparently that of many other customers, was contrary to the image of the airline's advertisements. While many employees of that airline are terrific—and they were terrific before they became "proud owners"—too many others don't act like owners, proud or otherwise.

Naturally, customers expect more of *owners* than of *employees*. After all, it's their business; an employee can't be expected to show the same commitment as an owner. While making your employees owners can improve performance (and by the way, this occurs only when systems and processes are in place that allow employee owners to effectively impact organizational direction), be aware that it raises customers' expectations and increases their irritation when employee owners don't act the part.

Be prudent when assigning and then advertising employee ownership. Ownership isn't about what you *call* employees; it is about how employees *act*.

Create a sense of ownership for your employees. Give them tangible incentives to perform. Link some part of their compensation with performance. Maybe even make them literally owners—but think twice before you create an advertising campaign around employee ownership.

6. Have Fun

Passengers on the 6:15 a.m. United flight from Denver to San Francisco are rarely at their perkiest. From experience, I know it can be a sleepy, uneventful flight. Of course, it depends on which flight attendant is on the plane's intercom.

On one such flight, as we approached San Francisco, we were treated to some announcements from the unorthodox flight attendant who'd been working the first-class cabin: "If you are having a hard time getting your ears to pop, I suggest you yawn widely. And if you are having a hard time yawning, ask me, and I'll tell you about my love life."

He went on: "We are on our final approach into San Francisco airport. If San

Francisco is your destination, I hope you'll have a safe drive home." And then, in his best disk-jockey voice, he added, "There is some blockage on the northbound 405 and there is a stalled car at the Market Street exit. But otherwise, traffic appears to be moving smoothly."

The usually sleepy passengers were waking up; there was laughter and giggling throughout the airplane. But there was more to come.

After we touched down, the flight attendant was back on the intercom for final instructions. "Unless the person next to you has beaten me," he quipped, "let me be the first to welcome you to San Francisco. You'll notice that the airport buildings are in the distance. We don't land next to the terminal because it scares the heck out of the people inside. That's why we land way out here. That means we'll need to taxi, so please don't stand up until we are parked at the gate and the seat belt sign has been turned off.

"For those of you who are 1Ks, Premiers, and Frequent Fliers—there are too many of you on board to mention by name, but you know who you are—we thank you for choosing United for your extensive travels. And if you'll leave me a recent picture as you deplane, I'll be glad to mail it to your loved ones so that they'll remember what you look like.

"My final hope is that when you leave the airplane, you'll do so with a big smile on your face. That way the people inside will wonder just what it is we do up here in the friendly skies."

Take a clue from this delightful flight attendant. Take some risks. Have some fun. And just maybe your customers will have fun too.

7. Recover Remarkably

I used to buy my home owner's and auto insurance through an insurance brokerage. I'd been doing business with this brokerage for nearly a decade when I finally got fed up with its increasingly poor service. The service rep assigned to me was immature and incompetent, and when my wife called for a quote on a new vehicle, it took the broker a week to call back. By then we'd taken our insurance business elsewhere.

I figured I owed the CEO of the business an explanation of why we'd left. So I called, presented a litany of the problems we'd experienced, and informed him we'd taken our business elsewhere. His response? "Mr. Sanborn, it sounds like there is nothing I can do to bring back your business. I'm sorry you decided to leave."

The fact is, he might have recovered my business—if only he had tried. Even the most jaded and upset customers might reconsider going elsewhere if the provider makes a sincere effort to regain their loyalty.

Given the cost of acquiring a new customer, to give up on saving a current customer's loyalty is a costly proposition. Even the best service providers aren't perfect. But when they make a mistake, they recover remarkably. Consider the following experience. . . .

Based on numerous pleasant stays at Ritz-Carlton hotels, I'd developed some high service expectations. However, one stay at the Philadelphia Ritz-Carlton fell far short of those expectations. I was disappointed at the surprising lack of customer service. I felt it my duty to share my disappointment with the general manager prior to my checkout. When I finished outlining my dissatisfactions, the general manager apologized—sincerely and without excuses.

But what he did next was most astounding. "Mr. Sanborn," he said, "I regret that I can't turn back the clock and prevent the problems that occurred from happening. Your room balance, of course, shows zero." I was puzzled. My bill had been more than $400! What did he mean?

He answered, "Sir, I would not expect you to pay for a stay at our property that was short of your expectations. And the next time you are in Philadelphia, I would like to invite you to stay with us again as our guest with my compliments. You'll be receiving a letter to that effect from me soon." And I did.

Needless to say, my disappointment was more than compensated for by this remarkable recovery. In my opinion, that's what makes Ritz-Carlton one of the best service providers in the world. Period.

Remember: it's rarely ever too late to save a customer's business—if you recover remarkably.

8. Involve Everyone in Improvement

Unique ideas and the ability to implement them drive your business. And a critical key to success is your ability to involve everyone in generating ideas for improvement, or taking advantage of what I call "cumulative expertise." Two of your best resources for such idea generation are employees and customers.

Dana Corporation is an auto parts maker. This company not only takes employee suggestions seriously, but also does an amazing job of mining the expertise of its work force. In 1996, Dana's 45,400 employees each submitted an average of 1.22 suggestions per month, for a total of 666,120 ideas for cutting costs, improving operations and productivity, and increasing profitability.

How often do you ask your employees for suggestions about improving service? And how well do they respond? I've seen employee suggestion boxes covered with cobwebs. If you aren't getting lots of suggestions, you aren't asking well.

How does Dana do it?

For one thing, it uses 70% of all suggestions. For most employees, implementation of their suggestions is the best reward. Employees everywhere are tired of making suggestions that are never used.

Second, Dana rewards those who make suggestions with luncheons and other awards. For example, a plant in Chihuahua, Mexico, rewards employees the equivalent of $1.89 for each idea submitted and another $1.89 if it uses the idea. (Of course, the amount of monetary reward that is appropriate depends on location and pay. Remember: you get what you pay for.)

How about customer suggestions? Consider formalizing a process for soliciting, rewarding, and implementing customer suggestions. Most customers would feel gratified if a service provider even simply acknowledged their suggestions. What I'm advocating is more radical. If you pay employees (people you're already paying) extra for their suggestions, why not pay customers (people paying you) for their best ideas?

Maybe it's time for you to involve everyone in improvement by offering them much more than the proverbial penny for their thoughts.

9. Make Teamwork Work

Forget the concept of "internal customers." Like so many in business, I used to buy into the quality improvement process definition of a customer as "the next person in the process." It sounded like a good idea at the time.

The problem with this philosophy is that the paying customer ends up at the end of the line. I soon realized that focusing on internal customers diverts your attention from the only customer who matters—the one who buys your product or service.

Don't misunderstand. I still believe that service is created from the inside out. Employees who don't feel well served probably won't serve well. But for the people inside your organization, the most appropriate description is "teammates," not "internal customers," because, frankly, providing "internal service" isn't the point. You don't get extra credit for that. Your real, live customers aren't going to say, "You know, they treated me like dirt, but they took such wonderful care of each other!"

Promote the concept of teamwork in your organization. Teamwork works when there's communication, cooperation, and a desire to work together toward a common goal. Rally your teammates around the goal of better serving customers and securing their undying loyalty.

10. Do Everything Better

When my younger brother graduated from high school, I gave him some of the only advice I would ever offer unsolicited. Inside his graduation card I wrote, "To be a success, do whatever you do better than anybody else who does it." I had no idea what career path my brother would follow, but I knew that being the best at whatever he chose would guarantee his success.

Recently, one of the world's most renowned restaurateurs was asked the secret of his restaurant's success. He said the secret is in doing everything they do as well as they can do it. He added that on his way to the top, he learned that it doesn't matter if you're making French fries, as long as you make them the best French fries anyone has ever eaten.

Take a look at what everyone else is doing—your direct competitors as well as the best service providers in other industries—and set a simple goal to do what they do better than they're doing it. Load up a mini-van of employees and take a field trip to a terrific service provider. Take notes. Capture the best ideas. And then put your own unique spin on them.

Ask everyone in your organization, "How can we do it more, better, faster, or different?" Make them sick of hearing this question, so they'll take you seriously. Take your cue from Midwest Express airline, where every seat is first-class-sized. Or from FedEx, which built its business on the concept of faster delivery—guaranteed. Or from Disneyland, which unabashedly calls itself "the happiest place on earth."

How Can You Be Exceptional?

Leave no stone unturned nor any idea untried. Do everything better. The challenge: exceptional customer service. A concept that's simple to understand. A goal that's hard to achieve.

To be anything more than a fleeting burst of brilliance, your organization must commit to a comprehensive service strategy. But beyond that, you must also commit to the hard work that follows. Your strategy must be implemented in such a way that everyone not only knows what to do to give exceptional service, but actually does it—consistently and persistently. That's the practice of exceptional service.

Summary of 10 Practices of Best Service Providers

1. Eliminate Irritants
2. Perform as Promised
3. Manage the Customer's Experience
4. Make Customers Insiders
5. Create Ownership
6. Have Fun
7. Recover Remarkably
8. Involve Everyone in Improvement
9. Make Teamwork Work
10. Do Everything Better

About the Author

Because of his ability to educate and entertain simultaneously, Mark Sanborn is known internationally as "the high-content speaker who motivates." He works with business organizations that want to reach the next level and individuals who want to perform at their best. Mark presents 90–100 programs annually on leadership, teambuilding, customer service, and mastering change.

He is the author of the books *Teambuilt: Making Teamwork Work* (Master Media, 1994) and *Sanborn On Success* (Griffin Publishing, 1995) and numerous videos and audio training programs. He contributed the article "Live Like Your Life Depends on It" to a collection of essays, *Only the Best on Success* (Win Publications).

In 1995 *Presentations* magazine featured Mark as one of five "Masters of the Microphone." He has earned the Certified Speaking Professional designation and received the Council of Peers Award of Excellence from the National Speakers Association. His Web site address is http://www.marksanborn.com.

21

BEYOND LOYALTY: INSPIRING CUSTOMERS TO BRAG

Michael E. Cafferky

How can you get thousands of people to promote your products and services at no charge? Tap the promotional power of your customers. Getting more out of your satisfied customers is not just a matter of chance . . . if you know how to do it right. This article explains a simple, three-step approach used successfully by many companies that are serious about word-of-mouth promotion.

Most companies want their business to be built primarily on the strength of a good reputation. We're engaged in a battle over the loyal hearts of consumers—consumers who hold the power to spread our reputation. Who wouldn't want to boast that most of their business comes because loyal customers brag about them to others? The challenge is in knowing how word of mouth really works and how to inspire loyal customers to brag for you.

Imagine the promotional power of 40% or more of your current customers enjoying a pleasurable social experience while bringing in new customers or recommending your products and services to others. That's the potential. Word of mouth is the lowest-cost form of promotion. Also, it is arguably the most compelling.

Consumers look for consistency and congruence between paid advertising and the word-of-mouth messages they get from others. When consumers sense or fear inconsistency or incongruence, they tend to believe the word of someone who's experienced with your product. Also, when consumers have difficulty understanding the meaning of your products or services, they turn to someone else for help. That someone else is usually someone who offers the kind of credibility and mutual interest found outside your company: another customer.

We all talk, but social scientists have found through studies that some people get listened to more than others. So who are the talkers, those champion customers of your company, who get listened to when they brag? And, if you can identify them, how can you move them beyond mere loyalty by inspiring them to brag about you?

Loyal customers who brag and get heard are the ones who are perceived as believable, genuine, experienced, and enthusiastic. That's why they're called "opinion leaders." They're believable because they have no stake in the success of your company.

For example, one of your customers says to a friend, "You wouldn't believe what that customer service department did for me. They went the extra mile." The friend begins to have a new interest and attitude toward your company. Even if that friend does not become a customer, she's likely to pass on the information to someone else in the context of informal conversation.

Positive talkers who leave an impact are self-confident. They have a high degree of social interaction and may be formal or informal leaders in their community. They want to know your company and its products as well as you do. These champion customers read magazines and books. They may watch videos that help them learn more about the marketplace. Most important, those who have successfully referred other customers to you in the past are likely to continue talking positively about you in the future.

What can you do to get beyond loyalty by inspiring them to brag? The following simple, three-step approach is used successfully by many companies serious about word-of-mouth promotion:

- Find the talkers and identify what they're talking about.
- Inspire them to brag.
- Thank them when they work for you.

Find Them

Companies that move beyond building loyalty take measures necessary to identify by name the known and expected loyal customers. Each type of business has its own way of capturing this information. While the method you use is less important than the fact that you apply your method consistently, here are a few examples of successful ways to gather this information:

- The clerk at the cash register asks for name and address.
- The customer service staff member takes an extra minute or two to interact with the customer who expresses gratitude for the solution provided.
- Gather names and addresses on response cards.
- Save all letters of appreciation from clients.
- Ask new customers who referred them to you.
- Conduct a staff meeting to brainstorm a list of names of suspected champion customers (loyal customers who you believe are bragging about you to others).
- Use product registration cards to flag prospective talkers.
- Interview known loyal supporters, asking for names of other people who recommend your products and services.
- Ask frequent customers whether they recommend you to others.
- Review published reports (in trade journals, newspapers, magazines, and directories) of individuals who meet the criteria of talkers and leaders.

Whatever you do, you must start with a written list of names and addresses of these opinion leaders. Without a list, your word-of-mouth marketing efforts will be unfocused. You may not be able to apply all the attributes of bragging opinion leaders to all customers, but use your best judgment. What you're looking for is leaders, those bragging loyal customers to whom others listen.

One category of opinion leader is the "product expert"—a customer who makes it his or her business to know a lot about one or two related products and services. Some product experts become opinion leaders because of their innate curiosity about the product. Others, because of their careers or because of particular consumer needs they have, frequently find themselves in the context of the product:

- They use the product often.
- They see it being used every day at work.
- They stay current on the latest developments in the field.
- They make it a hobby to learn about the products.

Sometimes known as "product enthusiasts" or "product aficionados," these experts enjoy reading magazines and books in their area of interest. They may build collections of items related to the product of their interest. They collect written materials that instruct them. Preferring hands-on learning, product experts want to experiment with new products. Innovators and early adopters, product experts enjoy seeing demonstrations of new technology. They want to learn about new methods. Because of their knowledge of the products, they're willing to purchase by mail. And, most important, because of their expertise, others turn to them for purchasing advice.

Another important category of champions are the customers who are looking for the best value for their money across a wide variety of products and services. These "market mavens" make it their business to help others (their families and close friends) to be wise consumers. While most market mavens can be observed among consumers, there are also market mavens within industries. Some of these shoppers appear as if they're only looking for low price. However, what they really want is good value for their money or the money of their company.

Market mavens maintain a general knowledge of their marketplace. Even if they're not experts in your particular product or service, they're wise value hunters, so other people look up to them because of their wide experience at buying. Market mavens are constantly on the lookout for information that they can pass on to their friends and business associates. They read advertisements. They soak up news stories about products. They research makes, models, prices, payment terms, and conditions. They initiate opportunities to help others select products. Then they often follow up to confirm that their advice was appropriate.

A third type of champion to whom others listen is the "influential." Educated and well-read, influentials are typically political leaders in their companies or communities. These are the captains of industry from the top echelon through middle management. They subscribe to thought journals. They read books and attend training seminars. They give speeches and participate in panel discussions. Influentials are sometimes innovators, using or testing new products ahead of others. And, most important, in the circle of their influence, these opinion leaders command a huge amount of good will, which they can extend on your behalf at a moment's notice.

Find Out What They're Talking About

As you make your list of champion loyal customers, find out what your champion customers are saying about you, so you can leverage this information to your great advantage. You can use their words and phrases in customer service work, in advertising, and in employee training. Actively search for endorsements (testimonials and recommendations). Use the data from customer service surveys to identify prized consumer values. Conduct focus groups to identify the most important values. Study the wording that customers use to describe your benefits, then incorporate those actual phrases and words when you communicate.

Using the words and phrases used by loyal customers provides a consistency that reinforces your own messages with customer reactions. Knowing what customers are saying allows you the unique advantage over competitors to inform your customers in ways that strengthen their ability to brag about you. For example, you may find in focus group studies that loyal, bragging customers mention only one or two key benefits, such as durability and selection. Through your direct marketing efforts with these individuals, you're able to inform their experience, suggesting new uses or new benefits for your products while using their way of thinking as the anchor for new information.

In addition to these uses of consumer perception, integrate this information into the rest of the company in the following ways:

- Transmit this information to your marketing and public relations department.
- Give copies to your advertising agency.
- Incorporate the information into new employee orientation or customer service training events.
- Discuss the findings with your sales manager.
- Establish a company-wide information bank for this type of information, so that all employees can contribute to the depository things that they hear customer say.
- Periodically review this data bank, comparing what you find with your company's mission, vision, and strategic objectives.

How Leaders Create Success for You

Leadership is the basis of successful word-of-mouth marketing efforts. Opinion leaders are perceived as giving helpful information to their listeners. They help prospective customers by reducing the time those customers spend looking for information about value and quality. With their own experience as evidence, they recommend success, thereby reducing the risk that someone else will have a bad experience. These champions are especially persuasive because they have nothing to gain by their positive talk. Prospective customers may know that your company exists—they see your advertising or meet a salesperson. But their attitudes, just before they make their decision whether or not to purchase from you, will be shaped by your opinion leaders, champion bragging customers.

When Positive Talk Happens

You know how conversations go. Someone begins with one topic, then after a few minutes someone mentions another topic, by free association. During these conversation swings, people usually talk about people, what happens to people, or something involving people. When the conversation naturally swings to your services and products, your opinion leaders will brag about you if they've been inspired. It's human nature.

You cannot control when they think and talk positively about you. However, you can influence them to brag by how you inspire them.

Eight Ways to Inspire Them to Brag

The value of word of mouth is in direct proportion to its frequency. The more often you can inspire positive word of mouth, the more powerful your reputation becomes.

Realize that positive word of mouth is built on a foundation of excellent service. Make sure your champion customers are treated like the champions that they are. Although consumer expectations are higher than in the past, in general, the hallmark issues that consumers cite as important in service have not changed much. They include: responsiveness, reliability, competence, access, courtesy, communication, credibility, security, and understanding. (Yet, since the importance to consumers of these and related values is constantly shifting in each industry, it's impossible for us to ever say with confidence that we've arrived at a level of total customer satisfaction.)

Here are eight ways to inspire positive word of mouth.

1. **Create champions.** Any opportunity you have to help people become better than they thought they could be is an opportunity to create word-of-mouth. Take customers under your wings and help them achieve beyond their dreams. After all, you're not in business to merely sell products and services. Through selling your products and services, you're helping people achieve their dreams, solve their problems, obtain meaning in their lives. It's only by moving beyond the issues of the immediate transaction with the customer that employees see the consumer's bigger picture and the meaning of the product or service in the consumer's life.

2. **Showcase your list.** Somewhere in your company showcase your champion, loyal braggers and their work by giving them the recognition they deserve, through photos and displays. This showcasing is an education constantly at work, reminding all employees that what they do each hour affects real people, who go beyond loyalty and brag about them to others.

3. **Educate champions**. An educated consumer is one of your most powerful forces in the market. Opinion leaders need specific information about you and your company to share with others. Make sure you educate every champion about what you sell, what you can get for them, the quality of your work and materials, the training of your staff, and other information they find important. Educate loyal customers about all the uses of the products and services they purchase from you. Inform them beyond their expectations and they'll be inspired to brag.

4. **Be an expert's expert.** Every consumer, whether or not an opinion leader, needs other people from whom to seek expert advice. If you're already an expert on some aspect of your products and services, continue studying and enhancing this expertise. Make the long-term commitment to become the local expert on something. You don't have to know all about everything. But the fact that you specialize in something significant to customers will help spread the word faster. When you make the commitment to go beyond the required knowledge of your products and your company, you create a resource that leads customers beyond their loyalty and into the arena of bragging.

5. **Involve champions.** Tell people something and they will forget it. Show it to people and they may remember it. Involve them in using it and through their new understanding they will become champions who brag for you. Give more hands-on demonstrations. Give loyal customers the chance to "test drive" samples of new products or new service processes that you supply. Ask them to bring their reactions back to you, so you can share in their enthusiasm. Involve champion customers in your classes and demonstrations, i.e., give them the opportunity to demonstrate to others. Let them brag about the success they've found with your products. Ask them why they chose your products over your competitors' products. This involvement reinforces the positive. It also provides a means to show appreciation for their support.

6. **Give more information about related interests.** Stock copies of authoritative magazine articles on various topics that you can share at a moment's notice with a champion. Even if the articles are not along the lines of your primary interests, you'll be helping these opinion leaders do their work for you. Give them inside information on your industry that will explain the trends that influence their life. They need this type of information to share with others who look to them for advice. Develop a simple card file on every champion customer, where you can record areas of special interest for future reference. Then call them on the telephone or mail a postcard to let them know what you found for them. This kind of personal service will overwhelm them into bragging about you to others.

7. **Ask confirmed champions to spread the word.** Tell them about products and services you'll have in the future and ask them to suggest your products to others. Provide them tools to spread the word: postcards they can send, leads on potential customers who would appreciate a recommendation, structured opportunities to talk for you. Some companies that take word of mouth seriously have formed panels of loyal customers with whom they meet periodically

to inform and inspire. This principle applies equally well to consumer products and services as to industrial products and services.

8. **Persist in turning every customer problem into an opportunity to create bragging.** When there's a problem, the natural reaction of most employees is to try to solve it. That's all—to reduce or eliminate the negative. But you should seize a problem as an opportunity to achieve a positive, by impressing the customer. After all, most customers are expecting only that the company will try to make things right. Go beyond that and you may have your problem customer bragging about you.

Thank Them When They Talk

If you are genuine, you can never thank your champions too often for the bragging they do for you. Find creative ways to show your appreciation for their hard work. Personally thank your known champion patrons when you identify a new customer who comes through their recommendation. Thank them on the telephone. Thank them in writing. Put up an internal bulletin board featuring the work of your champions. Recognition, tastefully and genuinely given, often will result in more referrals.

In reality, the only way to successfully compete head-to-head with a product that has a good reputation is to have a product with a better reputation. Often, that better reputation is developed merely because of bragging by loyal customers.

Keep your word-of-mouth marketing program simple to manage. Keep looking for names of bragging customers. Constantly look for simple ways to inspire champions. Never fail to thank them. You can always add more embellishment when you get more experience. Encourage everyone in your organization to work the program with you. Soon you'll be using the best advertising in the world—when you let your customers do the talking.

Appendix: The Laws of Consumer Bragging

1. People brag.
2. People brag because they feel.
3. People brag about things that have meaning.
4. People brag about things of mutual interest.
5. Some people get listened to more than others.
6. You can identify the talkers who get listened to in your business.
7. Word-of-mouth bragging is the primary means by which your reputation is spread.
8. Word-of-mouth bragging universally is considered the most compelling, the least costly, the most natural, and the best way to signal value to customers.
9. Word-of-mouth bragging is controlled by your customers.
10. Champion, loyal customers who brag about your reputation can expand and exaggerate your virtues or your faults when you cannot.
11. The central figure in word-of-mouth bragging is the "opinion leader."

12. Opinion leaders include people such as market mavens, product enthusiasts, and influentials.
13. By bragging, opinion leaders help you by helping themselves and others.
14. The stronger the social tie between an opinion leader and an opinion seeker, the more likely the opinion seeker will act on the recommendation of a bragger.
15. Opinion seekers depend upon opinion leaders to achieve their own goals.
16. Word-of-mouth covers the broadest range of interests and endeavors and covers the largest proportion of the population of any promotion method.
17. Three kinds of social connections spread word-of-mouth bragging: close friendships, casual acquaintances, and aspirational relationships.
18. Word-of-mouth bragging is at the same time your best offensive and defensive marketing weapon.
19. Negative word-of-mouth travels faster and farther then positive word-of-mouth.
20. Negative word-of-mouth is just as useful to potential customers as positive word-of-mouth in that it helps them discriminate on one or more product/service attributes.
21. Word-of-mouth bragging transfers the core meaning of a product/service from one person to another.
22. Between 20% and 40% of the population are opinion leaders.
23. Every customer carries the potential for bragging about you.

About the Author

Dr. Michael E. Cafferky is the author of *Let Your Customers Do the Talking: 301 + Word-of-Mouth Marketing Tactics Guaranteed to Boost Profits* (Upstart Publishing, 1996). He has also developed other educational materials promoting word-of-mouth marketing, and regularly conducts seminars on this subject. His interactive Web site is at http://www.geocities.com/WallStreet/6246. He is now writing his fourth book on the topic. Michael is also a Certified Healthcare Executive and has been in healthcare leadership for over 14 years. He is the author of the consumer book *Managed Care & You: The Consumer Guide to Managing Your Healthcare* (McGraw-Hill, 1995).

22

CUSTOMER SERVICE SORT CARDS: A TRAINING EXERCISE

Sharon A. Wulf

Many companies recognize the importance of improving their customer service, but encounter problems pursuing that objective. This article presents an exercise based on three processes—awareness, analysis, and action. Participants discuss their current service practices and the service practices they'd like to implement, in terms of the impact on the organization, then begin to plan actions toward their goals. If you've got one hour and a desire to serve your customers better, everything else you need is right here.

Overview

The purpose of *Customer Service Sort Cards* is to enable participants to focus on their current versus desired customer service priorities. The exercise helps:

- To improve teamwork among individuals who provide customer service,
- To create an awareness of current versus desired customer service, and
- To improve the level of customer service through specific actions.

This is an excellent group activity to stimulate customer service efforts. As a consensus-building tool, Customer Service Sort Cards is designed for people throughout the organization who have direct contact with external or internal customers. The target group includes:

- Front-line personnel who provide day-to-day service to external customers,
- Customer service representatives who regularly interface with customers,
- Sales teams, including sales associates,
- Telemarketing personnel,
- Account management teams responsible for customer satisfaction, and
- Departments that service external and internal customers.

Objectives for Exercises

The objectives of Customer Service Sort Cards are:

- To create ownership of and commitment to improved customer service.
- To begin to define action steps necessary to achieve the group's desired customer service priorities.

Procedure

This activity can be run by one session leader, who need not have extensive experience in training, since all the materials and directions for the session are included. Teams are formed with five to seven members each.

Duration

1 hour

Materials Required

The session leader must have:

- The Leader's Guide,
- Overhead transparencies or flip chart posters of Slides 1 through 3, and
- A flip chart with paper and markers.

Each participant must have:

- A copy of the Participant Handout,
- A pencil, and
- Notepaper.

Each designated team of five to seven participants must have:

- A deck of 16 Customer Service Sort Cards. (To make a deck, copy the two pages with the eight numbered rectangles each, then cut along the lines.)

Also necessary:

- An overhead projector and a projection screen for viewing the overhead transparencies or a flip chart stand with flip chart posters.
- A watch or wall clock.
- Tables and chairs for all participants and the session leader. (If possible, seat each team at a round table so the members may work comfortably.)
- A training room large enough to accommodate the participants and equipment. (Since the value of this activity is the discussion, it is important to

spread out the work groups to ensure that participants are not disturbed by the conversations of neighboring groups.)

Leader's Guide

Preparation

Prior to conducting the session, the session leader should do the following:

○ Prepare a copy of the Participant Handout for each participant.
○ Create a deck of Customer Service Sort Cards for each work team.
○ Review the teaching notes and participant materials.
○ Arrange the classroom so that each group of five to seven participants is seated at one table.

Session Outline

Section	Activity	Duration
Section A	Introduction	5 minutes
Section B	Customer Service: The Way It Is	20 minutes
Section C	Customer Service: The Way It Should Be	20 minutes
Section D	Next Steps	15 minutes

Section A: Introduction

Objectives

○ To formally welcome the participants to the session.
○ To introduce the topic of the session.
○ To engage the ideas, knowledge, and experience of the group members.

Estimated Time

5 minutes

Training Method

Introduce the purpose of the Customer Service Sort Cards exercise.

Step-by-Step Procedures

1. Welcome the participants to the session.
2. Display Slide 1. Explain that customer service is a requirement for success in today's competitive business environment.

3. Display Slide 2. State: "During this workshop, we will use the 3 "A" Model. The first A stands for Awareness. The second A stands for Analysis. The third A stands for Action. By discussing our current and desired service practices, we will become aware of the way it is versus the way it should be. After we have analyzed or reflected upon the impact on the organization, we can begin to plan our action."
4. Instruct the participants that each one of them has a Participant Handout for his or her use during and after the session. Each participant should take notes on information that will be useful for individual and group follow-up action.
5. Transition to Section B.

Comments

The purpose of the introduction is to encourage participants to actively participate during the session.

Adhere to the time guidelines. Different groups manage their time in different ways. As the session leader, it is your role to ensure that the participants stay focused and utilize time effectively.

Section B: Customer Service: The Way It Is

Objectives

- To identify the top four customer service action steps emphasized within the organization today.
- To identify the top four customer service action steps de-emphasized within the organization today.
- To discuss the impact on the organization.

Estimated Time

20 minutes

Training Method

Work in a designated team of five to seven people. Using the 16 Customer Service Sort Cards, identify the top four customer service action steps emphasized by the organization today.

Step-by-Step Procedures

1. Refer each participant to his or her own copy of the Participant Handout. Encourage them to take notes for future reference and action planning.
2. Display Slide 3. State: "Your designated work team has been given a deck of Customer Service Sort Cards. The cards define various essentials of customer

service: motivation, problem solving, internal assessments, customer satisfaction, internal cooperation, proactive systems, employment standards, decision making, customer feedback, service metrics, customer knowledge, feedback systems, service-oriented culture, empowerment, trained front-line staff, and good reputation. A definition for each one of these items is provided on the respective Customer Service Sort Card."

3. State: "Using the Customer Service Sort Cards, identify the top four customer service action steps emphasized by the organization today."
4. Lead the group in a quick discussion. Address the following:
   ○ How are these customer service action steps emphasized in the organization?
   ○ How does this affect the organization?
5. Instruct the participants to identify the top four customer service action steps de-emphasized by the organization today.
6. Lead the group in a quick discussion. Address the following:
   ○ How are these customer service action steps de-emphasized in the organization?
   ○ How does this affect the organization?
7. Transition to Section C.

Comments

This part of the session typically causes a great amount of discussion and disagreement. Encourage the participants to listen to opinions and thoughts that are different from their own view.

Do not allow one or two participants to dominate the conversation. Also, encourage the more senior manager in the group to share his or her thoughts only after others have expressed their views. This technique will ensure that new thoughts are expressed and not influenced by a senior manager's opinion. If the participants are conducting the exercise for a specific department or function, remind them to focus the discussion in relationship to that specific department or function. Adhere to the time guidelines.

Section C: Customer Service: The Way It Should Be

Objectives

○ To identify the top four customer service action steps that should be emphasized within the organization.
○ To discuss how these customer service action steps should be emphasized and why.

Estimated Time

20 minutes

Training Method

Work in a designated team of five to seven people. Using the 16 Customer Service Sort Cards, identify the top four customer service action steps that should be emphasized by the organization.

Step-by-Step Procedures

1. State: "Using the Customer Service Sort Cards, identify the top four customer service action steps that should be emphasized by the organization."
2. Lead the group in a quick discussion. Address the following:
   ○ How should these customer service action steps be emphasized in the organization?
   ○ How would their emphasis strengthen the organization?
3. Transition to Section D.

Comments

Remind the designated team to discuss the way it should be . . . and not the way it is.

All participants should be encouraged to discuss the statement shown on the Customer Service Sort Cards. If the participants are conducting the exercise for a specific department or function, remind them to continue to focus the discussion in relationship to that specific department or function.

Section D: Next Steps

Objectives

○ To begin to identify the required action steps to ensure improved customer service.

Estimated Time

15 minutes

Training Method

Discuss and record key action steps.

Step-by-Step Procedures

1. Ask the participants to record their recommended next steps.
2. Lead the group in a quick discussion. Address how the recommended next steps will enhance the service provided to the customers.
3. Assign a responsible individual the task of further defining each recom-

mended next step and reporting the information back to the group within 30 days.

4. Conclude the session by stating: "You cannot afford to merely let things happen. If you seek improvement, you will have to **make** things happen." Encourage each individual to continue to align his or her day-to-day actions and decision making with desired customer service priorities . . . or the way it should be.

Comments

To build the momentum developed during this exercise, you must plan and execute some follow-up action plans. Some suggestions include:

- ○ Conduct a follow-up meeting to further discuss and agree upon action steps.
- ○ Develop a quantitative Current Customer Service Profile and a Desired Customer Service Profile using the *Customer Service Action Plan* written by Sharon A. Wulf. (Contact HRD Press at 1-800-822-2801 for more information regarding this product.)
- ○ Schedule ongoing sessions to monitor the implementation of action steps and develop new action steps.

About the Author

Dr. Sharon A. Wulf, President of Enterprise Systems, Framingham, Massachusetts, works with organizations to create custom business and organizational development programs. She works with a wide range of client organizations, from Motorola and AT&T to the U.S. Postal Service. For the past 18 years, she has worked with management teams in North America, Europe, and Asia.

Since establishing Enterprise Systems in 1992, she has developed over 200 management development product. Her three recent products published by HRD Press—*Customer Service Action Plans* (1997), *Leadership in Action* (1996), and *Building Performance Values: A New Tool for Goal Setting and Planning Action in Groups* (1996)—assist groups in making optimal business choices.

Sharon also delivers "The Entrepreneur's Clinic," a nationwide teleconference series sponsored by the U.S. Department of Commerce. Her recent satellite broadcasts at National Technological University include "Creating Effective Teams" and "Negotiation for Business Success." She is a recipient of the Toastmasters International Communication and Leadership Award for her service to her community, state, and industry through communication and leadership.

Motivation

Enrolling and mobilizing all employees to participate in a customer-focused work environment

1

Problem Solving

When problems are identified, taking immediate and helpful action to solve them in a quick and effective manner.

2

Internal Assessments

Regularly surveying our staff to find out how satisfied they are with the work environment and asking for their suggestions to provide better service.

3

Customer Satisfaction

Listening carefully to our customers and immediately resolving issues that are causing dissatisfaction.

4

Internal Cooperation

Consistently cooperating with one another throughout the organization to work smarter, do more with less, and reach shared service goals.

5

Proactive Systems

Consistently making it easy for customers to do business with us by speeding up the purchase process, decreasing response time, and/or making our business a special place to visit.

6

Employment Standards

Employing people at all levels in the organization who feel responsible and empowered to do what needs to be done to service customers and keep them satisfied.

7

Decision Making

Involving employees at all levels in making decisions about aspects of their work that involve the customer.

8

Customer Feedback Actively listening to customers and using their input to improve our products and/or services. 9	**Service Metrics** Reporting service metrics so that employees are constantly aware of the importance of customer service and progress in achieving service goals. 10
Customer Knowledge Understanding and anticipating what customers need, want, or expect, and consistently giving it to them. 11	**Feedback Systems** Operating with a clear feedback system that encourages ongoing customer feedback, listening carefully to their suggestions, and implementing ideas to improve customer service. 12
Service-Oriented Culture Setting goals, committing resources, modeling behavior, and building a quality service culture to ensure total customer satisfaction. 13	**Empowerment** Training employees at all levels to perform as customer champions capable of using good judgment when quick action is needed to satisfy a customer. 14
Trained Front-Line Staff Constantly training front-line service personnel in both technical and interpersonal skills, including telephone, face-to-face interaction, and other customer relation skills. 15	**Good Reputation** Developing and maintaining a consistent reputation for credibility, reliability, fair treatment, and honesty by providing reliable delivery and honoring warranties and guarantees. 16

Customer Service is a requirement for success in today's business environment.

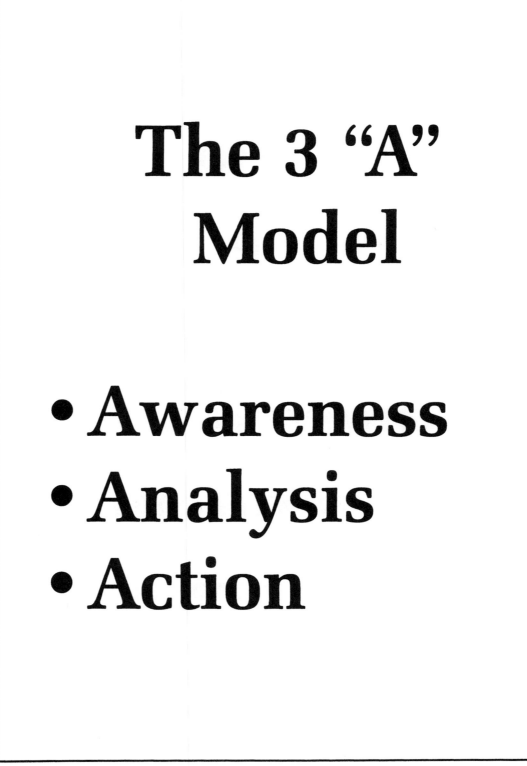

The Way It Is...
The Way It Should Be

1. Motivation
2. Problem Solving
3. Internal Assessments
4. Customer Satisfaction
5. Internal Cooperation
6. Proactive Systems
7. Employment Standards
8. Decision Making
9. Customer Feedback
10. Service Metrics
11. Customer Knowledge
12. Feedback Systems
13. Service-Oriented Culture
14. Empowerment
15. Trained Front-Line Staff
16. Good Reputation

Slide 3

Participant Handout

Section A: Introduction

The purpose of this exercise is to focus your organization's[1] current versus desired customer service priorities. The exercise helps to:

○ Improve teamwork among individuals who provide customer service.
○ Create awareness of current versus desired customer service action steps.
○ Improve the level of customer service through specific actions and commitments.

The objectives of *Customer Service Sort Cards* are to:

○ Create ownership of and commitment to improved customer service.
○ Begin to define actions steps necessary to achieve the group's desired customer service priorities.

---

1. If you are doing this exercise for your department or function, discuss the Customer Service Sort Cards in relationship to your department or function. If you are doing the exercise for your organization, discuss the Customer Service Sort Cards in relationship to the entire organization.

Section B. Customer Service—The Way It Is

Using the 16 Customer Service Sort Cards, identify the top four customer service action steps emphasized by your organization today. Write 1, 2, 3, and 4 in the appropriate space shown below.

Action Step	*Top Four*
1. Motivation	_____
2. Problem Solving	_____
3. Internal Assessments	_____
4. Customer Satisfaction	_____
5. Internal Cooperation	_____
6. Proactive Systems	_____
7. Employment Standards	_____
8. Decision Making	_____
9. Customer Feedback	_____
10. Service Metrics	_____
11. Customer Knowledge	_____
12. Feedback Systems	_____
13. Service-Oriented Culture	_____
14. Empowerment	_____
15. Trained Front-Line Staff	_____
16. Good Reputation	_____

2. How are these customer service action steps emphasized in your organization?

_____

_____

_____

_____

_____

_____

_____

_____

3. How does this affect your organization?

4. Identify the top four customer service action steps de-emphasized by your organization today. Write 1, 2, 3, or 4, in the appropriate space shown below.

Action Step	*Top Four*
1. Motivation	_____
2. Problem Solving	_____
3. Internal Assessments	_____
4. Customer Satisfaction	_____
5. Internal Cooperation	_____
6. Proactive Systems	_____
7. Employment Standards	_____
8. Decision Making	_____
9. Customer Feedback	_____
10. Service Metrics	_____
11. Customer Knowledge	_____
12. Feedback Systems	_____
13. Service-Oriented Culture	_____
14. Empowerment	_____
15. Trained Front-Line Staff	_____
16. Good Reputation	_____

4. How are these customer service action steps de-emphasized in your organization?

_____

_____

_____

_____

_____

_____

_____

_____

_____

_____

5. How does this affect your organization?

_____

_____

_____

_____

_____

_____

_____

_____

_____

Section C. Customer Service: The Way It Should Be

Using the 16 Customer Service Sort Cards, identify the top four customer service action steps that should be emphasized by your organization. Write 1, 2, 3, and 4 in the appropriate space shown below.

Action Step	*Top Four*
1. Motivation	_____
2. Problem Solving	_____
3. Internal Assessments	_____
4. Customer Satisfaction	_____
5. Internal Cooperation	_____
6. Proactive Systems	_____
7. Employment Standards	_____
8. Decision Making	_____
9. Customer Feedback	_____
10. Service Metrics	_____
11. Customer Knowledge	_____
12. Feedback Systems	_____
13. Service-Oriented Culture	_____
14. Empowerment	_____
15. Trained Front-Line Staff	_____
16. Good Reputation	_____

2. How should these customer service action steps be emphasized in your organization? How would their emphasis strengthen your organization?

_____

_____

_____

_____

_____

_____

_____

_____

Section D. Next Steps

1. Based on your discussion, what next steps do you suggest? How will these next steps enhance the level of customer service provided to your customers?

_____

_____

_____

_____

_____

_____

_____

_____

_____

_____

23

Strategies That Foster Customer Loyalty

Lisa Ford

The world is full of slogans, seminars, and books that focus on customer service. We understand that excellent customer service increases customer loyalty, which in turn boosts profitability and drives growth. Then why is customer service so often still so poor? It's a question of moving from attitude into action. This article stresses ways to change organizational culture to value customer loyalty, to do whatever it takes to earn this loyalty one transaction at a time.

What was your latest customer service slogan? "The customer is always right"? "The customer comes first"? "This is the year of the customer"? Have you had a recent customer appreciation week, given all employees lapel buttons stating "Yes, I can" to reflect their empowered attitude? Most organizations have involved their employees in a slogan or a customer service seminar. Everyone in management has bought and perhaps read the latest books on service.

So why is customer service still mediocre at best in so many organizations? Most of the slogans, seminars, and books seem to create the right attitude, yet no meaningful action follows. Words, including these in this article, don't create improvements. Informed action does.

The best people and companies know this. They've come to understand the links connecting excellent customer service, customer loyalty, organizational growth, and profitability. They know that the key to their long-term success is changing the organization's culture to one that prizes customer loyalty. Although it's true that service by itself does not guarantee loyalty, without it you greatly reduce your chances of retaining customers—the basis for building and sustaining growing, prosperous organizations.

In the United States I see three levels of service being delivered. Those three are *rude*, *indifferent*, and *exceptional*. Of these three, which do you mostly receive? "Indifferent" gets my vote.

Here's one of my recent encounters with indifference. While I was renting a car, the customer service agent folded the rental contract, told me how to find my car and in which space, and then said, "Thank you, sir." Wrong, since I'm a "ma'am"! Better yet, why not use "Thank you, Ms. Ford"? The misstatement indicated robotic, indifferent service. It also told me that this company does not have a culture that values me (and perhaps you) as its customer.

Most organizations are great at *processing* customers. Very few excel at *serving* and *satisfying* customers. We get processed all the time. Go to the bank and make a deposit. In most cases you get exactly what you expect—a correct receipt for your deposit and the amount of money you requested. Did anything occur to leave you with a positive impression of the bank that would keep you loyal? Most likely not. Perhaps your teller did not acknowledge you by name or thank you. Maybe the employees talked among themselves.

Exceptional service and satisfaction are required to create loyal customers. The process of being served is what's memorable. That *personalized transaction* is the key to customer retention.

Customer *service* is not enough. Customer *satisfaction* that leads to loyalty is the goal. "Loyalty" means you retain a customer and increase the business you do with that customer, developing a relationship so this customer will not be lured away to the competition with the promise of a lower price.

Most everyone knows the research and statistics, yet few take the numbers to heart. Research done some years ago tells us it costs five to six times more to attract a new customer than to keep a current one. Experts estimate the cost today as being closer to eight to ten times. Bain & Company reports that if a company retains 5% of its current customer base, its profits will increase between 25% and 125%! Have you noticed how many companies spend their time, money, and energy to attract new customers, while doing very little to keep their current customers? Although it's a fairly common practice, it's very short-sighted.

Here's a scenario that's probably happened to you in the last year. Let's say it's 7 o'clock in the evening and you've just sat down to dinner. The telephone rings. You answer and discover it's one of the long-distance telephone carriers offering a great deal with plenty of incentives to entice you to become a new customer. You stop the representative and say, "Time out! You already are my long-distance carrier." The rep responds, "Oops!" Then you ask, "Well, can I have that deal as a customer?" And the answer is "No." The offer is only for a new customer, not you, the established customer.

It's amazing how few organizations have figured out that marketing to current customers is good business. What about your organization? Does it work as hard to build the loyalty and business of current customers as it does to attract new ones?

Six Strategies for Building Customer Loyalty

Let's review what I believe are the six best strategies for building customer loyalty.

1. New glasses for everyone or See your service from your customer's eyes.

There's an old expression, "Perception is all there is." The customer's perception is reality, and perception is rarely neutral: it's either positive or negative.

When seating me in a St. Louis area restaurant, the host pulled out the chair, for which I was grateful, but I could see under the table that the floor was littered with crumbs and empty cracker packages. When I see the dining room floor, I now know what the kitchen looks like and what kind of food to expect. That's my perception—and it becomes the reality by which I decide whether to eat there again.

Here's the opposite. I take my car to a repair shop that always washes it upon completing the repairs. So when I arrive and see my clean car, I'm certain the car's been repaired properly! That's my perception—and it becomes the reality by which I decide whether to take my car there again.

The best companies are constantly taking the customer's pulse so they share in the customer's perception. Those insights drive their companies to higher levels of service delivery. The methods used to take the customer's pulse include surveys, customer councils to elicit feedback, and phone calls. All are very necessary and useful.

Here are a few creative approaches you might consider:

○ Work for a while in your customer's shoes. Weyerhaeuser, in Cottage Grove, Oregon, asked its employees to go spend a week as employees of their customers. Shipping managers worked on loading docks at distribution centers, while accountants worked as customer service reps at retail centers and as freight drivers. Their goals were to listen, learn, and provide insights on how they could improve their work back at Weyerhaeuser. After the improvements were implemented, their customers felt Weyerhaeuser's lumber was better than its competitors'. In a commodity business that competes mostly on price, what a great achievement!

○ Grab one of your surveys and fill it out as if you're a customer. Make sure the questions relate to experiences with your company. Is there room for customers to write comments? Boxes and numbers are usually not enough for them to accurately report their experiences. Make your rating scale different. Use the words "love" and "hate." Research shows when customers check the "love" box, they're loyal. Make sure you continue to do everything to deserve that love and nothing to lose it.

○ Consider using a "didn't get the business" survey. Send out the survey to customers who considered doing business with you but did not accept your bid or price quote. Such customers can give you valuable insights into why they chose someone else, which may often be for reasons other than price. You may discover that the reason was a lack of follow-through or insufficient knowledge. Or perhaps delivery was bad or particular features were missing. You'll find that most customers are willing to participate in such a survey.

○ Invite a customer to speak at your next meeting. This gives your staff "real-time" feedback. Let the customer describe his or her recent experiences with your company, including the good, the bad, and the ugly. This is certainly more effective than having someone from the marketing department show graphs from the latest surveys. Invite a customer at least quarterly.

○ When talking to your customer, whether via surveys, on the phone, or in person, ask, "If there were one thing you would like to see us change, that one thing would be. . . ." and "Who do you like doing business with and why?'' If this is a new customer, you have a great opportunity to find out ''Why did you choose us?'' and ''What did you dislike about your most recent supplier/vendor?'' A new customer is smartest after a purchase decision. Don't pass up a chance to gather some insights.

Seeing service from your customer's eyes means giving yourself an *external* view, rather than the usual *internal* one. We all need a new set of glasses on a regular basis. Your challenge: Ask customers for feedback—and act on it.

2. Make the customer's encounter with the company a delight *or* Redefine the customer's expectations of great service.

If you do *only* what's expected, there's no guarantee that the customer will return. Today's competitive world requires creating memorable experiences that differentiate you from the others. Very few companies have the luxury of offering a product or service that's so unique that customers remain captive.

Here are some memorable experiences:

- Direct Tire Sales, Watertown, Massachusetts, offers customers a free taxi ride or a loaner car to get back home or to work. That one policy causes customers to call and ask, ''Is it true you pay for the taxi ride to work?'' When they hear ''Yes,'' they seldom question the price of the tires. If that's not enough, the sparkling clean waiting area has complimentary coffee with real cream and fresh croissants along with current magazines.
- Georgia Power, an electricity company, creates a memorable experience based on its advertised guarantee: ''We will connect your service by the date promised.'' Here's how the company turns a simple guarantee into a surprising situation—and a memorable experience. Let's say you were promised the electricity would be connected on Tuesday. Then, to your dismay, it was not. You call the company to express your disappointment and possibly your anger. The customer service representative checks your records, then apologizes. Now the surprise: the rep continues, ''Here's what we'll do: we will have it on for you tomorrow and, since we did not live up to our promise and guarantee, we will credit your account with $100 for every day we are late.'' Your jaw drops. After you recover, what are the first words out of your mouth? ''Hey, take your time. I'll wait a few more days!'' This really exceeds the customer's expectation, since it's not what we expect from a utility company.
- A heating and cooling company has technicians who slip booties on over their work shoes before entering the customer's home. They lay a red carpet down on the work area around the unit. Attention to these kinds of details creates impressions that cement lifelong customer relationships.
- Great American Business Products in Houston offers a free gift to any customer who's put on hold to wait for the next representative. The hold recording tells customers this good news. The company can afford the gifts because customers seldom have to be put on hold. When it happens, the company

offers the gift as an apology and to make the wait worth the customer's time. Customers love the free gift—and the superior fast service.

○ A computer company offers any customer who's on hold for more than three minutes the choice of a phone card or a 30-day extension on the warranty.

○ A dental practice in Maryland hands out flowers to patients on Valentine's Day and lottery tickets to dads on Father's Day. This creative, wacky staff takes any opportunity to put on costumes. Patients schedule appointments around certain holidays, especially Halloween, simply for the memorable experience!

○ A large paper manufacturer includes a signed packing slip and actual photos of the shipping department employees responsible for the jobs. Their customers love the personal touch. It says "We care, and we're proud to serve you."

Your challenge: Identify six ways in which you've exceeded and redefined your customers' expectations of great service.

3. Till death do us part *or* Build partnerships.

Individualize, personalize, and customize. The days of the customer being the adversary are long gone. Customers seek partnerships that can last a lifetime. People being creatures of habit, customers prefer to keep their business in one place if they continue to feel they're receiving good value. Just as it's expensive for companies to attract new customers, it's also time-consuming to find new suppliers. So eliminate any reasons your customers might have to do that.

Consider these methods:

○ Sea 1st Bank of Seattle realized that the first few months of the relationship are crucial to customer retention. The day when a new customer opens an account, a thank-you letter is sent out to that customer, personalized by the employee who served him or her. At 14 days, the employee calls the customer to check on how things are going ("Did your checks and ATM card arrive?"). At 30 days, a survey is sent out to solicit feedback on the experience of opening the account. With these efforts in place, Sea 1st has retained five times the number of customers over a three-year period as it had before initiating the process.

○ A florist sends out a card to customers who have used its services to send flowers for a special day the previous year. The card reminds customers of what was sent last year and how a simple phone call would enable them to do the same this year. With each initial order, the florist asks the customer if he or she would like such a reminder card (obviously to prevent any embarrassing moments).

Consider how you might use computerized databases to let your customers know you remember their last transaction and you know their preferences. A customer should never have to tell you the same thing twice. Demonstrate to the customer that you're investing in the relationship and learning about him or her. When customers see you're intimate with them, they're more willing to take risks with you. That's very important as you try new things with your technology, products, and services.

Here's a simple example of a learning relationship. When you call the local pizza delivery place, the person who answers asks for your phone number and, with that information, then asks, "Would you like a large mushroom and pepperoni on a thin crust as you ordered last week?" The message there is that those people remember you and are ready to quickly accommodate your needs.

Most likely your company sells something much more complicated than pizza. Are you knowledgeable about your customer's preferences? The reality is that you'd better be, because your customer is comparing you with anyone who delivers superior personalized service.

Your challenge: What are you doing to learn about your customer? Can you use that information to create a partnership? A happy marriage is built on communicating, improving, and growing together as you continually learn about your partner. How do your customers feel about you? Are they willing to renew the vows? Or are they ready to divorce you?

4. Common sense required *or* Get back to the basics.

I won't belabor this point. The best organizations usually stand out because they're great at the basics and slaves to the details.

Here are four of the basics for you to evaluate.

Listening skills. One of my favorite sayings is "There is a difference between listening and waiting for your turn to talk." What is your habit? Do you look for the answer on the computer screen? Or do you listen to what's being said first and then seek the answer?

Phone skills. Have you called your company or department lately? The next time you do, listen and think about what your customer experiences. Are there endless recordings, rushed greetings, pleas to "Hold, please," or numerous transfers? Customers want to talk to only one person. They expect whoever answers the phone to be empowered and able to handle any type of question or problem—and do it fast and right the first time!

Research done by TARP/SOCAP (see the article in this book by John Goodman on the impact of service excellence) shows that customers calling 800 numbers with problems or inquiries report much higher satisfaction when they get an answer in one call. In the computer industry, for example, if a problem is solved in a single call, 68% of the customers are completely satisfied, but that figure drops to only 28% if it takes two or more contacts.

Does your company use the "one-voice concept" or "first touch—last touch" approach to satisfy customers? Your customer wants the personalization and continuity of dealing with one staff person and not getting the run-around. Ask yourself these questions about your phone handling:

○ Do customers get regularly dumped into voice mail without warning?
○ How quickly does the customer get a return call after leaving a voice mail message? (Some companies have a two-hour promise to return calls or a sunset rule, which means the call will be returned by the end of the day.)

○ Can your customer get a real live person easily? Customers are getting more comfortable with automation and telephone technology, yet they still demand personal attention when the situation requires it.

Finally, two other basic areas where customers expect a professional approach: **recovery skills**—the ability to deal effectively with angry customers—and **handling customer criticism.**

You know what the basics are. Just make certain you and the rest of the staff are practicing them daily. It's not always easy, but it's vital to keep your customers satisfied, and thus it's vital to your success as well.

If you're not paying attention to the details, it can be costly. And it's not just the cost of losing one customer. You need to remember that customers talk loudly and spread the word widely when dissatisfied. Everyone is familiar with the TARP research that says a satisfied customer tells four or five others, while a dissatisfied one tells 10 to 12.

That's not true today. Now the angry customer simply logs onto the Internet and tells thousands, possibly millions immediately. A dissatisfied customer is an incredible threat.

Your challenge: Create a sense of urgency to be obsessed with the basics and details.

5. Beyond warm bodies *or* Hire and train the best employees.

Recruiting strategy is a top priority. The first step in delivering superior service is to start with the right employees. Too often we've heard managers who are short-staffed say, "Hire anybody, get some warm bodies." I'm concerned with that attitude because it generally results in warm bodies and not much else. Now take the "warm bodies" comment a step further. If you're a newly hired employee hearing your new manager make that plea, then what are you? Obviously, only a warm body!

Steve Carline, CEO of a training firm, says, "We only hire creative, intelligent, and articulate people." The employees of this company know they're special and live up to Carline's expectations.

What the best service companies have discovered is "hire the attitude." As Herb Kelleher, president of Southwest Airlines, says, "People who can fly airplanes are a dime a dozen. People with great attitudes aren't." (See the article in this book on Southwest Airlines by Jody Hoffer Gittell.) It's a lot easier to train people in technical skills than in attitude.

So, during the interview process, ask questions that uncover how this candidate acts and thinks in customer situations. Here are two questions you can ask to get at a potential employee's attitude:

○ What's an example of you providing exceptional customer service?
○ What's an example of customer service that's frustrated you?

You can also create customer situations and ask candidates how they would handle them. Then look for answers that project a positive approach that resulted in win-win for the customer and the company. Of course, make sure that's your attitude as well.

When interviewing someone for a job that requires a lot of phone contact with your customers, do some of the job interview over the phone. Your candidate might be brilliant and charming face to face, but lackluster and abrasive on the phone.

Another simple guideline to hiring smart is not to oversell your company. Tell the candidate the highlights, of course, but also the frustrations of everyday life. If you can, hire this person for a day or two so he or she can get a feel for the environment. One company calls this process "realistic job preview." This gives everyone the chance to determine if the fit is right. The last thing you want is "buyer's remorse"—for your company, your new employee, or both. Turnover is deadly to customer satisfaction and retention.

Once the person is on board, training is crucial. Too many companies turn an untrained employee loose to serve valuable customers. This is deadly, for both the employee and customer. Customers get frustrated when dealing with someone who doesn't have solutions or the skills to handle tough situations. This usually leads to customer turnover and employee turnover as well.

Two quick examples of the benefits of training. Ryder Truck found that turnover for employees who participated in the company's new training program was 19%, far lower than the 41% rate for employees who did not participate. Motorola invests 3.2% of its payroll in training—an investment that results in a 30% gain in productivity.

Training for customer service reps should cover technical skills, but it should also cover how to listen effectively and how to deal with angry customers. Many companies teach employees how to "process the customer," but service and satisfaction skills are what will positively differentiate your company from your competitors. There is clear and convincing research that excellent customer service employees mean satisfied, retained customers.

Here's your challenge: Do you invest as much time in hiring and training new employees as you do in finding and attracting new customers?

6. Act like you mean it *or* Lead to inspire great service.

Everyone knows this one. As stated at the start, most companies have only the slogans right. Unfortunately, their actions are often not aligned with these slogans. The best organizations have made high levels of customer satisfaction a part of their team and department goals.

Here are some ways to help employees implement these goals:

- **Do job trading.** Invite employees from other teams to observe. Make certain your team goes out to other departments. This exchange can last from one day to a week. Companies successful with this idea make job trading a part of the performance appraisal; employees are responsible for setting up the exchange quarterly. If you have some departments in which walls and turfs still exist, job trading can help build a shared understanding of how everyone's work affects others.
- **Involve employees in ideas to improve service.** One manager asks his team,

"If you had my job, what three things would you do to improve customer satisfaction?" This manager is very diligent in following through and implementing the ideas she's given. Employees are an incredible source of ways to improve—when there's evidence someone's listening to them and putting their ideas into practice.

○ **Use slogans that are aligned with policies, procedures, reward systems, recruiting, and training.** Words can inspire when employees feel empowered to act accordingly. That's a culture that supports and inspires customer loyalty.

Exemplary leadership is perhaps the most important ingredient in your formula for success.

Here's your challenge: When was the last time leaders in your organization listened in on customer calls? If it's been a while, do it. And do the leaders of your organization speak convincingly and take actions that lead to high-quality customer service? Do they recognize the connection between this service and customer retention? If not, managers at all levels need to carefully consider who pays the bills and how the company can make sure they're satisfied.

Final Thoughts

Today's customer expects and demands more. Your customers will easily and often quietly take their business elsewhere if all you give them is basic service. If you don't want that to happen, pay attention. Create service that upgrades customer expectations. Build the partnerships that create customer loyalty. Remember: you earn this loyalty one transaction at a time. Exceptional service is not magic; it simply requires an unrelenting commitment to doing right by each customer.

About the Author

Lisa Ford is a speaker and seminar leader with 18 years of experience presenting to businesses, associations, and government. She speaks throughout the United States and internationally on topics of customer service, leadership, team issues, and change. Lisa is the author of the videotape series "How to Give Exceptional Customer Service"—the #1 selling business tapes in the U.S. for the last three years. Her other videos and audiotapes include "Developing a Customer Retention Program," "Building a Customer-Driven Organization: The Manager's Role," and "Personal Power."

24

THE CARE AND HANDLING OF THE MATURE MARKET

Patricia V. Alea and Rebecca Chekouras

There's a great market out there for your products and services—and it's growing larger and more powerful all the time. It's the world of people over age 50—the mature market. This article will help you better understand the critical character-istics of the mature market, so you and your employees will know more about what 50-plus consumers want and need and be better able to provide it.

Typically, when business people think of the mature market they make two fatal errors: they think *way too old* and they think *way too small*. Don't underestimate the aging of America and the implications for how you deliver customer service. This trend is going to dominate most businesses for the rest of your life.

In brief: the mature market is large, it's growing, it has all the money, and it's different from generations that have come before. This difference, this "newness" of the market, is predominantly expressed in the changing lifestages of today's 50-plus consumer.

Perhaps that doesn't sound like fast-breaking news, but these lifestages are packed with surprises for them and for you. Once you get a handle on the rich variety of lifestages and the resulting wants and needs among the 50-plus crowd, you'll begin to help them solve their problems, meet their challenges, and enhance their lives rather than simply trying to "sell them something." Your business struc-ture with them will be transformed from a *transaction*, in which suppliers are all alike and interchangeable, to a *relationship*, in which you become the value-added, differentiated supplier whom they trust.

This chapter will explain the key drivers—the hot buttons that influence this market. These drivers are connected to generational identity, age-related values, and the current social, cultural, and economic trends that color the way these consumers experience the world around them.

When you gain real understanding of these critical factors, your ability to serve the mature market will be better than best—it will be outstanding. But make no mistake. This is a tough, discriminating market. Pleasing mature customers is not about wearing a smiley face button and saying, "Have a nice day." In fact, that kind of behavior is likely to backfire. There's nothing superficial about 50-plus Americans as consumers and nothing more insulting to them than a "canned" or insincere approach. A deeper understanding of the mature market is your key to outstanding customer service. In an era when "quality" has become the price of entry, service has become the point of differentiation.

Understanding the Importance of the Mature Market

The following provides a review of several characteristics of the mature market and includes the points you need to share with employees about understanding and dealing with customers in this large and growing market segment.

It's Big and Getting Bigger

America is aging . . . and aging pretty well. At the beginning of this century, when life expectancy at birth was 45 years, 50 was old. Today, because of quantum leaps in longevity, that's just not true anymore. In 1900, most people didn't live long enough to become part of a mature population as we now know it. How many of us have heard stories within our families of those who worked hard all their lives, retired, and quite quickly died, as if the end of their "usefulness" marked them as finished? Today, it's common to live 20, even 25 years beyond retirement age.

Today, life expectancy at birth is almost double what it was a hundred years ago. By the year 2050 the "average" American will live to be 90! Every aspect of life as we know it will be impacted by this phenomenon. Imagine a society with a rapidly expanding mature market and a simultaneously shrinking youth market. That's America today and, in fact, that's the story in most industrialized nations. Our society is becoming dominated by mature Americans whose attitudes, needs, and preferences—that is, their consumption patterns—extend well beyond their work lives and influence the creation, production, and delivery of goods and services for an additional 10, 20, or 30 years.

Not only are people going to live significantly longer than previous generations, but there are going to be millions more doing so. No other trend that we will experience in our lifetime will be even half as influential.

When historians look back on the 20th century, what will astound them? It won't be the exploration of space, magnificent as that may be. It won't be the advent of computers, those marvels of our genius, or even the rise and fall of Communism. It will be the addition of 30 years to the human life span in the space of one century! We have virtually doubled the time a human being exists on this planet: more consumers, living twice as long. In this new paradigm, a relationship (multiple sales over a customer's lifetime) makes more sense than a transaction (a single sale at a single moment in time).

Right now there are 69 million people over the age of 50. By the turn of this century, as the enormous Baby Boom generation swells the ranks of older Americans, there will be 76 million—and by 2020 an astonishing 115 million. (You can chart the growth of the 50-plus population by going to the U.S. Census home page on the Internet at www.census.gov/.)

Learning how to serve the mature market is just plain good business, and the return on your understanding is going to increase over the decades to come. Yet, to date, surprisingly few have been willing to invest in this critical market segment.

Why this blind spot? Because most of us think we already understand "old people." So we go on treating them as we always have: we ignore them, patronize them, or expect them to adapt to (our) business as usual. The marketplace has traditionally (and relentlessly) focused on younger consumers, and advertisers (frequently young themselves) continue to underestimate the segment that has all the growth potential—the mature market.

The youth market is shrinking. The mature market is burgeoning: it's where the "juice" is. It's powerful. It's different from generations past. It's complex and multidimensional. And it's fascinating.

People today who are 50, 60, and 70 years old are pioneering previously unimagined ways to live. These pioneers don't think of themselves as old, at least not in the way their grandparents did. Think of it the way it's being lived. Aging Americans today have an additional 20 or 30 years added *not* to the *end* but to the *middle* of their lives. So we have a growing population with a new expectation about aging. They expect to live a long time and enjoy it.

Key Points to Share With Employees

- The mature market is the largest, wealthiest customer group in history.
- Expanded life expectancy means an extended middle age, not a prolonged old age.
- Consumer demands are exploding because more people living longer have enormous new needs.

It's a New Kind of Market

In the past, people lived what we might call "linear lives." That is, their lives followed a fairly predictable sequence of events, or lifestages, which were experienced once and not repeated. Similarly, each of these lifestages carried, implicit within its boundaries, a pattern of product wants and needs. For example, the customary path of a typical life looked like this: birth, education, first job, marriage, children, retirement, death. And a lot of people made a lot of money following this predictable, if somewhat sleepy pattern. Men came home from World War II. They married and needed life insurance, houses, and cars. Their children were born and needed clothes and schooling. Their children hit adolescence and needed fads and fashion. On and on, the wheels of commerce ground this grist.

Then, something happened. Their children, the Baby Boomers, lived their lives differently. The Boomers (we can hardly call them "Baby" anymore, now that they're between the ages of 34 and 52!) began living *cyclical* lives, repeating lifestages whenever they wanted: multiple marriages, multiple families, blended families, working moms moving in and out of the workforce, multiple educations as the demands of downsizing and advancing technology created a new idea in careers: retooling.

This is the new mature market that's moving into 50-plus at the rate of one person every eight seconds for the next 20 years. They think differently. They've lived differently. They are different consumers. Their demand for service is exponentially greater than their parents' was.

It's Powerful

As the 69 million Americans who are 50-plus today are joined every eight seconds by another Boomer, the financial impact of this complex generation continues to astound.

Although Americans over the age of 50 represent only 26% of the U.S. population, their economic impact is very impressive—and growing every year. Consider the following percentages for what they own and what they're buying:

Bank/S&L deposits	80%
Mortgage-free homes	70%
All stockholders in the U.S.	66%
Insured money market certificates	60%
Wall-to-wall carpet	57%
Disposable income	55%
Golf shoes	55%
Color televisions	53%
Recreational vehicles	51%
Furs	49%
Domestic cars	48%
Cameras	47%
Home furnishings	40%
Major appliances	37%
New cars (all)	33%

Those 50 and older, although just 26% of the population, control 65% of the total net worth of U.S. households—over $7 trillion. Hold these figures in your mind for a moment. Now tell yourself, "These numbers are only going to get bigger." And those people are going to spend much of that money on *living*, not just *surviving*. Now you're beginning to see the "demographic imperative" of the mature market.

Key Points to Share With Employees

- The mature market has more money and spending power than any other segment.
- People 50-plus are spenders, not browsers.
- Targeting the mature market is good business. Ignoring it is foolish.

Different From Past Generations

A woman we know who just celebrated her 50th birthday with a lavish party of 200 friends says, "I'm not a 'black balloon' type of gal." Aging no longer means a loss of vitality or diminished hopes and dreams. Rather, older Americans are refashioning their lives in unprecedented ways. It's getting easier to imagine the second half of life as possibly the best half. Although they're all pushing 50 or somewhere beyond that point, the Rolling Stones, Neil Diamond, Kiss, and Rod Stewart are among the top earners in rock and roll and, some would claim, still major creative forces in popular culture. Arnold Schwarzenegger is still all muscles. Diane Sawyer is still getting the scoop. The "new old" are not only retaining their energy, they're taking it to new heights.

A 50-something woman we know took her mother on a cruise last year. When filling out forms for the travel agency, the daughter inquired of her 82-year-old mother, "Do you want to be listed as 'single' or 'widowed'?" Her mother replied, "Just put me down as 'available.' " And she wasn't joking. What does it mean to know that a woman 80-plus is still hoping for romance? What are the implications for those 30 years younger? People today who are beyond age 50 are seeking new adventures, relationships, careers, and spiritual experiences. And that means they are consumers. They will buy products and services that advance those dreams— and they have the money to do it.

Key Points to Share With Employees

- Those you may see as "old" don't see themselves that way—and they don't purchase as "old" people.
- Reframe your vision to recognize their vitality, their *expanding* (not shrinking) product needs.
- Rehumanize mature customers by seeing them as individuals with unique plans, hopes, and dreams.
- If a woman who looks wrinkled is buying wrinkle prevention cream, respect her optimism.

Understanding Changing Lifestage Needs

When "mature" was 65 and retired, it was easy to lump together all people beyond that age as one market with similar wants and needs. That perspective will run you out of business today.

As tens of millions of Americans pass age 50, it's an ongoing challenge to sort out what is and what isn't predictable in terms of lifestage. Lifestage is the single greatest driver of product wants and needs. Aging is being reinvented, as we've said. The "new" mature market is infinitely more complex, filled with surprises, and it constitutes nothing less than a reinvention of the family.

Picture a man, mainstream, age 55, with a college degree and a $75,000 income. What is his lifestage driving him to put in his shopping cart? He could be looking at early retirement and enjoying an "empty nest" with a long-time spouse. He could be newly married and embarking on the challenges of a second family. He could be helping to care for grandchildren and supporting his parents at the same time, while working as hard as he can to retain financial stability.

The point is that it's impossible to know what anyone in the mature market wants and needs simply by looking at the old, linear model. Marketing today requires an understanding of the complexities of life options at the turn of this very new century.

One woman we know describes her family as "blended, extended, upended." She is 52. Her spouse of 15 years is 45. Her grown daughters are 25 and 27 and on their own. Their father, her long-ago husband, is 56. His new wife is 34 and their family includes a three-year-old and a baby who's only five months old. This "blended, extended, upended family" of eight represents over $100,000 in discretionary annual income. Unless your understanding of the mature market includes them, these dollars will go to someone else.

Not so long ago, life seemed to have clear and predictable stages: birth, education, marriage, work and family, and death. But because of our new, cyclical lives, today an individual is likely to have numerous career changes, more than one marriage, the periodic need for ongoing education in relation to work, and caregiving responsibilities for children, grandchildren, and aging parents. The extra 20–30 years in the middle of our lives can be packed with new goals and new needs. The changes in life activities vary greatly and are unique to each individual. However, new technologies provide us with ways of getting and using information that can allow us great insight into who these people are and how they live their lives. Within the general mature market, we can identify discrete segments: new relationships, empty-nesting, caregiving, new singlehood, grandparenting, retirement, and post-retirement careers.

As people enter a new lifestage, their product wants and needs change profoundly. It's the best time to win them as customers. Those who are *just turning 50* might be involved in new relationships or blended family formations. Late-stage parenting or adapting to stepchildren are not uncommon experiences among this group. Most are still highly involved in career roles and responsibilities and, while they may be experiencing some characteristics of aging, there is little acknowledgment of it. *Empty nesters*, in contrast, have new flexibility and spontaneity in their lives, are open to new experiences, and exhibit increasing awareness of the need for health-related and financial planning.

Caregivers, who are often responsible for consumer decisions for themselves and others in their families, are also known to need support and to desire escape from their responsibilities on occasion. Older people who are *single*—by choice or by chance—seek trusted advisors and increased social activity, and they're frequently building a tentative sense of new independence. Many older single women, for example, are fearful of high-pressure sales situations. And many are uninformed and intimidated about financial decisions. Sensitive marketers have begun to create "safe" settings in which they build confidence by establishing trust and by listening to the fears of such consumers before trying to sell them goods or services. An unanticipated reward for such marketers has been the rate of referrals they receive once they win the customer. Older single women routinely exchange advice on consumer decisions with their friends.

Modern *grandparenting*, another dynamic lifestage, creates the need for additional purchases for cherished grandchildren. For many in this segment, maintaining long-distance relationships includes increased travel, higher telephone bills, and even growing use of on-line computer services in order to e-mail the little ones.

Retirement has begun to mean a refocusing on life interests that have been set aside during busier times. The current 65-and-over population is increasingly likely to seek meaningful work, paid or volunteer, while it enjoys the highest level of discretionary income among all mature consumer segments. Their post-career years may find them taking up new hobbies, enjoying sports, and increasing travel expenditures while paying acute attention to medical and financial products and services.

Key Points to Share With Employees

- As the mature market expands, it evolves into a myriad of lifestages.
- Each lifestage segment represents new and specific consumer needs and desires.
- Products, goods, and services should be offered specifically and strategically in relation to lifestage.
- Take the time to learn about and meet lifestage needs by listening to customers.

Understanding the Key Drivers of the Needs of the 50-Plus Market

Now that we've established the importance of the mature market in size, variety, and power, and looked at some of the specific lifestages that drive the needs of those 50 and older, we can consider the general, shared characteristics. Factors such as cohort (generational identity), lifelong values, and socioeconomic trends that influence most Americans at the close of the 20th century further flavor the delicate mix of who this mature consumer is.

Cohort Identity

Cohort identity provides a fascinating perspective from which to view any consumer. Every age group has a set of shared cultural and historical experiences. These are "lasting marks" or indelible traits created by their common historical experience when coming of age. Cohort differences shade the ways we perceive and react to the outside world.

Just a few years ago, people of various ages were asked what kinds of smells or aromas brought up pleasing nostalgic memories of their childhood. Those aged 70 and over were likely to say "mowed grass" or "grassy fields on a summer's day," while those who were younger than 30 said things like "Playdoh" and "diesel fuel." The world of childhood had changed.

The same is happening with the world of 50-plus. A new cohort of "inhabitants" is moving in and the mature market is changing! Cohort recognition will allow you to shape your product to the market and create the communication and service breakthrough that will get your message past the daily marketing barrage with which they're inundated.

Boomers, those people born between 1946 and 1964, have proven themselves to be spenders and debtors who seek and enjoy immediate gratification. The sheer numbers of their generation have created lemming-like marketplace response.

They're accustomed to demanding and getting what they want. Boomers, although they number in the many millions, are highly individualistic and are notoriously cause-oriented. This generation is famously anti-authoritarian and mistrustful of "established" systems. They are, for the most part, comfortable with technology. After all, they invented most of it! To reach mature customers, sensitivity to generational values provides insight for establishing style and tone, choosing language, and creating promotions brought to life through an accurate reflection of who they are and how they see themselves.

Key Points to Share With Employees

- Cohort experiences provide you with "hot buttons" for getting the attention of consumers.
- Targeted products and services that reach customers' emotions are key to successful sales strategies.
- You can and should state features and benefits of your goods and services according to customers' values and priorities.

Common Physical Challenges, Uncommon Responses

As we age, our bodies, no matter how well we take care of them, show signs of wear and tear. But, as usual, the Boomers have "attitude" about the inevitable. What are the stereotypes that come to your mind when you hear these phrases: physical disability, hearing loss, memory lapse, heart condition, joint pain? You probably think "old" as in "helpless" or "cranky." Does "geezer" come to mind? Maybe you're more sympathetic. You're thinking "frail, slowing down."

Well, think again. Those who are beginning to grow older in the late 20th century may be enduring the symptoms of new physical challenges, but they're hardly deteriorating into "geezerhood." If previous generations gave in to physical deterioration and resigned themselves to a slower senior lifestyle, don't look for such surrender among today's "new old."

Some snapshots of the physically challenged:

- A 50-year-old executive with chronic back pain continues to travel the world giving corporate presentations while wearing a back brace beneath her Dana Buchman jacket. Between trips she uses massage and acupuncture to improve her condition.
- A 52-year-old veteran volleyball player ices her knees after each game. "They swell up," she says, "but I'm not quitting!"
- A 55-year-old dad has just finished his second rotator cuff surgery and is rebuilding shoulder strength in order to continue summer backpacking trips with his daughter, a forest ranger.
- A 56-year-old survivor of seven-way bypass surgery assumes an aggressive rehabilitation schedule and is able to join his friends in Montana eight months later for the annual tent-camping vacation.
- A 60-year-old professor shares a laugh with her students when she admits

she tried to calculate their grades on her TV remote control device. Her credibility remains high with the kids.

○ A 52-year-old mom, completely unable to hear specific conversations, enjoys the noise anyway in the Hollywood swing dance club where her daughters have taken her for a night out.

○ A 56-year-old lifelong skier who injures his spine in a fall relentlessly rebuilds stamina and is back on the slopes the following season. A little uncomfortable, a bit careful, but back!

Are you getting the picture? Stuff happens! And today's over-50 folks are ready and eager to deal with it and get back to their interests with renewed energy.

So how can you better serve people who are experiencing new challenges, who are willing to admit it, but who don't want to be identified with "disability"? People who may have a physical disability—temporary or permanent—but who are determined to keep their spirits intact?

The best approach is to understand that a *challenge* isn't a *crisis*. Offer ordinary consideration and attention to comfort and safety in your sales setting—for all your customers.

"Universal design" means *everybody* and, happily, everybody likes it. No one feels that they have been broken away from the mainstream, shunted because of some physical condition. Following the principles of universal design, provide readable signs, reduce noise, create brochures anyone can read, and offer information that's easy to understand for all your customers. No need to single out those over 50. When you see someone who looks confused, tired, and/or physically burdened, the chances are it will be a young mother with a toddler in tow. Sensitivity to the vision, hearing, dexterity, and special circumstances of all customers is just good business.

A 60-year-old woman we know who is in excellent health recounted a story of a shopping trip to a large city, during which she became increasingly weary as a result of holiday crowds and hours of gift buying. A sensitive young saleswoman who was about to ring the woman's sale and package her purchases took a look at her and asked, "Would you like to come to the back room and sit down while I wrap these things up?" The shopper was very pleased, not only with the chance to rest for a few moments but because the sales clerk, with one glance, could see and appreciate her weariness. She mentioned particularly that the personal and sincere offer didn't make her feel "old." Not everyone in a sales role has the opportunity to offer a special spot for a tired customer, but connecting with and truly acknowledging any customer's reality can make a big difference.

Key Points to Share With Employees

○ Check your sales setting for clear signage, distracting noise levels, and possible physical hazards—for the benefit of all customers.

○ Note the comfort level of your customers during transactions and offer to help anytime it's needed.

○ Talk to your customers. Find out if your setting is a part of the advantage you have to offer.

Mature Consumer Preferences

As people age, they accumulate multiple decades of consumer experience. Apart from the specific characteristics of lifestage and cohort, mature customers are likely to share some general attributes in the ways they make choices.

Broadly, mature customers . . .

. . . Are relationship-based buyers.

One customer described waiting over two months for a pest control company to help her deal with an invasion of bats in her attic. The company was unable to help her sooner because of an unusually high seasonal demand for its services. But she was unwilling to contact another firm because, as she put it, "They are the company I always use." The company offered her a substantial discount on the bill because of her loyalty and the relationship remained strong in spite of the inconvenience to the customer.

. . . Like to be acknowledged for their life experience and savvy.

An older man tells the story of his most recent automobile purchase. Instead of getting a high-pressure approach at the dealership he visited, the salesman spent a lot of time listening and even asked him to tell his stories of previous car selections. Most of us accumulate an auto history in our lifetimes and many of us enjoy remembering our favorite cars. This customer not only was allowed to indulge in his memories, he provided the salesman with clear statements about his values and the benefits of previous successful transactions. The salesman was then able to discuss directly and clearly which of the options available would create a satisfying purchase.

. . . Value convenience.

Although some older consumers are likely to have discretionary time to shop and compare for expensive, important items, most appreciate transactions that don't cause unnecessary wear and tear on them, either physically or emotionally. It saves time and reduces frustration if you clearly provide the right amount of information. The space in which sales transactions occur should be comfortable and convenient: customers burdened with a long wait in a standing-room-only environment may grow frustrated and go elsewhere. A local merchant with a picture framing business only recently realized that including information in his advertisements about convenient parking behind his store was a key benefit for older customers.

. . . Are concerned with quality over cost and willing to switch brands.

Mature consumers have learned many of the hard lessons of buying cheap and suffering the consequences. Their lifetime of experience has taught them that quality pays. Yet, as the marketplace multiplies its offerings, older customers are curious about new options and willing to spend the time necessary to research and find new and better products and services. And they listen to one another and share consumer experiences, both good and bad. When selling to such customers, it's important to acknowledge their expertise and ask about the experiences they've had. This approach creates an opportunity to discuss comparative advantages and to discuss product or service benefits that may be new and improved.

Key Points to Share With Employees

- Nurture existing relationships and reward loyalty.
- Build trust and gain insight by listening.
- Create purchase options that are respectful of limited time and endurance.
- Explain "new and better" options as the opportunity arises.

Trends and Influences at the Turn of a New Century

Quick! From the customer's point of view, what's the most critical need filled by customer service? And how does your customer see this need fulfilled in your store?

In a world where most products are rapidly becoming commoditized, service becomes increasingly the determining factor in the purchase decision. So let's understand right up front that the stakes are high. You're going to need to do better than "business as usual." You need to understand what drives the customer's perception of good service and, from that knowledge, evaluate and refine your practices.

Two distinct trends shaping the American consumer experience at the close of the 20th century are related to *time* and *fear*. These trends apply universally, but in a rapidly changing world, these trends are magnified for the mature consumer, as multiple demands on their time and attention erode their tolerance for "new for the sake of new" and make them more receptive when "new" translates into a clear and utilitarian benefit.

The Customer Service Equation From the Seller's Side

At its most basic level, your relationship with your customer is transactional, so it's critical to understand the dynamics of the transaction on both sides of the equation. For you, the merchant, customer service provides the platform for three critical marketing opportunities: extension of the original sale, opportunity to resell, and opportunity to create positive referral.

Customer service engages you (or if it occurs after the sale, re-engages you) with your best customer—the person who already buys from you. The cost of keeping a satisfied customer is significantly less than that of acquiring one who doesn't know you and has to be convinced there's a reason to buy from you. Service is your opportunity to resell that customer and, significantly, move that customer from one who's willing to shop your store to one who's willing to shop your store *and* willing to tell his or her friends to shop your store.

You know you can't build a business if, for every two people who walk in the front door, five are walking out the back. Now, imagine that those five customers you just lost are telling five of their friends to leave too. That's 25 negative impressions. While most marketers appreciate the power of positive referral, many underestimate the serious erosion caused by negative referral.

Every employee needs to internalize the simple truth that customer service is *selling* and that there's a sales obligation implicit in every interaction with a customer. Furthermore, and this is critical, each employee must understand in no uncertain terms just what it is he or she is selling in those interactions.

Management's obligation is to ensure that employees understand these two essential facts:

○ Each employee is selling—whether that employee is stocking the shelves of a grocery store, installing a car battery, or fielding a phone call.
○ What is being sold is larger and more important than just the store's product.

How is this so? Consider two examples: Nike and Domino's Pizza.

What is Nike selling? Sneakers? Not really. Athletic footwear is a hotly contested category and there are many brands, each claiming its shoe is somehow better than a competitor's shoe. The truth is that the top three brands are all good shoes, well made, featuring superior foot support and made of quality materials. Quality is not what differentiates among the top brands. Rather, quality is just the price of entry into the top brand rankings. Knowing it can't differentiate on product, Nike competes on something beyond product. While Reebok may be selling a sneaker, Nike is selling motivation.

Nike has carefully cultivated its product to become a sign of membership in an exclusive club of highly motivated athletes who are serious about what they do and impressive. Nike has "transformed" its shoes from footwear to admission into an "inner circle" that's not for everybody.

But, you may be thinking, this is a marketing campaign composed largely of advertising images and themes. How can *customer service* transform a product?

Let's look at a product that's even more of a commodity than sneakers—pizza. You can't even count all the brands available in some markets. And, to make matters more difficult, no matter how much glamour you try to surround them with, tomatoes, onions, and peppers are, well, just tomatoes, onions, and peppers. Domino's was the first to understand that, while it might be tough to sell pizzas on a grand scale, it's easy to sell convenience. Domino's stopped selling its customers tomatoes, onions, and peppers and started selling 30-minute delivery time anytime of the day or night.

The Customer Service Equation From the Buyer's Side

What is the most critical need filled by customer service? And how does your customer see your service in relation to this need?

Wants and needs arise within a context; they are not absolutes. That's why it's so important to understand your customer in the larger context of his or her life, rather than in a single, isolated moment in your store. Understand the major trends shaping the customer's shopping experience and you understand how to create a service atmosphere that can make a critical difference in the customer's store preference and loyalty.

When we examine these major trends and their impact on contemporary life choices, it becomes clear that the "invisible something" that is being sold by good customer service, like Nike's motivation, is a sense of control over the outcome of risk. You allow your customers to believe that, by shopping your store, they're making an investment in themselves.

With specific regard to customer service, the most critical trends shaping the American experience at the close of the 20ᵗʰ century are about *time* and *fear or anxiety*.

Time Trends

More Is Less. Technology promised to free up our time, but it's actually had the opposite effect. It takes time to seek out new technology, it takes time to evaluate its many options for purchase, it takes time to learn how to use it, and it takes time to adjust our daily living patterns to incorporate evolving technology into our routinized affairs. Then, technology changes and the process begins again. Almost diabolically, this process is accompanied by the anxiety of needing to make "right" choices—buying the wrong technology could leave you with a bigger problem than owning a Betamax. The perception now is that you could get bumped off a fast-moving track and be left behind, perhaps permanently. The irony we have created is this: consumption takes time—the more we produce, the more time we need for consumption.

Lowered Tolerance for Real Time. We live on the go, and most products that have achieved a permanent place in our lives have adapted to constant motion. Our audio tapes and CDs travel with us screwed into our ears. We eat hand-held foods. We work on our laptops and take calls anywhere on our cell phones, often responding to messages from our pagers. We have cordless phones at home, along with e-mail, voice mail, and answering machines. These devices have raised standards of speed in our daily life and thus lowered our tolerance for coping with expanded interactions of any kind. The more time it takes, the less we like it. Time is no longer something to be enjoyed and expanded; it has become something we compete against and force into submission.

Time as Quality. The two trends identified above have burdened our perceptions and, therefore, our expectations of time. As a culture we've become almost hysterical about our time. Dual-career families and time compromised at work by crushing demands for productivity have translated into a hugely exaggerated need for quality in the remaining, non-work time. Lifestyle has become as much a commodity as anything.

Fear Trends

Stress: The American Culture of Anxiety. People are worried. They feel their jobs are threatened unless they constantly retool their skills. Layoffs have become a fact of life. Most households require two earners just to make ends meet. Our culture seems to be more violent than ever. Science is uncovering hidden killers in our genes, waiting to strike out at the appointed hour, no matter how good we've been with diet and exercise. While the wealthiest technocrats live extravagantly, the ordinary family may be just one paycheck away from free fall.

Gap Between Rich and Poor. As America polarizes into the wealthy and the impoverished, the psychological fallout is middle-class fear. Despite the strength of the economy in the late 1990s, there is little relief for economic insecurities bred by distrust of large corporations that have made a name for themselves at the close of the century for downsizing the workforce and bloating executive compensation.

The Impact of Trends on Customer Service

The importance of these trends for anybody in business revolves around the element of risk associated with consumer purchase decisions. What consumers long for is *a sense of control*. They want quality goods that they can purchase conveniently and in the shortest time possible with the assurance that any problems will be immediately and satisfactorily resolved. No hassles. No risk.

The role of customer service is to minimize risk by creating in the consumers' minds the confidence that they've invested their time and money wisely by buying from you, that choosing you as a provider is, in fact, making an investment in themselves. An atmosphere of exceptional customer service gives consumers the impression of having control over the outcome of their decision to shop your store and buy from you. Their purchase has become one less thing to worry about and one less demand on their time.

Key Points to Share With Employees

- Technology must be used as an asset, not seen as an additional burden in the marketplace.
- Humanize the consumer environment to provide respite from anxiety.
- Create opportunities to reduce risk and solve problems.
- Offer assistance, but give the mature customer a sense of control over the outcome.

Conclusion

There's actually no conclusion, just an opening up of opportunities, both for people beyond age 50 and for the companies that appreciate their business. The key is the same as for good customer service in general: know and value your customers, then try to meet or exceed their expectations.

Once you recognize the great variety of lifestages and wants and needs among people over 50, you'll begin to help them improve their lives, rather than just trying to increase your profits. Your business should mean more than simply *transactions*; you should focus on *relationships*. It's not just a good thing to do: it's good business.

About the Authors

Patricia V. Alea, a teacher and an author, is a member of the distinguished panel of Age Wave speakers and is frequently invited by major corporations and associations to consult and speak about the growth and influence of the mature market in relation to strategic planning. Through the integration of direct marketing, publications, special events, customized services, and human resource management, she has helped clients significantly increase revenues and embrace innovation as a core value.

Rebecca Chekouras is Vice President of Research Services for Age Wave Communications Corporation in Emeryville, California, the leading provider of customized marketing solutions for companies targeting the mature market. Rebecca has researched and written extensively on the socioeconomic implications of an aging society. She has been an invited guest speaker at forums discussing the Boomer generation and has been quoted in leading publications, including *The Wall Street Journal*, *American Demographics*, and the *Los Angeles Times*.

25

CUSTOMER SURVEYS THAT DELIVER ACTIONABLE INFORMATION

Robert Shaver

If you want to improve your customer service, you need to know how the customer thinks and feels. It's as simple as that. But when it comes to surveying your customers, it's not simple at all. Surveys are often undermined by communication problems and by mistakes made in the survey process. This article explores the communication barriers and suggests a step-by-step approach to the survey process that will improve your results and help you get what you need so you can take the necessary action to better serve your customers.

A Request

Before you read this article, please take a minute for the following exercise.

1. Take a sheet of 8^1/$_2$ by 11 paper and fold it in half.
2. Rip out the upper left-hand corner of the sheet of paper.
3. Fold the sheet of paper in half.
4. Rip out the upper right-hand corner of the sheet of paper.
5. Fold the sheet of paper in half.
6. Rip out the lower left-hand corner of the sheet of paper.
7. Unfold the sheet of paper.
8. Compare the results of your efforts with the four examples shown in Figure 25-1 (at the end of this article).

Application of Your Learning

Let's take a look at what you can learn from this exercise and apply it to the task at hand: designing a survey that collects actionable information and enables corporate decision-makers to make better decisions.

Did you do the exercise? What is your best guess as to the percentage of readers who did the exercise?

I don't know the answer, but I would speculate that a very small fraction of the readers will actually do the exercise. Why? Unless you had to search for paper, the exercise should have required less than one minute. Is this too much to ask?

Think about *response rates* for your surveys. You tell the customer that you need but a few minutes of their time, yet the customer chooses not to give it. Why not? In my request, I said "please." But did you have any sense of why the exercise might be important or what might be in it for you, if you completed the exercise? Probably not. Is this also true for surveys you've received or sent out?

If you completed the exercise, how well did you do? Does your sheet look at all like any of the examples?

If one of your customers, or a member of your top management group, held up Example A in Figure 25-1 as evidence of what he/she expected, would you be able to explain why you failed to meet or exceed his/her expectations?

Having done this exercise with more than 100 audiences, I am confident that your sheet does *not* look like Example A. It seems reasonable to assume that you are an accomplished reader. The instructions are short, simple, and clear. So, what went wrong?

What's that you say? The instructions are not simple? not clear?

What could be more simple or clear than three folds and three rips?

Oh, I see! It makes a difference how you hold the paper, how you fold the paper, how you turn the paper, the size of the rips, and whether you unfold the paper each time you make a rip. I often do this exercise with audiences of 30 to several hundred people. In general, no two people will have the same outcome. In effect, we create a number of unique snowflakes—not exactly what we want for survey research.

How well do you communicate with others in the survey process? How clear and simple are the instructions provided by management to the researcher? How clear and simple are the instructions provided to the respondent? How often do your results look like snowflakes?

In this article, we will take a brief look at some of the reasons we miscommunicate, what the co-editor of this book, John Woods, in his book *Supervision* (South-Western, 1998) calls "barriers to shared understanding." In addition, I will identify several constructive steps we can take to enhance the quality (accuracy and completeness) of the survey process and the survey instrument and, ultimately, the value of the data gathered.

Communication Gaps as Threats

The survey process includes six important time periods. Within and between each time period, there are countless communication gaps that can threaten the quality of the survey process and the value of the results.

Think back to the last survey you conducted. Ask yourself:

A. Did the information *required* by management during Time Period 6 (T6) equal the information *requested* by management in T1? . . . by the researcher in T2? . . . of the data collection method in T3? . . . of the respondent in T4?

Time Period	T1	T2	T3	T4	T5	T6
Task	Initiation	Development	Administration	Collection	Analysis	Action
Primary Agent	Management	Researcher	Researcher	Respondent	Researcher	Management

B. Did the information required and requested in A equal the information *available and provided* by the respondent in T4?
C. Did the information required and requested in A and the information available and provided in B equal the information *obtained and understood* by the researcher in T5?
D. Did the information required and requested in A and the information available and provided in B and the information obtained and understood in C equal the information *received and accepted* by management in T6?

If the answer to any of these questions is no, how much confidence do you want to place in the quality and value of the survey results? How much confidence should others place in the findings and recommendations? How accurately has each agent in this process—manager, researcher, interviewer, and respondent—communicated with the others in this process?

To complicate this even more, the survey process may take six months or several years. Given the speed of change in some markets (for example, fashion or entertainment) and the rapid obsolescence of some products (for example, personal computers), the desired information in Time Period 6 may be very different from that requested in Time Period 1. Does the survey process provide sufficient flexibility to effectively address this?

Surveys as a Voluntary Social Encounter Among Strangers

Sudman, Bradburn, and Schwarz (1996), three distinguished researchers in survey design, have described the survey process as a "voluntary social encounter among strangers," a succinct summary of some of the key challenges of survey design.

We may offer monetary or other incentives to encourage the customer to participate, but surveys are usually *voluntary*. The potential respondent makes a decision to participate or not participate, to disclose or not disclose, to tell the whole truth or something less. Why should the respondent care about what you want? What's in it for the respondent? Why should potential respondents say "yes" to your request? The outcomes of these decisions are reflected in the response rates and the quality of the data provided by those who participate in the survey.

The survey process is a *social encounter*, strongly influenced by implicit rules that govern the content and process we use in communicating with *strangers*. Often, the survey respondents have no clue as to who is asking the questions or what uses might be made of their responses. Why should a respondent trust you with the information you're requesting? How do respondents decide what to share and what to withhold? Unfortunately, the unwritten rules governing disclosure to strangers are not sufficiently researched, documented, or understood. Learn to trust your "gut" on this. If you would not be willing to provide similar information to a stranger, why do you think respondents should be willing to provide this information to you?

To develop actionable surveys, it is essential that you walk in the respondents' shoes long enough to answer a few questions. Why should respondents be willing to give you their time and the information you requested? Why should respondents make the effort to retrieve the information you requested? Why should respondents trust you with the information you're seeking?

In the next two sections, we examine several constructive steps that can be taken to remove barriers to our shared understanding by enhancing the quality of the survey process and the survey instrument. The goal is to encourage a greater number of respondents to participate and to obtain actionable information from the survey process.

Constructive Steps: A. The Survey Process

You can influence the quality and value of the survey results by focusing attention on the survey process. Use the following series of checklists to evaluate one of your surveys—previous, current, or proposed.

A1. Time Period 1—Initiation of the survey. Management requests/directs that a survey be conducted. Does management commit the necessary time and resources to effectively communicate why a survey is needed and what it will be expected to determine? Does the researcher understand the real purpose of the survey? How effectively do management and the researcher communicate?

Does management . . .	*Yes*	*?*	*No*
. . . ask for surveys that will contribute to the big picture (e.g., an organizational SWOT)?			
. . . know where we are now? Where we want to go? The options available to get there?			
. . . clearly identify what is desired from whom? How it will be used? When it is needed?			
. . . provide budgeted resources (e.g., time, staff, money) that are consistent with the objectives?			
. . . invite the researcher to identify more effective or less expensive ways to collect the data?			

A2. Time Period 2—Development of the survey. Researcher translates management's request(s) into an effective survey design. Does the researcher ask the right questions and make the appropriate decisions?

Does the researcher . . .

	Yes	?	No
. . . conduct a search of available data sources? (What is available? What can we take for granted and not incur the expense of recreating?)			
. . . identify earlier findings or current beliefs that are in conflict and should probably be addressed?			
. . . select the right data collection method (face-to-face interviews, telephone or mail survey)? (The choice of data collection method has a large influence on the way the survey will be designed and the types of questions that can be asked.)			
. . . select a proper sampling design? (Who knows the answers to our questions? Who is most likely to be willing to participate in the survey? To which population do we want to be able to generalize the survey results?)			
. . . include questions that will help identify trends? (Most surveys collect snapshot data. By asking questions related to how our products or services have changed since previous use or purchase, we gather information about the direction we're going—i.e., better, same, worse.)			
. . . include questions that will help identify the competitors and how our product or service benchmarks against them?			
. . . include questions about how the customer uses the product or service? (A customer might feel that $5 is a good price for wine used for cooking, but expect to pay $30 for wine used as a gift.)			
. . . include open-ended questions that invite respondents to identify ways our organization might better serve them?			
. . . pilot-test the survey, the instructions, and the letter of transmittal? (If you don't have time or money to pilot-test, don't do the survey.)			

A3. Time Period 3—Administration of the survey. The data collection method will strongly influence the survey process and the outcomes. The data collection method is a series of trade-offs. Face-to-face interviews and telephone surveys can collect rich data while offering the interviewer a chance to clarify the questions and the respondent an opportunity to elaborate on the responses. On the other hand, both cost more than mail surveys and the interviewers may have unintended influences on the results.

Mail surveys have the lowest cost per respondent and eliminate interviewer bias by providing each respondent with exactly the same questions. On the other hand, mail surveys have the lowest overall response rates and provide no opportunity to clarify the questions or the answers.

Does the selected data collection method . . .

	Yes	?	No
. . . provide the best balance of trade-offs?			
. . . require all of the available resources? (Do you have resources to use more than one data collection method, to compare results?)			

	Yes	?	No
. . . provide the types of answers required in T1 and T2?			
. . . require use of interviewers? (If so, have the interviewers been trained to reduce interviewer bias?)			

A4. Time Period 4—Collection of the survey data. Control is shifted to the respondent. Months of work (T1, T2, and T3) to prepare for this moment—and the survey instrument may be evaluated by the potential respondent in a brief moment and found to be not worthy of his/her time. (We will devote considerable attention to additional steps you can take to enhance the respondents' reception in the next section on the Survey Instrument.)

Does the respondent decide to . . .	*Yes*	*?*	*No*
. . . participate or not? (The letter of introduction is important, but so too is the survey itself. Even if a respondent completes most of a survey, she/he may change her/his mind if asked questions that seem invasive, offensive, or unrelated to the reasons she/he agreed to participate.)			
. . . take the time to search his/her memory, other records, or other people for the requested information?			
. . . say "don't know"? (Rather than admit that they might not know, respondents will answer nonetheless. Have you provided the "don't know" option to discourage this?)			
. . . tell the truth? Or provide a more socially acceptable answer? (If you live with the illusion that respondents always tell the whole truth, read *Vital Lies, Simple Truths* by Daniel Goleman.)			

A5. Time Period 5—Data entry and analysis. The researcher summarizes and interprets the returned surveys.

Does the researcher . . .	*Yes*	*?*	*No*
. . . follow up to increase response rates?			
. . . create an audit trail for data collection, entry, coding, and cleaning that permits others to evaluate the quality of the methodology and decisions reached?			
. . . evaluate nonresponse errors and assess the degree to which the survey results can be generalized to a larger population?			
. . . develop a descriptive summary and report that's easily understood by others?			
. . . benchmark against archival, industry, or trade data?			
. . . provide actionable recommendations that are supported by the survey results?			

A6. Time Period 6—Completion and management action. The management group receives the survey results from the researcher.

Does the management group . . .	Yes	?	No
. . . evaluate the quality (e.g., accuracy, completeness) and value of the survey results?			
. . . identify previously unidentified threats or opportunities?			
. . . act to create value-added services or products? (If not, were the survey results actionable?)			

In the next section, we move from the survey process to the survey instrument. The emphasis will be on mail surveys, but nearly all comments will also be relevant for telephone surveys.

Constructive Steps: B. The Survey Instrument

The mail survey instrument consists of a cover letter, instructions, questions, response categories/scale, demographics, and a closing. Use the following series of checklists to evaluate one of your surveys—previous, current, or proposed.

B1. Cover letter/letter of transmittal—First impressions are important. Most refusals come here. Responding to surveys is a voluntary act that incurs costs for the respondent (e.g., time, effort, risk of disclosure). Your task is to establish rapport and motivate the reader to become a respondent.

Does the letter . . .	Yes	?	No
. . . look professional (e.g., quality of paper, first-class mail)?			
. . . explain what the survey is about?			
. . . explain why the information is important, without grossly overstating the importance?			
. . . identify who wants to know the information (i.e., real sponsor)?			
. . . include an implied or explicit promise of anonymity/confidentiality?			
. . . establish limits on who else the information might be shared with?			
. . . explain how the reader was picked?			
. . . explain why this particular reader's opinions are important?			
. . . show appreciation for the reader, his/her time, effort, and opinions?			
. . . indicate how long the survey might take? (Is this a reasonable request?)			
. . . include the due date and return procedures?			

. . . suggest how the reader, or others important to the reader, might benefit?			

B2. Instructions—Most respondents will make every reasonable effort to be good respondents, but they are not mind readers. The more unusual/complex the instrument, the greater the chance for misunderstanding.

Are the instructions . . .	Yes	?	No
. . . set apart from, but just prior to the actual questions?			
. . . clear, complete, and sufficient for even the least capable of the respondents?			
. . . sufficiently brief, so that the sophisticated respondent can skim them?			
. . . too long? (If so, the survey may be too complex.)			
. . . necessary? (If the form is very simple, instructions may be redundant.)			
. . . explicit regarding desired "accuracy"? (For example, are estimates OK? How is the respondent to reply if he/she doesn't know or if the question isn't applicable?)			
. . . biasing the responses? (Beware of including suggested responses.)			

B3. Questions: content and wording—This is usually the most difficult task in survey development. The socioeconomic characteristics of your respondents should have great influence here. Questions that might be appropriate for college students, for example, may not be appropriate for residents of a nursing home. The more diverse the respondent group, the more difficult it is to design a survey for the entire group. Every question should be designed to overcome the respondent's inability and/or unwillingness to answer.

Are the questions . . .	Yes	?	No
. . . necessary (e.g., focused directly on the issue to be measured)? (Will the respondent readily identify how each question relates to the stated purpose of the survey?)			
. . . written in a layperson's language? (Are technical terms, jargon, slang, words with multiple meanings—e.g., "value" or "conservative"—avoided? Would the *least* sophisticated respondent be familiar with the terms used?)			
. . . simple? (Unlike this checklist, which includes several double-barreled questions.)			
. . . stated as precisely, clearly, and briefly as possible?			

Are the questions . . .

	Yes	?	No
. . . going to discriminate among respondents? (For example, have you avoided questions that are likely to be endorsed by almost everyone—e.g., I like milk—or by almost no one—e.g., I like drugs?)			
. . . assuming too much knowledge on the part of the respondent? (For example, one spouse may not know the monthly expenses for a specific expenditure category if the other spouse usually makes these purchases.)			
. . . easy to answer?			
. . . covering major issues thoroughly, while quickly passing over minor issues?			
. . . applicable to all respondents?			
. . . asking the respondent to remember too much detail or a distant event?			

B4. Questions: sequence and layout—In general, always work from general to specific, from easy to difficult, from casual to threatening. You're writing a letter to a stranger; is the logic clear to the respondent? Beware of undesirable contamination (context effects) from earlier questions.

Does the survey . . .

	Yes	?	No
. . . start with easy (e.g., nonthreatening, noncontroversial) questions that validate the legitimacy of the survey to the respondent, establish rapport, and arouse interest?			
. . . look attractive and easy to fill out? (At first glance?)			
. . . have sufficient white space to avoid appearing dense, cramped, or cluttered?			
. . . group questions of similar content, similar scale, and similar instructions?			
. . . unfold, flowing smoothly from one section to another?			
. . . include necessary transitions/instructions to maintain rapport and direct the respondent when there are changes in direction?			
. . . include filter questions that measure familiarity (e.g., product use, past experience, opportunity to observe) before the topic questions? (These questions enable the researcher to filter out respondents who are not adequately informed.)			
. . . end with those questions that might be sensitive or threatening to the respondent? (Unless the questions are inappropriate, the established rapport and legitimacy may be sufficient to encourage the respondent to complete and return the survey.)			

B5. Response categories and scales—Categories and scales permit us to obtain responses that are comparable to one another. Where a logical middle position exists (e.g., neither, no change, average), include one. If "don't know," "not applicable," or "other" are appropriate responses, make the alternatives available to the respondent.

Are the response categories/response scales . . .	Yes	?	No
. . . simple?			
. . . exhaustive? (What evidence do you have that nothing important has been excluded?)			
. . . discrete and mutually exclusive? (Overlapping categories create confusion for the respondent and make data analysis very difficult.)			
. . . meaningful to the respondent? (Have you avoided the use of terms that have different meanings for different people—e.g., "usually," "normally," "frequently," "regularly"? Where appropriate, ask for actual counts over a recent period of time.)			
. . . anchored so as to avoid using universals, such as "always," "never," "all," "none"?			
. . . limited to fewer than 10 categories, and preferably seven?			
. . . comparable with other available data (e.g., historical or secondary data)?			

B6. Demographics—Second only to the opening letter, no section of the survey is more important to you or the respondent. This section enables you to discover who is responding. Are the respondents the people you needed to hear from? Do the respondents include your best customers? Noncustomers? These questions may be sensitive to the respondent, but they're essential if you want to identify segments in your market and evaluate the degree to which you can generalize from the respondents to a larger population (i.e., all potential customers).

It may help to explain that this information is voluntary or to reassure the respondent of the confidential nature of the survey. If the respondent objects to a particular question, she/he may still send you the partially completed survey. It also helps to explain why you're asking for this information (e.g., "To determine how consumption of popcorn and preferences vary among people of different ages, incomes, and occupations, we need information on . . . ").

Will the demographic questions . . .	Yes	?	No
. . . be sufficiently general so as not to be perceived by the respondent as a violation of the anonymity/confidentiality promise made in the opening letter?			
. . . be sufficiently specific to examine meaningful differences between groups?			
. . . protect the respondent's ego (e.g., prestige, self-image)?			
. . . permit comparisons with historical data or secondary data?			

B7. Closing—This is your last chance to make a positive impression, express your thanks for their gift to you, and request a prompt return of the survey. Does your survey do these?

Summary

Surveys are never perfect. There are no scientific rules that will guarantee an optimal questionnaire. Survey design is an art acquired through experience. The fine-tuning of a survey comes from the creativity and experience of a skilled researcher. The purpose of planning and careful execution is to avoid major errors and oversights. Minor errors should be treated for what they are—things that may require qualifiers in the interpretation of the results.

If you seek actionable information, take proactive steps to:

1. Enhance the quality of the survey *process* by reducing the communication gaps within and between each of the six time periods.
2. Enhance the quality of the survey *instrument* by paying special attention to:
   a) the reasons a respondent might be unwilling to participate,
   b) the reasons a respondent might be unwilling to take the time and effort to recall or locate the requested information, and
   c) sensitive questions that might discourage a participant from telling the truth to a stranger.

Suggested Readings and Resources

Pamela Alreck and Robert B. Settle, *The Survey Research Handbook: Guidelines and Strategies for Conducting a Survey.* 2nd Edition. Irwin Series in Marketing. Homewood, IL: Irwin 1995.

J.T. Dillon, *Practice of Questioning.* London: Routledge, 1990.

Arlene Fink and Jacqueline Kosecoff, *How to Conduct Surveys: A Step by Step Guide.* Newbury Park, CA: Sage Publications, 1985.

Daniel Goleman, *Vital Lies, Simple Truths: The Psychology of Self-Deception.* New York: Touchstone Books, 1996.

Allen I. Kraut (Ed.), *Organizational Surveys: Tools for Assessment and Change.* San Francisco: Jossey-Bass Publishers, 1996.

Seymour Sudman, Norman M. Bradburn, and Norbert Schwarz, *Thinking About Answers: The Application of Cognitive Processes to Survey Methodology.* San Francisco: Jossey-Bass Publishers, 1996.

Richard C. Whiteley, *The Customer-Driven Company: Moving From Talk to Action.* Reading, MA: Addison-Wesley Publishing, 1991.

About the Author

Robert Shaver is a faculty associate with the Management Institute, a continuing education unit of the University of Wisconsin School of Business. Bob has had 20 years of non-academic work experience in a wide spectrum of blue-collar and mili-

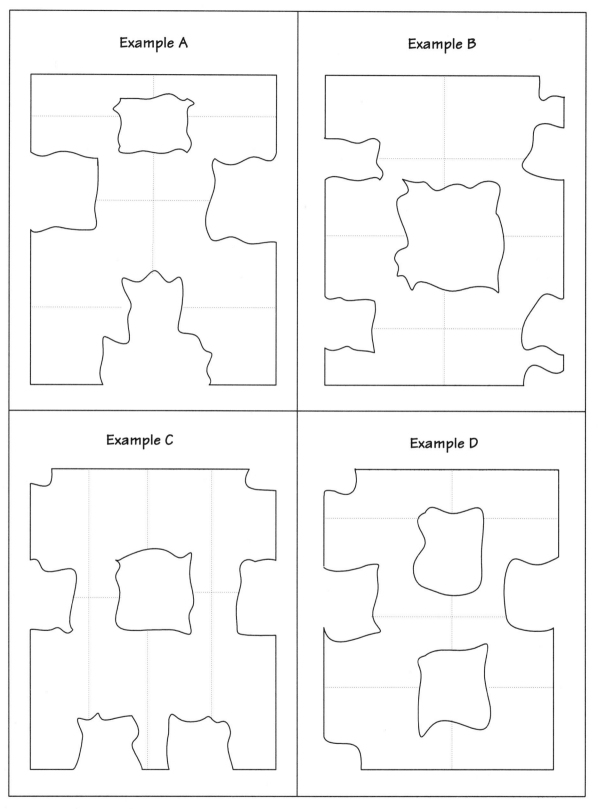

Figure 25-1. Snowflake exercise: four results.

tary jobs, including experience in automotive repair, construction, naval engineering, nursing homes, consumer and real-estate lending, and state government. He has nearly 10 years of managerial experience as a first-line supervisor and middle and senior supervisor.

Bob regularly works with companies throughout Wisconsin designing and delivering comprehensive, integrated training programs. His clients have included Wisconsin Physicians Service, CUNA Mutual Group, Wausau Papers, P.H. Glatfelter Paper, U-Care HMO, Aqua-Chem, Promega, and SSI Technologies, Inc.

Bob's research and teaching focus on survey research and design, motivation, managing change, problem-solving and decision making, creativity, and futures. He has developed and conducted employee-attitude surveys for several companies, including SSI Technologies, The Swiss Colony, Viking Insurance Company, and Wausau Paper Mills. Bob teaches regularly in the Management Institute Basic Management Certificate Series programs and has also taught undergraduate courses in decision-making and organizational behavior for the University of Wisconsin School of Business.

PART SIX

Customer Problems and Problem Customers

26

SERVICE RECOVERY: TURNING OOPS! INTO OPPORTUNITY

Ron Zemke

No company satisfies all of its customers all of the time. But how a company handles complaints makes a big difference in its ability to retain current customers and attract new customers, which makes a big difference in its profitability. This article by co-editor Ron Zemke focuses on recovery, on how you can keep customers after you've failed to meet their expectations—and leverage what you learn from their complaints into ways to improve the quality of your products and service.

Overview

The true test of an organization's commitment to service quality is the way the organization responds when things go wrong for the customer. Service recovery is about keeping customers coming back after the worst, or at least something very annoying, has happened. In simple terms, it's the special effort customers expect you to put forth when things have gone wrong for them.

Effective service recovery saves "at-risk" customers for the organization and becomes a hallmark, a way to distinguish the organization from its competition. It's a planned, systematic process that includes:

- A problem resolution process,
- A complaint and problem capture-and-analysis subsystem, and
- A way of feeding back information on systemic problems.

There is a growing body of data suggesting that companies performing high-quality service recovery for customers can realize substantial economic payoff. According to John Goodman, president of Technical Assistance Research Programs, Inc. (TARP), a Washington, D.C., research and consulting organization specializing in customer service research, at least three studies have found that customers who complain and have their complaints quickly satisfied are *more* likely to purchase additional products than are customers who've experienced no problems with the organization or with its products. (See the article by John Goodman in this book for more on this idea and how to quantify the sales and profit impact of not dealing effectively with customer complaints.)

Leonard L. Berry, J.C. Penney Chair of Retailing Studies, Professor of Marketing, Director of the Center of Retailing Studies at Texas A&M University, and one of the U.S.'s leading service quality researchers, is equally adamant about the importance of good service recovery: "The acid test of service quality is how you solve customer problems."[1] Berry explains that a series of studies that he and colleagues Valarie A. Zeithaml and A. Parasuraman have conducted over the past 10 years have consistently revealed that the best satisfaction scores come from customers who've experienced no problems, the second best from those who've had problems resolved satisfactorily, and the worst from customers whose problems go unsolved.

The impact of poor recovery goes beyond the disappointment and loss of a single customer. The salesperson or customer service rep who dismisses an unhappy or complaining customer with a perfunctory "I can't help you, that's our policy" positions the company to lose dozens if not hundreds of current and potential customers. The problem is that the complaining customer who's summarily dismissed doesn't simply go away. He or she takes every opportunity to tell anyone who will listen what rotten treatment he or she was made to endure at the hands of your company.

One study conducted by Performance Research Associates, Inc., found that 18% of customers were upset with treatment they received at the hands of a Midwestern phone company. These upset customers reported they had each told an average of 20 or more people of their plight.[2]

Frederick Reichheld and W. Earl Sasser[3] calculated the value of customer retention over a five-year period for nine industries. They considered not only base profit but profit from increased purchases, profit from reduced operating costs (attainable through increased knowledge of a customer's requirements over time), profits from referrals, and profits from price premium purchases. They found that a single customer who's been with you five years can be up to 377% more profitable, depending on your industry, than a customer you've only just wooed to your products or services! By focusing on customer retention tactics, such as service recovery, and reducing annual defections by a mere 5%, an organization can boost pretax profits 25% to 125%.

The message from all this research is pretty clear: do it right the first time. If you don't, you'd better be darned sure you do it right the second time. If you fail—if you've not met the customer's expectations twice—that's about all the room the customer will give you.[4]

1. Chip R. Bell and Ron Zemke, "Service Breakdown: The Road to Recovery," *Management Review*, October 1987, p. 33.
2. Unpublished study conducted by Performance Research Associates, Inc.
3. Frederick Reichheld and W. Earl Sasser, "Zero Defections: Quality Comes to Services," *Harvard Business Review*, September–October 1990, p. 105.
4. Chip R. Bell and Ron Zemke, "Service Breakdown: The Road to Recovery," *Management Review*, October 1987, p. 33.

What Customers Expect When Things Go Wrong

Customers have expectations for service recovery just as they have expectations for "normal" product and service performance. At Performance Research Associates, we conducted focus group and telephone interviews during 1991–1992 with over 1,200 customers, in a variety of industries, who'd experienced recent service breakdowns. We asked them what they experienced as positive from companies when they experienced a service breakdown. Our goal: to find out what customers experience as most memorable of the service recovery efforts they encounter when things have gone amiss for them. We found that, regardless of the type of service—business-to-business, consumer, professional, medical—the most memorable aspects of the successful service recovery were remarkably similar (Table 26-1).

As Table 26-1 suggests, the most memorable aspects of recovery are almost evenly divided between interpersonal or communications skills (seven items) and technical or problem-focused skills (five items). This leads us to the conclusion that memorable—and organizationally effective—service recovery is a fine mix of problem-solving and customer-handling skills. It's a set of actions focused on two objectives: making the customer's problem go away and doing it in a way that forms a memorable, positive impression on the customer.

We have developed a six-step process for handling disappointed and even disgruntled customers. Applied consistently by customer contact people, it has, in one controlled application, led to an overall 12% improvement in customer satisfaction with problem-solving.

What focus group members remembered and *found impressive*	*% of focus group members who commented on and were impressed by this action*
1. CSR* dealt with my upset.	79.0%
2. CSR apologized.	69.1%
3. CSR didn't become defensive, but showed humility and poise.	62.9%
4. CSR followed up after the complaint transaction.	56.8%
5. CSR showed skill at problem-solving.	53.0%
6. CSR, when appropriate, was proactive in admitting organization error, didn't try to shift blame.	44.4%
7. CSR acted in a fully responsible/empowered fashion on the customer's behalf.	40.7%
8. CSR showed good interpersonal skills, particularly listening.	40.7%
9. CSR showed empathy for the customer's plight and/or upset.	38.3%
10. CSR acted quickly to solve the problem, showed urgency.	35.8%
11. CSR created added value for the customer.	32.1%
12. CSR believed the customer, valued the customer's perception.	24.7%
*CSR = Customer service representative	

Table 26-1. What customers recall of effective service recovery incidents.

Step 1. Apologize for, or acknowledge, the fact that the customer is experiencing an inconvenience.

Apologizing without becoming defensive or shifting the blame to the customer is a key expectation and an important first step toward keeping a customer who's feeling aggrieved. Although a simple apology costs nothing to deliver, we find it forthcoming in fewer than 48% of the cases where a customer contacts a company to report a problem with a product or service.

An apology is most powerful when delivered *first person*. A sincere, non-robotic "I'm sorry for any inconvenience" or "Thank you for letting me know" suggests that whoever is making the apology is taking a personal, professional interest in the situation. In addition, there's compelling evidence that a simple apology can defuse a situation and prevent legal escalation.

Step 2. Listen, empathize, and ask open questions.

Customers do not want service professionals to join them in a tirade about "those guys in shipping who should be shot." Rather, customers are looking for a good listener who allows them to vent their frustrations, shows understanding of their upset, and who, by listening, offers tacit evidence of believing the customer's report of the incident or error.

Step 3. Offer a fair fix to the problem.

After the service professional has acknowledged and dealt with the emotional side of the service breakdown, customers want what went wrong to be made right. It's important that customers perceive the service provider as skilled, empowered, and interested in a timely resolution.

Contrary to common belief, customers typically bring a sense of fair play to the table when a service breakdown occurs and some recompense or compensation is appropriate. For example, when we asked telephone subscribers what they expected from the company when service failures occurred, we found that they distinguished between weekends and weekdays. They told us, in effect, that it was OK for the phone company to be more sluggish in its response to a failure on a weekend because, after all, "Sunday is a weekend, and most of them like to be home with their families just like the rest of us."

In one survey we conducted, we found that "asking the customer how he or she would like the problem solved" made a significant difference between "satisfied" and "very satisfied" customer attitudes toward a company's problem-fixing effort.

Step 4. Offer some value-added atonement for the inconvenience or injury.

We often refer to this step as symbolic atonement. The word "symbolic" is carefully chosen. It suggests that little things, when sincerely done, mean a lot to the customer. The customer does *not* expect us to offer to shoot the branch manager or provide a trip to Walt Disney World for keeping him or her waiting in the reception area an extra 10 minutes. The customer *does* expect us to make a reasonable, small gesture that acknowledges the inconvenience. Atonement is critical to satisfaction when the customer feels "injured" by the service delivery breakdown, when the customer feels victimized, greatly inconvenienced, or somehow damaged by the problem.

Step 5. Keep your promises.

Customers are frequently skeptical of a company's recovery promises. They tend to believe that service reps who make promises are more interested in getting the customer off the phone or out of the office than in solving the problem or fixing the customer's upset.

Be honest. Although customers may huff and bluster at the customer contact employee who gives them some bad news, they would rather have employees give them honest and realistic bad news than lie to them or even slightly mislead them. For example, customers would rather be informed that their flight may be up to 90 minutes late than be told of a 15-minute delay six times.

Step 6. Follow up.

Customers are very favorably impressed when a sales or customer service person follows up with them after the initial service recovery episode, to make sure that the implemented solution is still satisfactory. This "after the fact" service recovery satisfaction assessment is particularly important in breakdown situations where customers perceive that they may be "at risk" if they seem angry or upset. For example, research conducted by Philip A. Newbold and Diane Stover of Memorial Hospital in South Bend, Indiana, found that "because of fear of retaliation, some patients kept quiet (about service disappointments) until after discharge, particularly regarding nursing issues."[5] Follow-up gives the organization a second chance to solve the customer's problem if the first effort came up short of the customer's expectations and the customer was reluctant to voice the complaint a second time.

This step should also initiate an internal follow-up. Service representatives should be able to communicate inside their organizations to ensure that the solutions they put in motion are actually executed (e.g., the package was shipped or the account was credited) and to allow recurring problems to be tracked and removed from the delivery system.

Managing the Service Recovery Effort

In a small organization with a handful of sales or service people, the six-step process, plus a little coaching and supervision, should allow for significant improvements in customer satisfaction with problem-solving. Improving service recovery in a larger, multiple-site company is a more daunting process.

5. Philip A. Newbold and Diane Serbin Stover, "Patient Satisfaction Pilot Reveals Gains and Limits," *Healthcare Forum Journal*, November/December 1991, pp. 48–51.

Creating distinctive service recovery in a large organization requires management to develop a cultural milieu that supports and promotes service recovery and customer problem-solving as an important activity. It also needs to create vehicles for communicating the value of the service recovery and have guidelines for implementing and reinforcing the service recovery message.

Through our consulting work and via an organizational survey called the Service Management Practices Inventory (SMPI®) with a database of 70,000 respondents, we've looked carefully at the factors promoting distinctive service recovery. We've found that customers give the highest recovery scores to organizations where five things seem to be in place internally.

1. **There's training focused on recovery.** Employees are trained in the fine points of handling customer problems, are continually made aware of the most common kinds of problems customers encounter, and are skilled at enlisting the customer in generating acceptable solutions to the problem or complaint.

2. **There are recovery standards.** Formal standards and informal norms exist to reinforce the message that it's important to solve customer problems quickly and with a minimum of inconvenience for the customer. Front-line employees are encouraged to go "above and beyond" for the customer because employees who've saved a relationship with an upset customer are recognized for their efforts. For example, at Federal Express Corporation, employees who are commended by customers through letter or phone call are given "Bravo Zulu" awards (letters of commendation) in front of their peers and the performance is recorded in their personnel record.

3. **It's easy to complain to the organization.** We find that in recovery-oriented organizations there are systems, policies, and procedures in place that make it easy for customers to report problems or complaints and for employees to respond. Policies and procedures that narrowly define employee responsibilities and roles severely limit the initiative and risk an employee will take for a complaining customer. More recently, we're finding that technological restrictions—in the form of poor telephone, e-mail, and customer communication systems and limited computer information systems—severely limit service employees in their problem-solving efforts.

4. **Front-line employees are part of a system.** In organizations that are successful at recovery, front-line employees are confident that problems they solve will stay solved and that others in the organization will work as hard as they on the customer's problem. In our surveys, positive responses to the statement "I know that the customer will receive great service if I have to refer him/her to another department for help" have been found to correlate very highly to overall positive customer perceptions of an organization's recovery efforts. In organizations like the card service group of American Express, front-line employees meet regularly, without a manager present, to discuss difficult customer problems and to exchange information on solving customer problems.

5. **Employees believe they're part of a quality system**. In good service recovery companies, front-line employees are confident that everyone is as concerned as they are about quality and customer satisfaction. They believe that there's consensus in the organization about the importance of retaining customers and the value of recovery efforts in the organization's retention efforts.

In organizations where sales and customer service tend to operate independently, it's important that employees in customer service believe that the people in sales are as concerned with solving problems as the people in front-line service. In several instances, we've noted that informal communications between individual sales people and front-line service people very much promote this sense of mutual concern with recovery and retention. We've also found in several studies that customers are very impressed when sales people are knowledgeable about problems they've encountered and how those problems were resolved.

Creating a Service Recovery System

For service recovery to be more than a process for cleaning up after poorly performing products and slapdash service, it must also serve as a resource for systematic improvement of the primary processes for creating products and services. Berry and Parasuraman[6] have identified three major outcomes of an effective service recovery system:

- The identification of service problems,
- A process for resolving problems effectively, and
- A way for the organization to learn from the recovery experience.

We find this a robust framework, and we've adapted much of the guidance their framework provides. What follows is a detailing of the activities and mechanisms an organization needs to put into place to make maximum use of the service recovery effort, as we interpret it.

Identifying Service Problems

The purpose of the problem-identifying process is to capture historic and emerging information about organizational errors and problems in need of correcting and expunging, and to make sure that customers with problems are managed effectively. There are three basic "streams" of this information:

Customer Research. This is customer (not market) research, focused on customers with complaints. The key to effective customer recovery research is to look for the unfound, unusual, and unexpected. Asking unusual questions helps, as does analyzing historical information on customer satisfaction and dissatisfaction with problem resolution. For example, one managed care firm in the northwestern U.S. found that complaints offered to its member relations group represented only 15% of ac-

6. Leonard Berry and A. Parasuraman, *Marketing Services* (New York: Free Press, 1991).

tual customer complaints. The other 85% were voiced to doctors and clinic staff members who, overwhelmingly, did nothing with the information.

Effective tools for customer problem research are focus groups, paper-and-pencil and telephone surveys, customer intercepts, employee logs, and mystery shoppers.

Assessing Customer Complaints. It's important to examine incoming customer complaints in a timely fashion to spot emerging problem trends and newly developing delivery system deficiencies. The complaint handling system is also a vehicle for spotting and thinking through new situations that service reps will face in the near future.

Early warning, action planning, and planned follow-up opportunity are the keys to real-time customer complaint assessment.

Process Monitoring. Monitoring the process of serving customers and of handling customer complaints (in real time) is important to keeping the quality of transactions clean, positive, and on track. The goal is to look for spots where the systems for serving customers and creating recovery are bent, if not broken. It's about finding real and potential fail points and repairing them.

Good tools for the job are mystery shopping, simple observation, and creation of detailed service blueprints and maps.

Resolving Problems Effectively

Prepare the People and Keep Them "Fit." Good recovery depends on finding, training, and retaining good people—people with the strength to withstand the barbs of unhappy customers and the ability to search for solutions to customer problems in the customer's presence.

Effective people preparation begins with hiring. *Hire* the right people. Screen technical people for "customer" skills. *Train* employees in the psychology of customers, problem-solving, handling customers, and product knowledge. *Empower* employees to deal with customer problems and to resolve them on the spot. Give them time and tools to do the job the way you want it done. Technology is essential. Then, *reward* and *recognize* excellent performance.

Create Both a Recovery 'Track' and Solution Spaces. The recovery 'track'—a process, such as our six steps to service recovery—should emphasize apology, listening, empathy skills, rapid resolution, added-value treatment, compensation, and (where useful) customer education.

Solution spaces provide a specific protocol or model to follow in particular service breakdown situations. For example, most airlines have a protocol for overbooked flights, which tells employees exactly what types of compensation and alternative arrangements may be made for bumped passengers. Good solution space matrices suggest atonement that's valued and real. When airlines find enough "volunteers" to avoid bumping unwilling travelers, it's because their atonement offer (free tickets or travel vouchers) is a good match for the inconvenience of taking another flight. For the solution space to be effective in the eyes of the customer, the apology for inconvenience, the correction of the problem, and the offer of compensation must be treated seriously.

Learning From Recovery Experience

An effective service recovery learning loop sends information about product and service problems back into the service and product production system. The methods described earlier feed data into tracking and root-cause analysis processes that create usable information for confirming or correcting the functioning of the product and service delivery production system.

This organizational learning component has three features:

A Problem-Tracking System. The focus of a recovery tracking system is measurement of the customer retention and delivery improvement effort. It should answer two questions:

1. Does the problem resolution process actually result in customer satisfaction and retention?
2. Does feeding product and service breakdown information back to the production cycle result in improved products and service delivery?

Keys to an effective problem-tracking system are tracking contacts, assessing customer satisfaction with problem resolution, and analyzing problem trends.

A Root-Cause Analysis Process. Whether housed with the service recovery function or within the service and product creating system, information from the recovery process should feed into a root-cause analysis process.

Keys to an effective root-cause analysis system are training in analytical techniques, time available for data analysis, and permission to make process improvement suggestions.

Flexible Service Process Monitoring. A good service recovery system frequently uncovers service delivery fail points that were unidentified and thus not monitored. The service recovery function, therefore, must have the flexibility and permission to establish monitoring or feedback systems for these fail points.

Keys to successful service process monitoring are having the skills to establish such systems within the recovery system and permission to create new monitoring efforts as perceived to be needed.

Summary

In the final analysis, service recovery is a process designed, primarily, to save the at-risk customer and, secondarily, to feed useful information for problem prevention back into an organization's quality management/quality assurance process. Our key points are the following:

1. Recovery—returning an aggrieved customer to a state of satisfaction after a service or product breakdown—has a critical economic impact on your business.

2. Breakdown involves customer expectations of both outcomes and processes.

3. Recovering well when things have gone wrong increases customer loyalty and decreases marketing expenses.

4. Only your customer can tell you how annoying or victimizing a particular service breakdown has been. Only your customer can determine when appropriate recovery has occurred.

5. *Planned* service recovery ensures that each breakdown will be handled in a creative way that will satisfy customer and organizational needs.

6. Yes, you can—and should—plan for the unexpected.

7. When problems occur, customers expect you to apologize, give them a "fair fix," treat them like you care, and make atonement for injuries.

8. A good rule is "Fix the person, then the problem." Planned recovery helps you do both—and do them well.

9. It's critical to identify recurring problems so that you can make changes and corrections in your production processes and service delivery systems.

10. Planned service recovery improves overall service quality awareness and motivates employees to work on the customer's behalf to solve problems.

Creating service quality is a journey, not a destination. In our competitive world, customer expectations are constantly changing and rising—thanks in part to the never-ending contest to be first in the customer's esteem and first in the marketplace.

William James, the father of modern American psychology, commented, "The deepest principle of human nature is a craving to be appreciated." That's true of our customers, true of our peers, and true of our associates. And nothing is more appreciated than a problem solved faster, more easily, and more effectively than a customer dared hope.

27

COOLING THE CUSTOMER WITH HEAT

John Hartley

When a customer has a problem, your company has a problem. How do you handle customer problems? A survey has shown that 68% of customers who leave a company for a competitor do so because of an attitude of indifference on the part of a company employee. The simple, four-step approach advocated in this article can guide your employees and help you keep your customers.

Do you believe the old adage, "The customer is always right"? I don't—never have and never will. I do, however, believe "The customer is always the customer, and I want that customer to always be mine."

Have you ever stopped doing business with a certain company or individual? Have you asked yourself, "Why?" What made you quit doing business with them? More important, have you asked yourself why your customers leave your company and go to your competition?

Why Customers Leave

Not long ago I had dinner in one of Tampa's nicer steak houses. After having dinner, we went upstairs to their dessert room. I ordered a dessert, which was delivered as ordered.

After an appropriate wait, our waiter came in and asked if everything was to our liking. I had barely touched my dessert. I told him that the idea was to complement the dinner, not contrast with it, and that there were several things that I found unacceptable.

I try to do everything I can in a friendly manner, treating others as I would like to be treated, so I was not even remotely abusing our waiter nor was I embarrassing our table. Yet our waiter never said a word; he just backed out of the dessert room as I was telling him what was wrong. He was doing his best to escape a situation that he obviously had not been trained to handle. Yet a simple "I am sorry. Can I get you something in its place?" would have taken care of the problem. I did not pursue it further until later that evening, when I decided that I must either call the manager or never eat there again.

Since I truly enjoy dining there, I called the manager. His reaction was appropriate and satisfying.

In a survey, the American Society for Quality asked the question, "Why do your customers leave you and go to your competition?" The respondents gave the following answers:

Die	1%
Move away	3%
Influenced by friends	5%
Lured away by the competition	9%
Dissatisfied with product	14%
Turned away by an attitude of indifference on the part of a company employee	68%

Keep Your Customers by Taking the HEAT

Is your business losing customers? Are sales down and employee turnover up? Over the next few pages, we'll show you how to retain that 68% who are turned away by an indifferent attitude. The idea is called "taking the HEAT."

HEAT is an acronym for **H**ear, **E**mpathize, **A**pologize, and **T**ake Ownership. Teach your employees this principle, and you can retain the 68% turned away by indifference. And that can make a big difference in the success of your company.

Every employee who comes into contact with your customers will have at some point the opportunity to apply the HEAT principle. What that employee says or does will determine whether that customer is likely to remain yours or go somewhere else. If you're the only game in town and your customers have no choice but to come to you for your products or services, you don't need to read any further. However, if you're like most of us and your customers have a choice, then read on.

We've all been on the giving end of a complaint of one type or another. Do you recall what the people hearing the complaint did? Did they listen? Did they interrupt? Did they argue with you? Did they seem indifferent? Did they have an attitude? Did they pass you off to someone else? Worse yet, did they not even seem to care?

Now reverse the role, and try to recall what you did when you were on the receiving end of a complaint. Most employees, like our waiter, do not like to listen to complaints because they feel ill-trained to handle such problems.

By learning and applying the HEAT principle, you can turn a negative situation into a positive one. Using the HEAT principle works well either in person or over the phone and it allows you to first meet the customer's *personal* needs and then focus on meeting the *practical* needs.

Our customers will usually show *emotion* when they are dissatisfied. This is the key indicator that a customer is unhappy. Ask yourself, "Why is it difficult for employees to listen to customers express their emotion?" You may find that:

- The customers might be wrong or unfair.
- The customers might jump to conclusions.
- The customers may accuse the employees.

○ The employees may wish to defend themselves.
○ There may be other work that needs to be done.
○ The customers may well have a legitimate complaint.

Everyone who comes into contact with a customer, whether over the phone or in person, needs to remember that *emotion* often gets in the way of listening, problem-solving, and rational decision-making.

It is equally important during this emotional time that we recognize that our employees have needs as well. The basic need, of course, is to maintain and enhance their self-esteem. To accomplish this, our employees must:

○ Feel trained and qualified.
○ Feel successful.
○ Feel in control.
○ Feel they are empowered.
○ Feel valued in their abilities.
○ Feel they will be supported.

HEAT meets all of these employee needs.

How to Apply HEAT

When you have a customer with a problem or complaint and an employee who does not want to listen or take the complaint, we have a *gap*. How do you bridge the gap between the needs of our customers and the needs of our employees? By applying HEAT.

HEAT will allow you to meet the needs of your customers and your employees. Plus, there's a bonus: the HEAT process can be used outside the office, to help take some of the stress out of daily living. If you don't believe this, just try it once.

Here again, in all its simplistic glory, is HEAT:

H	Hear
E	Empathize
A	Apologize
T	Take Ownership

Hear

A dissatisfied customer wants to know that someone is willing to listen. It's important to be quiet, pay attention, and listen carefully to what the customer is saying, without being distracted or sounding impatient. *Do not interrupt!* To do so may cause the customer to argue, to withdraw, or to hang up or go away.

Empathize

After getting the opportunity to express dissatisfaction, the customer wants to know that someone understands and cares. Listen and respond with empathy to acknowledge the customer's feelings (upset, frustrated, disappointed) and the facts of the situation that are causing those feelings. To empathize effectively, we should:

- Acknowledge the customer's feelings.
- Acknowledge the facts of the situation.
- Let the customer know you heard him or her.
- Let the customer know you understand how he or she feels and why he or she is upset.

Apologize

The customer wants to hear that you're sorry about the problem or inconvenience. Expressing empathy before apologizing shows the customer that you understand the feelings behind the complaint, which legitimizes your apology. Unless the problem is your fault, you can apologize without accepting blame. You can say, for example, "I'm sorry that upsets you" or "This situation is unfortunate and I apologize for it" or "I'm sorry you feel you weren't treated fairly." However, be careful not to apologize too much. Doing so might make your firm appear incompetent. We should admit fault if it's clear the organization is to blame.

Take Ownership

Customers complain because they feel something needs to be done. If the problem can fixed on the spot, *do so!* If the problem cannot be fixed on the spot, *some* action needs to be taken. This may include calling in a supervisor or transferring the customer to the appropriate department. Commit to *follow up* if appropriate—and it would be hard to imagine an instance where some form of follow-up is not needed.

Benefits of HEAT

In summary, remember these "Cooling the HEAT Tips."

Hear. Allow the person to speak without interruption. Acknowledge what he or she says.

Empathize. I'm sure _____ (fill in the blank) was upsetting. I'd be upset if _____ (fill in the blank) happened to me.

Apologize. I apologize for the situation. I'm sorry you were inconvenienced.

Take ownership. I'd like to take care of this right away. Let me call my supervisor and get some help.

HEAT pays in . . .

- Customer loyalty,
- Business success,
- Employee satisfaction and retention, and
- Customer satisfaction.

Now, imagine applying HEAT in the following situation.

I stopped by a local franchise of a national fast-food chain, to have it "my way." At least I thought it would be "my way." I ordered a bacon, egg, and cheese biscuit from the drive-through window to take to work. When I arrived and was ready to enjoy my breakfast, I found that they had given me something other than what I ordered. Of course, it was too late to take it back, even if I'd been willing to take the time to make the drive.

The next morning I again ordered a bacon, egg, and cheese biscuit from the drive-through. When I drove up to the window, I asked the young lady (assistant manager, no less) to check if my order was right, because they'd given me the wrong thing the day before. She looked in the bag and said, "Yes, it is," and then handed it to me. She did not check to see if it was what I ordered, nor did she say one word about the previous day's mistake.

That's just another example of employees who are not being properly trained to handle the everyday business of business. Things would have been different if the assistant manager had known the power of HEAT. I now patronize a different local fast-food restaurant. Will the other restaurant miss me? I doubt it—nor will I miss it.

About the Author

John Hartley is a development coach with Promus Hotel Corporation in Tampa, Florida, ranked number one in the hotel industry in the American Customer Satisfaction Index, published by the University of Michigan School of Business and the American Society for Quality. John has spent 23 years in various customer service capacities, following eight years in the U.S. Army Security Agency.

PART SEVEN

Customer Service on the Internet

28

THE WORLD WIDE WEB WAS MADE FOR CUSTOMER SERVICE

Jim Sterne

You probably know all about how companies are using the World Wide Web. But most are making big mistakes, according to the author of this article, who also wrote the book Customer Service on the Internet. *He offers recommendations for any business that's serious about making the most of its Web site.*

The Internet has garnered a great deal of hype and media attention in the past two years. Some of it has been alarmist and some of it has been utopian. But the descriptions of the Internet as a whole new way to communicate that will change the way we do business have been right on the money.

It would be a crime to ignore a new way to communicate with your customers. Even so, most companies are building World Wide Web sites in order to communicate *to* their customers instead of *with* them. Most Web sites are created to provide an electronic brochure, essentially the Internet version of a sales pitch, a sort of online television ad. Yes, people can get the specific information they're interested in, but companies are giving little thought to two-way communication.

The Internet offers a whole new way to establish rapport with customers. Answering customer questions, solving their problems, and selling them additional products can now be computerized. It took a healthy bit of prodding to push banks into the 21st century with automated teller machines. Now, all companies can provide their customers push-button service without installing networks of cash machines. They can do it through the World Wide Web.

The Web offers an additional means of creating the all-important bond of trust and loyalty between buyer and seller. Companies are using the Web to sell products and services and give their customers another means of conducting business. The rewards have been lower customer service costs and higher customer satisfaction. These are clearly goals to be envied.

Portions of this article were adapted from *Customer Service on the Internet* by Jim Sterne (New York: John Wiley & Sons, 1996).

297

Customer Service: The Next Wave of the World Wide Web

A few years ago, Jerry Neece, then Senior Product Manager for Internet product marketing for Sun Microsystems, announced that Sun had saved an estimated $1.3 million in January 1995 alone through Web-based customer service. Approximately one-third of that was in human resources. Most of the savings was through delivering software fixes over the Internet, instead of creating magnetic tapes and installation documents and stuffing them into postal packaging. Not to mention the shipping costs. A year later, in January 1996, one employee said Sun could show a savings of $12 million each month.

Saving money by delivering information electronically might be enough for most bottom-liners. But the Internet is a two-way street. It's a communications medium. It's not a TV, a radio, or a magazine. It's much more like a telephone, giving us the ability to hear as well as be heard. You don't use the telephone to deliver a radio message and then hang up. You use it for conversation, be it chit-chat, problem-solving, or transaction processing.

Like the telephone, the Web also allows for conversation. Today that conversation is written. Tomorrow it will be audio. The day after tomorrow it will be visual. The audio and visual tools will help us take care of things on the Web as we do with our 800-numbers. The "complaint department" will simply be available in a new way. But the reason the Web is ideal for customer service today has to do with the text capabilities that are available today.

The magic of a well-constructed Web site is that it can provide the information a customer wants, when she wants it, and in as much detail as she wants. Customers can answer their own questions, in their own time, and to their hearts' content.

At first, this sounds wonderful merely because of the cost savings. You don't have to pay for the call to the 800-number. You don't have to pay for the person to answer the phone. You don't have to pay for the brochures and specification documents to be printed, stored, picked, packed, and posted.

But the true wonder comes from the heightened sense of satisfaction felt by the customer. Giving your customers the ability to get an answer to a problem, in sufficient detail and in minimal time, is a gift they'll receive gladly. A stronger bond of loyalty will be created, ensuring you a larger share of that customer's commerce.

Sticking to the principles of customer service, sticking to the principles of Web site development, and looking to others who have done well on the Web are the best ways to make the most of this new medium.

Getting Started

The tools of the Internet trade are the tools of the database administrator and the tools of the librarian. But first you have to be willing to help your customers in any way you can. Having a fully automated droid handle all customer inquiries would be wonderful, and it's a goal well worth pursuing. However, infinitely intelligent droids aren't available this year, so you'll have to start from the beginning.

It doesn't take fancy graphics or big budgets or sophisticated systems to produce results. It just takes an understanding that customer support is important. Good customer support doesn't have to be *expensive*, just *good*.

Keeping Up

Your task will be to start with something meaningful and move up the value chain. You'll continue to move up this chain as your customers demand more and your competitors offer it. You'll find that you must openly publish customer criticism, you must engage your clients in public discussions, and you must be willing to give them access into the very center of your company's electronic life-blood.

At the same time, your customers will reveal information about their likes and dislikes, their needs and their habits, like never before. They'll tell you what they think, but they'll also show you how they react. The knowledge you will glean from your customers is unprecedented.

The winners in the new world order will not just publish all until there are no secrets left. The winners will be those who know how to interpret what their customers are telling them via e-mail, discussion groups, and mouse clicks.

Making your company easier to do business with is today's great competitive edge. Customers expect the best price. They expect fast service. They expect to get answers instead of being put on hold until dawn. And they'll flock to buy from you if you can save them 10 minutes here and 20 minutes there.

Superior Customer Service on the Web: Eight Steps

Here, then, are eight steps to superior customer service on the Web.

1. Recognize that the world has changed.

The Web represents a fundamental shift in the way business communicates. The telephone changed the way we did business. The fax machine did it again. In time, the Web will bring together phone, fax, voice, and video—and it will all be necessary to remain competitive.

Bringing customers into your company through the Web will cause ripples of change throughout the organization. Your upper management must embrace this new media and stand behind your efforts to service the people who pay the bills—your customers.

Those ripples of change will include the way you run your business internally. You'll need Intranets to give your employees access to enough information that they can then service your customers.

2. Post a "frequently asked questions" document.

An amazing number of calls to your company revolve around the same issues. Talk to the people who answer the phone and find out what those questions are, then post the answers for all to see.

Your FAQ document can start simple. Then it can grow to include a knowledge base of answers. The software development tools company Intersolv (www.intersolv.com) posts its FAQ for all to see. If you have a problem using Intersolv software, ask the knowledge base. It's the place the company stores all the problems people have had and all the answers they've offered.

Determining which questions to place in your FAQ should be very simple, because your customer service people deal in frequently asked questions for a living. They know which questions are asked most often. They also know the answers. More important, they understand that a person asking, "Does it weigh more than 100 pounds?" is usually asking about delivery methods and costs. When somebody asks about delivery, the question is also about how long it will take to make the product useful. When somebody asks about warranties, the question is also about reliability.

The most significant rallying cry you can incorporate as you put together your FAQ is "Think like a customer!" Maybe even like a *prospective* customer. The customer doesn't care if your company is organized by product line, business unit, or spheres of political influence. The customer wants his or her question answered. Let your FAQ reflect how your customers, current or prospective, think of your company.

If your site is large enough, implement a search engine. It should be accessible from the home page and from any page on the site. It should be powerful and easy to use. Placing a search icon on your home page and a search button on the generic, site-wide button bar is straightforward and easy to do. Providing a search tool that is both powerful *and* easy to use is not straightforward and easy to do, but it's a great boon to your customers.

3. Respond to your e-mail.

The Internet is a communication tool rather than a broadcast medium. When customers use e-mail instead of the telephone, you need to be ready to respond. Make sure there are people assigned to answering e-mail and properly trained in its use.

As a start, offer multiple e-mail addresses for your customers. Some may want to talk to accounting@company.com. Some may need to converse with shipping@company.com or sales@company.com. Allow them to choose—and save yourself some sorting time and effort.

Provide some serious training for the people who will be answering your e-mail. It's a new communication medium. It's different. People react to the written word differently than to the spoken word.

When the guy on the phone says, "Gosh, Jim, I'm sorry. I'll get it out just as soon as I can. Really. We've got a backup here, but it looks like a couple of days to get it to you," I listen carefully to the level of confidence expressed in the tone of voice. If confidence is not high (perhaps overt emphasis on the word "couple"), then I make my plans knowing he's probably not going to come through.

If the statement, "It looks like it'll take a couple of days to get it to you," shows up in e-mail or in a letter, I plan on two or three days to delivery and plan accordingly. If the company doesn't deliver, I'm in a tight spot and I lay blame squarely on the guy who lied to me. If you're going to work in the modern world, you'll have to treat your e-mail with the respect it deserves.

When an issue is critical, a customer will usually call. If it's a contractual issue, they'll send a fax with its inherent status as a legal document. But if it's merely important—a product question, a service modification, a clarification of some kind—they'll send an e-mail. They don't need an immediate answer, but they're not doing it for the sheer joy of it either. They expect an answer within 24 hours and it's up to you to get it for them.

For the high end, look to tools like Mustang Software's Internet Message Center (IMC). Rather than try to use artificial intelligence to divine the subject matter of each incoming e-mail, IMC sorts incoming e-mail by the To: address (sales@company.com, support@company.com, and so forth), sends it to the right message pool, and gives it a number. IMC sends an auto-response back to the sender and waits for an 'agent' to read and respond to the message, all the while recording who's working on it and how much time goes by between receipt and reply.

The customer knows the message was received and has a tracking number, as well as any pertinent boilerplate information. The people responding to incoming mail can share the load, since you can have as many agents as needed. Management gets status reports about agents, customers, and productivity.

4. Create a place for discussion.

Take advantage of bulletin boards and e-mail lists to give your customers a place for online discussions. They know things about using your products that you don't and they can help each other use your products better. It's also a great way to learn what your customers are thinking.

Cisco Systems (www.cisco.com) sells Internet routers and switches. They *know* their customers are online. They've created a Customer Forum on their Web site, where people from all over the world can post questions and answers. If you have a problem with the way one of their routers works with one of your work stations running one of your Web servers using one of the major telecommunications companies' connections, there's a place to turn for help. You can turn to hundreds of Cisco engineers. But you might also turn to tens of thousands of Cisco customers.

5. Track your customers' visits.

Keep logs of what your customers look at, how they navigate, and what they search for. This will give you lots of clues about what interests them and how easy your site is to use.

After a review of their server logs, Hewlett-Packard (www.hp.com) changed its Web site to make it easier for many of its site visitors to find what they were looking for. People would come to the home page, click on the "Products" button, then the "Peripherals" button, and then the "Printers" button. Lots of people. So HP simply put "Printing & Imaging" at the top of the menu on the home page.

And pay attention to the most frequently asked questions. If you know what people are asking, you can provide the answers up front: in your marketing materials, in your instruction manuals, on your home page. Give them the answers before they ask.

6. Provide access to as much information as possible.

The ideal Web site has so much information that everybody who comes there can find something to help him or her. Every time you come up with more tips, advice, or pointers, be sure to post them on your Web site. Make your site the vault of all knowledge and your customers will get used to looking there first.

Don't publish everything on one page: that's like giving them a drink from a fire hose. Instead, offer the basics up front and let them drill down to the information they need, when they need it, and at their own pace. The person who's happy with a terse reply can click and run. The person who wants a more detailed explanation can get it.

7. Give customers access to live information.

The reason the FedEx Web site is always held up as a vanguard of business on the Web is because it allows direct access to live data. Your customers want to know more than just what colors your products come in. They want to know when you'll be able to deliver, if the problem they reported has been solved, and if the new version will be out soon.

A&A Printers and Digital Graphics (www.aaprint.com) prints brochures, posters, and direct mail pieces. A&A publishes its production schedule online. Anybody can go look and see how busy the pre-press department is and how stacked up the printing presses are. Got a rush job? Don't bother calling until Wednesday. But there's some slack time on Monday, if you can get your artwork in on time.

Then A&A posts individual job lists on their site. Punch in your customer number and take a look at the status of each job. Click on a particular job and see if there are any open issues, problems, or questions. Read the comments entered by the account executive or the press foreman. Add your own comments. Answer those questions and keep the project on track.

8. Treat your customers like individuals.

Your customers are unique. Not just each company you sell to, but each person in each company you sell to. Track them all as individuals. Your Web site can recognize individuals and treat them as such. It's time to put that database technology to its full purpose.

Greet them by name when they show up at your site. Show them what you've added to your site since the last time they visited. This isn't a generic "What's New" page. This is a call to the customer database to see exactly when this person last visited, to create a "What's New to You" page.

Just as Federal Express lets you track your packages, let your customers review their billing statements. Let them see the status of their back order. Let them make their purchasing decisions based on your stock-on-hand.

Seeing the World Through Customer-Colored Glasses

Successful customer service always means looking at your products, your company, and your customer service methods through your customers' eyes. Customers don't care how your company is organized. They just want you to answer their questions and solve their problems.

The most important task for a customer service Web builder is figuring out what the customer will want to see, will want to ask, and will want to get out of the experience. It may be well worth the effort to ask your customers directly, "If you were able to do business with us via our Web site, what sort of functionality would you most like to see?"

Customer Service Tomorrow

In the future, your lawn mower, your washing machine, and your car will all have the ability to notify you and the manufacturer when something is wrong. Factory equipment already has the sensors and communications gear to stay in touch with its creator. Temperature, tolerances, velocities, and throughput can all be monitored from afar to ensure superior performance.

Consider the following scenario:

"If you've rebooted and the same error came up before you ran the totals, then, well, I'm stumped," says Jeeves, the cartoon-like character in a small video window on Bob's screen. "So, I've logged your problem and I've routed it to a real person who can help."

Another window appears. "This is Melissa. She's just taking a quick look at our conversation and will be able to ask a few more intelligent questions than I can."

"It looks," says Melissa, reading intently and pausing to finish, "like the problem might be insufficient memory." She looks into the camera at the customer. "Did you upgrade to version 3.6?"

Sensing the head movement, Jeeves remains quiet to let the customer answer.

"Um, I think that was the first thing we tried. Right, Jeeves?"

"Yes, that was the first thing we tried, Bob. You're right. Melissa, is there another way to improve the memory without a hardware upgrade?"

"Let's try resizing the cache," she says and sends a small diagnostic tool down the line.

When the fix works to everyone's satisfaction, Melissa adds it to the Jeeves customer service database for future reference.

Customer service on the Internet is all about empowering your customers to be able to take care of themselves. There are a number of transformations happening in the world of computers and business that point to the customer-as-workmate:

- ○ Equipment costs are continuing to decline.
- ○ Online analytical processing is allowing decision support on the fly.
- ○ Internet access is allowing economic computer connections from anywhere.
- ○ Inference engines, case-based reasoning, and fuzzy logic efforts are paying off.
- ○ Object-oriented software is interoperating across different computer platforms.

○ Faster hardware and smarter software is allowing for flexible mass-customization.

These are the forces of technology coming together to allow change to happen. In addition, there are social forces at work:

○ Customer expectation inflation is rising at an enormous rate.
○ Employees are being empowered to make decisions closer to the customer.
○ Downsized executives are starting small, alert, agile companies ready to compete.

These transformations and these forces taken together, the commercial organization has no choice but to accept the inevitable: electronic customer service is at hand. Some companies will ignore it. Some will tolerate it. Some will roll with the punches. Some will make do. The real winners are the ones that embrace the technology—and their customers.

About the Author

Jim Sterne is the head of his own consulting company, Target Marketing. He has spent over 15 years in sales and marketing of technical products. For the past several years, Jim has devoted all of his attention to the Internet as a marketing medium. He has gathered information from online discussion groups as well as from his own experience as a founding partner of a regional Internet access provider. His currency is ensured by his activities as a marketing consultant to some of the world's largest companies.

In September 1994, Target Marketing launched the world's first "Marketing on the Internet" seminar series. This event included five speakers and was delivered in eight major cities. In November 1995, Jim published his first book, *World Wide Web Marketing* (New York: John Wiley & Sons). His second book, *Customer Service on the Internet*, was published in October 1996 (New York: John Wiley & Sons). He completed his third book on this subject in September 1997, *What Makes People Click: Advertising on the Web* (Que). Jim Sterne is a public speaker and consultant, helping clients set Internet marketing goals and determine strategies.

29

USING THE INTERNET TO MEASURE CUSTOMER SATISFACTION AND LOYALTY

John Chisholm

"A revolution in customer satisfaction measurement is imminent," according to the author of this article. He explains how organizations can use the Internet to get feedback from their customers more easily, quickly, cheaply, and accurately. But which medium is better for your customers—e-mail or the World Wide Web? And how can you make the most of the potential of the Internet? This article offers some solid answers to the basic questions.

Delivering excellent service requires that managers continually survey customers for feedback and promptly respond to it. In the past, phone interviews and postal mail questionnaires have been the most common methods of surveying customers. Today, the Internet is enabling customers to provide feedback more easily, quickly, cheaply, and accurately than ever before.

Yet many practitioners are still unaware that, due to the Internet, a revolution in customer satisfaction measurement is imminent. At its current rate of growth, the Internet will become the most widely used means of measuring customer satisfaction early in the 21st century.

In this article, we'll address why the Internet is so rapidly replacing conventional means for customer satisfaction measurement (CSM). We'll review the design of surveys used for CSM and the kinds of analyses that customer satisfaction specialists can do on survey results to assess an organization's operational performance, strategic advantages, and competitive limitations. These design and analysis considerations apply equally well, whether the survey is conventional or on the Internet. We'll address where Internet surveys can best be used, the different kinds of Internet surveys currently possible, and the pros and cons of each kind. Finally, we'll examine as a case study the first worldwide customer satisfaction survey conducted on the Internet by a Fortune 500-class company, a milestone that occurred in 1997.

Although the techniques covered here are on the leading edge in early 1998,

Internet technology is advancing so quickly that sections of this article may be out of date by the time you read them. To view an updated version of this document at any time, visit http://www.CustomerSat.com.

Internet Advantages

The Internet offers many advantages over conventional postal mail and telephone surveys for CSM. The following factors contribute to the high response rates and respondent satisfaction and lower costs that characterize Internet-based CSM:

- Complete survey results are typically available two to three weeks after deployment, with partial results available in days, hours, or even real time.
- Customers can complete questionnaires whenever they choose, from wherever they choose, in any time zone. No scheduled phone interviews or face-to-face appointments are required.
- Keyboard, mouse, and computer screen make answering surveys easier than handwriting responses, especially open-ended ones, and faster than with a questionnaire read over the phone.
- Human interviewer influences that can bias responses are eliminated.
- The cost of deploying the surveys, tabulating the responses, and capturing verbatim open-ended responses is a fraction of the cost of conventional interviews.

Customer Access to the Internet

In deciding whether to use the Internet for CSM, the first question is how many of an organization's customers will be able to receive and respond to an Internet survey. Before all else, Internet- or Intranet-based CSM requires that a sufficient number of customers have access to the Internet or an Intranet to be representative of an entire population.

The number of industries in which this requirement is generally met is significant and growing rapidly. First are technology industries—software, computers, networking, technical publishing, semiconductors, and biotechnology—where using the Internet for CSM either already is or is rapidly becoming feasible. Second, an increasing number of non-technology businesses offer Internet-based services, where customer access to the Internet is implicit. These services include online reservations, securities trading, information retrieval, and online gaming and other entertainment. Third, for internal customer services where many or all of the internal customers (employees) use corporate e-mail, an Intranet-based survey is practical, even if employees have no access to the external Internet. Finally, Internet-based CSM is just becoming practical at this writing for some mainstream consumer products and services that are not computer-oriented. At its current rate of growth, the Internet will be an important CSM vehicle for *all* consumer products and services before this book is out of print.

Types of Survey Questionnaires and Their Design

CSM measures satisfaction with either *relationships* or *transactions*. Customer *relationships* refer to experiences over an extended period (typically a period of three months to a year). All aspects of the customer-vendor relationship—including service quality, product quality and value, and ease of doing business—may be measured. A customer *transaction* is a single unit of service, typically extending over only a few minutes, hours, or days. Measures of satisfaction with *relationships* provide *strategic and operational* knowledge; measures of satisfaction with *transactions* provide primarily *operational* knowledge.

Transaction-oriented questionnaires typically ask a subset of the questions in relationship-oriented questionnaires. Either type of survey, deployed either via the Internet or conventionally, usually has three parts:

- *Overall measures of satisfaction*, such as "What is your overall level of satisfaction with our product or service?" "How likely would you be to recommend our product or service to a friend or colleague?" and "How likely would you be to purchase our product or service again?"
- *Ratings of key performance attributes*, for example: "How satisfied are you with the promptness of service you received . . . the courtesy of our staff . . . the accuracy of our service . . . the completeness of our solution . . . the speed of our system?" Pre-survey interviews and online focus groups can be conducted with a sample of customers to determine these key performance attributes.
- *Demographic questions*, which will be used to segment survey responses by category, for example: "What are your company's annual revenues?" "In what geographical region are you located?" "What is your industry?" "Which of our product(s) do you use?" "For how long have you been a customer?" Any significant differences in satisfaction within any of these customer segments will be revealed by cross-tabulating the results by each of these respondent categories. Being able to pinpoint needed performance actions to a specific customer segment helps make survey results *actionable*.

Many customer satisfaction surveys ask the respondent not only to rate the company's *performance* for each attribute but also to rate the *importance* of each attribute. Asking both of these variables enables surveyors to measure *gaps* between importance and performance (gap = importance rating—performance rating). To prioritize them for management attention, attributes are ordered from largest to smallest gap. Attributes with both high importance and performance (satisfaction) ratings are key strengths; attributes with high importance but low performance ratings should be key concerns for management.

Either instead of or in addition to asking about importance explicitly, survey analysts may *derive* the importance of attributes by computing the correlation between an attribute's rating and overall satisfaction. This approach assumes that overall satisfaction is a variable dependent upon the key performance attributes, which are assumed to be independent variables (or linear combinations of independent variables). Factor and regression analyses are used to determine the degree of correlation for each attribute. *Asking explicitly* about importance indicates which attributes customers *believe* are most important. *Deriving* importance determines which attributes actually *drive* overall satisfaction and loyalty.

Conventional wisdom for postal mail and phone surveys is that the use of open-ended questions (such as "What can we do to most improve the value of our service to you?") should be limited, because such questions are time-consuming for respondents to complete and the responses are costly to record and tabulate. But with Internet surveys, respondents can complete open-ended questions quickly using keyboard and mouse and, since their responses arrive in electronic form, there's no need for manual data entry. Consequently, customer satisfaction specialists may use open-ended questions more freely in Internet than in conventional surveys.

A final issue of Internet survey design is dealing with international languages and cultures. Since Internet surveys can be so readily distributed around the globe, they may well be received by respondents whose local languages and cultures vary widely. Today, English is by far the most widely used language on the Internet; but as Internet usage grows, so will the use of other languages. Conducting worldwide surveys in multiple languages can help respondents understand questions—and it may even be necessary for meaningful responses. But since languages do not translate exactly, aggregating survey results gathered from questionnaires in different languages may not be meaningful. Similarly, attitudes toward and assessments of customer service vary widely among cultures. Consequently, aggregating survey results across cultures may be problematic even if all questionnaires are in English. Because of these issues, CSM specialists choose, in many cases, to tally and analyze Internet survey responses from different countries separately.

E-mail Survey or Web Survey?

Internet surveys can be conducted using e-mail, the Web, or a combination of the two media. Each approach has advantages and limitations.

E-mail Survey

E-mail surveys use questionnaires in plain text (ASCII). The surveys may be used for anyone with an Internet address, whether or not that person has access to the Web (Figure 29-1). They're also easy to complete. Respondents simply edit the messages, typing in characters at designated places to answer either closed-ended or open-ended questions, and click on "reply." Respondents do not even have to be connected to the Internet while completing the survey: they may download the message and complete the survey off-line. If they download the survey into a laptop or notebook, they can complete it on a plane, a commuter train, or almost anywhere.

The electronic equivalents of paper surveys, e-mail surveys also have limitations. The use of words alone (your instructions) cannot keep a respondent from, say, choosing both "yes" and "no" for a question when only one response is meaningful. Responses cannot be validated until the completed survey has been e-mailed back and received by the surveyor, which may be hours after the respondent has

To answer a question, type an x between the brackets, anything like this [x] or [XX]. For fill-in-the-blanks, type between the brackets like this: [your response]. Please make no other changes to this survey.

I. Program Overall

    1. Considering all factors (marketing and sales assistance, equipment programs, technical consulting services, training, education, and costs of services), what is your *overall* level of satisfaction with the Software Partners Program?

        [ ] a) Very satisfied
        [ ] b) Satisfied
        [ ] c) Neither satisfied nor dissatisfied
        [ ] d) Dissatisfied
        [ ] e) Very dissatisfied

    2. How likely will you be to renew your membership in the program?

        [ ] a) Very likely
        [ ] b) Likely
        [ ] c) Neither likely nor unlikely
        [ ] d) Unlikely
        [ ] e) Very unlikely

    3. If you answered d) or e) to either question above, why? [ ]

    4. What can we do to most improve the Software Partners Program overall? [ ]

II. Program Features

    5. Of the following features of the program, which *one* is most important to you?

        [ ] a) Marketing and sales development
        [ ] b) Equipment programs
        [ ] c) Technical consulting
        [ ] d) Training and education
        [ ] e) Other, please specify . . . [ ]

    6. How satisfied are you with the marketing and sales development programs (sales support, solutions catalog, trade shows, advertising, communication activities)?

        [ ] a) Very satisfied
        [ ] b) Satisfied
        [ ] c) Neither satisfied nor dissatisfied
        [ ] d) Dissatisfied
        [ ] e) Very dissatisfied

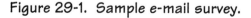

Figure 29-1. Sample e-mail survey.

completed the survey. Instructions for skipping (e.g., "If no, go to question 34") must be explicit, just as in paper surveys. These factors can reduce the quality of data from an e-mail survey and can make it necessary to clean the data.

A final limitation of e-mail surveys is that some PC e-mail software products (such as Lotus cc:Mail) limit the length of the body of an e-mail message to 20,000 bytes of text, which equates to anywhere from 30 to 60 questions, depending upon the amount of text in each question.

Web Surveys

Web surveys use hypertext markup language (HTML), the language of the Web, and are posted on a Web site. Web surveys have four advantages over e-mail surveys:

○ Radio buttons, check boxes, and data entry fields—which are possible in HTML but not in the ASCII text of e-mail surveys—keep respondents from selecting more than one choice when only one is meaningful and from otherwise typing where no response is intended by the surveyor.
○ Skipping can be automatic, based on a respondent's answers, eliminating the need to spell out instructions.
○ Responses may be validated as they are entered.
○ Additional survey elements—such as graphics, images, animations, and links to other Web pages—may be integrated into or around the survey.

These factors make completing the survey faster and more interesting, and result in higher-quality data.

For survey research to be meaningful, surveyors must be able to control the selection of respondents. This requirement is met by e-mail surveys, which surveyors distribute to designated addresses. To control selection with Web surveys, e-mail invitations are used. Surveyors send e-mail messages containing the Web address (Uniform Resource Locator or URL, usually in the form "http://www.company.com/etc") of the survey page to respondents, who can view the survey page either by clicking on the URL or by copying and pasting it into their Web browser. When used with e-mail invitations, a Web survey is best posted in a hidden location on the Web, so that uninvited Web surfers are unlikely to find it.

Positively Identifying Respondents

Surveyors also need to ensure that customers do not respond multiple times ("stuff the ballot box"). Again, e-mail surveys can be readily designed to meet this requirement: questionnaires can be encoded, if desired, to match returned responses with outbound e-mailings. For Web surveys, any of three approaches may be used.

One approach is to use a "cookie," a marker file that a Web page can leave in a user's browser to indicate, in this case, that the user has completed a survey. Whenever somebody accesses the Web page, the survey checks the user's browser for the cookie. If it's not there, the user can complete the survey. But if the cookie is there, the user is not allowed access to the survey.

Cookies are easy for surveyors to use, but they have four limitations:

○ Many Internet users are uncomfortable with cookies and have learned to reject them, which would mean rejecting the survey.
○ Respondents can complete the survey, then delete the cookie and return to the Web site to complete the survey again.
○ Cookies are computer-resident, so a person can circumvent cookie controls simply by accessing the survey from another computer.
○ Cookies are usually tied to a Web browser, not to an individual; so if a personal computer is shared by multiple legitimate respondents, only one of them could complete the survey.

A second approach is for the surveyor to provide the respondent a password along with the Web survey URL. The respondent enters the password into a field that pops up before the Web survey page appears in the respondent's browser. Passwords are more reliable than cookies, but respondents have to remember and key in cumbersome passwords, which can reduce response rates.

The newest approach—Positive Respondent Identification™ (PRI) technology from CustomerSat.com—integrates e-mail, Web, and database technologies into a single solution. A Web program generates a unique URL for each respondent pointing to the survey page on the Web. Each respondent is then e-mailed an invitation containing the personalized URL. Afterward, the respondent clicks on the URL or copies and pastes it into his or her Web browser: there's no need to remember or type in any password. The Web program then reads the URL and checks it against a database. Checking confirms that respondents are authorized to complete surveys and keeps respondents from completing surveys more than once. The database is updated after every respondent completes the survey.

Customer Confidentiality and Anonymity

Without the assurance of confidentiality, many customers will not respond candidly, or perhaps at all. In a confidential survey, a response may be linked to a customer name, but only by a survey researcher for purposes of survey management. An anonymous survey goes further: a response cannot be linked to a customer name at all.

To respond candidly, customers must *trust* that the survey is conducted confidentially. The use of an independent survey firm to conduct the survey helps build this trust. In many cases where organizations have changed from performing CSM themselves to using an independent survey service provider, key attribute ratings have changed relative to each other and declined overall, as customers have become more candid.

For the greatest customer comfort levels, e-mail surveys are best sent by an independent survey service provider and returned to that provider, rather than sent out by and/or returned to someone in the organization. The survey provider then delivers summary and statistical results and verbatim responses to the company, without revealing the identities of individual respondents. For similar reasons, Web surveys are typically hosted on an independent survey service provider's Web site, rather than the organization's Web site.

Simple e-mail surveys can be made anonymous by instructing respondents to send responses to an anonymous remailer, a mail-forwarding service that removes the sender's e-mail address from a message. Simple Web surveys—HTML pages— that make no use of respondent controls are also anonymous. But in these cases, surveyors cannot ensure that customers respond only once and cannot send reminders to non-respondents.

The various forms of respondent control—cookies, passwords, and Positive Respondent Identification—may be used even in anonymous Web surveys. For example, a survey researcher using PRI may generate a unique URL for each customer, and then delete the corresponding customer name in the database. All that's recorded is whether a particular URL has been used or not, not the customer's identity.

Survey Response Rates

Given the state of the Internet as of this writing, Web surveys by e-mail invitation tend to experience lower response rates than e-mail surveys. There are several reasons for this:

- In many organizations, either because of technical constraints or corporate policy, employees have access to Internet e-mail, but not to the Web.
- E-mail comes directly to the respondent, while it takes several steps for the respondent to get to a Web survey: clicking on, copying and pasting or typing in a URL, and waiting for a page to download from Web server to PC. These steps take time and, however simple, confuse some respondents.
- Respondents generally need to be connected to the Internet while completing a Web survey; they may not be off-line, as with e-mail surveys.

For all of these reasons, Web surveys tend to experience lower response rates than e-mail surveys.

The response rate for a Web survey with e-mail invitations depends in part on the percentage of the respondents with *Web-enabled e-mail clients*. A Web-enabled e-mail client is PC e-mail software that allows a user to click on a URL in an e-mail message to access that Web page. With an e-mail client that's not Web-enabled, a respondent must manually copy and paste the URL from e-mail message to Web browser to access the Web page.

Response rates are higher for respondents whose e-mail clients are Web-enabled. As of this writing, all recent releases of e-mail software from leaders Microsoft, Netscape, and IBM/Lotus, as well as some 40%-50% of the Internet e-mail clients currently installed worldwide, we estimate, are Web-enabled. These percentages will rise rapidly in 1999, as users of earlier versions of e-mail software upgrade to newer versions. As this happens, we expect that response rates for Web surveys will get closer to those for e-mail surveys.

Measuring Response Rate Differences

To measure the difference in response rates between e-mail and Web surveys, CustomerSat.com conducted a test in mid-1997 as part of a satisfaction survey of participants at a leading Internet technology conference. The survey measured satisfaction with the conference program, facilities, meals, registration, city location, and performance relative to other conferences. Approximately 70% of the respondents, who were highly Internet-savvy, used Web-enabled e-mail clients. CustomerSat.com surveyed half of the 600 participants via e-mail and half via Web surveys with e-mail invitations. The response rate to the 30-question survey, without benefit of pre-notification or reminders, was 24% for the Web survey with e-mail invitations and 30% for the e-mail survey. We believe the Web survey response rate would have been lower had not such a high percentage of the respondents had Web-enabled e-mail clients.

Not only are respondents more likely to respond to e-mail surveys than to Web surveys, they're likely to respond *sooner*. Almost 80% of the early responses in the test (those received within six hours of deploying the survey) were e-mail survey responses. Apparently, it's easier to postpone or ignore clicking on a link in an e-mail message than to ignore reading the e-mail message itself.

Because of the extra effort (albeit small) required to respond to Web surveys with e-mail invitations, as compared with e-mail surveys, we hypothesized that average satisfaction rating scores would be slightly lower and variances slightly higher for Web survey responses than for e-mail responses in the above test. Our reasoning: respondents whose satisfaction lies between the two extremes are less likely to go to the extra trouble required to express their opinions than those who feel very strongly—either favorably or unfavorably—about the survey. This would increase the variance in ratings. Also, very dissatisfied customers are more likely than very satisfied customers to go to extra trouble to express their opinions. However, we found no appreciable difference in the average scores and variances between the two groups. The extra time and steps required to complete a Web survey appear not to be so significant as to affect rating scores.

Rules of Thumb for Decision Makers

Here are the rules of thumb for choosing between the two main types of Internet surveys:

Choose e-mail surveys for:	*Choose Web surveys with e-mail invitations for:*
○ Shorter surveys (< 20,000 bytes)	○ Longer surveys (> 20,000 bytes)
○ Less Internet-savvy respondents	○ More Internet-savvy respondents
○ E-mail-based online services	○ Web-based businesses and services
○ Simple skip patterns and edit checking	○ Complex skip patterns and edit checking

Respondent Incentives

A respondent incentive—something of value that a respondent receives for completing a survey—can significantly raise response rates. The ideal incentive is one that's highly valued by the respondent and cost-effective for the service organization to provide and fulfill. An incentive that often meets these requirements is a random drawing for a selection of the organization's products or services. This type of incentive offers two major advantages for the organization. First, an organization can usually provide its own products or services at cost. Second, with a random drawing, the organization needs to fulfill only a limited number of incentives, rather than one for every respondent, thereby reducing costs. However, care must be taken to ensure that the choice of incentive does not bias responses by motivating some customers to respond but not others.

Displaying Survey Results in Real Time on the Web

With conventional surveys, it typically takes weeks or longer for survey results to be tabulated and reported. With the Internet, survey results can be displayed and updated in real time as responses are collected. Typically, charts, frequency distributions, lists of open-ended responses, and even cross-tabs of survey questions are presented in password-protected locations on the Web. This technique, especially valuable for transaction-oriented CSM, enables customer service managers to monitor feedback from customers in real time and take immediate action if, say, satisfaction with a particular product or in a particular geographical region falls below a minimum acceptable level.

Customer-interaction systems—also known as "customer care" or "front-office systems"—are enterprise applications that enable service and support staff to serve customers more effectively. These systems, built around a customer contact data base, provide staff with automated access to customer histories, status of orders and problems, support for work flow among staff members, and ready access to technical information required to address customer needs. Leading customer-interaction system vendors include Aurum, Clarify, Remedy, Scopus, Siebel, and Vantive.

CustomerSat.com has extended such systems with real-time, transaction-oriented CSM. The closing of a customer case, problem ticket, product sale, or similar event in the customer-interaction system triggers the e-mailing of a survey to the customer. Survey results are generated in real time and posted in a password-protected Web location, providing a seamless link between customer service and CSM.

Combining Internet-Based Data Collection With Conventional Techniques

The same techniques used to recruit, qualify, and probe respondents with conventional surveys may be used with Internet surveys. In addition to e-mail, surveyors may use telephone, postal mail, and fax to invite and further guide respondents to a Web survey. Respondents may complete a Web survey when a telephone staff person calls or they may bookmark a survey Web page to complete later. If the respondent does not complete the Web survey within a reasonable time, a reminder can be e-mailed or left as a phone message. The telephone staff person's role evolves from one of *interviewer* to *facilitator*. The length and cost of the phone call is dramatically reduced.

Only very limited probing of open-ended responses is possible online in Web surveys today. To compensate for this limitation, a phone call may allow follow-up probing of open-ended Web survey responses. If about one out of 10 questions is open-ended, and only one out of 10 open-ended responses requires probing, use of the Internet can reduce required phone interview time and cost by a factor of 100, as compared with conducting an entire survey via phone. As an added benefit, most interviewer bias, either unintentional or intentional, is eliminated.

Fortune 500 Company Case Study

In 1997, Advanced Micro Devices (AMD) conducted what was, to the best of our knowledge, the first annual, worldwide customer satisfaction survey by a Fortune 500-class company whose primary medium is the Internet. AMD is a global supplier of integrated circuits for the personal and networked computer and communications markets. AMD produces processors, flash memories, programmable logic devices, and products for communications and networking applications. Founded in 1969 and based in Sunnyvale, CA, AMD had revenues of $2 billion in 1996.

Prior to 1997, AMD had for many years conducted its annual customer satisfaction, loyalty, and value survey of over 200 of its largest customers through face-to-face and phone interviews and postal and fax questionnaires. In search of a more effective and streamlined approach for its 1997 survey, and to make providing feedback more convenient for its customers, the company turned to CustomerSat.com, whose principals had conducted hundreds of Internet surveys since 1993.

CustomerSat.com specializes in measuring customer satisfaction and conducting market research using e-mail, the Web, and combinations of the two media. Members of CustomerSat.com have achieved numerous firsts in Internet surveying, including the first automated collection, reading, and tabulation of survey responses by e-mail, the first real-time calculation and display of cross-tabs on the Web, and the first positive identification of respondents to Web surveys.

Because AMD's customers were almost exclusively involved in the manufacture of electronic equipment, almost all of them had ready access to the Internet. A list of e-mail addresses for most of AMD's largest customers was assembled from various corporate databases. Phone and fax were used to collect e-mail addresses for other customers.

To determine the key performance attributes that the questionnaire would measure, pre-survey interviews were conducted with a sample of AMD customers. The survey covered six major AMD product lines—microprocessors, non-volatile memory, networking, communications, programmable logic products, and embedded processors. The length of the survey—over 90 questions—dictated the use of a Web survey with e-mail invitations, rather than an e-mail survey. Because customers were accustomed to conversing about AMD products and technology in English, the survey was conducted in English worldwide.

For marketing purposes, AMD was interested in what attributes customers *believed* were most important as well as what attributes actually drove their overall satisfaction and loyalty. So, the importance of each attribute was both asked explicitly and derived using factor and regression analyses. Demographic variables used for cross-tabs included size of customer organization, primary market, type of customer (manufacturer, distributor, or reseller), respondent job function, length of time product(s) had been used, and geographical location.

After HTML programming, Web scripting, and test, the survey was hosted on CustomerSat.com's Web site. (A copy of the survey questionnaire, no longer active, can be viewed at http://www.CustomerSat.com/amd.htm.) Invitations were sent out, primarily by e-mail, to the customers over a two-week period from AMD's director of customer quality systems.

It took less than 30 days to achieve over 200 responses, the targeted number, to the 95-question survey. Respondents included vice presidents and directors of AMD customer companies. During the 30-day period, reminders were sent as needed by e-mail and voice mail. Of the customer companies whose feedback was solicited, the overall response rate was close to 50%.

The invitations to the survey gave customers the choice of responding by Web, e-mail, fax, or postal mail. Of those who responded, 93% did so via the Web. Most of those who responded by means other than the Web were outside of North America, in countries where access to the Web is less widely available. Others worked for companies that restricted or blocked access to the Web. To these customers, the questionnaire was either faxed or e-mailed as an HTML attachment.

Customers were enthusiastic about the Web survey. Some of their comments were:

"Survey was easy to fill out."
"This is a good tool for measuring customer satisfaction."
"This is an effective way of providing feedback."
"This Web site is a convenient way to do the survey."
"This is certainly a very efficient method. . . . Good job!"

Several customers commented on the speed with which they could complete the Web survey. While a face-to-face or phone interview would have required 45–55 minutes of a customer's time, the Web survey could be completed in 12–15 minutes. One of the survey questions asked whether the customer would be willing to be contacted for follow-up probing, if required. Combining the Internet with selective, follow-up probing by phone—pinpointed to the respondent and question—provides all of the advantages of phone interviews at a fraction of the cost.

Bruce Hicks, AMD director of customer quality systems, concluded, "The Web survey process allows us to gather vital data from customers in much less time and at great savings to both AMD and our customers. Over time, more and more of our customer satisfaction measurement will shift to the Internet."

About the Author

John Chisholm is president of CustomerSat.com, a Menlo Park, California–based customer satisfaction measurement and market research firm specializing in the Internet (http://www.CustomerSat.com). John has 20 years of experience in operations, marketing/research, and strategy. Before founding CustomerSat.com, he founded Decisive Technology, a developer of Internet software, and served as vice president of marketing for Ventura Software and NetFrame Systems. He serves on the market research council of the Association for Interactive Media.

30

INTERNET SELF-SERVICE SUPPORT: BEYOND SEARCH ENGINES TO "SMART ANSWERS ON THE 'NET"™

Keith Loris

As more and more people become familiar and comfortable with the Internet, they're expecting companies to provide immediate customer support for their products and services. A recent market research study reports that the top three things end users want from corporate Web sites are interactive customer support, solutions to specific product or service problems, and on-line access to technical information. How can companies satisfy increasing demands from their customers without straining their resources?

The Internet lets you access information on just about anything: stock quotes, news, travel, weather, health tips, investments, vacation spots, people, places, companies—almost any topic imaginable. The Internet delivers direct access to a wide world of information right at your fingertips, 24 hours a day: no more waiting on hold, no more waiting for the right person, no more waiting in line—no more waiting, period.

The explosive popularity of the Internet has spawned a huge demand for immediate and direct access to quality information. And it hasn't taken long for companies to realize that these same expectations hold true in the world of customer support and service. It's a natural progression: if people can use the Internet to get timely information about companies and products, then why can't they use the Internet to get immediate support on the products and services they use?

According to a recent report from the market research firm Gartner Group, the three most important things end users want from corporate Web sites are:

1. Interactive customer support,
2. Solutions to specific product or service problems, and
3. Online access to technical information.

Microsoft Corporation has shown that, when end users get effective online support, Web-based support usage grows while traditional phone-based support is reduced. As *Infoweek* reported (May 19, 1997), "Microsoft is stepping up its Web-site support because company research shows that more than twice as many customers are now getting help online rather than over the phone."

And this is a growing, long-term phenomenon. *PC Week* reported (May 19, 1997) that the market research firm Dataquest Inc. of San Jose, California, had projected that by 1998 more than half of all support problems will be handled on the Web. *PC Week* noted that only 26% were handled that way in 1996.

True Internet Self-Service Support

As inviting as it may sound to respond to these customer requirements by simply placing technical support information on a Web site, companies must recognize that true Internet self-service support requires more than just giving end users (employees or customers) access to a support database or FAQ (frequently asked questions) list. Instead, it requires technology that interactively and intelligently guides end users through the problem-solving process in a way that's easy, fast, and usable, regardless of their technical sophistication.

Support databases, after all, were originally designed for experienced technicians who are well trained in both support procedures and information retrieval. Technicians know how to phrase a precise database query that delivers a focused response that's meaningful and understandable. End users, on the other hand, are not good at clearly describing their problem ("it's broken" is a common initial description, as in Figure 30-1), nor are they good at quickly finding the most appropriate answer from a long list of potential solutions.

Problems With Search Engines

Most companies rely on a simple search engine to provide access to their online information. Unfortunately, the inadequacy of this retrieval technique is highlighted in the study "On-Site Searching," written by Jared M. Spool of User Interface Engineering (*UIETips* [e-mail publication], 23 October 1997).

The author asked users to find specific information on various Web sites. Although the majority of users tried to use the search engine provided by each Web

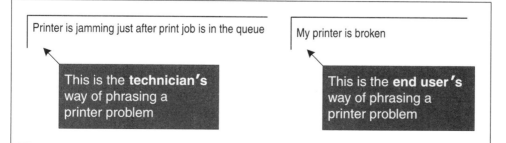

Figure 30-1. Two ways of describing a problem.

site, the study reported, "Search engines didn't make finding information easier, they made it harder. When users found information without a search engine, they did 50% better than when they tried to use a search engine." Spool concluded that "overall, having a search engine on a site doesn't seem to make the site more usable."

One of the major reasons users were unable to find their information was that they didn't know how to narrow their search. "They would often type in very broad terms, such as 'Videos' when looking for a video about the Wild West to get a friend," Spool continued. "This is the equivalent of walking up to a librarian and just saying 'Travel' and expecting they'll instantly find the book on Hawaii that you are interested in."

With the massive quantity of information currently available on the Web, the challenge facing corporations today is no longer getting information to end users—it's getting just the *right* information to them. Let's face it: information overload often makes the Information Superhighway look like the proverbial haystack; you'll never be able to find the needle without some helpful guidance. And a passive support database on your Web site will create the same information overload and the same level of frustration for end users.

In addition to the risk of overwhelming end users with information, a number of other problems emerge when you provide direct access to your support database. Since the database was originally developed for sophisticated support technicians, it often uses technical terms and jargon that may not be understood by end users. And there's a security risk in giving end users access to an internal database. In fact, some companies that have put their database on the Web have discovered, to their chagrin, that it contained information (about sales projections, forthcoming products, product deficiencies, etc.) that should not have been made public.

Assistance for End Users

Most of us would agree that the Internet is an incredibly powerful tool that's dramatically changing the way we do business. And yet, for self-service customer support to be successful, end users need assistance in identifying their specific problems and selecting the most appropriate solutions. True self-service support must automate problem-solving while providing assistance that's similar to what end users get when speaking with an experienced support technician over the phone. On-line support must simulate the question-and-answer process, custom-tailoring the experience for each user. Figure 30-2 illustrates how a screen might look to a customer.

"The Internet and the World Wide Web are becoming increasingly important tools for delivering world-class customer service and support (CSS)," said Carter Lusher, VP and research director for Customer Service and Support Strategies at Gartner Group. "Phase one of exploiting the 'Net for CSS is making information available to customers and permitting simple tasks like submitting trouble tickets and messages. Phase two consists of forward deploying active problem resolution capabilities directly to customers so that customers can solve their own problems. Frankly, the age of the passive Web site has passed. Interactivity is critical now."

Self-service support is possible today because the Internet allows end users to

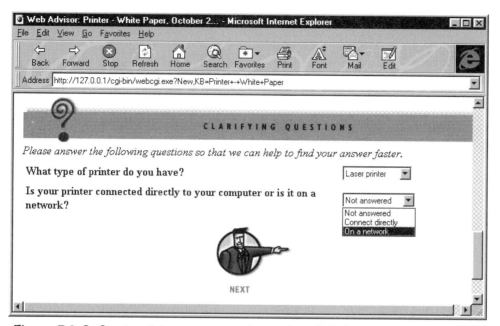

Figure 30-2. Customizing support through a Q & A process.

access high-quality, consistent support information at essentially no cost. And for the first time, there are software tools for the Internet that provide an intelligent, easy, and effective way for end users to solve their own problems. As one can imagine, empowering employees or customers to resolve their own problems without contacting the help desk quickly makes a service organization more productive and dramatically lowers its costs.

For customer support, this latest wave of technological innovation ushers in the era of Internet self-service support that's reminiscent of earlier technologies that brought self-service to industries as diverse as telecommunications, gasoline retailing, and banking. (Remember the days when we relied on operators to dial phone numbers, attendants to pump gas, and tellers to dispense money?)

The Traditional Customer Support Model

Let's compare Internet self-service support with the traditional customer support model. Traditional phone- and LAN-based customer support representatives (CSRs) receive a telephone call from a customer, listen to the customer's problem, and then use a database or help desk software to recommend a solution to the problem. At a basic level, the CSR's function is to translate the customer's problem into language that the support database can understand, run a database query, retrieve the query results, and interpret the results for the customer.

This model requires a significant amount of time and investment to guarantee that all CSRs receive regular and consistent training. In addition, management needs to ensure that policies and procedures are developed and laboriously monitored for consistent response time, conversational style, and quality of advice. To be successful, the management team and the organization's IS department have to focus on managing the process (how support is provided) and concentrate on optimizing the use of help desk resources.

The Power of Self-Service Customer Support

Once you empower end users to solve their own problems, however, the emphasis dramatically shifts from managing the process to solving the problem. After all, with self-service customer support, management's only concern is to ensure that end users have their problems resolved—intelligently, efficiently, and accurately.

Internet self-service customer support introduces a new concept—"level-zero" support—a level of support that does not require assistance from the support technician. Nonetheless, a good self-service support system integrates with level-one support. The system enables end users to resolve a problem on their own while allowing them to escalate the problem directly to the support desk if they choose. It can also capture all of the valuable information from the self-service session and send it to the support desk. At this point, the level-one staff can immediately pick up the problem, see the steps that the end user has already taken, resolve it, and then e-mail the solution to the customer. Figure 30-3 shows a request for assistance screen.

Self-service customer support dramatically reduces the number of calls about common problems while freeing the support staff to handle the more unusual calls.

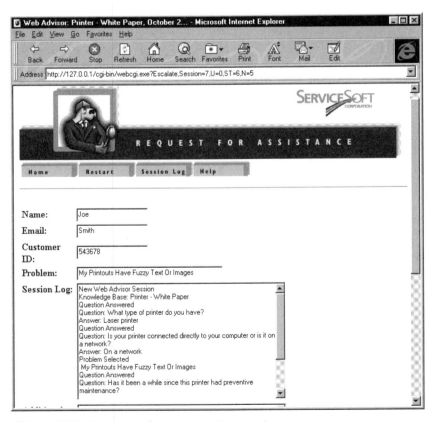

Figure 30-3. Screen for requesting assistance.

Since most support calls consist of repetitive problems, a self-service customer support system can immediately begin paying back its investment by automating your 10 most common problems first, then the next 10 problems, and so on.

Consequently, call avoidance is one of the biggest and most important benefits of self-service customer support. The potential savings are significant, because the average support call costs about $30, according to research conducted by the Help Desk Institute. In addition, companies are now experiencing an increase in the number of support or service calls and a rapid growth in the cost of each call.

Self-service customer support lowers call volume and, at the same time, raises the level of customer satisfaction. End users can solve their support problems at their own convenience, 24 hours a day, from anywhere in the world. They are empowered with interactive, consistent, expert advice. And they no longer have to wait on hold for a support technician. For customer-satisfaction driven organizations, self-service customer support is now a must.

"The benefits of customer service and support delivered via the 'Net and Web include: raising customer satisfaction, reducing costs, gathering intelligence, increasing support staffing flexibility, and moving toward TERM (technology-enabled relationship management)," Lusher said. "Furthermore, due to the inexorable increase in the demand for customer service and technical support, organizations that do not exploit the self-service capabilities of the Web will find themselves stuck in a losing battle against costs. As a consequence, using the 'Net for customer support is rapidly moving from 'nice to have' to 'must have.'"

Suitable for All Levels of Sophistication

With the traditional support model, end users articulate their problems to the CSR in different ways, depending on their skill levels or technical knowledge. The requirement to address different levels of sophistication does not change with self-service support, because end users still range from external customers with very limited product knowledge to internal, expert technicians. Just as the CSRs adjust their questions and advice to fit a caller's skill level, a self-service application must do the same. The application must be neither too complicated and overwhelming for the novice customer nor too simplistic and condescending for the expert.

This ability to tailor questions and provide advice to people with varying skill levels and knowledge is critical to the success of a self-service application. Without this, end users will not be able to solve their own problems, because novices will reject "hard" or confusing advice and experts will not accept patronizing suggestions. Different questions may need to be asked, or the same advice phrased in different ways, in order to meet the needs of different people.

Merely supporting this diverse range of end users, however, is not enough. The support system can be designed to handle the entire range of users, from novice to experienced, as shown in the screen shot (Figure 30-4). And the way the system supports your end users should be intuitive and natural, regardless of each end user's knowledge level. Furthermore, the system should allow end users to seamlessly progress from level to level as they learn. In fact, a well-designed self-service application will not only solve the initial problem, but also help train users by show-

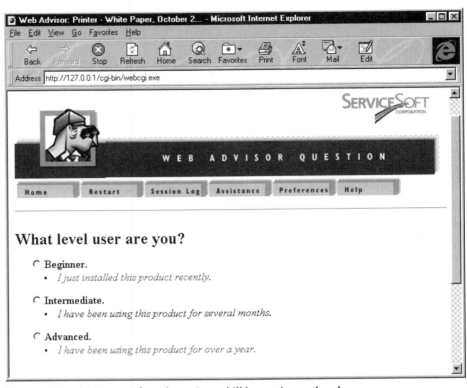

Figure 30-4. Screen for choosing skill/experience level.

ing them the steps involved in problem-solving, so they can more easily solve their own problems in the future.

How can a single system provide advice for a variety of different skill and experience levels? The answer is found in the ability to provide your end users with a range of problem-resolution methods and let them choose the method with which they feel most comfortable. Just as "one shoe size does not fit all," there's no single best way to solve a problem. This flexible approach to problem resolution is called Expert Reasoning™.

Expert Reasoning: The Key to Problem Resolution

Here's how it works. Expert Reasoning, pioneered by ServiceSoft Corporation, uses a unique approach to problem resolution that identifies the customer's needs and the corresponding solution faster and more precisely than any other method.

Expert Reasoning is the problem-resolution methodology behind ServiceSoft's Knowledge Builder™—the application used to build knowledge bases—and Web Advisor™—the navigation tool that accesses the information in the knowledge base and guides end users through the problem-resolution process.

Expert Reasoning represents a powerful synthesis of the four main problem-resolution methodologies—natural language retrieval, case-based reasoning (CBR), decision trees, and expert models. The new methodology combines the search capabilities of natural language retrieval, the simplicity of decision trees, the flexibility of CBR, and the power of expert system modeling in an intuitive, easy-to-use, non-threatening environment. More than a database search engine, Expert Reasoning intelligently suggests questions, processes answers, and guides end users to the most efficient solution.

Best of all, with Expert Reasoning, end users do not have to select or understand which problem-resolution method (i.e., natural language retrieval, CBR, decision trees, or expert systems) is being used. Expert Reasoning automatically "does the right thing."

No Expertise Required

Expert Reasoning is designed for end users—people with no special knowledge of databases or the subject matter of the knowledge base. The only prerequisite is an ability to use standard Web browsers. Using Expert Reasoning, Web Advisor guides end users through a simple question-and-answer process, similar to a conversation with a CSR, to determine the precise problem and most appropriate solution.

One of the most important functions performed by a CSR is to make the problem description more specific. If an end user calls up with a general problem description ("the printer's broken"), the representative will ask questions to determine the specific problem ("there's a paper jam") and suggest the appropriate solution.

Expert Reasoning employs similar techniques to lead an end user from a general problem description to a more specific problem description and finally to an appropriate solution to the problem. Its intelligent algorithms figure out which questions to ask next, respond to user's answers, and interactively lead the end user in a series of steps and screens to the correct solution.

Building a Knowledge Base

A knowledge base captures and organizes problem-solving information so that existing knowledge can be applied to new problems. Until recently, building a knowledge base was a challenging and time-consuming experience. It required expert technicians who were well-versed in the art of programming languages, writing scripts, and case-based reasoning theory. The process required specialized training and a serious commitment of time and resources that didn't always pay off.

Today, with Knowledge Builder and its Expert Reasoning methodology, building knowledge bases requires only expertise in content. In fact, the best knowledge bases are built by content experts—people who have knowledge and experience in the subject matter. In a help desk environment, it's usually the help desk technician; in a service environment, it's usually the CSR.

Knowledge Builder, with its Expert Reasoning methodology, offers an intuitive development interface that allows anyone to create the knowledge base for Web Advisor with no need for programmers, CBR experts, or even Web masters. A service technician can easily create an Expert Reasoning knowledge base by using elements (objects) that are familiar to every CSR—'problems,' 'causes,' 'solutions,' and 'questions.' The power behind Expert Reasoning is the natural way it uses these elements to intelligently recreate the process that a CSR uses to solve problems.

Technology Leaders

Self-service support enables organizations to provide a higher level of service to their end users anywhere in the world, 24 hours a day. End users are empowered to solve their support problems independently and receive immediate, consistent expert and guided advice.

Internet self-service support is raising customer satisfaction while lowering call volume—the primary objectives of any support organization. This new class of customer support is a strong differentiator in a very competitive marketplace.

Taco Bell Corporation, a leading international Mexican food franchise, is a good example of a company embarking on self-service customer support via its corporate intranet. Taco Bell uses ServiceSoft's self-service support software to eliminate some of the 4,000 to 6,000 calls the help desk receives every month. The company's 1,000 + corporate-level employees consult their intranet site to solve their own problems with off-the-shelf software or proprietary Taco Bell applications.

According to Don Weiner, a technical analyst at Taco Bell's Information Technology Group, "Web Advisor looks familiar to our end users; it's intuitive, interactive, and inviting enough for them to use. By empowering our users to solve their problems independently, we expect to significantly reduce the current volume of monthly calls and save an incredible amount of help desk resources."

An example of Internet self-service customer support is Four11 Corporation, the top "people finder" on the 'Net. Four11 used ServiceSoft's Knowledge Builder to quickly create an online support knowledge base for RocketMail, its free e-mail service introduced in March 1997. Web Advisor accesses this knowledge base to provide quality technical support on-line, thus eliminating many of Four11's costly support calls.

RocketMail has been growing rapidly and "we needed a solution that keeps up with this growing level of activity and allows us to provide immediate and accurate assistance to our users," said Katie Burke, marketing director at Four11 Corporation. "Web Advisor and Knowledge Builder allowed us to create sophisticated, interactive help desk applications that deliver fast, accurate online support."

These are just two of the many organizations that are using self-service customer support to solve their service dilemma. Most support departments are faced with a seeming contradiction: they must lower costs while keeping up with increasing demands for high-quality support.

Internet self-service customer support is one of the most efficient ways for a company to resolve this paradox because, for the first time, tools exist that allow companies to quickly and easily deploy powerful self-service applications on the Web. Forward-thinking companies are now recognizing the competitive advantage provided by delivering support information in an interactive environment that empowers end users to solve their own problems.

About the Author

Keith Loris is vice president of marketing and new business development at ServiceSoft Corporation, the leader in self-service customer support with Web Advisor and Knowledge Builder software. He has more than 10 years of experience working with large and small high-tech companies, including serving as vice president of technology for the Desktop Document Systems Division of Xerox Corporation, where he was responsible for all core Optical Character Recognition technology as well as the Natural Language Processing business.

PART EIGHT

Customer Service and the Rest of the Organization

31

Coordinating Services Across Functional Boundaries: The Departure Process at Southwest Airlines

Jody Hoffer Gittell

What can you learn from an airline? A lot! A recent study compared organizational practices and performance outcomes at four airlines. The results described in this article reveal lessons about cross-functional coordination and ways of overcoming functional boundaries to deliver better service.

When customers demand services delivered in a more timely and seamless way, organizations often must overcome functional boundaries to meet the challenge. Created by differences of expertise and status, and often by the systems put into place to manage performance, functional boundaries are not easily overcome.

This article takes a close look at cross-functional coordination of the departure process at Southwest Airlines to discover how managers can make well-integrated service delivery a reality. Southwest's service quality ratings are as high as or higher than those of its competitors, while turning planes faster and with fewer staff, even after making allowance for its simpler approach to airline travel.[1] To achieve these outcomes, Southwest draws upon well-established customer service concepts for managing front-line customer service providers. Southwest is well-acquainted with the concept that highly satisfied service providers help to create highly satisfied customers.[2]

But that's only part of the story. Although customer service managers tend to focus their attention on the interface between service providers and the customer,

---

1. Jody Hoffer Gittell, "Cost/Quality Tradeoffs in the Departure Process? Evidence from the Major U.S. Airlines," *Transportation Research Record*, No. 1480, 1995.
2. James Heskett, Earl Sasser, and Leonard Schlesinger, *The Service Profit Chain: How Leading Companies Link Profit and Growth to Loyalty, Satisfaction and Value* (New York: The Free Press, 1997).

that's not the only interface that's critical to the overall service experience. Excellent service also depends upon the interactions among the employees—among all of those people who are engaged in producing and delivering the service, whether or not they interface directly with the customer. Many of these interactions are partially or fully hidden behind the scenes in the typical service experience, but their results are often all too apparent to the customer.

This article reveals what happens behind the scenes at Southwest to produce an effective service experience, identifying organizational practices with strong— sometimes unexpected—impacts on coordination. Whether they're operating in res-taurant, hotel, healthcare, or other service settings, customer service managers can identify employee interactions that are critical to service excellence and then design organizational practices to support them. Though the story is set in the airline indus-try, its lessons are relevant wherever multiple functional groups must interact in a timely, seamless way to deliver excellent service.

The Departure Process: Performance and Practices

Coordination is the management of interdependencies among tasks and among the people who perform them. It's critical to performance whenever people are engaged in interdependent tasks—that is, when the successful completion of a task assigned to one party depends on the successful completion of a task assigned to another party.

The airline departure process is a highly interdependent work process. Unload-ing, servicing, and reloading a plane with passengers, baggage, cargo, and fuel in a short period of time, then sending it off with accurate information about flying con-ditions and about the composition and placement of the load, requires the coordi-nated efforts of pilots, flight attendants, ticket agents, gate agents, operations agents, baggage handlers, cargo handlers, fuelers, caterers, cabin cleaners, and mechanics. It's a tremendous organizational challenge.

A recent study of the airline departure process compared organizational prac-tices and performance outcomes at American, Continental, Southwest, and United Airlines.[3] Even after adjusting for its simpler approach to airline service, Southwest's departure process was found to be significantly more efficient and effective. Its ad-justed aircraft turnaround time was 37 minutes, as opposed to 51 minutes for the overall sample, while its staffing ratio was only 43 station employees per 1,000 daily passengers enplaned, compared with 77 per 1,000 for the overall sample. Likewise, its on-time performance, baggage handling, and customer satisfaction ratings were significantly higher than for the three other airlines in the study.

How were these superior performance outcomes achieved? While the leader-ship of Southwest's CEO Herb Kelleher cannot be discounted, this study suggests that much of the success is achieved through the design of sound organizational practices.

According to this study, 60% of the differences in quality and 90% of the dif-ferences in efficiency were due to differences in organizational practices and the resulting differences in cross-functional coordination (see Figure 31-1). The coordi-

---

3. Jody Hoffer Gittell, "Horizontal Relationships and the Quality of Communication: Coordinating the Airline Departure Process," *Harvard Business School Working Paper*, 1997.

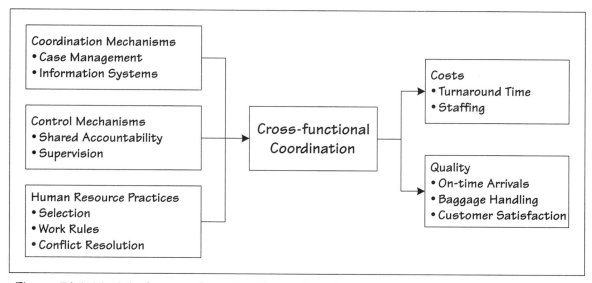

Figure 31-1. Model of cross-functional coordination.

nation mechanisms that made a difference included the use of case managers and information systems. Key control mechanisms included shared accountability for outcomes and a supportive role for supervisors. Finally, the critical human resource practices included careful selection of employees for their teamwork skills, flexible work rules that permitted employees to help each other across functional boundaries, and a strong emphasis on horizontal conflict resolution.

Coordination Mechanisms

How is the flow of information managed? This is the job of coordination mechanisms.

Airlines traditionally use operations agents to manage the flow of information about a particular flight. This is the equivalent of a case manager, where the "case" is a flight rather than an individual customer. Operations agents gather passenger information from ticketing and gate agents, baggage information from the baggage agents, fueling information from the fuelers, weather and route information from central dispatch, aircraft readiness information from maintenance, cargo information from freight agents, catering information from the caterers, and so on. Then they compile that information and transmit it to the parties that require it. Two interrelated organization design decisions are how many cases (flights) an operations agent will manage simultaneously and how much of the communication will be automated through the use of information technology.

Southwest has chosen to staff this case manager position at levels unheard of in the industry. Each operations agent manages only one flight at a time, from 45 to 60 minutes before the flight's arrival until about 30 minutes after its departure. This level of staffing is considered wasteful from the perspective of other airlines, such as American, which centralizes its agents in a single location and schedules them to manage from 10 to 15 flights at a time.

At the same time, Southwest uses automated information technology very sparingly—none of the key linkages among functional groups was conducted primarily through an automated format. The operations agent's job includes face-to-face contact with each of the other key functions involved in the departure process, including the pilot, whom the operations agent personally visits in the cockpit just prior to departure. This approach appears to be useful in building a network of relationships that's conducive to good communication under stressful conditions. "The operations agent is the team leader while the aircraft is on the ground," said one of Southwest's chief pilots. "It's a real good job—a lot of stress."

Looking at the sample more broadly, this study found that high levels of case manager staffing were linked to high performance, while heavy reliance on information technology for communication among functional groups was linked to low performance.

Bottom Line

High levels of case manager staffing pay off in terms of both quality and efficiency. Though information technology can facilitate communication, it's not an effective substitute for a human interface.

Control Mechanisms

How are employee actions aligned with organizational goals? This is the job of control mechanisms.

A major preoccupation when managing the airline departure process is assigning responsibility for delays. Typically, a single department must ultimately be held responsible for each delay, unless the cause can reasonably be ascribed to weather or other nonhuman factors. This approach, called functional accountability, is designed to prevent carelessness and to ensure that people will be held accountable for their mistakes.

The unfortunate outcome, according to findings from this study, is that finger-pointing prevails and time is spent unproductively assigning blame for delays. "What usually happens is a communication breakdown, but we have no code for that," said a ramp supervisor at American. "If you ask anyone here, what's the last thing you think of when there's a problem? I bet your bottom dollar it's the customer. And these are guys who bust their butts every day. But they're thinking, 'How do I keep my ass out of the sling?'" At other airlines, people reported holding back from helping when a delay appeared imminent, since helping might make them appear to be responsible for causing the delay.

Southwest has tried to overcome this problem by creating a team delay. "The team delay is used to point out problems between two or three different employee groups in working together," said the vice president of operations. "If you see everybody working as a team and it's a team problem, you call it a team delay. It's been a very positive thing." With the team delay, there's always the possibility of taking joint responsibility for a delay, when in fact the problem appears to go beyond the failures of a single functional group.

It's not surprising to most people that shared accountability across functions has a positive effect on cross-functional coordination and on the performance of processes that rely on cross-functional coordination. There remains the question, however, of why it's been so difficult for most airlines to institute shared accountability for delays when it appears quite sensible.

Southwest Airlines employees are involved in a profit-sharing program and United Airlines adopted a team delay when it instituted employee ownership: these two cases would suggest that perhaps shared monetary incentives are the secret to making shared accountability effective. But American Airlines has had profit-sharing programs for its employees since 1989, and yet it's perhaps the most adamant about sticking with strict functional accountability. When an American station manager tried to move to a shared accountability system, he was told that the station would still have to report to headquarters the single department deemed responsible for each delay, thus undermining the credibility of the local innovation.

What's more surprising, perhaps, is the effect of supervision on cross-functional coordination. High ratios of supervisors to front-line employees were linked in this study to strong departure process performance.

This is unusual in the airline industry: most airlines, particularly American and United, had been moving aggressively toward lower levels of supervision, in the name of cost-cutting and empowerment. In some sites, they had moved to levels as low as 2.4 supervisors per 100 front-line employees, for a span of control of about 40. One negative side-effect identified by this study was that supervisors had only the time to focus on the "bad apples" and little time to give useful feedback to the large majority of their direct reports. Yet in processes that are highly interdependent, more feedback is needed, so each employee can interpret the effects of his or her actions on overall process outcomes.

Southwest has dramatically higher levels of supervision than other airlines—more than 10 supervisors per 100 front-line employees, for a span of control of about 10. This higher level of supervision has not only increased the potential for useful feedback but, by making the managers more available, has served to increase the flow of information in the other direction as well. Higher levels of supervision also make it more probable that any given front-line employee can reasonably aspire to a management position, particularly in an airline like Southwest, which is dedicated to promotion from within.

Bottom Line

Shared accountability improves cross-functional coordination. That may seem obvious, but implementation of the idea may be hindered by the fear that managerial control will be compromised. High levels of supervision, in the context of an organization that emphasizes the feedback or coaching function of supervisors, also boosts cross-functional coordination.

Human Resource Practices

How are cross-functional relationships managed? This falls under the category of human resource practices, particularly employee selection, flexible work rules, and conflict resolution.

In the airline industry, employees are typically selected for their functional expertise. In recent years, selection criteria have been expanded to include customer orientation for most of the customer contact positions. But one criterion for employee selection that's typically been overlooked in this industry is the ability to work as part of a cross-functional team—which would seem important when the job involves working with other functions in a highly interdependent process.

One reason for neglecting this ability is that airlines generally prize qualities that run directly counter to the goal of teamwork across functions, as in the case of pilot selection at American. "There is a certain amount of hostility that pilots face from the other functional groups," said an employee relations manager. "The personality of the pilot generates that hostility. We look for command presence, for the most self-assured, arrogant people we can possibly find."

Another reason that teamwork is not a major selection criterion for many airlines is that work rules in the industry often restrict employee groups from doing each other's work. "The work groups are so well defined that they are not allowed to help out, so we don't look for that [when hiring]," said a supervisor at American. "It would cause problems."

At Southwest, by contrast, teamwork is an explicit hiring criterion for every major work group involved in the departure process. "Something we look at is people who are very team-oriented from prior work experience," said a ramp manager. "Do they limit themselves to the job, or go above and beyond? . . . The concept of teamwork is tough. You really don't know if a person will be able to cross over from his or her primary responsibility and do other things. We get a feel for people who will go above and beyond."

Even those who are typically selected for their technical expertise are subjected to the teamwork criterion at Southwest. "Our pilots aren't stiff because we don't hire pilots who are stiff," said a flight department administrator. "We do target selection for mechanics," said a personnel manager. "We're looking for experience, but also for someone who is going to be able to work with others in a good environment." The hiring process was the first step toward belonging at Southwest and Kelleher characterized it as having a "patina of spirituality."

Consistent with the concern for teamwork in the hiring process at Southwest is the absence of work rules that exclude work groups from doing each other's work. Although Southwest was the most heavily unionized carrier in the study, it had a strict policy against including 'covered work' in its contracts. "There are no work restrictions in our contracts," said a Southwest manager. "Most airlines have very restrictive work rules, will list in the contract very detailed job definitions. . . . We don't have the 'it's not my job' mentality. We have very thin contracts." According to a ramp manager, "Our contracts here don't have covered work. The job descriptions all say at the end, 'or whatever you need to do to enhance the overall operation.'"

In a stressful process like airline departures, where multiple work groups must interact under time constraints to get the plane out, conflicts are likely to arise among work groups. This likelihood is exacerbated by a history of status differentiation among the work groups involved in the departure process. "Gate and ticket agents think they're better than the ramp," said a ramp supervisor at American. "The ramp thinks they're better than cabin services; (they) think it's a sissy, woman's job. Then the cabin cleaners look down on the building cleaners. The mechanics think the ramp are a bunch of luggage handlers."

Yet despite these factors that generate conflicts among employee groups, conflict resolution procedures in the airline industry, as in many industries, are typically designed to address vertical rather than horizontal conflicts. When there's a conflict between a member of management and a nonmanagement employee, there's an elaborate grievance procedure available for airing and resolving it. Yet there's a relative neglect of procedures for addressing conflicts among front-line employees.

In contrast to the industry norm, Southwest takes horizontal conflict very seriously. "What's unique about Southwest is that we're real proactive [about conflict]," said a station manager. "You're going to have conflict," said a customer service manager. "You try to get them to talk it out. They can bring it up to the supervisors and myself. Hopefully they'll do it in a positive tone. Maybe a wrong call was made in the heat of the moment. You give them the other side of it."

According to a gate agent, "If it's a real conflict, we bring the people together and we don't leave here until it's resolved. If it's a conflict across groups, we might have an information gathering meeting where we all sit down." These information gathering meetings were quite common at Southwest for resolving conflicts across work groups; in some locations they were called "Come to Jesus Meetings," suggesting that conflicting parties were expected to bare their souls if necessary to reach reconciliation.

Bottom Line

The management of cross-functional relationships should not be taken for granted. Through careful selection of applicants for teamwork abilities, work rules that promote helping across boundaries, and conflict resolution practices aimed specifically at horizontal conflicts, these relationships can become a source of competitive advantage.

Conclusion

The study of airline departures extends in an important way what we know about service. When service delivery requires coordination among multiple functions, it's not enough to focus on the employee/customer interface. Employees are a potential source of competitive advantage in service settings, but this competitive advantage is not only realized in the interface with the customer, in the much-discussed "moment of truth."

Interactions among employees—particularly in the highly interdependent processes that characterize much of service delivery—are also an important focus for managerial attention. When service delivery processes require timely, seamless interactions among employees, companies succeed by designing the organizational practices that facilitate the coordination of those interactions.

That's not difficult, as we see from this study of Southwest Airlines and its peculiar use of case management, information systems, supervision, conflict resolution, and shared accountability. This approach is guided by consistent attention to the quality of relationships and communication across functional boundaries, but it challenges several well-established management practices. Though customer service managers may not have the authority to institute such far-reaching practices on their own, they can nevertheless be effective advocates for adopting better practices and indispensable in implementing them.

About the Author

Jody Hoffer Gittell is Assistant Professor of Business Administration at the Harvard Business School. She works on organization design, human resource, and coordination problems in service settings. She is a member of the Service Management Interest Group and teaches Technology and Operations Management in the M.B.A. program. She recently completed a study of cross-functional coordination of the airline departure process, with the participation of four major airlines. In June 1997 Jody launched a study of the coordination of patient care, with the participation of nine large hospitals in Boston, New York City, and Dallas. This study tests key ideas from the airline study of cross-functional coordination, extending them to the delivery of patient care across both functional and organizational boundaries.

32

SWING WITH YOUR TRAPEZE BUDDY: WORKING TOGETHER INTERNALLY TO SERVE EXTERNAL CUSTOMERS

Mark Rosenberger

It's become common for people in business to talk about "internal customers." The author suggests that another term might be better—Trapeze Buddy. The metaphor expresses teamwork, communication, precision timing, and the "extra effort" mentality, as well as the serious consequences of letting somebody down. This article recommends some ways to improve those significant relationships.

"Hey, you caught me! Just the way you said you would! We're flying through the air with the greatest of ease!"

Does this describe your life with the people you count on? Or are you spending much of your time picking yourself up off the concrete after being dropped?

If you're being caught more often and dropped less often, then you're working like Trapeze Buddies. On the other hand, if you spend way too much time falling, this will be the tool to keep you flying!

You're most likely familiar with the term "internal customer" to refer to the people you work with. However, I've never been convinced this term delivers the needed impact and importance service plays—both inside and outside the successful organization.

The metaphor of the Trapeze Buddy conveys the idea of teamwork, communication, precision timing, and the "extra effort" mentality. The concept also clearly conveys the grave consequences of not coming through and dropping the person who's counting on you to complete a task or a function or to provide information so he or she can do the job.

The Metaphor

I remember going to the big-top circus with my parents. We nervously awaited the flying trapeze artists, who would dazzle us from high above the arena floor. The talented artists would jump, fly, spin, and catch one another with precision, often only inches from disaster. Each time they missed a catch, my heart leaped and I gasped in horror as I watched my circus hero tumble to the safety net below. I'm willing to bet they planned some of the falls just for effect. Believe me, it worked!

My anxiety level reached an all-time high the year I went to the circus and the trapeze artists refused to use the safety net. I hung on their every move. The artists worked hard to put on a thrilling show and we all know it didn't happen without hard work and practice.

What a perfect analogy for each of your jobs! Every day you climb the ladder, stand on the platform, and then swing out toward the middle. The entire time you're hoping . . . for what to happen? The answer is obvious: at a predetermined, agreed-upon time, someone from the other side will swing out and catch you!

Yet how many times have you climbed the ladder, stood upon the platform, and swung out toward the middle, only to hear some excuse like the following? "I *wanted* to have that information for you." "I *tried* to get it done on time." "We *almost* have it complete, but the computer went down."

It really doesn't matter what the excuse happens to be; you know the outcome. You're already spinning in the air because you were counting on someone to come through and now, once again, you've been dropped. Oh, and by the way, in most businesses there are no safety nets. In fact, where you work, there are probably spikes sticking up! And you're heading toward them, fast!

Lessons From the Circus

We can glean many insights from the circus artists and apply them to our real-world work situations. Your internal customers or Trapeze Buddies are counting on you to come through and catch them as they swing out and spin from their trapeze bars. Understanding the principles applied by our circus models will help ensure that we're caught more often and dropped less often. Let's face it: we're all tired of being skewered and we welcome the opportunity to be caught.

Exploring the Trapeze Buddy model will enable you to discover new insights and enhanced team performance. This article will guide you and your team through a five-step process for creating a new perspective and a set of skills that will improve your performance and reduce your falls.

Step 1. What's in It for You?

The first step in the process is to ask and answer the question, "What's in it for me?" Great question! What might be in it for you, your team, and the company if you could count on being caught more often and dropped less often?

Why ask this question? Because it's natural and necessary for enthusiastic participation. When everyone on the team understands the benefits of playing together at this new level, they all willingly participate. Conversely, you don't address this question and people see this approach as "the new flavor of the month," resistance will be greater and the positive results will suffer.

The benefits of this new Trapeze Buddy perspective are numerous, including the following:

- Less stress on the job
- More proactive time, less reactive time
- More fun on the job
- Fewer headaches and hassles
- Fewer problems and complaints
- Happier customers
- Less rework
- Increased productivity
- Reduced employee turnover
- More repeat business
- More referrals
- Improved morale
- The ability to attract and hire the best people
- Job security
- More revenue and increased profits
- Improved customer loyalty

Are any of these benefits of interest to you? If you enthusiastically answered, "Yes!" you'll immediately see the benefits of applying the Trapeze Buddy model to your world. (If you answered "No," put down the book and crawl back under your rock!)

Write down three "Personal Benefits" important to you. Use the above ideas to create your "PB" or draw from other experiences you've discovered.

What's in It for Me: "Personal Benefits"

1. _____

2. _____

3. _____

4. _____

5. _____

6. _____

7. _____

8. _____

9. _____

10. _____

Now that you've answered the question, "What's in it for me?" we can proceed to step two: our definition of Trapeze Buddy.

Step 2. Trapeze Buddy Defined

Simply stated, a Trapeze Buddy is "anyone you count on or rely upon to complete a task or a function or to provide you with information so you can get your job done."

Can you think of anyone who meets this definition? Most likely, lots of folks come to mind. But don't stop there, because a Trapeze Buddy is also "anyone who counts on *you* to complete a task or a function or to provide *them* with information so *they* can get *their* job done." Even more people should come to mind now!

We're interdependent. Every day you count on dozens of people to come through so you can accomplish your mission. Conversely, dozens of people are counting on *you* to come through so they can fulfill their responsibilities. Trapeze Buddies are inside and outside your organization.

Think again about that definition: "anyone you count on or who counts on you"! This definition includes vendors, suppliers, co-workers, and even the customer. It includes managers, people on the front lines, and even the folks behind the scenes. It takes into account the obvious and the not-so-obvious in every organization. The definition also includes family and community members. You have *lots* of Trapeze Buddies.

The definition is important because, in one form or another, it touches everyone in the organization. No one can say they're "just a. . . ." There are no "*just a*'s": we're all Trapeze Buddies to someone! Everyone counts and everyone makes a contribution.

Try this. Copy the definition and place it around the office as a constant reinforcement of the concept.

Step 3. Mind Mapping

You've discovered you have lots of Trapeze Buddies. The next step in our process is to take them from your head and put them on paper. The process is called Mind Mapping. It'll help you clearly see your many interdependent Trapeze Buddy relationships.

The process is simple. In the diagram in Figure 32-1, place your name in the center circle. Each of the circles surrounding your name represents a person or department that's your Trapeze Buddy. Notice the arrows in the diagram go in both

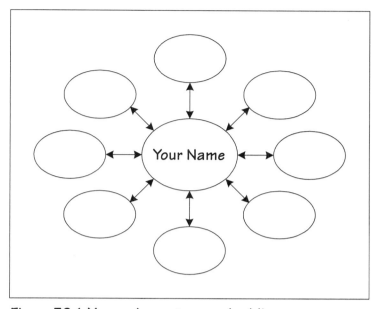

Figure 32-1. You and your trapeze buddies.

directions. Why? Most likely, you're counting on one another and you're all interdependent. Your job is to list all your Trapeze Buddies, inside the organization and outside the organization, the obvious and the not-so-obvious. You'll need more circles than the diagram offers, so draw a line and create more circles.

The game is to discover and list as many Trapeze Buddies as possible. And don't try to take a shortcut: it doesn't count to write the words "Everyone in the Company" or "Everyone in the Universe" on your list. Trust me. You'll benefit by taking the time to create and diagram your Trapeze Buddies. Every member of the entire team should take several minutes and individually map out his or her partners.

The next step is to review your findings with the other people on your team. The goal is to identify as many Trapeze Buddies as possible. One by one, each person in the group simply reviews the Trapeze Buddies he or she has discovered. The others in the group listen; if they hear one that could be on their list, they write it down. Use the input of others to trigger ideas for you. Your list should be even longer after this review exercise.

The next step is to "star" the three to five Trapeze Buddies you feel are most important to your success. Yes, I know they're all important. But for the sake of a future exercise, you'll want to narrow the scope a bit. "Important" can mean several things. For example, you interact with them frequently; therefore, you feel they're important. Place a star next to their name. Or it could be somebody whose support matters a lot: if that person happens to drop you, it really hurts and takes a long time to recover. Place a star next to his or her name.

You've now mind-mapped your Trapeze Buddies and highlighted the most important three to five. Look at your diagram. What do you notice? Is your list pretty long? Are there lots of opportunities to be dropped? Did you include family members, friends, and community relationships? Did you include the phone company, copier repair person, and overnight delivery service? Hopefully you've listed the receptionist and the cleaning service for your office and/or home.

As you proceed through your day, you'll notice even more Trapeze Buddy relationships. Add them to the list. The game is to mind-map all our Trapeze Buddy relationships. You'll be impressed with the number.

You're now ready to move on to Step 4: Trapeze Buddy Success Distinctions.

Step 4. Trapeze Buddy Success Distinctions

It's now time to begin designing our game plan for being caught more often and dropped less often. We'll begin the process by exploring *how* real Trapeze Buddies interact with one another.

It's probably safe to assume that trapeze artists interact with one another differently than we do in most business settings. As well they should, since they're literally risking their lives! To understand the differences and uniqueness is to understand the *distinctions* between trapeze artists and our own performance. We'll call these "Trapeze Buddy Success Distinctions."
A distinction is defined as:

1. The condition of being different; difference.
2. What makes or keeps distinct; quality, mark, or feature that differentiates.

The objective of this step is to answer these two questions:

○ What can we learn from the circus performers and apply to our world?
○ What are the distinctions our circus heroes use that will work in our environment?

The following process will help you understand trapeze artist distinctions. Here's the scenario. You and/or your entire team (this is a great group exercise) have been assigned as the official Trapeze Buddy "coaches" at your place of business. Your job is to study our circus performers. Based on your findings, you will then provide coaching to your team about how to be caught more often and dropped less often.

For example, you have a new hire who comes to the team. The new employee will learn the ropes sooner or later, we hope. But "later" can be very painful and expensive. So, from day one, you're going to provide coaching that will enable the new hire to perform at a high level with his or her new Trapeze Buddies. What will you tell your new hire? How will you coach that person? The answers will most likely come from the trapeze artist success "distinctions" you discovered.

Begin with these questions. What's critical to a trapeze artist's success? What attitudes, behaviors, skills, and levels of performance need to be in place to ensure success? As you put yourself in the new performer's shoes, you'll notice yourself asking, "What needs to be in place for us to perform at a high level?" The answers to these questions are your clues.

Communication

Allow me to prime the pump with an example of a Trapeze Buddy Success Distinction—*communication.* Your team discovers *communication* as being an attitude, behavior, or skill needed to perform at a high level. Excellent! It makes sense that trapeze artists must communicate to put on an awesome show. So you place the word "communication" on the list of coaching ideas.

But wait! You cannot stop after simply writing the word "communication." We're looking for the distinctions that allow trapeze artists to perform at a high level. We want to understand how they might communicate differently than we do. We want to understand the *distinctions* of communication in order to enhance our own performance. After all, each of us communicates at work every day!

After listing "communication" on our coaching chart, we now look for the high-performance distinctions. For example, communication can be in the form of a monosyllabic grunt. Is this the type of communication used by our trapeze artists? You can bet your paycheck it isn't! Trapeze artists communicate at a high level. They communicate with *precision*. They recognize that a major reason for being dropped is poor communication. A misunderstanding, an assumption, or a missed detail can be deadly! Given this insight, what are the distinctions of effective communication? How will you coach the new hire on the skill of communication?

Our trapeze heroes would offer the following insights into the distinctions of their communication:

- It's **precise**. It's void of slop, fluff, or play-it-safe terms.
- It's **timely**. You don't want to tell me an important detail after I'm already spinning.
- It's **accurate** and **complete**.

Trapeze artists incorporate three communication keys: *verify, clarify,* and *confirm.* Let's explore these items in more detail to glean additional insights.

Verify. Does everyone have the same understanding of the communication? Are all the expectations in agreement? Has the timing been double-checked? Does everyone understand their roles and responsibilities in the process? Is the flight leaving on time? Does the hotel have your room reservation? Is the meeting happening when and where you think it is? These are all great illustrations of questions used to verify. Add to the list of questions with your own situations and circumstances. Compile a checklist of items that you would benefit from verifying.

Try this. One powerful verifying technique is to ask a Trapeze Buddy to share back with you his or her understanding of your communication. You'll know immediately if your communication was received in the manner intended!

Clarify. You'll know very rapidly if your communication is on target after the verifying technique described above. If communication is uncertain or confused, now is a great time to insert clarity. A few extra minutes early in the communication can save hours of headaches, hassle, and trauma on the back end. The key to precision communication is not just for you to say something, but rather for your Trapeze Buddy to understand it—and to understand it in the manner intended. That's precision communication. Of course, if they don't "get it," now's the time to add clarity.

Confirm. A win-win strategy for Trapeze Buddies is to confirm agreements and deadlines *while there's still time to act*. Why wait until it's too late to remind, reinforce, or confirm an important issue, deadline, or topic with the people you count on most? If you're playing for win-win, there's no reason why you wouldn't confirm and confirm early. If you're waiting "to see if they come through," you're playing some game other than win-win. Our objective here is to minimize the chances of being dropped and maximize the opportunities to be caught. A friendly reminder can save countless hours of headaches and hassles.

Try this. Reach agreement with Trapeze Buddies that you will support one another with important timelines and reminders. Time-activate reminders far enough in advance so people can come through and accomplish what they promised as agreed. Confirming will be a useful tool for all Trapeze Buddies.

Timing

What additional attitudes, skills, behaviors, and performance standards will your new hire need to understand before he or she can perform effectively as a Trapeze Buddy? You've added one key performance element to your list: communication. What else will you place on your Trapeze Buddy Success coaching form?

The members of your team put their creative minds together and someone offers "timing." Excellent! Is timing important to trapeze artists? You bet! And is timing important in your business or industry? You bet it is! Customers have expectations. Co-workers have expectations. Timing is essential to the successful, smooth operation of every business.

The next step is to define the distinctions associated with *timing* for your organization. We're helping the new hire understand exactly what "timing" means. Does it mean to answer the phone in three rings, to return calls within three hours, or to get the document to you by a certain time? What does "timing" mean in your organization? Don't assume the new hire (or anyone else on the team for that matter) understands what perfect timing is.

Try this. Map out the key timing issues critical to your company's success. What are the performance standards associated with timing? Create a handout that helps the new hire see and understand the critical timing issues in your organization. Detail his or her participation and responsibility in the timing processes. Use this "timing sheet" as a tool to ensure Trapeze Buddy success.

If for some reason you won't be able to come through on a deadline or agreement as promised, for goodness' sake, let your Trapeze Buddy know *before* he or she leaps off the platform and begins spinning! That buddy will have many more choices and options if he or she knows before it's too late. Once a trapeze artist is in mid-air, the choices are rather limited. Usually it's just face down or face up on the concrete. Both options hurt!

Take time to add more ideas to the Trapeze Buddy Success Distinctions profile now, in Figure 32-2.

You've now worked with your team to create Trapeze Buddy Success Distinctions. You're now able to communicate with other Trapeze Buddies about needed distinctions for success. You're able to speak with a new employee in specific terms about how he or she can contribute to the overall success of the organization.

The entire team can work at further refining the performance so no one gets dropped! That's a powerful tool if used with the entire team. We're ready to take the game to the next level: designing a Trapeze Buddy report card.

Step 5. The Trapeze Buddy Report Card

The premise here is simple: people walk around with mental report cards scoring our performance every day! Customers are evaluating your performance based on the criteria most important to them. If you score an "A" on these high-criteria topics, you earn another opportunity to serve them.

There are score cards being used in many situations every day. A classic example is with "significant other" relationships! I'm well aware my wife has a mental "This Is How I Know Mark Loves Me" score card. I'm learning that if I score an "A" on the topics most important to her, I get to sleep indoors! I'm also aware that if I

Key Distinction	Specific Performances	Priority
1.		
2.		
3.		
4.		
5.		
6.		
7.		
8.		
9.		
10.		

Figure 32-2. Trapeze buddy success distinctions.

do what's on her score card but don't perform in the manner desired, I'll be sleeping outside. An example is in order: I know a major, high-criteria topic on her score card is for me to tell her I love her, adore her, and appreciate her. And she wants to be told often! Now, do I need to tell her "just right" that I do in fact love, adore, and appreciate her? You know I do. If I come home feeling mad, bent out of shape, irritated, and moody (quite a pleasant picture!) and a snooty tone comes out as I rudely say, "Love you!", do I score any points? You know I don't score points; in fact, I'm willing to bet I've scored negative points and I'll be sleeping outside. There are several items on my wife's score card. If I score an "A" on the entire list, who wins? We both win!

Trapeze Buddies have report cards as well. There are items they need from you and others to perform their job brilliantly. The Trapeze Buddy report card will help identify the win-win elements needed by each partner.

Look at the sample report card (Figure 32-3). Select one important Trapeze Buddy and place his or her name on the top line. Down the left-hand column, write the topics, issues, attitudes, behaviors, or performance standards needed by this particular Trapeze Buddy. Answer the question, "What does this person need from me in order to perform his or her job brilliantly?" Jot your ideas down in the left-hand column.

Once you've completed the exercise, push for a 10% improvement. Ask your Trapeze Buddy to "verify and confirm," to "delete from and add to the list" so you have a clear picture of how to win with your Trapeze Buddy. Your Trapeze Buddy should be doing the same activity for you: What do you need to perform your job brilliantly?

Together, you're creating a win-win relationship by gaining a clear understanding of what's most important to both of you. Complete this exercise with your five, 10, or 100 most important Trapeze Buddies. You'll be amazed at the positive impact.

Name of Trapeze Buddy: _____

Success Distinction	Priority	Performance

Figure 32-3. Trapeze buddy report card.

Try this. You've created a list of Trapeze Buddy success distinctions. Can any of these be added to the Trapeze Buddy report card? Make sure your report cards include items such as professionalism (whatever that means in your industry), accuracy, completeness, timeliness—all essential Trapeze Buddy elements.

Conclusion

By taking your team through the five Trapeze Buddy steps, you'll be on your way to being caught more often and dropped less often. But a word of caution: just like the circus counterparts, the process will require practice—plenty of practice!

Once you get the hang of swinging together, you'll be pleasantly surprised with the amazing show you'll put on with your Trapeze Buddies. You'll hear people shouting, ''Hey, you caught me! Just the way you said you would! We're flying through the air with the greatest of ease!'' Keep swinging!

About the Author

Mark Rosenberger is the founder and Director of WOW! Training and Consulting. Mark is a professional speaker who has appeared before groups in North and South America. He has developed several training programs used in schools and corporations across the United States, including The Customer Loyalty System, Team Selling, How to Stay Sane in an Insane World, Tele•Consulting, The Service Audit, and the Service University. He is the author of the recently published book, *The PLUS 10% Game: 52 High Impact Leverage Points to Enhance Sales, Customer Loyalty, and Teamwork.*

33

THE COMPANY-WIDE, SALES-FOCUSED ORGANIZATION

Gary Connor

Your business depends on selling your goods and services. So, do you realize that those sales efforts may be compromised and undermined . . . by your employees? This article can help you understand those hidden problems and take care of them, once and for all, so that all your employees are working with the perspective of your sales representatives in mind.

Ed Edwards was pleased to have finally ended the saga of the aging copier. He had put off replacing his old machine as long as possible, until his staff finally threatened to revolt. Ed was a tough buyer, interviewing five copier vendors. He wanted the new copier to meet all three of his criteria: it had to be economical, it had to be proven technology, and it had to accommodate all of his copying needs.

Trouble began when the copier was delivered. "You're the first one on your block to have this baby," said the truck driver. "This is really cutting-edge stuff."

So much for proven technology, thought Ed.

Later that morning, when the technician came to set up the unit, Ed asked how to copy on 11 × 17 paper. Looking surprised, the technician said, "Well, you *can* do that. But this machine wasn't really meant to use that size paper. Let me show you how to fool it, though."

So it really *won't* do all of my applications, thought Ed.

The final blow came when he called in his first supply order that afternoon. "Wow! You sure have the Rolls-Royce of copiers," said the order clerk. "Not too many of them out there in that price range. You must have one heck of a sales rep."

Strike three, thought Ed, as he phoned to cancel the order.

Three well-meaning support staffers effectively killed a sale, each trying to either compliment or help the customer. What was lost really went far beyond one sale. It cost a sales representative and his company their reputation with this client for the foreseeable future.

In an age when product differentiation is slim and pricing is similar, the credibility of the rep and his or her company is what can make or lose the sale. Developing a company-wide sales mentality requires a fundamental shift in the way the organization views its sales force and the sales process.

Education

A sales-focused organization views everything it does at some point through the eyes of the rep. The first step in closing that gap is to educate the supporting forces as to why sales people are the way they are.

It's Not We vs. They

In some companies, the sales force is seen as a necessary evil. "The reps don't play by the rules." "Those people will say anything to get a sale, then we're left trying to make good on their promises." These are comments frequently heard in a company without a sales mentality. Sales representatives are seen as some sort of dishonest entities who exist only to make the keepers of the system miserable.

The reality is that the members of the sales force *are* different. They are hired because they're aggressive, resistant to rejection, outgoing, and highly creative. These are traits that can make them the polar opposite of the administrative and technical people who support the sales effort. What's valued in the one culture is hated in the other. Through comments and innuendo, this perception can even be passed on to the customer.

The Sales Representative Doesn't Work for Only You

When asked who employs them, most sales people will give you the name of their company. The reality is something different: they are essentially self-employed. The sales rep is a negotiator trying to meet the demands of his customer while dealing with the constraints placed on him or her by the organization. That places the rep in a position of being accountable to both and forces a split loyalty. The rep is sincerely trying to do what is best for both the client and the company . . . and make a living at the same time.

No Sales = No Pay

A frequent frustration to sales support functions is a lack of detail on the part of the rep. Granted, you can find this trait in any profession, but there may be an underlying reason peculiar to sales.

Commissioned sales people are paid *only* when they're selling—not for paperwork, not for technical support, not for delivering supplies, and not for setting up the company picnic. This focus is sometimes seen as "anti-team" by others. It's not. It's just what you're paying them to do.

Making Your Organization Sales-Focused

So how do you go about undoing years of anti-sales attitude on the part of your company? It takes a total refocus, from attitude to systems to training.

Two-Way Empathy

An office equipment company was witnessing a growing gap between its sales force and the collections department. Collections was faced with a very short "days outstanding" goal and was quick to cancel a sale to help reach that goal. The staff were also upset with the lack of sales support they received when trying to resolve a collection problem.

The solution came about when both groups "swapped jobs" for a day. Sales reps were brought in to work with a collector for a day. They gained an appreciation of the pressure on the collectors and realized that they really weren't trigger-happy when it came to canceling sales for non-payment.

When the collectors spent a day in the field, they began to appreciate the balancing act every rep plays between the company and the client's needs. Several said that they gained a new respect for the sales profession that day.

At the conclusion of the "swap," both groups brainstormed creative solutions that both lowered the "days outstanding" and reduced the number of canceled sales.

A Systems Approach

The sales focus must be built into every system.

Customers don't buy products. They buy the results those products deliver. Yet seldom does a company's systems tell anyone *why* the customer bought.

Think back to the scenarios at the beginning of this article. If the delivery person had known that this customer wanted "proven technology," he wouldn't have commented about the copier being cutting-edge. If the installation technician had known all the applications the customer needed, he wouldn't have been taken by surprise and would have been prepared to show how all the applications could be accommodated. If the supply clerk had known that economy was important to this client, she wouldn't have used the Rolls-Royce analogy.

All of that information could be supplied by a small section of the order form in which the sales representative could list the customer's buying motives. Additionally, that buyer profile would give the next representative handling that account valuable insights.

Tell Your Reps the Bad News

Several years ago a copier company launched a new "top of the line" product. The machine had more features than you could imagine and the reps were told it was the new "premier machine."

Within weeks of the first installations, severe reliability problems surfaced. Most of those occurred when the customers were doing high volumes of standard $8^1/_2 \times 11$ paper. The customers were upset, the reps were upset, and the technicians were upset.

Although the machine had a wide range of applications, the problems were happening because the overall volume capacity of the new model was far lower than the current machine with fewer features. In their efforts to excite the sales force over the new product, marketing had decided not to mention this volume restriction.

Sales representatives need to know the good and the bad. Give them all the information, even if you feel it may suppress some sales. They will be better positioned to help the customer, and you will gain respect for your honesty.

Make Everyone a Sales Person

When a sales person closes an order, he or she is actually just beginning the sales process, a process that continues until that customer orders again. Whatever his or her title may be, every employee who comes in contact with that customer supports that sales process.

Given that reality, how well trained in selling skills are your non-sales people?

A document outsourcing company I recently visited includes all new employees in its sales training classes. From engineers to secretaries, these non-sales people fully participate, right down to role-playing and handling objections. They gain an appreciation for the process and empathy for the sales person. They come to realize that everyone is part of the sales process.

Interesting to note: that company has had a number of internal career changes into sales as a result of the training.

Top to Bottom

A sales-focused organization is more than a slogan. It cuts to the core values of the company and its view of the sales process. This organization looks at its sales people as the front line and supports them. It builds sales information into every aspect of its systems.

A sales-focused organization makes certain that *all its employees* know they are part of the sales process.

About the Author

Gary Connor has over 25 years of sales, sales management, and sales training experience with three Fortune 200 companies. He is president of The Connor Group, Inc., which specializes in custom-designed sales and sales management programs. The author of *Buyer's Side Selling: Sales Performance Enhancers From the Customer's Perspective*, a sales training program, and co-author of *Sales Games and Activities for Trainers* (McGraw-Hill, 1997), Gary is a nationally known trainer and speaker.

34

Customer Service: A Key to Innovation Success

Scott Davis

Business experts generally maintain that a key to lasting success is innovation. You may think that your company is dedicated to innovation. But are you using your customer service representatives to help drive the innovation process? If not, then you're missing out on a lot of advantages, according to the author. This article presents an eight-step process for developing new products, starting with customer sales reps as market research resources.

Corporate leaders across America are beginning to realize that a critical lever to long-term growth is innovation. They're discovering that the only surefire way to ensure long-term stability, achieve shareholder growth goals, maximize employee happiness, and stay at the forefront of their industry—with a sustainable, dependable position—is to innovate.

They also realize that innovation needs to go beyond being a project and, instead, become part of a company's mainstream and that they need to shed their short-term mindsets and expand their thinking into the future.

Successfully innovative companies have recognized that risks are inherent, failure is OK, rewards and recognition are critical, and involving senior management enhances innovation efforts.

One key tool for future success that has not been leveraged widely, a tool in which we are firm believers, is the use of your customer service reps to help drive the innovation process. These reps are closest to your customers, hear their day-to-day gripes, understand their perceptions of your company, and, for many customers, are your company face. Why not start to view them as your market research arm—instead of spending exorbitant dollars on outside market researchers?

That's right, your reps can be your market research arm. Customer service reps have the ability and the tools (i.e., their skill sets, the telephone, and a fax machine) to conduct research with your current customers, lost customers, and future customers. The type of research they conduct can revolve around product/service satisfaction, perceptions of your products versus competing products, brand research, and needs and wants that are not currently being met. Researching needs and wants and identifying problems, we believe, are the right starting place for any company wishing to launch market-based, needs-driven new products and services.

Obviously, to maximize your innovation hit rate, you need to develop your own formula for success. The best new product companies in the world—3M, Rubbermaid, S.C. Johnson and Son—have adopted processes that have altered their success potential from luck (i.e., 1 out of 10 successes) to probability (i.e., 7 out of 10 successes). These companies ensure they always have an active, live pipeline, filled with a balanced portfolio of new products, from low-risk/low-return to high-risk/high-return. They treat innovation as a valuable corporate asset.

Leveraging a new products process within your company that is iterative and easy to understand will only better the chances that your entire organization will "adopt" it. While there are many processes out there, and we certainly do not mean to offer ours as the only choice, the eight steps outlined below constitute the process that we have consistently found that effectively takes a company from customer-driven needs and wants assessment to final commercialization.

As stated earlier, we firmly believe that your customer service arm can be key in enabling this process to work effectively and efficiently and may even serve to reduce overall cycle-time.

An Eight-Step New Products Process

The following outline provides the basics of this approach. Each of the first four steps will then be detailed in the following sections of this article.

1. Planning and Direction-Setting. Develop a new products strategy that includes earnings and revenue growth gaps to be filled by new products, the roles you want new products to fulfill, and an assessment of past new products to benefit from lessons learned. In addition, total team integration and an agreed-upon work plan are critical to ensuring that everyone is working together from the start.

2. Market Problems and Needs Exploration. Leverage your customer service reps to conduct exploratory, qualitative research with consumers to explore and identify their needs, gripes, complaints, and hassles in a given product category. These problem areas provide a focus for generating ideas.

3. Problem-Solving and Idea Generation. Generate new solutions and creative approaches that address consumer problems. An *idea* describes the purpose of the new product and outlines the benefits that the new product will provide to consumers. Often ideas can come from customers, and customer service reps should make it a part of their job to note and report these ideas.

4. Concept Development and Business Analysis. Screen the ideas, then develop the better ideas into "three-dimensional" descriptions of a product. A *concept* should describe the product features and attributes, intended use, and primary benefits perceived by consumers. It outlines the core technologies that will be used and states general technical feasibility. It addresses how the product might be positioned against competition and defines the primary purchaser.

Step 4 provides another opportunity to involve customer service reps. However, instead of using the telephone alone, incorporate the fax machine or direct mail with concept renderings. This will allow you to garner more detailed feedback.

Business analysis, tied to the feedback you receive, will help your team to formulate a market and competitive assessment that projects the potential size and attractiveness of the new product concept. Include a rough-cut, three-year pro forma that estimates future financial performance.

5. Prototype Development. Complete development of the product, including product performance and consumer acceptance tests.

6. Plant Scale-Up. Determine roll-out equipment needs and manufacture the product in quantities large enough to identify "bugs" and problems. Run additional product performance and quality tests.

7. Commercialization. Introduce and sell the product. Initiate awareness-building and trial simulation programs to reach the targeted consumer base.

8. Post-Launch Checkup. Monitor performance of the new product at six and 12 months after launch and evaluate potential changes or improvements.

The First Steps Are the Hardest

In our many years of experience, working on scores of new product development projects, cutting across multiple industries, we have consistently found that most companies have difficulty with Steps 1–4. In fact, more often than not, companies have a very strong development and commercialization process, but admit to being weak in determining *what* to develop.

To this end, the rest of this article highlights the key elements of those first four steps. Think of this as an overview of the "cookbook" your company should consider adopting for developing new products going forward. Every time you go through this process, you should update your "cookbook" and add new "recipes." As you read this process, think about the contributions customer service reps can make because of their communication with customers.

Step 1. Planning and Direction-Setting

Objectives, Step 1
The purpose of Step 1 is to improve your new product success rate by developing a strategy and identifying the best process for new product development within your organization. This strategy leverages the strengths and weaknesses of historical new product development efforts. In addition, Step 1 should clearly identify specific new product goals and objectives to be achieved over a three- to five-year period.

Step 1 generally requires about four weeks to complete and entails the following major activities:

- Conducting product and company diagnostics to assess past new product performance and leverage lessons learned. Feedback from customer service can be valuable here.
- Developing an initial new product strategy, including a new product vision, new product roles and goals, screening criteria, and a financial growth gap.

End Results, Step 1
1. An agreed-upon new product strategy.
2. A cross-functional project team. (Someone from customer service might be a member.)
3. Research categories to explore and a work plan for executing that exploration.

Activities, Step 1

1. Developing an Agreed-Upon New Product Strategy
The strategy includes financial goals, roles, screens, and vision.

Overview
A new product strategy is an overall description of the role that new products will play in achieving the company's growth goals. Specifically, it defines: the financial growth gap and goals that new products are expected to meet, strategic roles that describe the functions of the new products, and screening criteria that will be used in determining which categories and new product concepts are most attractive to pursue.

Financial Growth Gap
A financial growth gap is developed by first understanding the amount of sales revenue senior management expects from new products at the end of a specified period (typically three to five years). Key inputs for determining this "gap" are interviews with senior managers, historical new product performance, current company planning documents, and category performance learnings. The purpose of developing this growth gap is to provide management with a common understanding of the expected financial contribution of new products.

Vision and Strategic Roles
A new products vision and strategic roles help a company identify the specific areas in which new products will compete and the potential ways they can help support existing business lines and establish new markets. Key inputs include interviews with management, company planning documents, and research on consumer and market trends, often carried out in part by customer service.

The purpose of developing a new product vision is to define the market for new products. The purpose of developing strategic roles is to pinpoint the methods for defending and expanding the company's current business.

In general, there are two types of roles that new products play in a corporate strategy. *Requisite roles* direct a company to develop new products that defend and bolster its current line of products. These are generally line extensions, revisions, and new-to-the company products. *Expansive roles* direct a company to think outside of the box and develop products that will truly expand the business in which it competes. Expansive roles most often direct a company to look at new markets, new benefits, new technologies, and so on. Obviously, the returns are greater when developing expansive products, but the level of risk is higher.

Screening Criteria

Screening criteria are measures for evaluating the potential of new product opportunities. Key inputs include management perspectives, historical screens, and risk analysis. The purpose for determining new product screening criteria up front is to help prioritize ideas generated during the project and to provide guidelines for objectivity, discipline, and rigor in selecting the ideas that will move forward to concept development and business analysis.

Stated Senior Management Commitment

Arguably, the most critical output of this activity is garnering top management commitment to proceed with the new product initiative. This includes a consistent and visible commitment to invest resources, adherence to a formal process as well as strategic and financial screens, continuous direction-setting, and autonomy for new product managers.

End Benefits and Outputs

Ideally, a new product strategy should include:

1. A desired three- to five-year target for revenue from new products,
2. A specific vision and strategic roles for new products,
3. An estimate of development expenditures and investment capital needs for at least the next two to three years, and
4. Top management's expectations for and commitment to new products.

2. Forming a Cross-Functional Project Team

Success will only be achieved if *the team* drives out the answer.

Overview

If you do not have respect and trust among team members, if you do not have adequate resources to complete this initiative within the agreed-upon time period, if you do not have cross-functional representation or the levels of commitment described earlier, you may be doomed for failure. We have consistently found that poor team dynamics and poor "handoffs" more often than not result in failure.

We believe this new products team has to represent every functional area. Obviously, team members will play different roles at different times on this project. Dedication should range from 20% to 40%, depending on the role. Customer service reps will play a much larger role in Steps 2 and 4 than in Steps 1 and 3.

Team Formation: Actions to Take

We suggest conducting a number of values-related exercises and teaming events within this step, to maximize team effectiveness. Some of the exercises we have used with the greatest impact include:

- Setting a team vision and a team pledge,
- Agreeing upon team values and norms,
- Understanding one another through tests and exercises (e.g., Myers-Briggs),

○ Getting to know one another's spouses or friends,
○ Agreeing upon specific roles and responsibilities for each team member as well as a totally integrated work plan.

End Benefits and Outputs

While many will balk at the idea of conducting these exercises, we have consistently found that those teams that take the time to go through this in Step 1 are more likely to succeed in Steps 2, 3, and 4. Again, trust and strong communications are the two most important elements of any good relationship, and we would heavily suggest that this is a worthwhile investment for your team in the short and long run.

3. Agreeing upon Research Categories to Explore

This activity forms a plan to follow throughout the rest of the process.

Overview

In this stage, the team will make important strategic decisions, prior to going out into the field to conduct exploratory research. The team will also finalize the work plan and determine the exact resources needed to complete the entire project.

Research Categories

A research category is nothing more than an area to explore. Strategic roles, category trends, and secondary research are designed to help the team decide upon no more than 15–20 research categories to pursue. This important step gives the team, and especially customer service reps, the direction they need to successfully explore several different problem areas with customers in Step 2.

End Benefits and Outputs

Reaching total agreement on the next steps is one of the most exciting and binding experiences the team will face. The research categories and the work plan result in a contract between the team and the rest of the organization.

Step 2. Market Problems and Needs Exploration

Objectives, Step 2

The purpose of Step 2 is to uncover and determine important "needs and wants" that are currently not being met, or not being met well, in the market. This step helps the team to focus idea generation and concept development around the issue areas with the highest potential for marketplace success.

Step 2 is time-intensive and research-driven. It generally requires about eight weeks to complete. Its major objectives include:

○ Identification of high-intensity unmet needs, wants, and opportunities, based on research with primary decision-makers and decision-influencers.
○ An understanding of key trends and drivers impacting the various categories, based on non-consumer research and secondary research.

End Results, Step 2
1. A comprehensive understanding of the marketplace.
2. Five to seven strategically focused customer opportunity areas that will serve as a basis for Step 3 idea generation.

Activities, Step 2

1. Developing a Comprehensive Understanding of the Marketplace
Team members became grounded in market data.

Overview
This step primarily involves interviewing. While we have found that one-on-one and focus group interviews tend to be very effective, because of resource restraints (both time and money), leveraging your customer service reps is a fine alternative. To be successful, though, it is imperative that all customer service reps receive thorough, up-front interview training before they start the interviews. Additionally, because of the intensive interviewing and tight time frame of Step 2, one team member should own the overall interview/research plan.

Customer service interviewing in Step 2 is structured by Iterative Qualitative Analysis (IQA). This is a process whereby reps interview, analyze, restructure and refocus, interview again, analyze again, revise again, and so on, in waves, to form a funnel that starts broad and narrows down to the highest-potential opportunity areas.

Conducting Qualitative Research
Wave 1 is typically broad in scope and focuses the team on understanding each research category. It reveals how buyers currently purchase the product and what they think about both the product and the brands in the market/industry. Systematically compiled information from customer service can be very helpful here.

After the team analyzes Wave 1 findings, Wave 2 refocuses efforts. The purpose is to dig even deeper, to better understand specific problems and frustrations within each research category, and also to uncover new categories that may have been overlooked in Wave 1.

Wave 2 analysis generally allows your reps to develop "problem statements," which they then present to interviewees in Wave 3 to confirm both the accuracy of the problem and its relative intensity compared with other big issues. Wave 3 research is used, if needed, to further prioritize opportunities and to make sure the team is in full consensus with Step 3 idea generation.

Conducting Non-Consumer Research
While most of the effort in Step 2 is directed at conducting primary research with decision-influencers, equal time is spent on conducting non-consumer research. Through secondary and selected primary research (with industry experts, associations, and the like), the team can "round out" its understanding of the market.

Specific types of information that should be addressed in non-consumer research are: marketplace trends, emerging technologies, competitive profiles, and industry facts and figures. This information will allow the team to enhance its understanding of the market and evaluate the areas for greatest opportunity.

2. Selecting Five to Seven Strategically Focused Customer Opportunity Areas
This will serve as a basis for Step 3 idea generation.

Overview
Once all the data has been collected, we recommend that the team, led by customer service reps, invest a solid week in analyzing and synthesizing the data and reaching consensus on a plan for Step 3. This should involve a total integration of learnings from primary research with decision-makers and decision-influencers as well as secondary research.

Opportunity Area Prioritization
The team should select the highest-potential opportunity areas for Step 3 idea generation, based on market need intensity of the unsolved problems and/or opportunities addressed in each category.

Step 3. Problem-Solving and Idea Generation

Objectives, Step 3

The purpose of Step 3 is to generate high-potential new product ideas based on the market needs and wants uncovered in Step 2. The emphasis in Step 3 should be on generating as many ideas as possible that will potentially solve problems and satisfy needs identified by consumers during the exploratory research conducted in Step 2. The top 25–30 ideas will move forward to Step 4, concept development and business analysis.

Step 3 generally requires about four weeks to complete. The major objectives for this step are:

- Develop a comprehensive list of ideas to address needs and opportunities identified in Step 2.
- Evaluate each idea against the consumer and strategic screens and the technology and manufacturing screens identified in Step 1.
- Choose 25–30 top-tier ideas to take into Step 4.

End Results, Step 3
1. A series of idea generation sessions conducted.
2. A list of 25–30 top-tier new product ideas for concept development and business analysis.

Activities, Step 3

1. Conducting a Series of Idea Generation Sessions
This process will help the team come up with several hundred ideas.

Overview

The primary objective of Step 3 is to generate new product ideas. The forum for doing this is a series of *idea generation sessions.*

These are not focus groups. The structure is similar—one or two moderators, eight to 10 participants, and a recorder taking notes— but the purpose is different: a focus group identifies consumer problems, while idea generation sessions identify solutions for problems and ways to satisfy identified consumer needs. As in Step 2 research, all idea generation sessions are conducted by team members.

Setup and Background

Typically six to eight idea generation sessions are conducted during Step 3. Six or seven of these sessions are likely to be conducted with different functional areas of the company, such as marketing, R&D, packaging, sales, and customer service. The team should also pursue a separate session with senior management that will provide an open, non-threatening forum to foster creativity at the highest level. Conducting a session with this group also continues the "buy-in" process that is so critical to new product development.

In addition to internal idea generation sessions, one or two sessions should be held with the market (consumers, customers, decision-influencers, etc.). These groups sometimes generate the most "out of the box" ideas, since they are not working in the industry and have no preconceived paradigms.

These idea generation sessions will generate several hundred targeted, new product ideas. Some of these ideas will be complete, while others may still be in "idea fragment" form. Concurrent to these sessions, the team will need to continually edit and maintain the list of ideas to ensure that the ideas captured are complete, robust new product ideas.

Idea Screening

There are two types of idea screening that should be conducted in Step 3. The first screens an idea must pass are *consumer and strategic screens.* These screens assess the degree to which ideas satisfy or address new product strategic roles and consumer needs and wants. The second type of screens are *technology and manufacturing screens,* which assess the degree to which ideas leverage available technologies and manufacturing and/or packaging processes. Typically, only the top 75–100 ideas are subjected to this screen, which is why the consumer and strategic screens are conducted first.

2. Narrowing the List of Ideas to the Top 25–30 Ideas

In typical projects, there may be 50–60 ideas that pass all the screens, fit the strategic roles set up in Step 1, and seem like winners. Unfortunately, it would be unrealistic to attempt testing that many ideas as concepts in Step 4. Only 25–30 ideas can successfully be tested and assessed in a month's time by any strong research team. The team is responsible for filtering the 50–60 ideas down to only 25–30.

Step 4. Concept Development and Business Analysis

Objectives, Step 4

The purpose of Step 4 is to identify two or more high-potential concepts ready for further development in Step 5, based on iterative consumer input and business attractiveness.

This step generally requires about eight weeks to complete. Its two major objectives are:

○ Shape the highest-potential concepts from Step 3 via iterative consumer input.
○ Conduct business analysis on the top five to seven concepts, to develop a full understanding of the potential for each of these strong concepts.

End Results, Step 4
1. Two (or more) high-potential concepts with "mock-up" designs/formulations that mesh with the existing category portfolio and are ready for full product development.
2. Five (or more) additional high-potential concepts that are "deferred" and documented for future consideration.

Activities, Step 4

1. Developing High-Potential Concepts

This includes "mock-up" designs/formulations that mesh with the existing category portfolio and are ready for full product development.

Overview

Think of Step 4 as inside-outside-inside. The first part of this step entails turning the 25–30 ideas into robust concepts. The second part involves testing those concepts and prioritizing the top five to seven. The last part involves conducting business analysis on those five to seven concepts and narrowing them down to the top two or three that should move forward into development.

Concept Development and Testing

To determine the highest-potential concepts for business analysis, the team will conduct iterative consumer research, similar to that conducted in Step 2. Prior to this research, however, the team needs to fully develop each of the 25–30 ideas into concepts, with written descriptions and renderings. These concept descriptions will become the stimuli for consumer research.

Customer service reps, using either the fax machine or direct mail, will begin Iterative Qualitative Analysis to reveal the most attractive concepts. These waves of research again act like a funnel, sifting out the best concepts for successive waves and leaving the weaker ones behind. Wave 1 addresses all 25–30 concepts; these concepts undergo team analysis, to narrow down to the top 12–16 concepts for Wave 2. Wave 2 analysis determines the top five to 10 concepts. Wave 3 solidifies with the market the high potential of these concepts. About five to seven concepts are selected during Wave 3 for business analysis.

Conducting Business Analysis

In Step 4, the team must ensure that all ideas remaining in consideration for development display strong market and business attractiveness, based on extensive preliminary assessments of design, cost, and sales. These assessments include market potential, technical and design scenarios, and cost and manufacturing potential, all of which lead to business case financial scenarios.

The team is ready to develop a business case for each of the five to seven concepts. Each business case should include the following components:

- Concept statement and renderings
- Market sales scenarios
- R&D (technology) scenarios
- Packaging scenarios
- Manufacturing scenarios
- Business financial analysis scenarios.

Business case development should begin with three-year sales estimates. The team may consider the following guidelines for developing sales potential estimates:

- Consumer-based trial and repeat estimates leveraging historical launches
- Share estimates based on the existing and potential market size for the consumer benefit offered by the concept
- Benchmarking against businesses with similar characteristics, including "normal" sales growth benchmarking.

The team should develop technology, packaging, and manufacturing scenarios to estimate the cost of materials for developing a product. In most cases, the team will have several options for each scenario and should calculate each one. Scenario development is designed to help the project team create a list of possible options, including costs for input in the financial scenario calculations.

Financial scenarios should be developed using all of the above input. The objective of these financial scenarios is not to determine an exact launch pro forma financial plan, but rather to help select the most attractive ideas to move forward into development. It's too early to make a refined estimate of exact costs or develop the accuracy needed at that level.

2. Selection of the Top Two or Three Concepts

This rigorous analysis and the market-based research will point the team toward two or three concepts that it will recommend to move forward. However, it should also construct plans for the other concepts, as they also show potential.

The Next Steps

At this point, the concepts move on into the final four steps of this new product development process:

5. **Prototype Development**
6. **Plant Scale-Up**
7. **Commercialization**
8. **Post-Launch Checkup**

As stated earlier, many companies have a very strong development and commercialization process. The problem is that they have difficulty determining *which* ideas to move forward. We feel confident that the four steps detailed in this article will help them develop a process that will considerably reduce that difficulty and improve their chances of success.

About the Author

Scott Davis is a partner with Kuczmarski & Associates. He leads the firm's focus on brand equity management as a key component of delivering customer value. He has led projects dealing with the creation of customer-focused innovation strategies with some of the top brands in the United States. His work has been cited in numerous publications, including *USA Today* and *The Wall Street Journal*. Scott also serves a contributor for *Crain's Small Business* "Business Advisor Column." His work has been published in several marketing-oriented journals.

35

GREAT INTERNAL SERVICE
CREATES GREAT
EXTERNAL SERVICE

H. Lee Meadow

What's the goal for your customer service people? It should be to try, in every interaction with a customer, to provide better and more memorable service than the last time. Not only that, the author of this article contends, but the "better and more memorable" service begins within your company, in the interrelationships of your employees.

Introduction

Customer service is a proactive attitude that can be summed up as: *I care and I can do.* It means that, as a customer service provider, I enter every interaction seeking to provide better and more memorable service than the last time. With that in mind, consider the following three service encounters:

Service Encounter 1. It's 9:00 Monday morning. Tom Saunders, director of purchasing, is calling his sales representative at Acme, Inc., to check on the status of the parts order he placed over three weeks ago. The receptionist answers, "This is Acme, Inc. How may I direct your call?" Tom replies, "I need to speak with Sharon Riser." The receptionist responds, "Sharon is on leave. May I direct your call to one of the other sales representatives?" Tom replies, "Please!" The call is then transferred to Frank Ramsey in the sales department. Tom explains, "I understand Sharon Riser is on leave, but I need to know the status of my order." Frank replies, "I'm sorry, but Sharon has her own system, and I have no idea how to get that data for you." Tom responds, "But Sharon promised me delivery no later than last Friday. I need to know where the order is, so may I speak to your sales manager?" Frank tells Tom, "That's Sam Smith, but he's at a trade show and won't be back until next week." Tom then asks, "Well, is there anyone I can speak with to find out about my order?" Frank answers, "I'm sorry, Mr. Saunders, but you'll have to wait until Sharon comes back from leave on Thursday." Tom then thanks him sarcastically and hangs up frustrated with Acme, Inc.

Service Encounter 2. Sheila Donald, director of the Ace accounting department, has just received a bill from Alltime Heating and Air Conditioning Company for installing an A/C unit. She can't understand why the bill is $5,000 more than expected. The contract states the terms as $12,150, with 3/10, net 45 days, but Alltime is now billing at 2/10, net 30, for a total of $17,200. Sheila needs to get the billing corrected, so she calls the Alltime billing department. Bud Thomas answers with a simple "Hello." Sheila identifies herself and tells Bud, "There's a discrepancy in the bill I received and our agreed-upon purchase price and terms. Is there anything you can do to help us?" Bud says politely, "Hold on and I'll get your file." Bud finds the file on the computer and the paper copy, then tells Sheila, "I've got your information in front of me. How can I help you?" Sheila explains the problem. Bud confirms that the bill doesn't match the price or terms in the contract. He tells Sharon, "I'm very sorry about this. I'll have to check with my boss to see what we can do." Sheila responds angrily, "What do you mean 'what you can do'?! There's a mistake, and I expect it to be corrected immediately!" Bud replies, "I agree there's a mistake, but since the MIS department has issued the bill and they have a separate database, I can't correct the problem. Only Anne Taylor, my boss, can work with the MIS director, and Anne won't be in until tomorrow." Sheila tells Bud, "I expect you or someone else to handle this problem *today*! I want to speak to Anne's boss." Bud answers, "David Fine, VP of accounting, is not available. You'll have to wait until Anne gets back." Sheila then tells Bud, "Well, you tell Anne to call me, or I won't pay this bill at all." Bud then retorts, "I don't understand your anger! I can't do anything because I don't have the authority or the ability to correct the problem. You'll just have to call back." Sheila tells Bud, "No, you have Anne call me first thing tomorrow!" Bud promises to leave the message and then hangs up. Bud "forgets" to pass along the message, and nobody calls Sheila.

Service Encounter 3. Tom Davis, an electrical contractor, needs some lighting equipment for his new building project. He drops by The Electrical Supply House, the area's largest electrical equipment wholesaler, since he's working on a building in the area. Although he's done over $6,000,000 of business with the firm the last eight years, it's all been by phone; this is the first time he's visited the wholesaler's site. He stands at the counter for a while, watching several employees behind the counter area, talking and walking around. They notice him waiting, but nobody offers to help him. After five minutes, he yells out, "Would someone please help me?" One of the workers tells him, "Hey, buddy, wait your turn! We've got other important stuff to do first!" Tom then overhears the man tell another employee, "If we've got to stop for every guy who wants a light switch or a box of fuses, we'll never finish stocking this inventory, and the boss will kill us!" Tom stomps off, swearing that he'll never do business with The Electrical Supply House again. Two months later the sales department realizes that there haven't been any orders from Tom, who's accounted for well over $800,000 annually in supplies and equipment—about 7% of the wholesaler's business. The sales rep responsible for the Tom Davis account doesn't understand why Tom has stopped doing business with him, so he drops by to investigate—and Tom curtly tells him to get lost.

Reviewing These Encounters

What happened in these three service encounter scenarios happens in some form every day in many businesses, government agencies, and not-for-profit organizations. These scenarios show several problems:

- There's a significant lack of visionary leadership in customer service.
- It's most likely that the employees are as dissatisfied as the customers they're serving.
- There are no partnerships within and among the parties involved.
- There's no attention to building quality customer service.
- There are significant signs of information silos that undermine the proper handling of customer inquiries and problems.
- The companies don't have an open communication system, which further undermines customer service.
- Internal and external processes appear to be randomly developed and reactive, at best.

This article focuses on issues and examples that will help customer service managers and their staff improve their operations and build the necessary internal and external partnerships that will result in improving the organization's financial strength. We'll start with some basic leadership and customer service concepts that customer service organizations need to understand and make part of their operating philosophy. Then, we'll consider ways to manage customer expectations and methods for developing appropriate service response systems. We'll conclude with suggestions for managers on improving customer service and creating a loyal bond between server and customer.

A Review of Basic Leadership and Customer Service Issues

The Business Environment

To understand where customer service fits within any organization, the customer service manager must understand three key elements—customer satisfaction, continuous improvement, and financial performance—at work in a very turbulent and ever-changing environment. These are elements that are dynamically linked, as shown in Figure 35-1.

The business first develops initiatives that continuously improve the organization's processes, people, and market offerings. These improvements are derived from two data flows between customer metrics and internal metrics and lead to some level of perceived customer satisfaction. The key to this figure lies in understanding that customer satisfaction drives financial viability—not the other way around, as many business leaders believe. In turn, an organization's financial performance provides the resources for further improvement initiatives to increase customer satisfaction.

Figure 35-2 depicts a process model that delineates an approach to operations

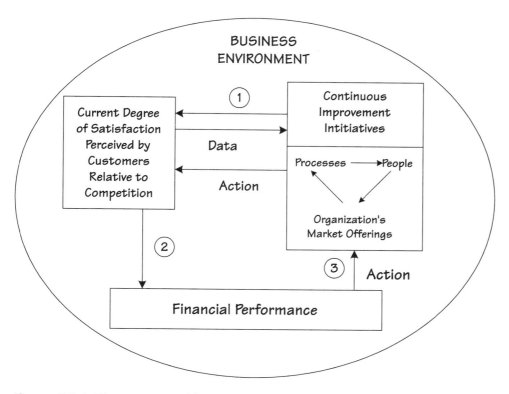

Figure 35-1. The context of business today.

that customer service leaders should strive to achieve. This figure shows the link between internal customer service and financial performance, with a customer-driven philosophy and vision necessary for financial viability.

In the first stage of the process, *Internal Customer Service*, the organization's leaders focus on serving the needs of its internal customers (i.e., employees). The better the leaders and internal customers know themselves and the organization, the more responsive the organization and employees can be to employee needs.

Internal Customer Service leads to the second stage, *Internal Customer Satisfaction*, which creates a bond of trust between the organization and the employee, so the employee is more likely to buy into the organization's mission and vision. The greater the job satisfaction, the better the performance and the more amenable the employee is to reacting to changing conditions in the business environment.

In this stage, leaders should focus on *Internal Customer Partnerships*, building a "we're all in this together" atmosphere, a team orientation within and among departments, functions, and/or areas. The orientation is not on individual achievements, but on team or organizational achievements. The leaders encourage the creation of internal customer service processes that look inside-out. They focus on helping employees understand the need to work as partners, to help each other meet their objectives. Each partner should understand the need to serve the next partner in the customer service process, to help that partner "shine" (i.e., be the best he or she can be).

This partnership continues through the customer service cycle process, so that

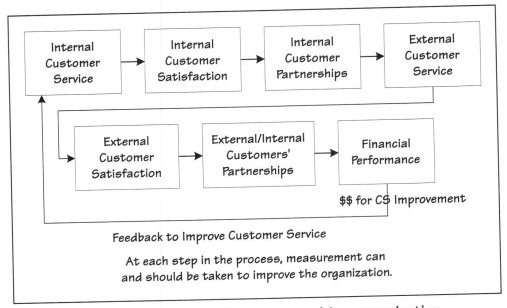

Figure 35-2. A process model of a customer-driven organization.

the internal partner who works directly with the external customer can provide the services or market offerings expected by the customer, in the *External Customer Service* stage.

Once the internal partners begin to focus on external customer service, processes can be improved to deliver outcomes that meet and exceed external customer expectations, so the customer feels a bond with the organization, building customer loyalty. This *External Customer Satisfaction* stage focuses on helping all internal customers understand external customer expectations and on creating an open communication system that allows a free flow of information, good and bad, up and down the hierarchy. And the focus of this communication is on improving customer service processes.

With that communication system in place, internal customers can probe for external customer expectations. When those expectations are warranted or realistic, the organization can respond accordingly. When those customer expectations are unreasonable, the organization can develop marketing communications to help educate the customers about what they should expect. Doing this well requires not only an open internal communication system, but also an open communication system connecting the organization and its customers and allowing for a free flow of all types of information (good or bad) that will help both parties prosper.

When customer service meets or exceeds the customer's expectations, it builds trust between the organization and the customer, which leads to greater customer loyalty. The next stage in the model, then, is developing value-added *External/Internal Customer Partnerships* that serve both the organization and the customer. Key to such partnerships is the philosophy that neither partner can succeed unless the other partner succeeds.

When external/internal partnerships are created and nurtured, then both partners benefit. For the external customers, this means better service. For the organization, this means greater customer loyalty and better financial performance. This proposition was tested by Frederick F. Reichheld and Thomas Teal, who reported the results in their seminal work, *The Loyalty Effect: The Hidden Force Behind Growth, Profits, and Lasting Value* (1996).

As the gains in customer partnerships lead to better financial performance, the organization can invest to further improve customer service processes. If the process is measured at each key juncture, that information can help all parties direct customer service improvement efforts. Monitoring the process via metrics of customer service, satisfaction, and partnership will determine what improvements to make that will further enhance the relationship.

Management and Leadership

To create the system just described, organizations must change from traditional management hierarchies to a more modern leadership orientation that focuses on *self-directed employee action* and on providing an environment that enables employees to use their skills, intelligence, and abilities to operate the various processes for which they're responsible.

Leadership revolves around self-directed individuals and work teams with a common focus and vision. Each internal customer's job is to make all other internal and external customers shine and make every interaction positive and memorable. Employees are encouraged to "step outside the box" and take actions to better serve the customer. This orientation allows for mistakes, expects, and, frankly, encourages them, in that mistakes show that employees are taking chances on behalf of the customer, and this provides a chance to learn to make improvements. Today's leaders understand that employees must feel free to fail if they're going to find ways to succeed and improve customer service processes. Thus, these leaders encourage employees to turn an "I care" attitude into "I can do" behavior.

Keys to Creating a Customer Service Orientation

Here are eight basic points central to changing the organization so that everyone understands and practices the value "customer service is everybody's business." In making these changes, remember that change is disruptive, so start with easy changes that turn into easy successes, then work into the more difficult changes. Success breeds success: little achievements can help employees feel more secure about attempting more difficult improvements. Substantial changes take time: what modern leaders seek is a continuous improvement process, not an entire re-engineering effort.

1. **Change can begin at any level, even the lowest**. The quality movement has enforced the message that unless "top management" commits to improvement initiatives, no change is possible. This is a myth. Although commitment at the top makes improvements easier and faster, change can take place at any level. In fact, many of the most admired departments and organizations owe their successes to changes that were initiated at the bottom. Focus on

your own span of control. Don't worry about what others are doing or may think. Good results will win people over.

2. **All employees must focus on customer service**. This means defining quality customer service *not* in terms of your *efforts*, but in terms of the *results* for the *customer*. It also means not just working *hard*, but working *smart*. A goal should be to exceed customer expectations. If you and your employees aim only at meeting expectations, your service won't build trust or develop partnerships—it will simply be OK. Seek to exceed your customers' expectations, and they'll remember you positively. This means you'll be proactively improving processes (not just reacting to problems), and customers will share information with you so you can further improve your processes.

3. **Customer service starts with *internal* customers, then moves to *external* customers**. The point here is that if *internal* customers get good service and are satisfied, it naturally translates to providing good service to *external* customers. Conversely, if *internal* customers (i.e., employees) are dissatisfied, it is nearly a sure thing that they will not go out of their way to meet and exceed the expectations of *external* customers.

4. **Your organization must be focused inside-out**. Thus, the leader must consider his or her internal customers as the most important customers, because they determine the level of service provided to external customers. Good leaders build teams that buy into the organization's vision, and they show that a concern for customer service applies to all customers, external and internal.

5. **The outcomes of customer service/satisfaction/partnering depend largely on information and satisfaction/expectation measurement**. If there's any downside to being customer-focused, it's that measurement must be continuous and constantly monitored and interpreted by *all* persons responsible for customer service outcomes. You never have enough information, so you must constantly use as many methods as possible to collect information about your customers (internal and external) and keep up with changing needs and expectations. When you involve *everyone* in interpreting the data, that sense of ownership helps build consensus and facilitates buy-in for changes.

6. **Customer change (internal and external) is constant, unpredictable, and difficult to control**. Thus, leaders must help their staffs learn how to manage in an ever-changing environment, with ever-changing expectations and rules for reacting appropriately to change. Leaders must develop teams, and then give them the time to learn how to succeed—because teams don't always come together immediately. Team processes should emphasize the long term: all the preliminary work is an investment that will pay off over time.

7. **Encourage and facilitate open communication at all levels**. Communicate all non-proprietary information to internal and external customers and enable all customers to make decisions that will raise their level of service and/ or satisfaction. Make sure everyone understands that bad news is as important as good news. Leaders who are not open to bad news cannot hope to

encourage their employees to take chances to serve their customers or make improvements.

8. **Remember: leaders can't** *empower,* **just as leaders can't** *motivate.* All they can do is create an enabling environment that will allow their employees to take charge. Until your internal customers accept the need to extend the bounds of their actions, no "empowerment directives" will have much effect. Leaders must provide information and tools and help employees learn to acquire new information and develop new tools and methods so they can do their jobs better. In an enabling environment that encourages change, employees will take better advantage of their abilities to help themselves, the organization, and their customers.

Who Is Your Customer?

All of this brings us to the question, "Who should you consider your customer to be?"

The traditional model defines a customer as the one who pays for your services. Although this definition may not be comprehensive, it's correct. People who pay you for what you provide are your customers, also variously known as taxpayers, constituents, patients, clients, ratepayers, and guests.

Another answer to this question divides customers into internal and external: the external pays for what you provide, while the internal works with you to provide it. This second model has recently become the norm for developing customer-focused organizations and clearly emphasizes the need for collaboration and cooperation within organizations. However, this definition may be too narrow, as well.

I want to offer the following answer to the question, "Who is my customer?"

Anyone who interacts with me, either purposely or by accident!!!

This answer shows that we should build customer-driven relationships with all the persons we encounter, and it sets an implicit goal: What can I do to make the encounter memorable and positive or to improve a continuing relationship to help the other person(s) shine and build lasting value-added partnerships? Whether the customer is internal or external, or whether he or she pays or not, or even whether the interaction is intentional or accidental, the key to this model is developing dyadic or one-on-one relationships that determine how you or I personally will deal with anyone.

Think of the example service workers and their managers set when they treat everyone as a customer to be served. When you treat strangers with a "What I can I do to make you shine?" attitude, when your approach is "I care about you, regardless of who you are," it's difficult for others around you not to take the same approach, which helps build trust, the basis for a partnership.

Scenario

Consider the following example of a process based on customer service, inside and out. This process depends on two rules and a simple computer program. The first rule: if a phone is ringing, answer it ASAP, even if it's not yours. The second rule: no voice mail goes unanswered for more than one hour during the workday, and no one goes home until he or she has responded to all voice mail messages. The computer program—installed on all computers, whether using a Windows environment or a Macintosh platform, networked or not—keeps three screens/files resident in the background of all computers, allowing any worker to use toggle switches to easily pull up screens and access customer databases.

Now let's consider a hypothetical situation. A customer service office in a mid-sized warehouse facility has just undergone a downsizing. The smaller staff has to handle an increasing load of customer service problems, complaints, and requests. Further, the budget for training has been cut, so there's no additional training. Everyone is working harder than ever—yet when you call them, they can always handle the call.

Why? Because the workers have developed an "I care" and "I can do" work ethic that says that, regardless of the circumstances, they should be able to take care of whatever comes up. Everybody is expected to answer calls and attend to voice mail messages, because the customer matters most. The computer system allows anyone to handle any call, even if he or she doesn't know the caller or anything about the circumstances.

Every employee in the office has a phone and a computer nearby, with a voice mail back-up system to catch calls when they're busy or out of the office. Everybody, including the manager, has mapped out his or her normal job tasks, so that any co-worker can easily understand from the map the processes and activities involved in those tasks. Also, all the employees keep all data-related screens updated for all customers or accounts, so that no information is older than five working days. Then, any employee can use any computer to access customer information in seconds, to meet any need.

The following situation shows the process in action.

Mary Smith calls Bob Jones at 10 o'clock one morning, but he's away from his desk. Susan, working several desks away, comes over to answer the phone. "Hello, my name is Susan. Bob is not at his desk. How may I help you?" Mary then describes her problem, while Susan toggles up the first screen that Bob has created for just this type of call. The screen is divided into three sections: in the left half a list of possible problems, in the right half a list of suggested solutions for the problems, and space at the bottom of the screen for leaving notes for Bob.

Susan matches the problem to a suggested guideline or solution. She then writes a note for Bob at the bottom of the screen, to tell him about the call so he can remain up-to-date with the Mary Smith situation. This message goes immediately to Bob's e-mail in-box.

What if Susan finds that Mary's problem doesn't fit any of the categories noted on Bob's first screen? That depends on whether Mary is a current customer or a new customer.

If Mary is a current customer, Susan can toggle to a second screen, for a database hypertext screen arranged alphabetically by name. Susan clicks on the hypertext line indicating Mary Smith's name and up pops a screen containing all the data known about Mary Smith and the status of all the projects anybody in the organization is working on with her. Susan then can give Mary the latest information about her project or problem and the status of any previous queries or job tasks requested. If Mary is satisfied, Susan then writes a note in the space provided at the bottom of the screen, to tell Bob how she dealt with Mary using the second screen. This message goes immediately to Bob's incoming e-mail message directory.

What if Mary Smith is a new account or raises a new problem? If Bob were here, he'd engage Mary in a Q&A session to find out exactly what she wanted. So, Susan toggles to a third screen, where Bob has provided the protocol he uses with new customers and unusual problems. The screen is divided into two halves, with independent displays. The top lists the questions Bob would ask, in the order he'd follow. The bottom allows space to record the answers.

When the conversation ends, Susan tells Mary that when Bob returns he'll learn about her call and deal with any issues she's raised. She then closes the screen and the contents of both the top and the bottom halves go immediately to Bob's incoming e-mail directory.

The process used in this office makes it much more likely that the staff can satisfy their customers. In this example, Mary receives better service than if Susan were only able to take a message—or if Mary just reached Bob's voice mail. Bob looks great even when he's away from the office. Susan shines even with this stranger. Further, Mary no longer has to worry whether Bob is in or not. And if Susan selects the wrong solution, Bob can work with Susan so that she can better handle similar calls in the future. If Susan has problems with any of the screens, she can work with Bob to build a better set of help screens.

With this process, everyone in the group has a stake in the situation and everyone can work together to improve customer service.

How Does My Customer Assess My Service Quality?

There are hundreds of ways to assess the quality of service. Despite all the differences, especially between internal and external customers, the criteria used to assess service usually break down into the following general areas:

- Dependability, accuracy, reliability, timeliness,
- Assurance, locus of control, confidence,
- Perceptual indicators,
- Willingness, responsiveness, caring manner,
- Concern, empathy, equity, attention to customer needs.

With all the research done over the past decade or so, these factors seem to be the key criteria customers use to measure service and their satisfaction. They represent many of the issues that interact to influence customer perceptions of service. Here's what they mean in terms of what the customer thinks.

Dependability, accuracy, reliability, timeliness. Am I getting the highest-quality tangibles and/or intangibles? Are they being provided at the right time, to the right place, and in the right condition? To what extent does this meet my expectations?

Assurance, locus of control, confidence. How much do I feel in control of the situation? Do I feel like I'm at the mercy of the person or the organization? Or do I feel like I can determine the outcome?

Perceptual indicators. What impression do I get from the server's appearance and communication style and from the atmosphere of the service situation? Do these aspects convey the look, feel, smell, and sound of quality?

Willingness, responsiveness, caring manner. Does the person or the organization seem willing to deal with me, responsive to my concerns and expectations, caring about me and my unique needs?

Concern, empathy, equity, attention to customer needs. Do I feel like the person or the organization understands my service issues, cares about them, is paying attention to them and to me, and is treating me fairly? Is there evidence of sincere concern? Do I feel comfortable that the person or organization understands my needs, problems, and desires and can relate to them?

How Do I Lead a Proactive Customer-Service–Driven Organization?

In this section I'll provide some suggestions for managing service encounters proactively, with value-added processes. Though they may not all apply to your particular circumstances, you should find enough guidance to orient your service activity with an "I care" and "I can do" attitude, to develop long-term customer-server partnerships.

Managing Customer Expectations

What matters, as mentioned earlier, is not what the server puts into the service but what the customer takes away from the experience. The typical customer wants performance that not only meets his or her expectations, but exceeds them. That's what you should want, too. If you fall short of those expectations, you may lose the customer. If you just meet those expectations, there's nothing memorable on which to build a partnership. But if you exceed your customer's expectations, the service encounter becomes positively memorable and the customer is likely to continue with you.

Quite simply, the ideal outcome is when the customer's perceptions (what he or she gets) outweigh his or her expectations (what he or she wants). If there's only a balance between the two, the experience is neutral, not memorable. If the perceptions fall short of the expectations, the experience is negative and the result is dissatisfaction.

To build customer service to levels that cause excitement and great satisfaction, which should in turn lead to further interactions with the customer, you must manage the customer's expectations. To do so, you must measure those expectations continuously: before providing the service or producing the goods (to ascertain customer wants and desires and needs), while providing the service or selling the goods (to keep current on customer expectations), and after the service or sale (to determine the match between perceptions and expectations). If you measure continuously, you can always know what it will take to exceed expectations or, if those expectations are unrealistic, educate the customer.

Create an Environment That Encourages Leadership Among Employees

In the traditional management model, the manager possesses all the information and the power to make decisions; the workers seek out the manager to obtain information and permission to act. This serves as a control mechanism to minimize employee mistakes, but it also slows the decision-making process and causes information bottlenecks. This model of traditional decision-making can be depicted two ways.

Figure 35-3 shows how the traditional manager limits employees through detailed job descriptions and copious specific procedures. The rationale is that restricting decision-making authority reduces the chances of mistakes. Unfortunately, this model leaves customers (internal and external) dissatisfied and possibly angry.

In the second depiction of traditional management (Figure 35-4), the organization is a hierarchy with the leaders on top and the customers and the service workers at the bottom. Employees who survive in this environment work to please their managers, not to satisfy the customers. This breeds arrogance and neglect of customers.

These models, found in many organizations in all sectors of the economy, create both internal and external customer dissatisfaction, which in turn can lead to financial failure. To build a customer service-focused organization, you need to abandon these traditional models. Figures 35-3 and 35-4 should be replaced by Figures 35-5 and 35-6, which show how organizations are run by self-directed customer service teams (employees) and managers whose role is to make each of these teams "shine," so they can better manage customer-server relationships and customer expectations. The organization and the customers communicate freely, which promotes mutual understanding and partnerships.

Figure 35-5 shows how the leader creates an environment with a defined but

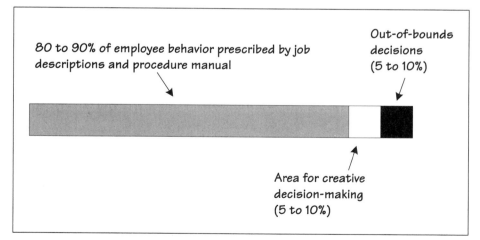

Figure 35-3. Decision making in a traditional organization.

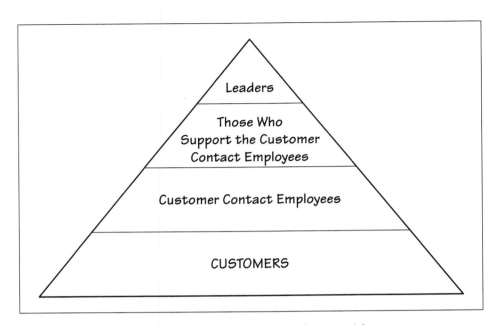

Figure 35-4. The traditional organizational pyramid.

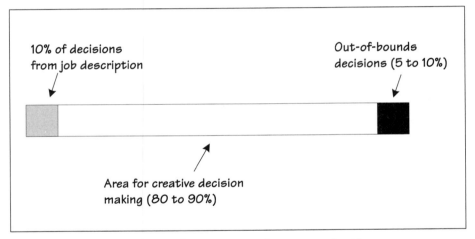

Figure 35-5. Decision making in a modern organization.

large latitude for creative decision-making, limited job descriptions and procedure manuals, and definite out-of-bounds behaviors (e.g., illegal, immoral, unethical, or customer-unfriendly actions and decisions). To further reinforce this model, the leader replaces the traditional procedure manual with a guidebook, organized around a list of problems and permissible actions, to help standardize actions and control costs. (In essence, the procedure manual is reorganized to be more user-friendly for customer service employees).

The system allows employees to deviate from the guidebook, under certain conditions. First, they must report any deviations, to establish personal accountability. Second, they must also report the outcome of the deviation. That way, successful actions can be incorporated into the guidelines, while unsuccessful actions can pro-

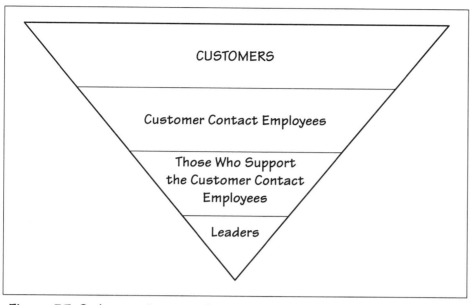

Figure 35-6. A superior organizational pyramid.

vide lessons, with the focus either on showing how an established guideline might have been more successful or on devising a new guideline for such situations. In essence, leaders focus on the mistakes, not on the employee who made the decision.

Figure 6 shows how the leaders help the support units shine, the support units help the customer contact employees shine, and the customer contact employees—with information and decision-making autonomy—help the customer shine. This increases the chances of exceeding customer expectations, the server-customer interaction is both positive and memorable, and trust builds that will serve as a foundation for building customer-server partnerships.

This modern design for self-leadership helps to reduce the costs of dissatisfied employees, both overt—the 5%–10% caused by turnover, absenteeism, disobedience, etc.—and covert—the 90%–95% caused by passive resistance to leadership, doing the minimum, and lack of a customer care focus. In essence, you're giving internal customers what they need to shine and the orientation to also provide outstanding service to the external customers they deal with.

A Method for Building Buy-in by Employees Who Serve Others

One way to help employees buy into the goal of exceeding customer expectations is to work on building a team with a common vision. The vision begins with a general direction provided by the leader; the employees develop the details and action statements. This process, called "sharing the vision," can hold a team together during good and bad times.

A model for sharing the vision is shown in Figure 35-7. The process is an interactive cycle, constantly updating the vision based on new information that's shared and interpreted by the employees.

The result: an orientation toward an internal organizational culture and an ex-

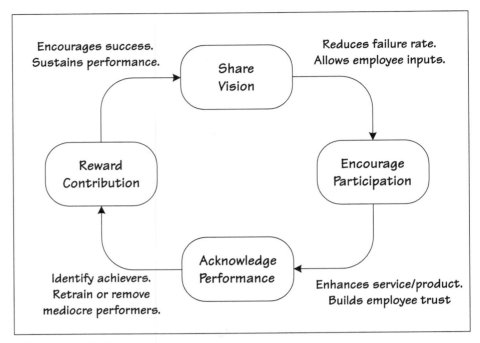

Figure 35-7. Team vision development process.

ternal customer service vision that conveys and supports an "I care" and "I can do" attitude. That culture and that vision are the basis for improving the satisfaction and loyalty of both internal and external customers.

Eliminate Behaviors That Cause Negative Reactions

Over the past 20 years, I've encountered many ways to dissatisfy customers. Leaders and service workers must constantly focus on avoiding such behaviors as I've labeled "the sins of service," especially those listed below.

1. **Apathy**—a "just don't give a damn" attitude
2. **Brush-off**—"try to get rid of this pest" standard operating procedure
3. **Coldness**—curt, unfriendly, inconsiderate, or impatient attitude
4. **Condescension**—treating customers in a patronizing manner
5. **Robotism**—a "thank you have a nice day, next!" manner
6. **Rule-bookism**—"a rule is a rule—no exceptions" standard operating procedure
7. **Run-around**—sending the customer elsewhere, "we don't handle that here" standard operating procedure
8. **False advertising**—promise of service quality without means to deliver

It's not easy to avoid these "sins," because there are many forces at work to reduce our motivation, there are customers we don't like, there are organizations that foster static conditions, there are people who won't buy into service, and there are people within and outside the organization who will purposely mislead us or even lie to us to protect themselves from any heat that might be caused by being customer-focused.

Leaders who show by example the virtues of avoiding these "sins" can at least make service encounters neutral. Though that's certainly not as good as memorable, it's better than making negative impressions! By avoiding these "sins" and helping others do so, you can lay a foundation for building a proactive environment for more consistently exceeding customer expectations.

Managing the Service Process to Create Positive Memorable Outcomes

Jan Carlzon, the CEO of Scandinavian Airlines Systems, years ago coined the term "moment of truth." Every service has a process with a beginning and an end, he contended, and if you string the service parts together you get a service cycle. From a customer's viewpoint, Carlzon explained, every service cycle contains moments of truth, instants when a customer comes into contact with any aspect of the server or the server organization. That contact means a chance for the customer to form an impression about the quality of service and, potentially, the quality of the serving organization as well. Moments of truth that are memorable Carlzon called *critical*, because they either establish or change the customer's impressions.

Organizations should try to manage the customer's expectations so that all moments of truth are critical, so the customer is excited or delighted. A moment of truth can be modeled as a dyadic relationship: the customer and the employee both bring into the service context attitudes, values, beliefs, wants, feelings, and expectations. To succeed, the organization, its customer service employees, and its leaders must manage those moments of truth.

To manage them is understand them, which means the organization must gather information about both its customers and its service employees and assess how each party can interact to make the service more positively memorable. The information gathered about customers—the inputs to a customer's frame of reference—can be grouped in the following way:

- Past experience with this organization or similar organizations,
- Beliefs about what this organization does for customers,
- Expectations formed by customer's previous experiences,
- Attitudes, beliefs, ethnic norms, and values,
- Recommendations or warnings from other customers.

The information gathered about its employees—the inputs to an employee's frame of reference—can be grouped in the following way:

- What the organization has told the employee to do,
- Rules and regulations set for employees and customers,
- The employee's level of emotional maturity,
- Expectations of customer behavior based on past experiences,
- Attitudes, beliefs, ethnic norms, and values,
- Tools and resources used to deliver customer service.

When the information collected is used to improve customer service, the result is a win-win outcome for the customer and the employee. The customer is more satisfied and the employee can feel better about his or her work.

Conclusion

I've tried to demonstrate that customer service is really a leadership concept that depends heavily on self-directed employees who, because the organization has exceeded their expectations as internal customers, seek to exceed the expectations of external customers. In other words, external customer satisfaction and partnering depend on internal customer satisfaction and partnering, which depend on leadership. Successful partnerships between servers and customers strengthen the financial condition of the organization, which can continuously invest in improving service and growing and solidifying those partnerships.

Let me conclude with some thoughts to summarize this article and help you focus your efforts in developing a customer-driven orientation. My research and my experience have revealed the following characteristics of customer-service-oriented individuals and/or organizations.

1. *Customer-driven organizations* realize that a quality market offering (tangible or intangible) delivered at a fair price or at a reasonable cost is the starting point for building service success that will lead to value-added service satisfaction and future partnerships.
2. *Customer-driven organizations* know that it's the process of striving for quality, not the attainment of a specific quality goal, that produces service satisfaction. (As the saying goes, it's the journey, not the destination.)
3. *Customer-driven organizations* know all their customers and treat every interaction as a customer service opportunity, a chance for both parties to benefit. The leaders know that information is *gold* and that they never have enough information about their customers, internal or external. They also realize that improvement must be a continuous process, since customer needs and expectations constantly change.
4. *Customer-driven organizations* focus on managing expectations through managing moments of truth. They think in terms of the effects of their actions on the customer, rather than on their jobs, tasks, procedures, and costs. They aim to create value-added partnerships that benefit all parties!
5. *Customer-driven organizations* understand that service must happen on the inside before it can happen with external customers.
6. *Customer-driven organizations* develop self-directed leadership skills rather than job descriptions. They believe that the role of leaders is to help the support staff shine, so they can help the service staff shine, so they can help the customer shine!
7. *Customer-driven individuals and organizations* know how to manage change through continually acquiring information that helps them uncover trends and changes in customer expectations. They realize that they must use the information to anticipate and proactively manage change, rather than reacting to the surprise of change.

In conclusion, if you buy into the propositions and methods offered by this article, you will do the following:

○ You will listen to, understand, and respond to all parties you interact with and treat them as customers.
○ You will develop a common vision that all who serve can share.
○ You will establish a continuous improvement process that will keep your organization up-to-date and financially viable.
○ You will set standards and measure performance, not to assess blame but to pursue continuous improvement in your service processes.
○ You will select and train employees so that they develop the "I care" and "I can do!" attitude that makes all of these concepts and actions work.

These are the keys to building successful customer-server partnerships. The effort involves the cooperation of leaders, managers, support staff, and service personnel, because customer service is everybody's business.

About the Author

Dr. H. Lee Meadow is Professor of Marketing and former Chairman of the Department of Management and Marketing for the Lumpkin College of Business and Applied Sciences at Eastern Illinois University. He has over 20 years of collegiate-level teaching and management experience. He has consulted extensively in the areas of marketing, management, and selling in retailing organizations (Sears), technology (Motorola), higher education (Metropolitan State College and the University of Northern Iowa), health care (Kishwaukee Hospital, Sarah Bush Lincoln Health System, and Home Health Care, Inc.), insurance (State Farm, Country Companies), state government (Maryland and Massachusetts), and federal government (U.S. Army, U.S. Air Force, and U.S. Office of Personnel Management).

He has developed a wide array of executive development programs, such as creating quality customer service programs, developing visionary leadership, strategic planning and its implementation, and improving service marketing strategy.

Lee received his Ph.D. in Marketing from Virginia Tech. He is the author of numerous professional and academic articles, with some of his publications covering such topics as developing effective strategies for delivering customer satisfaction and total quality; operating health care customer service programs; establishing effective value-added marketing strategies; understanding buyer behavior; linking marketing, aging, and public policy; and creating marketing delivery systems for the senior citizen market.

Appendix A

BENCHMARKING YOUR CUSTOMER SERVICE OPERATIONS WITH FINDINGS FROM THE 1996 ICSA BENCHMARKING STUDY

This appendix presents 20 tables reproduced from a study undertaken by the International Customer Service Association. The purpose of the study was to gather information on different aspects of customer service in different types of companies. The study was designed to explore key benchmarks in areas such as personnel/ training, service level, and order processing.

The study results include much more information than in the tables included here. But those chosen for inclusion deal with issues of interest to all customer service managers, from functions performed by customer service to employee turnover to complaint handling. You can use the data in these tables to compare your company's operations with those of others across many industries.

These tables are reproduced with the permission of the International Customer Service Association, 401 N. Michigan Avenue, Chicago, IL 60611. To learn more about the ICSA, check its Web site (http://www.icsa.com). The entire contents of the benchmarking study are listed there.

ICSA Table 1. Functions performed by customer service.

	1996			1993			1991		
	Total	Mfg	Serv	Total	Mfg	Serv	Total	Mfg	Serv
	%	%	%	%	%	%	%	%	%
Inquiries (general)	96	96	96	95	96	93	89	94	96
Liaison with Other Depts	89	94	81	88	93	81	89	95	78
Order Status Inquiries	84	97	63	82	95	62	82	96	60
Phone Order Processing	83	95	63	78	93	55	80	91	62
Price/Availability	79	93	58	79	91	61	77	90	55
Fax Order Processing	76	93	48	70	89	41	—	—	—
Returns/Claims Processing	73	91	46	73	85	56	71	86	46
Mail Order Processing	63	76	43	59	75	35	45	56	27
Field Sales Support	60	76	35	65	80	43	69	81	48
Sales Literature Requests	59	66	48	56	62	46	51	57	43
Service Quality Monitoring	55	50	63	—	—	—	—	—	—
Service Quality Reporting	53	52	55	—	—	—	—	—	—
EDI Order Processing	52	72	21	42	62	12	—	—	—
Inside Rep Training	51	57	43	53	55	48	55	57	52
Technical Support/ Troubleshooting	43	48	34	48	47	48	—	—	—
Inside Rep Supervision	38	43	31	41	45	37	39	41	35
Contract Admin/Processing	27	31	20	35	41	26	—	—	—
Direct Inside Selling	22	24	18	21	21	20	20	20	21
Credit and Collection	20	16	25	18	18	20	18	13	25
Sales Lead Qualification	17	17	17	18	19	18	16	13	20
Other Inside Supervisory	13	13	12	18	21	15	20	20	20
Other	8	9	7	13	11	17	18	16	20
No Answer	1	1	2	1	1	1	1	1	2

Blanks indicate question did not appear in study noted

ICSA Table 2. Average percentage turnover in different customer service positions.

	1996		
	Total	Mfg	Serv
	%	%	%
Customer Service Director	—	—	—
Customer Service Manager	1	1	2
Asst Manager of Customer Service/CS Supervisor	1	—	1
Order Processing Manager/ Supervisor	—	0	—
Senior CS Rep Assistant CS Supervisor	2	2	2
Customer Service Representative	9	7	11
Technical Service Representative	1	—	2
Order Entry Clerk	2	2	3
Customer Service Clerk	3	3	3
Other	2	1	2

New Categories for 1996

	Total	Mfg	Serv
Information Systems Personnel	—	1	—
Training Personnel	—	—	1
Consumer Affairs Personnel	—	—	0
Logistics Personnel	—	—	—

Blanks = less than 1%

ICSA Table 3. Standard maximum rings allowed before a call is answered.

	1996			1993			1991		
	Total	Mfg	Serv	Total	Mfg	Serv	Total	Mfg	Serv
	%	%	%	%	%	%	%	%	%
1 ring	2	1	3	2	1	4	4	3	6
2 rings	14	13	17	20	20	19	25	25	25
3 rings	48	51	43	42	43	40	53	54	50
4 rings	6	5	7	7	6	8	9	9	8
5 or more rings	2	1	3	3	2	3	2	3	1
No answer	29	29	28	27	26	25	8	6	11
Average number of rings	2.90	2.92	2.85	2.84	2.82	2.81	2.79	2.82	2.72

ICSA Table 4. Use voice mail for external calls?

	1996			1993			1991		
	Total	Mfg	Serv	Total	Mfg	Serv	Total	Mfg	Serv
	%	%	%	%	%	%	%	%	%
Yes	64	69	57	53	55	51	44	52	30
No	34	30	40	42	42	43	54	47	66
No answer	2	1	3	5	3	6	2	1	4

ICSA Table 5. Percentages of calls that are . . . .

	1996			1993			1991		
	Total	Mfg	Serv	Total	Mfg	Serv	Total	Mfg	Serv
	%	%	%	%	%	%	%	%	%
Abandoned	3	3	4	4	3	4	4	3	5
Delayed	14	12	17	12	11	14	11	10	13
Answered by Recording	13	11	18	19	17	24	16	13	21

ICSA Table 6. Change in number of customer service positions in past year.

	1996			1993		
	Total	Mfg	Serv	Total	Mfg	Serv
	%	%	%	%	%	%
Increased	38	34	45	38	32	49
Decreased	21	23	17	20	25	11
Remained the same	40	43	35	38	42	32
No answer	2	1	3	4	1	8

ICSA Table 7. Have CSRs received formal training?

	1996			1993			1991		
	Total	Mfg	Serv	Total	Mfg	Serv	Total	Mfg	Serv
	%	%	%	%	%	%	%	%	%
Yes	81	80	82	71	75	66	69	68	70
No	18	19	17	23	23	25	26	29	19
No answer	1	1	2	5	2	8	5	3	10

ICSA Table 8. How often do CSRs handle problems without transferring the customer to another department/person?

	1996			1993			1991		
	Total	Mfg	Serv	Total	Mfg	Serv	Total	Mfg	Serv
	%	%	%	%	%	%	%	%	%
Almost always	50	48	52	66	66	65	67	68	65
More than half the time	18	16	20	23	26	21	22	25	17
About half the time	3	3	3	4	3	4	2	1	2
Not very often	2	1	3	1	—	3	2	2	2
No answer	27	30	22	4	2	6	6	3	11

ICSA Table 9. Does your organization track complaints?

	1996			1993			1991		
	Total	Mfg	Serv	Total	Mfg	Serv	Total	Mfg	Serv
	%	%	%	%	%	%	%	%	%
Yes	71	72	69	68	70	68	58	59	54
No	26	26	27	27	27	26	37	38	37
No answer	3	2	4	5	4	6	5	3	9

ICSA Table 10. What was the percentage of
complaints received per number of inquiries in 1996?

	1996		
	Total	Mfg	Serv
	%	%	%
Less than 5%	21	18	26
5% to less than 10%	8	10	6
10% to less than 30%	9	9	10
30% to less than 50%	2	3	2
50% or more	1	1	3
No answer	58	61	54

ICSA Table 11. Approximate percentage of complaints because of . . . .

	1996			1993			1991		
	Total	Mfg	Serv	Total	Mfg	Serv	Total	Mfg	Serv
	%	%	%	%	%	%	%	%	%
Product quality (conformity to specs, performances, etc.)	28	31	21	26	29	22	29	31	25
Early/late delivery	17	16	19	12	13	11	17	20	11
Shipping error (wrong product, wrong quality, incorrect shipper, etc.)	16	18	12	19	23	12	17	19	12
Order entry mistake	14	13	15	14	12	17	10	9	12
Packaging error	6	6	6	5	6	4	5	6	4
Other	19	16	26	22	16	35	23	16	39

ICSA Table 12. Toll-free lines established for . . . .

	1996			1993			1991		
	Total	Mfg	Serv	Total	Mfg	Serv	Total	Mfg	Serv
	%	%	%	%	%	%	%	%	%
Customers to call in general	85	86	84	76	78	76	73	76	68
Customers to phone in orders	75	86	59	72	80	61	70	78	57
Customers to call in technical questions/problems	68	74	58	70	72	68	—	—	—
Customers to fax orders	42	49	29	34	41	26	33	41	21

Blanks indicate question did not appear in the study noted

ICSA Table 13. Do you have a carrier/service delivery evaluation or rating system?

	1996			1993			1991		
	Total	Mfg	Serv	Total	Mfg	Serv	Total	Mfg	Serv
	%	%	%	%	%	%	%	%	%
Yes	45	60	23	41	49	29	44	49	37
No	33	31	37	39	38	39	37	40	31
Not applicable	17	8	32	14	11	19	12	8	19
No answer	4	2	8	7	2	13	7	3	13

ICSA Table 14. Do you track on-time delivery of your product or service?

	1996			1993			1991		
	Total	Mfg	Serv	Total	Mfg	Serv	Total	Mfg	Serv
	%	%	%	%	%	%	%	%	%
Yes	57	71	36	56	65	42	64	73	52
No	36	27	49	37	33	43	28	25	32
No answer	7	2	15	8	2	15	8	2	16

ICSA Table 15. If you track on-time delivery, is it based on . . . ?

	1996			1993			1991		
	Total	Mfg	Serv	Total	Mfg	Serv	Total	Mfg	Serv
	%	%	%	%	%	%	%	%	%
Customer's original requested delivery date	52	51	53	63	62	63	62	59	69
Negotiated delivery date	34	36	28	37	40	29	35	41	20
Repromise date	5	5	2	10	11	8	5	7	2
No answer	10	8	16	6	4	11	5	4	10

ICSA Table 16. Do you measure customer satisfaction?

	1996		
	Total	Mfg	Serv
	%	%	%
Yes	75	74	77
No	20	23	15
No answer	5	3	8

ICSA Table 17. How do you measure customer satisfaction?

	1996		
	Total	Mfg	Serv
	%	%	%
Customer satisfaction surveys (written)	80	78	84
Telephone interviews	48	73	55
Person-to-person interviews	32	38	23
Other	8	9	7
No answer	0	0	0

ICSA Table 18. Do you record complaints manually or through a computer system?

	1996			1993			1991		
	Total	Mfg	Serv	Total	Mfg	Serv	Total	Mfg	Serv
	%	%	%	%	%	%	%	%	%
Manually	35	35	36	47	46	49	50	52	44
Through a computer system	51	54	45	41	45	37	45	41	51
No answer	14	11	19	12	10	14	6	7	5

**ICSA Table 19. What is the level of the highest person
who reviews detailed information on complaints?**

	1996			1993			1991		
	Total	Mfg	Serv	Total	Mfg	Serv	Total	Mfg	Serv
	%	%	%	%	%	%	%	%	%
CEO/President/Principal/ Partner	32	29	38	27	21	37	27	22	36
Vice President	23	25	19	23	24	23	25	25	26
Manager	21	22	21	21	26	15	21	23	17
Director	16	20	10	17	20	12	19	21	15
Other	3	1	5	1	1	2	3	3	2
No answer	5	4	8	10	8	12	4	5	3

**ICSA Table 20. Does your company have a
formal customer retention program?**

	1996			1993		
	Total	Mfg	Serv	Total	Mfg	Serv
	%	%	%	%	%	%
Yes	17	10	28	18	10	30
No	76	85	62	75	85	61
No answer	7	5	10	7	5	9

Appendix B

Magazines, Journals, and Newslettters That Deal With Customer Service

This appendix includes a listing of periodicals that cover customer service issues and news. It's not meant to be comprehensive, but to serve as a point of departure. We've organized this listing into two categories:

○ Periodicals dedicated to customer service in general.
○ Periodicals that focus on customer service in a specific economic sector or business function.

For each listing, you'll find subscription rates, addresses, phone numbers, fax numbers, e-mail addresses, and World Wide Web URLs. You'll also find a brief description of the periodical. If you have an interest in any one of these, you can usually get a sample copy by contacting the publisher.

Customer Service—General

Blue Ribbon Service: The Winning Approach to Customer Care
The Economics Press, Inc.
Bi-weekly pamphlet
Subscription: $50.70
12 Daniel Road
Fairfield NJ 07004
Phone: 800/526-2554, 973/227-1224
Fax: 973/227-8360
Web: http://www.epinc.com/prods/brs.htm
E-mail: info@epinc.com or order@epinc.com
Shows front-line staff the importance of good customer service and methods of providing that service.

Customer
Australian Customer Service Association
Newsletter
Subscription: free to association members
P.O. Box 423
Kew
East Victoria 3102
Australia
Phone: (03) 9899 4071
Fax: (03) 9899 4011
Web: http://www.downwrite.com.au/acsa
E-mail: acsa@melbourne.starway.net.au
Keeps association members up to date on industry information, meeting highlights, and the latest customer service practices.

The Customer Communicator
Alexander Communications Group, Inc.
Monthly four-page newsletter
Subscription: $167 in U.S., Canada, and
Mexico; $207 elsewhere; copy: $14
Customer Service Group
215 Park Avenue South, Suite 1301
New York NY 10003
Phone: 800/232-4317, 212/228-0296
Fax: 212/228-0376
Web: http://www.alexcommgrp.com/csg/
csg.html
E-mail: info@alexcommgrp.com
Helps customer service representatives develop the skills, techniques, and motivation to be more productive. Included with each subscription is the manager's copy of *The SkillSharpener*, which provides 19 half-hour interactive training sessions, with sample handouts, work sheets, and role-play scenarios. There are two volumes of *The SkillSharpener*, selling for $36.95 each or $58.95 for both, prepaid.

Customer Relationship Management
Society of Consumer Affairs Professionals in Business
Quarterly magazine
Subscription: free with membership ($195)
801 N. Fairfax Street, Suite 404
Alexandria VA 22314
Phone: 703/519-3700
Fax: 703/549-4886
Web: http://www.socap.org
E-mail: socap@socap.org
Formerly called *MOBIUS*, this magazine covers topics such as customer loyalty and retention, measuring customer satisfaction, staff training and development, consumer behavior, call center management, and developing and using consumer databases.

Customer Satisfaction Technology
Alexander Communications Group, Inc.
Monthly 12-page newsletter
Subscription: $197 in U.S., Canada, and
Mexico; $227 elsewhere
Customer Service Group
215 Park Avenue South, Suite 1301
New York NY 10003
Phone: 800/232-4317, 212/228-0296

Fax: 212/228-0376
Web: http://www.alexcommgrp.com/csg/
csg.html
E-mail: info@alexcommgrp.com
Focuses on improving customer service and satisfaction through technology.

Customer Service: A Journal of Theory, Research and Practice
International Customer Service Association
Bi-annual journal
Subscription: free with membership ($195);
copy: $25
401 N. Michigan Avenue
Chicago IL 60611
Phone: 800/360-ICSA (4272), 312/321-6800
Fax: 312/845-1084
Web: http://www.icsa.com
E-mail: icsa@sba.com
Educational supplement with in-depth articles by experienced customer service professionals. Each issue focuses on a particular theme; recent issues have been devoted to technology, outsourcing, training and education, building teams, call center management, and reengineering customer service.

Customer Service Manager's Letter
Bureau of Business Practice (Simon & Schuster)
Semi-monthly eight-page newsletter
Subscription: $179.20
24 Rope Ferry Road
Waterford CT 06386
Phone: 800/243-0876, 860/442-4365
Fax: 800/772-7421, 860/434-3078
Web: http://www.bbpnews.com
E-mail: bbp_editorial@prenhall.com
Interview-based articles provide managers with proven methods and best practices in customer service.

Customer Service Newsletter
Alexander Communications Group, Inc.
Monthly eight-page newsletter
Subscription: $137 in U.S., Canada, and
Mexico; $167 elsewhere; copy: $12
Customer Service Group
215 Park Avenue South, Suite 1301
New York NY 10003
Phone: 800/232-4317, 212/228-0296
Fax: 212/228-0376

Web: http://www.alexcommgrp.com/csg/
csg.html
E-mail: info@alexcommgrp.com
Reports on practical, action-oriented techniques and tactics for improving customer service operations. Helps customer service directors, managers, and supervisors get support from top management, train and motivate their staff, set standards, compile information, measure improvements, and benchmark to make their operations more effective.

Customer Service Professional
Kaset International
Monthly four-page newsletter
Subscription: $155 (five copies, with one copy of two-page *Customer Service Coach*)
8875 Hidden River Parkway
Tampa FL 33637
Phone: 800/735-2738, 813/977-8875
Fax: 813/971-3511
Web: http://www.kaset.com/pubscsp.htm
E-mail: john.smilanich@kaset.com
Intended as a tool package for supervisors and their employees.

Customers First
The Dartnell Corporation
Bi-weekly newsletter
Subscription: $89.97; copy: $2.95
4660 N. Ravenswood Avenue
Chicago IL 60640-4595
Phone: 800/621-5463, 773/561-4000
Fax: 800/327-8635, 773/561-3801
Web: http://www.dartnellcorp.com/
custfrst.html
E-mail: dartnell@dartnellcorp.com
Provides employees with an organized plan of action for building customer relations through innovative techniques and an emphasis on the importance of good customer relations.

Executive Edge
Select Press
Monthly newsletter
Subscription: $69.95
P.O. Box 37
Corte Madera CA 94976
Phone: 800/765-4625, 415/924-1612
Fax: 415/924-7179

Web: None
E-mail: selectpr@aol.com
Covers quality customer service and marketing techniques.

Executive Report on Customer Retention
Alexander Communications Group, Inc.
Semi-monthly eight-page newsletter
Subscription: $199 in U.S., Canada, and Mexico; $229 elsewhere; copy: $9
Customer Service Group
215 Park Avenue South, Suite 1301
New York NY 10003
Phone: 800/232-4317, 212/228-0296
Fax: 212/228-0376
Web: http://www.alexcommgrp.com/csg/
csg.html
E-mail: info@alexcommgrp.com
Provides information for "customer satisfaction strategists" on such issues as monitoring and measuring customer satisfaction, changing to a customer-focused corporate culture, benchmarking, using complaints and customer feedback to improve satisfaction, calculating the ROI for service improvements, and putting vision and mission statement into action.

First-Rate Customer Service
The Economics Press, Inc.
Bi-weekly four-page newsletter
Subscription: $45; copy: $1.95
12 Daniel Road
Fairfield NJ 07004
Phone: 800/526-2554, 973/227-1224
Fax: 973/227-8360
Web: http://www.epinc.com/prods/frcs.-
htm
E-mail: info@epinc.com or order@epinc.com
Gives customer service personnel advice that helps them do their jobs with an enthusiastic, customer-oriented attitude.

ICSA News
International Customer Service Association
Quarterly newsletter
Subscription: free with membership ($195)
401 N. Michigan Avenue
Chicago IL 60611
Phone: 800/360-ICSA (4272), 312/321-6800
Fax: 312/845-1084
Web: http://www.icsa.com

E-mail: icsa@sba.com
Vehicle for communicating association news, ideas, and business trends in customer service and for developing the theory of total quality service and service management.

Perceptions & Realities
Karten Associates
Quarterly eight-page newsletter
Subscription: $36 U.S., $42 Canada, $46 elsewhere
40 Woodland Parkway, Suite 217
Randolph MA 02368
Phone: 781/986-8148
Fax: 781/961-2608
Web: http://www.nkarten.com/newslet.html
E-mail: NKarten@compuserve.com
This newsletter is devoted, as the subtitle explains, to "Perspectives on Superior Service & Win-Win Relationships." The editor, Naomi Karten, is the author of *Managing Expectations*. Articles from this newsletter are posted on the Web site.

Quality Customer Service
Siefer Consultants, Inc.
Monthly newsletter
Subscription: $319; copy: $15
525 Cayuga Street
Storm Lake IA 50588
Phone: 800/747-7342, 712/732-7340
Fax: 712/732-7906
Web: None
E-mail: siefer@ncn.net
Strategies and tips to improve customer service and account retention.

Re-Designing Customer Service
Organizational Development Corporation
Monthly newsletter
Subscription: $144
P.O. Box 312
Mukwonago WI 53149
Phone: 800/634-1884, 414/363-9848
Fax: 414/363-9828
Web: http://www.pitnet.net/odc/index.html
E-mail: odc@pitnet.net
Focuses on service and quality issues, with case studies, real-life examples, and success-ful strategies, to maximize profit, sales, and cash flow.

Success in Service
Bureau of Business Practice (Simon & Schuster)
Monthly four-page newsletter
Subscription: $21
24 Rope Ferry Road
Waterford CT 06386
Phone: 800/243-0876, 860/442-4365
Fax: 800/772-7421, 860/434-3078
Web: http://www.bbpnews.com
E-mail: bbp_editorial@prenhall.com
For employees, this newsletter focuses on better serving customers and building long-lasting relationships through personalized service, satisfying displeased customers, and active listening.

Supervisor's Guide to Improved Customer Service & Retention
Clement Communications, Inc.
Bi-weekly newsletter
Subscription: $162.50 in U.S.; copy: $5.75
10 Conchester Road
Concordville PA 19331
Phone: 800/345-8101, 610/459-1700
Fax: 800/459-1933, 610/459-5092
Web: http://www.clement.com/csr.htm
E-mail: motivate@clement.com
News and information for supervisors to help improve their staff's customer service skills.

Customer Service—Specific Areas

Call Centers

Call Center Magazine
Flatiron Publishing
Monthly magazine
Subscription: $14 in U.S., $25 in Canada, $50 in Europe, and $60 elsewhere
12 W. 21st Street
New York NY 10010
Phone: 800/627-3435 (sales), 800/999-0345, 212/691-8215
Fax: 212/691-1191

Web: http://www.callcentermagazine.com
E-mail:
mary@nyoffice.mhs.compuserve.com
Features products and services for call center
and help desk managers, to help them
choose, buy, implement, and manage technology.

Call Centre Focus
Callcraft
Bi-monthly magazine
Subscription: free to qualified telebusiness
professionals; £45 otherwise
The Loft
Dean House Farm
Church Road
Newdigate
Surrey RH5 5DL
United Kingdom
Phone: 01306 631661
Fax: 01306 631412
Web: http://www.callcentre.co.uk
E-mail: info@callcentre.co.uk
Serves the call center industry in the U.K.
Also provides "Telebusiness now" (telebusi-
ness news on-line worldwide) through Web
site.

Effective Telephone Techniques
The Dartnell Corporation
Bi-weekly newsletter
Subscription: $89.97; copy: $2.95
4660 N. Ravenswood Avenue
Chicago IL 60640-4595
Phone: 800/621-5463, 773/561-4000
Fax: 800/327-8635, 773/561-3801
Web: http://www.dartnellcorp.com/
effective.html
E-mail: dartnell@dartnellcorp.com
Training bulletin to help telephone teams
build profitable customer relations through
contacts in sales, telemarketing, customer
service, and other functional areas.

Computer Service and Support

Service News
United Publications
Monthly newspaper
Subscription: $55 U.S. and Canada,
$125 elsewhere

106 Lafayette Street
P.O. Box 995
Yarmouth ME 04096
Phone: 207/846-0600
Fax: 207/846-0657
Web: http://www.servicenews.com
E-mail: aharris@servicenews.com
This publication is devoted to the $73 billion
information technology service, support, and
training market. The publisher provides a
free-subscription on-line version at the Ser-
vice News World Wide Web site.

Financial

Cross Sales Report
Siefer Consultants, Inc.
Monthly newsletter
Subscription: $319; copy: $15
525 Cayuga Street
Storm Lake IA 50588
Phone: 800/747-7342, 712/732-7340
Fax: 712/732-7906
Web: None
E-mail: siefer@ncn.net
Cross sales and customer service ideas for
financial institutions. Techniques to improve
sales and cross sales of bank products and
services.

Help Desks

LifeRaft
The Help Desk Institute
Bi-monthly newsletter
Subscription: $36 for HDI members,
$96 for non-members
1755 Telstar Drive, Suite 101
Colorado Springs CO 80920-1017
Phone: 800/248-5667, 719/531-5138
Fax: 719/528-4250
Web: http://www.helpdeskinst.com
E-mail: csc@sbexpos.com
The "professional journal of the help desk
industry" promises insider analysis on
trends, tips and techniques, and case studies
on a wide variety of support organizations.
The Web site features selected articles from
this newsletter.

Insurance

CSR Advisor
Standard Publishing Corporation
Monthly newspaper
Subscription: $126; copy: $10.50
155 Federal Street
Boston MA 02110
Phone: 800/682-5759, 617/457-0600
Fax: 617/457-0608
Web: None
E-mail: None
Provides customer service representatives in the insurance field information on serving their clients.

Manufacturing

Service Management
National Association of Service Managers
Monthly newsletter
Subscription free with membership,
$50 otherwise
P.O. Box 712500
Santee CA 92072-2500
Phone: 619/562-7004, 888/562-7004
Fax: 619/562-7153
Web: http://www.nasm.com/newslett.html
E-mail: nasm@nasm.com
A publication for after-market product service/support personnel in all manufacturing industries, from the oldest professional non-profit association of product service executives.

Marketing

Journal of Customer Service in Marketing & Management: Innovations for Service, Quality, and Value
The Haworth Press, Inc.
Quarterly journal
Subscription: $40 in U.S., $52 in Canada, and $56 elsewhere (individual); $60 in U.S., $78 in Canada, and $84 elsewhere (corporate)
10 Alice Street
Binghamton NY 13904-1580
Phone: 800/HAWORTH, 607/722-5857
Fax: 607/722-6362

Web: http://www.haworth.com
E-mail: getinfo@haworth.com
Features innovations for service, quality, and value for the customer, client, or patient.

Printing

Signature Service
Society for Service Professionals in Printing
Monthly newsletter
Subscription: free with membership,
$89 otherwise
433 E. Monroe Avenue
Alexandria VA 22301-1693
Phone: 703/684-0044
Fax: 703/548-9137
Web: NA
E-mail: NA
For customer service representatives in the printing industry.

Sales

American Salesman
National Research Bureau
Monthly magazine
Subscription: $42.35; copy: $5.75
200 N. 4th Street
Burlington IA 52601-5305
Phone: 319/752-5415
Fax: 319/752-3421
Web: None
E-mail: None
Topics cover all areas of sales, including customer service.

Telephone Answering Services

Answer
Association of Telemessaging Services International
Bi-monthly magazine
Subscription: $50
Lockbox Department 3471
Washington DC 20042-3471
Phone: 202/429-5151
Fax: 202/223-4579
Web: http://www.atsi.org/icenter
E-mail: atsi@dc.sba.com
Telecommunication news affecting the live telephone answering service industry.

Appendix C

CUSTOMER SERVICE RESOURCES ON THE INTERNET

The Internet is now established as a source of information resources on virtually everything, including customer service. It's impossible to provide a comprehensive list of materials available online. We've tried to provide a good sampling, a representative snapshot of customer service resources at this point.

Since many World Wide Web sites have links to other sites, with the sites listed below you're just a few clicks away from many more sites. The same is true of discussion lists: you're often just a query away from other lists, as your cyber colleagues will generally suggest other lists that might interest you. At the end of our list of lists, we provide more resources to help you get what you need from the 'Net. Finally, for those who might be daunted or confused by the terminology, we've included an introductory glossary.

Our directory consists of two categories of online resources:

- **World Wide Web Sites**. These are sites hosted by associations, companies, and other organizations. You access these sites (pages) using a Web browser such as Netscape Navigator or Microsoft Explorer. We've divided the sites into Resources (information, tools, experts) and Examples of Customer Service (how a few companies are using the 'Net to attract and serve customers).

- **Internet Discussion Groups**. These are free mailing lists that allow members (subscribers) to send e-mail messages to a central location, which then copies the messages to all members of that group. Some mailing lists are for distribution only: they send members information (usually publications or other resources), but don't allow members to post messages.

The Internet has grown and expanded greatly in the last few years. There's probably something for everybody and information to meet every need—if you can find it. Some of the discussion groups bring together experts, and we can gain a lot from their exchanges; others are more like discussions around the water cooler. Some Web sites are treasures, while others are basically infomercials or more glitter than gold. Also, discussion groups and Web sites are time-sensitive. The groups are like any other type of association: the value to any member depends on what the other members are contributing at any given time. Many of the sites suffer from inadequate maintenance as they age; some move to other addresses or just disappear.

Web Sites—Resources

The World Wide Web is full of products, services, and information for customer service professionals. The sites listed here are among the best and most interesting that we've found.

American Customer Satisfaction Index
http://acsi.asqc.org/
Over 150 companies and agencies have been measured in the ACSI, developed by the National Quality Research Center in the University of Michigan Business School and the American Society for Quality.

American Productivity and Quality Center
http://www.apqc.org/
This is the "International Benchmarking Clearinghouse," focusing on benchmarking and the development of best practices. It offers training and other resources in many areas, including customer satisfaction. The site includes articles from the Center's magazine, *Continuous Journey*.

BayStone Software
http://www.baystone.com
This company features an integrated suite of Customer Interaction Software applications to automate sales, marketing, customer support, and quality assurance functions—at a site that's pleasant to visit.

The Benchmarking Exchange
http://www.benchnet.com
TBE is primarily for members only, but visitors can get a free 30-day trial "subscription" to "the world's largest and most comprehensive benchmarking, quality and process improvement, and knowledge management network."

The Business Research Lab
http://busreslab.com
This site features several sample surveys that can be downloaded: Attitude, Awareness and Usage Questionnaire, Employee Satisfaction Questionnaire, E-Value2 Employee Questionnaires, and do-it-yourself surveys.

Call Centre Managers Forum
http://www.callcentres.com.au
If you operate a call center, this is a good site to frequent. It features a bibliography of books, archives of articles posted on this site, links to other sites, and virtual conference rooms ("Virtual Experience Exchange"), where visitors can discuss call center issues, personnel matters, job opportunities, and hardware and software.

Center for Customer-Driven Quality
http://www.cfs.purdue.edu/Conscirt/quality.html
The Center, established in the Department of Consumer Sciences and Retailing at Purdue University in 1992 and directed by Richard Feinberg, does "industry-sponsored research in world-class customer service strategies with a special focus on achieving customer satisfaction, increase retention of customers, and higher profit margins with call centers." This site may disappoint visitors, however.

The Customer Care Institute

http://www.customercare.com

This is an international organization serving customer service professionals, focusing on issues in customer service, consumer affairs, telemarketing, and help desk professions. The organization provides information, research, advisory services, benchmarking, and networking opportunities, as well as publishing booklets and organizing forums, workshops, and conferences. Although the site seems to be in early stages of development, it seems like one that deserves a return visit—if only for its online forum, with participants from around the world.

CustomerSat.com

http://www.customersat.com

If you're interested in Internet surveys, this is the place to begin. This site is focused on using the Internet for customer satisfaction, employee satisfaction, and market research. (The president, John Chisholm, contributed the article "Using the Internet to Measure Customer Satisfaction" to this book.)

The Customer Satisfaction Measurement Association

http://www.flash.net/~benchmar/csma.html

The CSMA is "an association of companies that conducts benchmarking studies to identify practices that improve customer satisfaction and the overall operation of members." Membership is free.

Customer Service Review

http://www.csr.co.za

This is a monthly, electronic newsletter. Subscriptions are $79 for a year, $44 for six months. The publishers claim to surf the Internet daily and scan 400 editions of "top global business publications" every month, to provide essential information with a practical, hands-on focus.

Customer Value, Inc.

http://www.cval.com

This site is designated "The Official Customer Value Analysis Web Site," promoting Bradley Gale and "the art and science of measuring customers' needs and wants and finding ways to serve those expectations better than the competition."

Edge on Line

http://www.edgeonline.com

This is the site of the magazine *Entrepreneurial Edge*. Under "business builders" are articles on customer service, and the "virtual network" gives visitors a place to post questions, exchange ideas, and offer advice. (The vice president of operations for *Entrepreneurial Edge*, Susan Smith, contributed the article "How to Create a Plan to Deliver Customer Service" to this book.)

The Enterprise

http://www.theenterprise.org

Billed as a "career quality network," this is "a national effort to recognize and certify workforce development organizations committed to delivering high-quality, customer-focused job training and reemployment services throughout the United States." It publishes a quarterly newsletter, *Enterprise Forum*, available online.

Free Word-of-Mouth Marketing Tips Home Page

http://www.geocities.com/WallStreet/6246

At this site, the author of *Let Your Customers Do the Talking* (1996) provides a bibliography, links, and quotations on the virtues of satisfying customers and gaining the benefits of word-of-mouth marketing. (The author, Michael E. Cafferky, contributed the article "Beyond Loyalty: Inspiring Customers to Brag" to this book.)

The Help Desk Institute
http://www.helpdeskinst.com
Billed as "your worldwide link to support services resources," this site features the KI Bookstore and the Internet edition of *Support Services Buyer's Guide*, as well as selected articles from the HDI bi-monthly newsletter, *LifeRaft*.

International Customer Service Association
http://www.icsa.com
The ICSA publishes *ICSA News* and *Customer Service: A Journal of Theory, Research and Practice*. This site features a good idea—an "applause" page for recognition of people and companies that have provided exemplary customer service.

International Quality & Productivity Center
http://www.iqpc.com
This site would be worth visiting only for the listing of conferences, which can be searched by key word.

National Association of Service Managers
http://www.nasm.com/newslett.html
The NASM, founded in 1955, is the oldest professional nonprofit association of product service executives. This site features back issues of the association's monthly newsletter, *Service Management Update*, "a publication for after-market product service/support personnel in all manufacturing industries."

The Resource Center for Customer Service Professionals
http://www.the-resource-center.com
This site is intended to serve help desk, customer service, technical support, and call center professionals, by providing a place to find books, newsletters, videos, training kits, self-study courses, and seminars.

Retail Business Consulting
http://retailbiz.com
This small company in Redmond, WA, provides services to local businesses, but it also uses this site to publish *Service Bytes: Strategies for Building Your Business*, a newsletter for the Internet community.

The Right Answer
http://www.therightanswer.com
A fun and useful site, set up by The Right Answer, Inc., to be a customer service resource center. It's the home of The Right Answer Society, a Web-based organization: free membership includes a monthly newsletter. The site also features training tips, a Q & A forum and a chat room, job search assistance, customer service links, a monthly award for customer service professionals who go above and beyond for their customers, and a CS Web of the month (recent picks: Blockbuster Video, L.L. Bean, Explore Technologies, Pacific Bell, and Ben & Jerry's). (The president of The Right Answer, Inc., Donna Hall, contributed the article "Problem-Solving Tips for Telephone Representatives" to this book.)

Rockbridge Associates, Inc.
http://www.rockresearch.com
This company, which provides market research resources, features at this site several articles by the staff on research into customer satisfaction.

Sierra Customer Response Management (Lynk Software)

http://www.lynkview.com

This company offers a way to take better care of your customers—and its site shows concern for its customers. The design is simple, understated, and well-organized. Information is easy to find and there are explanations. Visitors can even download an evaluation copy of the software.

Society of Consumer Affairs Professionals in Business

http://www.socap.org

This site, sponsored by SOCAP, "the Champion and Service Leader for the Bottom-Line Impact of Customer Satisfaction and Loyalty," features articles from *Customer Relationship Management* (formerly *MOBIUS*). Article reprints can be ordered in topic packages, which include "call center management," "customer loyalty, retention, and satisfaction measurement," "staff training and development," "consumer behavior," and "consumer database development, maintenance, and uses." There's also a catalog of books for customer service.

SurveyExpress

http://www.surveyexpress.com

This company offers a totally automated customer satisfaction survey service, including an alert that allows action within 24 hours of a complaint. A demo is available by phone.

Targeting Marketing of Santa Barbara

http://www.targeting.com

This site is worth visiting just for the articles by Jim Sterne. Anybody interested in using the Internet to better serve customers—current or potential—should read what Sterne writes about what works and what doesn't. (Sterne contributed the article "The World Wide Web Was Made for Customer Service" to this book.)

Technical Assistance Research Programs (TARP)

http://www.tarp.com

This customer service research and consulting firm proclaims its goal as "making customer satisfaction a profit center." This site serves primarily as a simple brochure explaining its services. (The president of TARP, John Goodman, contributed the article "Quantifying the Impact of Great Customer Service on Profitability" to this book.)

The Tele-M@rket

http://www.telemkt.com

"Your Gateway to the Call Center Community," this site features a virtual conference center, an events calendar, white papers, legal and government materials, and business links.

TelePlaza

http://www.teleplaza.com

This site is devoted to teleservicing, serving people in call centers, telemarketing, and customer service. It organizes, categorizes, and indexes industry information on the Web, featuring news, training opportunities, trade questions, and job postings.

Working Relationships, Inc.

http://www.customerretention.com

This site promotes the full line of customized research services available through Working Relationships, but it also offers some good freebies, including the *Customer Care Bulletin* online and a quick quiz for visitors to measure their "Customer Sensitivity Quotient." (The president, JoAnna Brandi, contributed the article "Unleashing the Power of Customer CARE in Your Organization" to this book.)

World Opinion

http://www2.worldopinion.com/home.qry

Although it may not quite yet be "The World's Market Research Web Site," as proclaimed by its sponsor, Survey Sampling, Inc., this site provides helpful links to research companies and associations—and shows thought and taste in its design.

Web Sites—Examples of Customer Service

These sites are just a sampling of the many good sites that show how companies and other organizations can use the World Wide Web to serve their customers, both current and potential.

Amazon Books

http://www.amazon.com

The biggest virtual bookstore in the universe—and an excellent example of how to partner for better customer service and greater profits.

Defense Logistics Services Center

http://www.dlsc.dla.mil

Straightforward and simple, as might be expected of a military site, yet attractive—even the notice that use of the site is monitored.

Federal Express

http://www.fedex.com

A good example of what to do and how to do it. Although the graphics slow access, this site features a good site map and attractive pages. Visitors can open an account, find shipping rates, prepare shipments, track their packages, and download free shipping region locator software.

Kodak

http://www.kodak.com

A wonderful site—easy to use, interesting, and (of course!) colorful. Visitors can send multi-media postcards, get advice on taking pictures, go shopping, and get customer support, including FAQs. The site includes a search engine and—a nice touch for credibility—a link to the Better Business Bureau Online (http://www.bbb.org).

ServiceSoft Corporation

http://www.servicesoft.com

Although this site is basically a promotional brochure for the company, it's a very good example of how to create a products and services site—easy to use, well-organized, colorful but not overwhelming . . . and each page ends with several questions to guide the visitor. (Keith Loris of ServiceSoft contributed the article "Internet Self-Service Support: Beyond Search Engines to 'Smart Answers on the 'Net™' " to this book.)

Discussion/Distribution Lists

There are surprisingly few discussion lists devoted to customer service. To compensate, you may find it worthwhile to participate in the virtual conferences hosted by such sites as the Customer Care Institute (http://www.customercare.com), Call Centre Managers Forum (http://www.callcentres.com.au), and Edge on Line (http://www.edgeonline.com)—all listed above.

Help Desk discussion list
address: listserv@wvnvm.wvnet.edu
message: subscribe hdesk-l firstname lastname

Quality discussion list (TQM in manufacturing and service industries)
address: listserv@pucc.princeton.edu
message: subscribe quality firstname lastname

TNS Customer Service discussion list
address: majordomo@mail.sdsu.edu
message: subscribe customer-service

TQM-D discussion list (quality in manufacturing and service industries)
address: majordomo@quality.org
message: subscribe tqm-d

The NetNurturing™ Letter distribution list (growing customer relationships through the Internet)
address: troberts@troberts.com
subject: subscribe NNL
or
subscribe through Web site: http://www.troberts.com

Innovation Line distribution list
address: majordomo@po.databack.com
message: subscribe innovationline-text

Customer Edge distribution list
subscribe through Web site: http://www.customeredge.com

Customer Service Newletter distribution list
address: cmassoc@citi.net
subject: subscribe
message: subscribe
or
subscribe through Web site: http://www.citi.net/home/cmassoc/cmassoc.htm

Going Beyond These Resources

Sometimes better customer service means more self-service. That's the case with Internet resources, at least. So, to help serve you better, we're including some instructions so you can find other discussion lists and Web sites to meet your specific needs.

To find other discussion lists, you can use the search functions of the following Web sites:

http://www.liszt.com
Through this site you can search among over 70,000 mailing lists by word or by category.
http://www.neosoft.com/internet/paml
This site allows searches for publicly accessible mailing lists.
http://catalog.com/vivian/internet-group-search.html
This site is operated by Vivian Neou, author of the book *Internet Mailing Lists Navigator*.

http://tile.net

Billed as The Comprehensive Internet Reference to Discussion Lists, this site also allows searching for ftp sites and Usenet newsgroups.

http://www.lsoft.com/lists/listref.html

CataList is "the *official* catalog of listserv lists," with information on about 15,000 public lists, out of some 60,000.

To find other Web sites, you can use any of dozens of search engines. The following are among the best at this time:

http://www.hotbot.com
http://altavista.digital.com
http://www.yahoo.com
http://metasearch.com
http://www.dogpile.com

This site runs simultaneous searches using the most popular engines.

http://www.reference.com

This site allows searches of Usenet and mailing list archives.

http://www.gosearch.com/inet.html

This site allows easy access to 10 of the most established search engines, including several for finding discussion lists.

http://www.isleuth.com

The Internet Sleuth provides the tools for any type of Internet search, including Web directories and search engines, Usenet, and discussion lists.

A Beginner's Guide to Internet Terminology

The following glossary contains only the terms that beginners might encounter and not understand in using discussion lists and the Web. We give simple, practical explanations, following the lead of Jim Clauson and his CyberGlossary © 1995–97. Our intent is simply to help Internet novices get out and access the many resources in areas of customer service.

baud or baud-rate—the rate at which data is transmitted electronically, with 28,800 bps now considered the minimum for using the Web

bookmark—a software capability that allows the user to save popular Internet addresses in a file, so they can be used with just a click

bps—bits per second, the measurement of electronic data transmission

browser—a software package for accessing Web sites, either textual (e.g., Lynx) or (more likely) graphical (e.g., Netscape Navigator and Internet Explorer)

BTW—by the way (e-mail shorthand)

client—your end of the Internet system, connected at the other end to the host or server

command address—the address of a discussion list at which commands are issued to the host computer

cookie—a file placed in the client computer by certain Web sites, to better serve the user who visits that site

cyber, cyberspace—terms derived from "cybernetics" to refer to the Internet and related matters

discussion groups—communities of people with a common interest, communicating through newsgroups or listservers (currently about 7,000 such lists)

domain name—the part of an e-mail address following the '@' sign, identifying the host server and *within the U.S.* the type of host (.com = commercial, .edu = educational, .org = nonprofit organization, .gov = government, .net = computer network) or *elsewhere in the world* the country (e.g., ca = Canada, uk = United Kingdom, au = Australia)

dotted quad—a form of Internet address (also known as the IP Number), as interpreted by computers but rarely used by humans, in the form of four numbers separated by decimal points (e.g., 199.68.1.48)

download—to retrieve a file from a remote host

DNS—Domain Name System, the Internet system that translates text addresses like human @home.com into numerical addresses (IP Numbers) like 109.63.4.84), with the acronym DNS generally used as part of an error message when a browser cannot connect with the desired host address

e-mail or email—electronic mail, text messages sent by from one computer to another through a network of computers

emoticons — creative faces formed sideways by punctuation marks to show emotion in e-mail messages, e.g., :-) smiley face, ;-) winking, :-(frowning, and dozens more

FAQ—Frequently Asked Questions, questions and answers kept in a file available for many discussion lists and Web sites, to efficiently provide basic information about the list or site

flame—(verb) to post a message to a discussion list or newsgroup expressing a passionate, often offensive reaction to a post and generally regarded as a violation of netiquette, (noun) an inflammatory message

flame war—a series of flames, wasting space and time and alienating members of the discussion list or newsgroup

ftp—file transfer protocol, a utility for transferring computer files through phone lines

gopher—a means of arranging and accessing data files, similar to a table of contents, in gopher sites (or holes), a system less and less in use

home page—the first level of access at a Web site, the most basic address

host—the computer to which your computer (the client) connects, to make use of some service (discussion list or newsgroup, Web site, telnet, gopher . . .)

html (or htm)—Hyper Text Markup Language, the code used to construct Web pages, making use of links, images, animation, and sounds

http—Hyper Text Transport Protocol, the fixed set of messages that allow a client and a host server to communicate through a hypertext link

hyperlink or hypertext link—words or phrases in a Web document that can be chosen by a visitor to cause another document to be retrieved and displayed

hypertext—generally, any text that contains links to other documents

IMHO—in my humble opinion (e-mail shorthand)

Internet—an international, loosely connected network of networks of networks of computers

IP number—Internet Protocol number (also known as a dotted quad), a form of Internet address, as interpreted by computers but rarely used by humans, in the form of four numbers separated by decimal points (e.g., 199.68.1.48)

K—kilobyte, rough translation of 1024 (10^2) bytes, used in measuring file size or data transmission speeds

link—hyperlink or hypertext link, words or phrases in a Web document that can be chosen by a visitor to cause another document to be retrieved and displayed

listservers—list-processing software systems that support discussion lists or newsgroups (e.g., listserv, majordomo, listproc, maiser, mailbase . . .)

lurk—to participate passively in a discussion list, reading messages but not posting—behavior normal and even recommended for newcomers to a group

netiquette—an informal, consensus-based set of rules of conduct, generally discouraging flaming and unsolicited or blatant advertising on discussion lists or newsgroups

newbie—an affectionate term applied to someone new to the Internet, especially when the novice makes errors or violates netiquette

newsgroups—a very large number (currently about 8,000) of informally managed, open discussion groups

post—(verb) to send a message to a discussion list or newsgroup, (noun) a message

posting address—the address of a discussion list to which messages are sent (posted) for other members of the group

search engine—a tool used to quickly search the World Wide Web for sites matching specified text or other criteria (for examples, check out our listing of search tools above)

server—a computer that hosts a specific service for the use of clients

shareware—software intended to be used free of charge, subject to specified stipulations

site—a page or set of pages on the World Wide Web

spam—to post inappropriate messages (generally advertisements) to discussion lists or newsgroups, an annoying violation of netiquette

surf—to use a browser to move around the Web from site to site following page links

telnet—any of several terminal emulation programs that allow a user to operate a remote system, such as an online library card catalog

URL—Universal Resource Locator, an Internet address in a standard format—access method://host:port/path.filetype:

for Web sites
http://info.cern.ch:80/default.html
for newsgroups
news://alt.hypertext
for file transfer protocol
ftp://wuarchive.wustl.edu/mirrors
for telnet
telnet://fedworld.gov

Usenet—an Internet predecessor that currently handles many of the newsgroups

Web browser—refer to "browser" entry

WWW or W3 or Web—generally the entire network of resources that can be accessed using http, gopher, ftp, telnet, Usenet, and other tools, but more particularly the system of http servers that allow text, graphics, and sound to presented together, using chained menu structures and links

DIRECTORY OF CONTRIBUTORS

Patricia V. Alea
Alea and Associates
708 Leonard Street
Madison WI 53711
Phone: 608/238-8017
Fax: 608/238-8017
E-mail: pvalea@aol.com

Kristin Anderson
Performance Research Associates
1820 Foshay Tower
821 Marquette Avenue South
Minneapolis MN 55402
Phone: 612/338-8423
Fax: 612/338-8536
E-mail: KrisLeeAnd@aol.com

Tom Atkinson
The Forum Corporation
1 Exchange Plaza
Boston MA 02109
Phone: 617/523-7300, 617/371-3347, 800/
        FORUM 11
Fax: 617/973-2001
E-mail: tatkinso@forum.com
Web: www.forum.com

Janelle M. Barlow
TMI, USA
181 Carlos Drive, Suite 102
San Rafael CA 94903
Phone: 415/499-5500
Fax: 415/499-5512
E-mail: JABarlow@aol.com
Web: www.tmius.com

Chip R. Bell
Performance Research Associates
25 Highland Park #100

Dallas TX 75205-2785
Phone: 214/522-5777
Fax: 214/691-7591
E-mail: prawest@aol.com

JoAnna Brandi
Working Relationships, Inc.
7491 North Federal Hwy, Suite 304
Boca Raton FL 33487
Phone: 561/279-0027
Fax: 561/279-9400
E-mail:
jbrandi@customerretention.com
Web: www.customerretention.com

Kathleen Brown
Mandel Communications
1425 Hidden Valley Road
Soquel CA 95073
Phone: 408/475-8202
Fax: 408/475-4365
E-mail: edm@mandelcom.com
Web: www.mandelcom.com

Anne Bruce
AddVantage Learning, Inc.
15889 Preston Road, Suite 2089
Dallas TX 75248
Phone: 214/503-6800 ext 500
Fax: 972/960-9766
E-mail: ABruceAL@aol.com

Michael E. Cafferky
2052 Gemstone Drive
Walla Walla WA 99362-8206
Phone: 509/529-7098
E-mail: miccaf@wwgh.com
Web:
www.geocities.com/WallStreet/6246

Rebecca Chekouras
Age Wave Communications
2000 Powell Street
Emeryville CA 94608
Phone: 510/652-9099
Fax: 510/652-8245
E-mail: rchekour@agewave.com
Web: www.agewave.com

John Chisholm
CustomerSat.com
140 Sand Hill Circle, Suite 100
Menlo Park CA 94025
Phone: 650/234-8000
Fax: 650/854-2135
E-mail: jchisholm@CustomerSat.com
Web: www.CustomerSat.com

Gary Connor
The Connor Group, Inc.
140 Merlin Court
Fayetteville GA 30214
Phone: 770/719-4992
Fax: 770/719-8427
E-mail: gbc@mindspring.com

Scott Davis
Kuczmarski & Associates
1165 North Clark Street, Suite 700
Chicago IL 60610
Phone: 312/988-1533
Fax: 312/988-9393
E-mail: scottd@ennovate.com
Web: www.ennovate.com

Lisa Ford
Ford Group, Inc.
140 Seville Chase
Atlanta GA 30328
Phone: 770/394-4860
Fax: 770/394-0034
E-mail: lford@mindspring.com

Jerry Fritz
Management Institute
Grainger Hall
University of Wisconsin
975 University Avenue
Madison WI 53706-1323
Phone: 608/262-7331
Fax: 608/262-4617
E-mail: jlf@mi.bus.wisc.edu
Web: www.wisc.edu/mi/1ff.html

Jody Hoffer Gittell
Harvard Business School
Baker 185
Soldiers Field
Boston MA 02163
Phone: 617/495-6768
Fax: 617/496-7167
E-mail: jgittell@hbs.edu

Reginald W. Goeke
VALTec Group, Inc.
601 Grand Street
Morgantown WV 26505
Phone: 304/296-5350
Fax: 304/296-7312
E-mail: valtec@valtec-group.com
Web: www.VALTec-Group.com

John Goodman
TARP
1300 Wilson Boulevard, Suite 950
Arlington VA 22204
Phone: 703/524-1456 x 132
Fax: 703/524-6374
E-mail: jgoodman@tarp.com
Web: www.tarp.com

Donna Hall
The Right Answer
P.O. Box 415
Ansonia Station
New York NY 10023
Phone: 800/254-1128 x 01
Fax: 718/296-4393
E-mail: donnahall@therightanswer.com
Web: www.therightanswer.com

John L. Hartley
Promus Hotel Corporation
7920 Woodland Center Boulevard
Tampa FL 33614
Phone: 813/243-7510
Fax: 813/243-7534
E-mail: jhartley@promus.com
Web: www.promus-inc.com

Keith Loris
ServiceSoft Corporation
1 Needham Place
50 Cabot Street
Needham MA 02194
Phone: 781/449-0049, 800/737-8738

Fax: 781/449-0107
E-mail: leila@servicesoft.com
Web: www.servicesoft.com

Dianna Maul
TMI, USA
2522 N. Proctor, Suite 132
Tacoma, WA 98406
Phone: 253/761-7444
Fax: 253/761-8286
E-mail: DiannaMaul@aol.com
Web: www.tmius.com

Gordon W. McClung
VALTec Group, Inc.
601 Grand Street
Morgantown WV 26505
Phone: 304/296-5350
Fax: 304/296-7312
E-mail: valtec@valtec-group.com
Web: www.VALTec-Group.com

H. Lee Meadow
Dept of Management and Marketing
237 Lumpkin Hall
Eastern Illinois University
Charleston IL 61920-3099
Phone: 217/581-7262
Fax: 217/581-7265
E-mail: cfhlm@eiu.edu

Rebecca L. Morgan
Morgan Seminar Group
1440 Newport Avenue
San Jose CA 95125-3329
Phone: 408/998-7977, 800/247-9662
Fax: 408/998-1742
E-mail: RLMorgan@aol.com
Web: www.RebeccaMorgan.com

James S. Pepitone
Pepitone Worldwide
3 Lincoln Center
5430 LBJ Freeway, Suite 210
Dallas TX 75240-2622
Phone: 214/343-3500 x 300
Fax: 214/343-3519
E-mail: ceo@pepitone.com
Web: www.pepitone.com

Douglas R. Pruden
Marketing Metrics, Inc.
305 Route 17

Paramus NJ 07652
Phone: 201/599-0790
Fax: 201/599-0791
E-mail: dpruden@marketingmetrics.com
Web: www.marketingmetrics.com

R. Eric Reidenbach
VALTec Group, Inc.
601 Grand Street
Morgantown WV 26505
Phone: 304/296-5350, 601/264-1707
Fax: 304/296-7312
E-mail: eric@valtec-group.com,
    102331.3303@compuserve.com
Web: www.VALTec-Group.com

Mark Rosenberger
WOW! Performance Coaching, Inc.
10608 Loire Avenue
San Diego CA 92131
Phone: 619/578-7900, 888/969-9682
Fax: 619/578-7065
E-mail: wowseminar@aol.com

Mark Sanborn
Sanborn & Associates, Inc.
695 S. Colorado Blvd, Suite 415
Denver CO 80222
Phone: 303/698-9656, 800/650-3343
Fax: 303/777-3045
E-mail: markspeaks@aol.com
Web: www.marksanborn.com

Eberhard E. Scheuing
College of Business Administration
St. John's University
Grand Central and Utopia Parkways
Jamaica NY 11439
Phone: 718/990-6770
Fax: 718/990-1868
E-mail: NA

Robert Shaver
Management Institute
Grainger Hall
University of Wisconsin
975 University Avenue
Madison WI 53706-1323
Phone: 608/262-7357
Fax: 608/262-4617
E-mail: rrs@mi.bus.wisc.edu

Jim Sterne
Target Marketing
1130 Arbolado Road
Santa Barbara CA 93103
Phone: 805/965-3184
Fax: 805/965-8687
E-mail: jsterne@targeting.com
Web: www.targeting.com

Michael Vandergriff
The Vandergriff Consulting Group
2205 Argyle Circle
Plano TX 75023
Phone: 972/964-6413
Fax: 972/612-5823
E-mail: michael@vandergriffgroup.com
Web: www.vandergriffgroup.com

Terry G. Vavra
Marketing Metrics, Inc.
305 Route 17
Paramus NJ 07652
Phone: 201/599-0790
Fax: 201/599-0791
E-mail: tvavra@marketingmetrics.com
Web: www.marketingmetrics.com

Nora Weaver
Integrated Customer Service
Delta Air Lines
1030 Delta Boulevard
Atlanta GA 30320
Phone: 404/715-2892
Fax: 404/715-5887
E-mail: nora.weaver@delta-air.com
Web: www.delta-air.com

John A. Woods
CWL Publishing Enterprises
3010 Irvington Way
Madison WI 53713-3414

Phone: 608/273-3710
Fax: 608/274-4554
E-mail: jwoods@execpc.com
Web: www.execpc.com/cwlpubent

Sharon A. Wulf
Enterprise Systems
1257 Worcester Road, Suite 301
Framingham MA 01701-5217
Phone: 508/626-2233
Fax: 508/626-9038
E-mail: sawulf@enters.com

Marlene Yanovsky
TARP
1300 Wilson Boulevard, Suite 950
Arlington VA 22204
Phone: 703/524-1456 x 126
Fax: 703/524-6374
E-mail: myanovsky@tarp.com
Web: www.tarp.com

Ron Zemke
Performance Research Associates
1820 Foshay Tower
821 Marquette Avenue South
Minneapolis MN 55402
Phone: 612/338-8523
Fax: 612/338-8536
E-mail: zemke@aol.com
Web: None

Georgette M. Zifko-Baliga
The Institute for Quality Center
11375 Bean Road
Munson OH 44024
Phone: 440/285-7226
Fax: 216/285-9563
E-mail: gzifko@imperium.net
Web: www.neohio.net/iqc/index.html